Innovations in Science and Mathematics Education

Advanced Designs for Technologies of Learning

✳ ✳ ✳

Innovations in Science and Mathematics Education

Advanced Designs for Technologies of Learning

✳ ✳ ✳

Edited by

Michael J. Jacobson
Allison~LoBue Group, L.L.C.

Robert B. Kozma
SRI International

LEA LAWRENCE ERLBAUM ASSOCIATES, PUBLISHERS
2000   Mahwah, New Jersey   London

Lawrence Erlbaum Associates, Inc., Publishers
10 Industrial Avenue
Mahwah, NJ 07430

Cover design by Kathryn Houghtaling Lacey

Library of Congress Cataloging-in-Publication Data

Innovations in science and mathematics education : advanced designs for technologies of learning / edited by Michael J. Jacobson, Robert B. Kozma.
p. cm.
Includes bibliographical references and index.
ISBN 0-8058-2846-X (cloth : alk. paper)
1. Science—Study and teaching—Technological innovations. 2. Mathematics—Study and teaching—Technological innovations. 3. Educational technology.   I. Jacobson, Michael J. II. Kozma, Robert B.
Q181.I654   1999
507'.12 —dc21   99-29076
                                                    CIP

Books published by Lawrence Erlbaum Associates are printed on acid-free paper, and their bindings are chosen for strength and durability.

Printed in the United States of America
10 9 8 7 6 5 4 3 2 1

Contents

Contributors

Alex J. Angulo
Harvard University
Graduate School of Education
210 Longfellow Hall, Appian Way
Cambridge, MA 02138
Alex_Angulo@gse.harvard.edu

Anthi Archodidou
University of Illinois at Urbana–Champaign
51 Gerty Drive
Champaign, IL 61820
(217) 244-6497
archodid@ux6.cso.uiuc.edu

Katy Ash
Carlow International Inc.
3141 Fairview Park Drive
Falls Church, VA 22042
(703) 698-6225
kash@gmu.edu

Kenneth Brecher
Boston University
Department of Astronomy
725 Commonwealth Avenue
Boston, MA 02215
(617) 353-3423
brecher@bu.edu

Mary Ann Christie
The Concord Consortium
37 Thoreau Street
Concord, MA 01742
(978) 371-5851
maryann@concord.org

Elaine B. Coleman
Center for Technology in Learning
SRI International
333 Ravenswood Avenue
Menlo Park, CA 94025
elainec@unix.sri.com,

Chris Dede
Graduate School of Education
George Mason University
Fairfax, VA 22030
(703) 993-2019
cdede@gmu.edu

John Frederiksen
University of California at Berkeley
School of Education
4423 Hall
Berkeley, CA 94720-1670
(510) 642-6367
frederik@socrates.berkeley.edu

Roy R. Gould
Smithsonian Astrophysical Observatory
Harvard-Smithsonian Center for Astrophysics
60 Garden Street, MS 71
Cambridge, MA 02138
(617) 496-7689
rgould@cfa.harvard.edu

Mark Guzdial
Georgia Institute of Technology
College of Computing
Atlanta, GA 30332-0280
(404) 894-5618
guzdial@cc.gatech.edu

Beth Hoffman
Education Development Center, Inc.
55 Chapel Street
Newton, MA 02458-1060
(617) 618-2127
bhoffman@edc.org

Paul Horwitz
Senior Scientist
The Concord Consortium
37 Thoreau Street
Concord, MA 01742
(978) 371-5856
paul@concord.org

Shari Jackson
The Concord Consortium
37 Thoreau Street
Concord, MA 01742
(978) 369.4367
shari_jackson@alum.mit.edu

Michael J. Jacobson
Chief Cognitive Scientist and Senior Consultant
Allison~LoBue Group, L.L.C.
1882 Sugarstone Drive
Lawrenceville, GA 30043
(678) 377-8844
mjjacobson@earthlink.net

Jim Kaput
Department of Mathematics
University of Massachusetts–Dartmouth
Dartmouth, MA 02747-2300
(508) 999-8321
JKaput@umassd.edu

Robert B. Kozma
Center for Technology in Learning
SRI International
333 Ravenswood Avenue
(415) 859-3997
Rkozma@unix.sri.com
Menlo Park, CA 94025

Joe Krajcik
Associate Professor, Science Education
School of Education
University of Michigan
Ann Arbor, Michigan 48109-1259
(313) 647-0597
krajcik@umich.edu

Marcia Linn
University of California at Berkeley
School of Education
4523 Tolman Hall #1670
Berkeley, CA 94720-1670
(510) 643-2303
mclinn@socrates.berkeley.edu

R. Bowen Loftin
Virtual Environment Technology Lab
University of Houston
Houston, TX 77023
(713) 743-1238
bowen@uh.edu

Barbara Means
Center for Technology in Learning
SRI International
333 Ravenswood Avenue
Menlo Park, CA 94025
(415) 859-3997
barbara_means@qm.sri.com

Jeremy Roschelle
SRI International
333 Ravenswood Avenue
Menlo Park, CA 94025-3493
(650) 859-4771
roschelle@acm.org

Philip M. Sadler
Harvard College Observatory
and Graduate School of Education
Harvard-Smithsonian Center for Astrophysics

60 Garden Street, MS 71
Cambridge, MA 02138
(617) 496-4709
psadler@cfa.harvard.edu

Marilyn Salzman
US WEST Adv. Tech.
4001 Discovery Drive
Boulder, CO 80303
(303)541-6454
mcsalzm@uswest.com

James D. Slotta
University of California at Berkeley
School of Education
4523 Tolman Hall #1670
Berkeley, CA 94720-1670
(510) 643-2303
slotta@socrates.berkeley.edu

Elliot Soloway
College of Engineering, School of Education, and
School of Information
1101 Beal Avenue
University of Michigan
Ann Arbor, MI 48109-2110
(734) 936-1562
soloway@umich.edu

Walter Stroup
Department of Curriculum and Instruction
University of Texas
Austin, TX 78712
(512) 232-3958
wstroup@mail.utexas.edu

Jennifer Turns
The EduTech Institute
Georgia Institute of Technology
Atlanta, GA 30332-0280
(404) 894-5618
Jennifer@chmsr.isye.gatech.edu

Barbara White
    4645 Tolman Hall #1670
    School of Education
    University of California
    Berkeley, CA 94720-1670
    (510) 873-8104
    bywhite@socrates.berkeley.edu

Preface

There has been, of course, great interest in recent years in the uses of technology in education, and currently considerable resources are being expended to connect schools to the Internet, purchase powerful (and increasingly affordable) computers, and so on. However, the mere availability of powerful, globally connected computers is not sufficient to insure that students will learn, particularly in areas that pose considerable conceptual difficulties such as in science and mathematics. The true challenge is not just to put advanced technologies in our schools, but to identify advanced ways to design and use these new technologies to enhance learning. The chapters in this volume represent a snapshot of current work in the field that is attempting to address this challenge.

We hope that this book will be provide valuable and timely information to a wide range of individuals, including science educators, educational and cognitive researchers, educational and instructional technologists, educational software developers, educational policy makers, and the general public. We also expect that this book will prove a suitable supplemental text in undergraduate and graduate level courses dealing with educational technologies, science education, and applied cognitive studies.

ACKNOWLEDGMENTS

We express our thanks to the Allison~LoBue Group, L.L.C., Learning and Performance Support Laboratory (LPSL) at the University of Georgia, and SRI International for their support during the preparation of this book. We are indebted to Alex J. Angulo for his commendable editing and editorial assistance on the chapters in this volume. Also, Kirstin Hierholzer provided helpful editing assistance on earlier versions of the chapters. Finally, we would like to thank Naomi Silverman, Nadine Simms,

Lori Hawver, and the entire Lawrence Erlbaum Associates staff for their
hard work and assistance in the production of this volume.

—*Michael J. Jacobson*
—*Robert B. Kozma*

1

Introduction:
New Perspectives on Designing
the Technologies of Learning

Michael J. Jacobson
Allison ~LoBue Group, L.L.C.

Alex J. Angulo
The University of Georgia

Robert B. Kozma
SRI International

From phenomena of seeming simplicity to those of unimaginable complexity, scientific research at the turn of the 21st century is advancing our understandings of the natural world at a breathtaking pace. Many of these findings are not mere incremental accumulations of "scientific facts." New perspectives are being articulated, dealing with phenomena ranging from quarks to the origin of life, that often challenge our everyday notions of the world. Much of this knowledge is difficult to understand, yet it significantly impacts our daily lives nonetheless, changing the foods we eat, the work we do, and the global conditions of the world in which we live. An understanding of these ideas is important, for both students in school and for an informed citizenry. Unfortunately, scientific knowledge formulated even prior to the 20th century—from Newton's laws of motion to Darwin's theory of evolution by natural selection—has proven challenging for students to learn. Making the sciences of the 21st century understandable will no doubt prove to be an even greater challenge.

Addressing challenges such as these has been an important component of the "innovations and explorations" described in the chapters of this volume. To help students deeply learn important scientific and mathematical knowledge, these research projects have designed and

1

developed many innovative technological tools and have explored the consequent learning processes and outcomes associated with the use of these tools. Although the chapters were written independently of each other, an overarching perspective is reflected in all of them. They each argue for the unique facilitative quality that appropriately designed technological tools provide students to not only acquire an understanding of science and mathematics but also to creatively construct, authentically experience, and socially develop and represent their understanding. Overall, this book is intended to provide not only an overview of what is possible with technological learning tools, but also a principled sense for how these tools may be designed, and why they may foster deep understandings of difficult scientific and mathematical knowledge and ideas.

CHAPTER OVERVIEWS

Kozma's chapter 2 examines the inherent quality of representation and social construction in learning and understanding chemistry. Kozma also argues for the representational and social nature of all scientific knowledge and for the prospects of technology to provide environments that support student thinking, discourse, and understanding. His chapter explores the relations between novice and expert views of chemistry and shows how these relations inform the design principles for the software application *MultiMedia and Mental Models in Chemistry* or 4M:Chem. "A central theme of the chapter," he states, "is the way that technology can augment the cognitive and social processes of scientific understanding and learning." The results from his research exemplify the emerging possibilities of computer software that supports students in the process of collaboratively constructing understandings of chemistry in particular, and of science more generally.

   A central assertion of the chapter 3, by Roschelle, Kaput, and Stroup, is that the mathematics of change and variation can be made accessible to a much wider range of students through the design of visualizations and simulations for collaborative inquiry. In contrast with the traditional course of study, they argue that the mathematics of change and variation (MCV) should be included earlier in the curriculum for students of all abilities. Roschelle, Kaput, and Stoup state that "the mission of our SimCalc project is to give ordinary children the opportunities, experiences, and resources they need to develop extraordinary understanding and skill with MCV. ...[W]e aim to democratize access to the mathematics of change."

Jackson, Krajcik, and Soloway summarize their 4 years in developing and testing a model-building software program in chapter 4, "Model-It: A Design Retrospective." The chapter discusses the project's founding premises rooted in active learning theory and learner-centered design, the design criteria of the software, and findings from the program's actual use in a Michigan high school. The purpose of the Model-It program "has been to support students, even those with only very basic math skills, as they build dynamic models of scientific phenomena and run simulations with their models to verify and analyze the results." Throughout the design and development phases of the project, the researchers attempted to "model" Model-It after the way scientists themselves learn from constructing qualitative and quantitative models of natural phenomena.

Chapter 5, by Jacobson and Archodidou, describes an approach for designing hypermedia tools for learning that they refer to as the Knowledge Mediator Framework (KMF). This framework, which is based on cognitive theory and research, consists of four major design elements (representational affordances of technology, represent knowledge-in-context, reify the deep structure of knowledge, and intra- and inter-case hyperlinks for conceptual and representational interconnectedness) and a set of correlated learning activities. The chapter describes a web-based learning tool derived from this framework, the Evolution Knowledge Mediator, and presents the results of a study of conceptual change and learning with an earlier system based on the KMF. Jacobson and Archodidou also consider the potential for using KMF tools as part of collaborative, online learning activities.

Genetics provides the vehicle for teaching scientific reasoning in the research reported by Horwitz and Christie in chapter 6. They discuss the design and use of a "computer-based manipulative" they call GenScope, and discuss how the program supports scientific thinking by students as they observe and manipulate graphic objects based on an explicit scientific model. The overall goal of the GenScope project is to help students understand not only scientific explanations, but also to gain insight into the nature of the scientific process. Following a discussion of linguistic and pedagogical barriers to learning science in the traditional classroom, GenScope's open-ended learning environment is proposed as a method for overcoming these difficulties. Horwitz and Christie include an evaluation of GenScope's effectiveness as an in-the-classroom resource. This chapter also provides a very concise account of one of the most difficult scientific concepts for students to learn—modern genetics.

Slotta and Linn (chap. 7) describe their research into making Internet resources accessible to students as an aid to understanding science. In their discussion of Knowledge Integration Environments (KIE) and Scaffolded Knowledge Integration, they illustrate the use of technology to frame autonomous learning, knowledge integration, and critical thinking skills when approaching content on the Internet. "We focus," they write, "on those aspects of KIE that support students in critiquing Internet evidence." Their chapter reports on a study involving eighth-grade science students and how they made sense of the World Wide Web, based on highlights from their *Sunlight, SunHEAT!* project.

Chapter 8 by Guzdial and Turns focuses on computer-supported collaborative learning (CSCL). Guzdial and Turns have studied methods to improve and to monitor improvements in the learning of science and engineering through the use of CSCL environments. In particular, they summarize their work with the CaMILE project (*Collaborative and Multimedia Interactive Learning Environments*): "Features in our current version of CaMILE make it possible for us to provide students with support for writing notes, support for tracking and monitoring discussion activity, and support for understanding the purpose and context of the discussion." The authors discuss research into the development of measures that characterize message interactions at a higher level of aggregation than individual messages. They then used these aggregate measures to compare and contrast the use of the CaMILE CSCL tool in multiple classes involving hundreds of students and thousands of notes.

The potential for networked technology in the study of astronomy is a central feature of Sadler, Gould, Brecher, and Hoffman's chapter 9. They illustrate student use of MicroObservatory, a state-of-the-art project that utilizes remotely accessible telescopic equipment via the Internet. These researchers describe how network technology that allows students to have access to professional quality scientific tools encourages high school student collaboration and the possibilities of promoting long-term interest in astronomy and the sciences. "This technology," they argue, "has the potential to revolutionize the teaching of science and to attract a new and larger generation of youngsters to become lifelong 'fans' of the scientific enterprise." The new remote telescopes represent advances in current telescope technology, part of a new generation of professional level scientific instruments accessible for students through the Internet.

Means and Coleman, in chapter 10, concerning the GLOBE project, describe ways in which technology can support authentic student participation in scientific investigation. In their discussion of GLOBE research, students are encouraged to collect environmental information and then post the data on the World Wide Web. They note that "GLOBE seeks to promote elementary and secondary school students' learning of science by involving them in real scientific investigation, following detailed data collection protocols for measuring the characteristics of their local atmosphere, soil, and vegetation." The lively participation involved in the project is reflected in the 4,000 schools across 55 countries that have signed on to be a part of this effort. Informed by the theoretical perspective of "anchored instruction," GLOBE has the scientific objectives of the collection of data and the educational objectives of the promotion of science learning and environmental awareness. Their review of the impact that the project has had on students points toward the creative possibilities for authenticating science learning through the use of technology.

Facilitating student's conceptual understanding of physics and of the scientific inquiry process is the focus of the White and Frederiksen's chapter 11. The authors discuss their research in the context of a 7-year study in urban classrooms and the progress they made with student learning concerning scientific inquiry goals, processes, and strategies. They argue for the potential that the ThinkerTools software has in assisting student's understanding of the Newtonian physics of force and motion by way of models and simulations. This software assists students in monitoring and reflecting on their own theory building as well as facilitating conceptual change, scientific inquiry, and further reflection. Based on their research, White and Frederiksen conclude that "a synthesis of cognitive theory with the development of new technological tools and the design of new instructional approaches can transform the nature of science education for both students and teachers." Furthermore, they propose "[i]t may even play a role in transforming how scientists themselves engage in and think about the scientific enterprise."

Chapter 12 by Dede, Salzman, Loftin, and Ash represents some of the latest and most extensive research concerning the educational applications of virtual reality technology. Through the experiential nature of virtual reality technology in their project *ScienceSpace,* they challenge typical naive student intuitions about Newtonian physics, allowing them to "construct new understandings of science" based on their experiences in the virtual environment. Informing the original design and evaluation of their project is a learner-centered philosophy that likewise guides the evolution of their technology. They discuss the learning gains in using virtual technology from the results of their studies and outline recommendations for further research.

TECHNOLOGIES OF LEARNING: THEMATIC STRANDS

As can be seen, the chapters in this volume explore the demanding conceptual aspects of learning science and mathematics—and the varied contexts in which this learning occurs—in a variety of innovative ways. A diversity of content areas, technologies, designs, theoretical perspectives, methodologies, and pedagogies are represented in the chapters. Yet weaving through this diversity of research into the design and use of technological learning tools may be seen at least four main thematic strands: *representations and symbols, design of technological tools and learning environments, collaborative interactions and learning communities, and assessment and learning processes.* This tapestry of thematic perspectives is reflected in varied and rich ways in the chapters.

The theme of *representations and symbols* is a central one in many of these chapters, one that has two dimensions: external and mental. The range of external representational and symbolic systems covered in these chapters is extensive: calculus, physics, electrostatics, quantum mechanical molecular bonding, chemical equilibrium, genetics, evolution, ecosystems, astrophysics, and engineering. Kozma suggests that there is "an integral relationship between the signs and symbols of a science and the understanding that scientists have of their domain." Furthermore, to paraphrase his comments about representations and chemists, "using and understanding a range of representations is not only a significant part of what scientists do—in a profound sense it is science." However, merely using technology to provide external representations of complex scientific knowledge is decidedly not enough. Horwitz and Christie articulate a goal that is shared in the other chapters: "We want our students to grasp not only scientific explanations of phenomena, but also the nature of the scientific process itself. In short, we want to teach them how to think like scientists."

However, the need to teach students to "think like a scientist" assumes that they often do not think in such a way. Thus a second dimension of the representations and symbols theme concerns mental representations. Slotta and Linn remark that

> In our view, students come to science class with a repertoire of models of scientific phenomena as suggested by work of Piaget (1970), diSessa (1988, 1993), and others. We use the term "model" loosely to refer to ideas, conjectures, principles, visualizations, and examples from everyday life. All of these mental constructs are drawn upon by students in support of their reasoning, and we refer to their totality as a "repertoire of models."

The concern with the learners' "repertoire of models," mental representations, or mental models is found in several of the chapters. For example, Kozma is concerned with mental models of chemistry, Roschelle and Kaput with children's conceptual and linguistic resources, Jacobson and Archodidou with mental models of evolution, Horwitz and Christie with mental schemata or conceptual frameworks, White and Frederiksen with conceptual models of physics, and Dede and associates with causal mental models. The analysis of both domain-specific symbols and students' mental representations influenced many of the technological design decisions and learning activities described in these chapters.

The second theme is *design of technological tools and learning environments*. Although these projects have been concerned, first and foremost, with issues of learning, representation, and pedagogy, they have sought to explore ways that technological tools could be designed and used to help address these issues. (This is in contrast to much of the technology and education literature in which "technology" is the focus.) The chapters in this volume depict a richness of technologies that includes simulations and visualizations (e.g., Kozma, this volume; Roschelle & Kaput, this volume; Jackson, Krajcik, & Soloway, Horwitz & Christie, this volume; White & Frederiksen, this volume), hypermedia, the Internet, and the World Wide Web (e.g., Slotta & Linn, this volume; Jacobson & Archodidou, this volume; Means & Coleman, this volume), remote scientific instrumentation (Sadler, Gould, Brecher, & Hoffman, this volume), telecommunications and computer-supported collaborative learning (e.g., Guzdial & Turns, this volume; Means & Coleman, this volume), and virtual and immersive environments (Dede, Salzman,

Loftin, & Ash, this volume). As discussed in the respective chapters, these projects are based on principles of design or design frameworks that are grounded on constructivism or sociocognitive theory. Overall, these chapters each share a concern for the principled design of the technologies of learning.

An important subtheme of design of technological tools and learning environments relates to scaffolding, which is articulated in various ways in these chapters. Jackson, Krajcik, and Soloway provide an overview of the literature related to scaffolding, and then propose three categories of technological scaffolding: supportive, reflective, and intrinsic. *Supportive scaffolding* refers to ways that the software or learning tool assists the learner in doing the task, such as modeling, guiding, or critiquing. *Reflective scaffolding* helps the learner to reflect on the task, the degree of success at doing the task, how to generalize from the task to other situations, and so on. Their third category of scaffolding, *intrinsic*, begins to alter the nature of the task by changing the focus of the learner's attention or by providing alternate conceptualizations for thinking about the task. Other perspectives on scaffolding are reflected in chapters in this volume as well. Jacobson and Archodidou describe hypermedia design features that provide conceptual scaffolding intended to make aspects of the deep structure of knowledge clear and explicit to the learner, and to demonstrate dimensions of conceptual interconnectedness across diverse cases and problems. They also discuss ways that their Knowledge Mediator learning tool can provide metaconceptual scaffolding (i.e., an awareness of one's mental representations and inferential processes) as part of learner-centered activities. Slotta and Linn describe how their KIE provides scaffolding support that may be cognitive, procedural, or metacognitive (cf., Jackson, Krajcik, & Soloway, this volume). The notion of scaffolding the inquiry process is at the center of the research in the White and Frederiksen chapter, and Dede and his colleagues consider ways that virtual reality may be designed to scaffold learners to form causal models as they engage in dynamic activities in the virtual environment.

The remaining two thematic strands deal with aspects of the overall learning environment in which technologies are used. The theme of *collaborative interactions and learning communities* is prominent in many of the chapters. The Kozma chapter and the Guzdial and Turns chapter provide excellent discussions of theory and research that persuasively advocate the importance of social interactions and discourse. Kozma writes, "designers should provide students with environments that restructure the discourse in science classrooms around collaborative knowledge building and the social construction of meaning." Each of the chapters in this volume provides models of how technological tools may be designed and used in environments to affect such collaborative knowledge building and socially mediated construction of meaning. Social and collaborative models are particularly emphasized in the chapters by Kozma; Jackson, Krajcik, and Soloway; Slotta and Linn; Sadler, Gould, Brecher, & Hoffman; Guzdial and Turns; and White and Frederiksen. New directions in collaborative learning with emerging technology are considered by Dede, Salzman, Loftin, and Ash, who outline research they are planning that would provide immersive collaborative learning opportunities for distributed learners in their ScienceSpace virtual reality environments.

The final thematic strand is *assessment and learning processes*. Obviously, it is vitally important that we know whether significant learning has taken place. This concern is of special relevance given the increasingly challenging nature of the scientific and mathematical knowledge with which students must become conversant in the 21st century. Several chapters describe research that involved the use of problem solving measures to assess learning (e.g., Kozma; Roschelle & Kaput; Jacobson & Archodidou; Horwitz & Christie; White & Frederiksen; Dede, Salzman, Loftin, & Ash). In addition to assessing individual learning outcomes, Guzdial and Turns propose a methodology for the aggregate analysis of student participation in computer discussion groups that spanned thousands of notes from hundreds of students. Other assessment methodologies involved the analysis of student project outcomes, such as designing models (Jackson, Krajcik, & Soloway), gathering and critiquing evidence from the Internet (Slotta & Linn), and conducting scientific research with remote instrumentation or distributed data collection (Sadler, Gould, Brecher, & Hoffman; Means & Coleman). Finally, assessment with standardized achievement tests is also one of the dependent measures employed by White and Frederiksen.

However, it is also necessary to understand the dynamics of the conditions under which learning occurs with technological tools. There is a need to identify "process data" and "causal mechanisms" in establishing the relation between the use of technology based interventions and learning. Much of the research to date has been pretest to posttest "outcome data" in which an experimental design can be used under the assumption one can infer a change in the learner's knowledge was due to the intervention. Unfortunately, outcome data obtained under these conditions, while important, does not specifically establish what it was about the intervention that caused the learning. That is, outcome data alone does not establish a causal mechanism. This is particularly problematic in dynamic learning environments where a technological learning tool has multiple components, and where it would be valuable to understand what learner–tool interactions had an impact and how it occurred. Chapters in this volume dealing with issues such as these include Kozma and Rochelle and Kaput.

CONCLUSION

Collectively, these chapters present a wide range of explorations into innovative ways to enhance learning with technological tools, as well as a considerable amount of research and practical experience. They are representative of the major trends in learning technology research today and also point toward the emerging research directions of tomorrow. We believe the approaches to designing and using technology described in these chapters represent potential solutions (or directions toward solutions) for many of the substantive issues that must be addressed to use technological tools and learning environments to improve students' understanding of advanced scientific and mathematical knowledge. It is our hope that these chapters—with their multiple perspectives on theory, technological design, pedagogy, learning, and research—will stimulate further explorations and innovations that will help all students deeply understand not only the concepts, but the excitement of discovery that is the true nature of modern science and mathematics.

ACKNOWLEDGMENTS

Work on this chapter was supported in part by a grant to the first author from the National Science Foundation under Grant No. RED 9616389 and by resources of the Learning and Performance Support Laboratory (LPSL) at the University of Georgia and SRI, International. The opinions expressed here are those of the authors and do not necessarily reflect the positions or policies of the sponsoring groups. Also, we acknowledge the helpful comments by Phoebe Chen Jacobson on an earlier version of this chapter.

2

The Use of Multiple Representations and the Social Construction of Understanding in Chemistry

Robert B. Kozma
SRI International

THE IMPORTANCE OF REPRESENTATION IN SCIENCE

Much of the phemomena that are of interest to the scientific community are those that exist at scales beyond our temporal, perceptual, or experiential limits. Whether the phenomenon is cosmological, geological, biological, or chemical, our window on the world is really very small. For example, it is estimated that the universe has taken 15 billion years to evolve to its current state from the primordial big bang. It has taken Earth's surface about 200 million years to form the current continents from the supercontinent Pangaea. Our early huminid ancestors began their distinct evolutionary path about 7.5 million years ago. Obviously, changes on these temporal scales are not directly accessible to us within a lifetime of 70-some years, yet understanding changes of these magnitudes is the motivation for many important lines of scientific research.

Even within more contemporary time frames, our access to scientific phenomena is limited by our perceptual mechanisms. For example, we see light waves in the range between 400 nm (violet) to 700 nm (red). Many substances absorb light energy within this range and reflect complementary wavelengths that enable us to see them. However, many other substances either do not absorb light energy or do so at wave-lengths beyond this range and thus they are invisible to us.

Size and distance also present formidable challenges to direct percep-tion. Even with optical magnification, it is physically impossible for us to see anything smaller than 2×10^{-5} cm, yet the largest atoms are about 5.0×10^{-8} cm in diameter; the diameter of the smallest atom, hydrogen, is 6.4×10^{-9} cm. At the other extreme, the universe is about 10 billion light-years across and expanding at the relative rate of 50 km per second per megaparsec. However, the furthest astronomical object that we can see with the naked eye is M 31, the Andromeda Galaxy, which is only about 2.5 million light-years away from us.

Expansion of the universe, tectonic plate drift, the evolution of species, and molecular structure and reactivity are all scientific phenomena that are not available to direct experience. Yet, understanding these phenom-ena is crucial to the development of scientific knowledge. Science in the 21st century will be even less accessible to our direct perceptions and actions as we push the boundaries of current knowledge.

Consequently, our understanding of scientific phenomena will be increasingly dependent on our ability to access and interact with them indirectly. Currently, much of what scientists understand is derived from physical signs, frequently mediated by instruments of some sort, such as the red spectral shift of moving galaxies, sonar mapping of the undersea volcanic ridges that separate continents, carbon-13 dating of skeletal remains, genetic comparisons across species, and nuclear magnetic resonance (NMR) spectra of molecular structures. Our understanding is further mediated by the symbolic expressions created to represent these phenomena, such as verbal descriptions, numerical equations, coordinate graphs, structural diagrams, and so on.

Tools and symbol systems have played an important role in the development of science. Historically, significant progress in scientific understanding has been associated with the introduction of new tools or instruments that have allowed scientists to go beyond their experien-tial and perceptual limitations. Progress has also been associated with the creation of new representational forms that have allowed scientists to think and communicate differently about scientific phenomena. In chemistry, for example, the perceptual inability to distinguish among invisible gases impeded the understanding of pneumatic chemistry, as well as that of other more visible chemical phenomena, such as combus-tion and acidity, until the late 18th century (Brock, 1992; Partington,

1989). The invention of the pneumatic trough, eudiometer, gasometer, combustion globe, and ice calorimeter, used with the earlier technology of the balance, allowed 18th century chemists to isolate gases and to collect precise quantitative data about these invisible substances. Lavoisier combined the ability to separate chemical substances with a new way of representing them—a new nomenclature and symbol system—to bring about a revolution in chemical thought by focusing on the imperceptible, elemental composition of substances. In creating new representational forms, Lavoisier moved the discipline of chemistry beyond a science of substances to the modern science of molecular composition and structure.

Goals of the Chapter

The focus of this chapter is on the inherently representational nature of scientific understanding and the development of new ways of representing science that support this process, particularly ways that support students' learning. I examine the role that representations play in science and the expertise that scientists have developed in using representations to do their work and to understand scientific phenomena. By way of contrast, I examine the difficulty that students have in understanding science and in using scientific representations.

A central theme of the chapter is the way that technology can augment the cognitive and social processes of scientific understanding and learning. I discuss design principles for such technological environments that use the surface features of representations to help students understand deep, underlying scientific principles. I examine a particular software application in chemistry—MultiMedia and Mental Models in Chemistry or 4M:Chem—that implements these principles, and I evaluate the impact it has on students' understanding. The chapter ends by extending this discussion to show how students can interact with each other and with the computer software to socially construct an understanding of chemical phenomenon.

REPRESENTATION AND EXPERTISE

Representations and Scientific Expertise in Chemistry

Creating an understanding from signs and symbols is much of what scientists do. This is often an arduous and effortful activity. For example, in our ethnographic study in industrial and academic chemical laboratories (Kozma, Chin, Russell, & Marx, in press), we observed chemists working individually and together using a range of signs and symbols to understand the results of their syntheses. Among the signs they used were the colored traces of thin layer and column chromatography and the characteristic arrangement, shape, and clustering of peaks on the printouts of mass and NMR spectroscopy. The symbolic representations that these chemists created included structural diagrams, equations, and chemical formulas.

The chemists in our study used these various signs and representations to converge on an understanding of the scientific phenomena that were the objects of their research. We observed chemists moving back and forth between these symbols and signs, for example, between the structural diagrams of target compounds and NMR spectra of their results, to speculate on the composition and structure of the products they had synthesized. Sometimes they used the features of diagrams to generate hypotheses about the structure of compounds and then confirm or reject these by examining the clustering and position of spectral peaks; other times their interpretation of specific features of spectra would be aided by sketching out a diagram that might explain them. Sometimes they would confirm that they had synthesized their desired products; at other times they would find that they had not and they would go back and take the experiment in a different direction. The chemists would at times agree on the interpretation of signs and representations; whereas on other occasions they would disagree and deliberate.

In this way, the chemists of our study were much like the researchers in a genetics laboratory studied by Amman and Knorr-Cetina (1990). Scientists in this laboratory gathered around recently exposed X-ray films of DNA or RNA fragments. As they examined the film, they pointed, made verbal references to marks on the film, drew inferences, raised objections, asked questions, returned to the film, provided replies, and so on until a conclusion, but not necessarily a consensus, was reached. This socially constructed sense of "what was seen" was reproduced when the data were transformed into evidence that appeared in scientific papers or in oral presentations. These observations and those of our ethnographic study confirm the unsettled, problematic, fallible, human social activity of "science in the making" or "science of the unknown" (Latour, 1987; Lemke, 1990) and the role that representations play in this negotiated process.

These findings also suggest an integral relation between the signs and symbols of a science and the understanding that scientists have of their domain. The use and understanding of a range of representations is not only a significant part of what chemists do—in a profound sense it is chemistry (Hoffman & Laszlo, 1991). Perhaps that is why chemists are so skilled at using multiple representations. In our experimental laboratory (Kozma & Russell, 1997), we found significant differences between expert and novice chemists in their ability to create an understanding of chemistry using a variety of representational forms, particularly language. In this study, we gave practicing chemists (i.e., experts) and college chemistry students (i.e., novices) two multimedia cognitive tasks. In the first task, subjects were asked to view a number of computer displays in one of four representational forms (graphs, molecular-level animations, chemical equations, and video segments of experiments) and to group these displays into meaningful sets. As in other studies of expertise (Glaser, 1990; Glaser & Chi, 1988), our expert chemists were able to create large, chemically meaningful clusters. In doing so, experts frequently used three or four different kinds of representations to create their groups. In addition, experts used conceptual terms to describe or label their clusters, terms such as "gas law," "collision theory," and so on.

For the second task in our study, subjects were asked to view a series of representations of chemical phenomena presented in one form and to transform each into another form (e.g., transform an animation into a corresponding graph, a video of a reaction into an equation). Experts were much more able than novices to transform any given representation into a chemically meaningful representation in another form. They were particularly skilled at providing an appropriate linguistic transformation, or description, for a representation given in any other form, much more so than novices.

The results of our laboratory study of representational expertise in chemistry corresponds to those in other scientific domains, such as climatology (Lowe, 1987) and biology (Kindfield, 1994). For example, Lowe found that meteorologists were much more able to accurately reconstruct a weather map from memory than were non-meteorologists. Perhaps more significant is how experts and non-experts differed in the strategies they used to recall the elements of the weather map. Meteorologists recalled elements in patterns based on underlying meteorological principles; non-meteorologists recalled elements based on the similarities of their surface features. Kindfield compared biologists with more or less advanced training in genetics in their spontaneous use of diagrams to reason about subcellular biological processes. She found that geneticists used their diagrams in a flexible way to help them think through the immediate reasoning task. Their diagrams, in turn, cued relevant knowledge that was used to solve the problem. Undergraduate biology students, on the other hand, used diagrams in a rigid way and could not map them onto the problem they were trying to solve. Kindfield has taken these findings as evidence that advanced representational skills and conceptual knowledge co-evolve or mutually influence one another in the development of understanding of a scientific phenomena, a position supported by the findings from our studies.

In summary, experts are able to use a range of signs and symbols to create an understanding of scientific phenomena. They move fluidly back and forth between representations and use them together to solve problems. Furthermore, these representations are used within a community of other scientists to state hypotheses, make claims, draw inferences, ask questions, raise objections, and reach conclusions.

Representation and the Understanding of Novices

Whereas chemists in our laboratory study (Kozma & Russell, 1997) demonstrated their expertise in the use of various representations, novices lacked both the underlying knowledge of chemists and their representational skills. Whereas the expert chemists were able to create large clusters, the novices created significantly smaller clusters. Whereas the experts also used three or four different representations to create their groups, the groups composed by novices more often included only one or two different types of representations. Whereas the experts also used conceptual terms to describe their clusters, the descriptions of novices were more often based on the surface features of the representations in the cluster—features such as color, objects depicted, graph labels, and types of representations (e.g., "red molecules bouncing around," "graphs of pressure and concentration," etc.). Finally, novices were much less able than experts to transform a given representation into another form. In brief, whereas experts were able to use their deep conceptual understanding and their representational skill to create chemically meaningful clusters that connected different representational forms, the understanding of novices was more dependent on and bounded by the surface features of particular representations and they could not connect chemical phenomena represented in one form to the same ones represented in another form.

The reliance of novices on the surface features severely impedes their ability to understand scientific phenomena and reason about them. First, students' understanding is often constrained by the physical aspects of a scientific phenomena, and there is frequently little about these surface features that correspond to underlying chemical entities or processes. For example, Krajcik (1991) interviewed ninth-grade students and asked them to draw how the air in a flask would appear if they could see it through a very powerful magnifying glass. A large majority of the students did not draw air as composed of tiny particles; rather, they simply drew wavy lines to represent the air in the flask. Similarly, Nakhleh (1992) found that 11th-grade students who had completed a unit on acids and bases drew waves, bubbles, or shiny patches when asked to draw how an acid or base would appear under a very powerful magnifying glass. In these studies, students could not move beyond the surface features of the physical phenomena to develop an understanding of the underlying chemical entities and processes.

Second, novice understanding seems to be constrained by the surface features of symbol systems and symbolic expressions used to represent science. Unfortunately, there is little about the surface of these symbols that corresponds to the underlying chemistry concepts. Students also lack the representational competence to make the mappings from symbols to these abstractions. Consequently, scientific symbols often do not help and frequently interfere with students' understanding of chemistry. For example, in a study by Kozma, Russell, Johnston, and Dershimer (1990), college students had a variety of misconceptions about chemical equilibrium that corresponded to the symbol systems that they were using. Many students had the notion that at equilibrium, chemical reactions stop. There is nothing about the surface features of the symbol used to represent equilibrium (i.e., $\Leftrightarrow$) that would convey its underlying dynamic nature. In a study by Yarroch (1985), high school chemistry students were interviewed on the meaning of chemical equations. Even though they were able to balance chemical equations, most students had little understanding of the chemical meaning of these symbols. They were not able to differentiate between subscripts and coefficients in the chemical equation $N_2 + 3H_2 \rightarrow 2NH_3$, and they represented $3H_2$ as 6 connected dots, rather than as 3 diatomic pairs. Students do not seem to be able to connect the symbolic expressions used by scientists to the scientific phenomena they are meant to represent. As Krajcik (1991) pointed out, although students are frequently good at manipulating chemical symbols, they often treat them as mathematical puzzles without possessing a understanding of the chemistry that corresponds to these symbols.

As science of the 21st century becomes more complex and less available to direct perception and interaction, the challenge will be to help students move beyond their dependence on surface features to develop both their representational skills and their understanding of these increasingly complex scientific phenomena. In doing so, science educators must find new symbol systems and symbolic expressions that will allow students to make connections between the things that they can see and manipulate and the underlying invisible science.

Building on Surface Features:
Multiple Linked Representations

In general, the relations between many symbol systems and their fields of reference are arbitrary ones (Goodman, 1976). That is, the specific features of a symbolic element may not have any direct correspondence to those of an entity it represents. For example, there is nothing about the word "cat" that directly corresponds to the species or a particular animal to which it refers. Rather, the word cat is a token or symbol that merely stands for a particular animal or for the species. The arbitrary relation between this symbol and its field of reference has been assigned by cultural convention. Its meaning is acquired by use in the context of various cats to which the symbol refers.

The creation of meaning by connecting a symbol and its referent in the context of use is particularly important for novices to a domain. Because novices rely on surface features and because there is nothing about the features of the word cat that correspond to its referent, it would be difficult for someone to assign meaning to this word if it was first encountered outside the context of a referent. The use of the word in conjunction with a specific referent allows the novice to assign meaning to it based on the surface features of the referent. Once the connection between a symbol and its referent is established, an image of a cat can be evoked when the word is used, even when a specific referent is not present.

Likewise, acquiring meaning for words and for other symbols that scientists use is difficult for novices because the field of reference is frequently not available, often for reasons described at the beginning of this chapter. Terms like "expansion of the universe," "evolution of the species," or "molecular reaction" are difficult to understand in large part because students are not able to perceive the phenomena to which they refer. This fact and the dependence of novices on surface features suggest the need for new symbol systems and symbolic expressions that have surface features that more directly and explicitly correspond to scientific entities and processes that are inaccessible because of limitations of time, distance, size, or perception.

Our research and development (Kozma, Russell, Jones, Marx, & Davis, 1996) draws on the assumption that technology can be used to design new symbolic representations with surface features that correspond to and behave like scientific entities and processes. The capabilities of computers play an important role in the design and use of these new representations (Kozma, 1991). The symbolic capabilities of the computer can be used to create graphic elements that in some way correspond to abstract entities that do not otherwise have a concrete, visible character—entities such as "force," "genotype," and "molecule." The computer also has the important capability of being able to "proceduralize" the relations among these symbols. Arrows, balls, and other symbolic elements can be programmed to behave in ways that correspond to the behavior of forces, genotypes, and other abstract concepts. For example, a velocity arrow can become longer or shorter, depending on the direction of acceleration. As a consequence, learners can manipulate these symbols, observe the consequences of their actions, and come to assign meaning to these symbols as they correspond to the underlying scientific concepts.

Within these software environments, these new symbolic expressions can be linked to other representations that correspond to real-world situations or to the more formal symbolic expressions used by experts. These referential links between different representations in the software environment can help students make the mental connections necessary to integrate conceptual entities, real-world situations, and symbolic expressions used by experts. As a consequence, students can come to have scientifically accurate meanings for the words and for other symbols that scientists use but that otherwise have rather arbitrary relations to scientific phenomena.

The Design of Representational Environments for Education

Several researchers in this volume (White & Frederiksen; Horwitz & Christie; Dede, Salzman, Loftin, & Ash; Roschelle, Kaput, & Stroup) have designed computational environments that illustrate these ideas. White and Frederiksen (chap. 11, this volume), for example, designed a software program, entitled ThinkerTools, in which students operate on symbolic elements to develop a Newtonian understanding of the relation between force and motion. The activities in this software environment use symbolic elements that stand for real-world objects (e.g., spaceships or billiard balls, as represented by simple picture graphics), as well as for abstract concepts, such as force or acceleration. For example, a symbolic object, such as a spaceship, moves across the screen and an additional symbol is used to represent the object's change in velocity over time (i.e., its acceleration). Acceleration is represented by a "dot print" that trails the object and consists of a series of dashed lines, the length of which is proportional to its velocity at a given time. As the student uses force (represented by a key press) to act on an object, another symbol, called a "datacross," decomposes the force into its xy vectorial components. As the learner applies more force (additional key presses) to the object, he or she would see not only the resulting effect on the object as it moves, but a dynamic decomposition of the force into its orthogonal vectors (i.e., the datacross) and a dynamic representation of the change in velocity over time (i.e. its dot print). By interacting with this symbol system, students can acquire an understanding of the relation between force and acceleration as it is traditionally represented in a force–acceleration equation and as it is acted out in the world. White and Frederiksen demonstrate that this environment is effective in helping even young students understand the complex concepts of force and acceleration.

With ThinkerTools, White and Frederiksen are helping students to understand the relation between force and acceleration by designing symbolic entities that correspond to these abstractions and then creating links between these symbolic entities that correspond to the underlying science. Links can also be created across different representational systems. These cross-representational links can help students to extend their understanding to include aspects of the phenomena uniquely represented in the second system, as demonstrated by another environment described in this volume.

Horwitz and Christie (chap. 6, this volume) have developed an environment called GenScope that helps beginning biology students understand the relation between genotype and phenotype, among other pedagogical goals. The genetic model that underlies this environment is represented at five levels: DNA, chromosome, organism, pedigree, and population. At each level, students can symbolically operate on this genetic model and see what happens to a fictional species of dragon. For example, the chromosome level describes phenomena that take place on the scale of a single cell. This level represents the underlying model in two ways—a cellular display in which chromosomes of one specimen of dragon are seen as animated "spaghetti strands," and a diagrammatic display that represents chromosomes with their associated genes in much the same form as they are found in textbook diagrams. Students can combine a cell from a male dragon with one from a female to create a fertilized zygote, which then becomes a new organism. Students can observe the resulting processes of mitosis (cellular reproduction) and meiosis (gamete formation) as QuickTime movies of real cells taken under a microscope running synchronously with computer-generated animations of chromosomes replicating and segregating.

This level of representation is linked with other levels. For example, the student can move up from the chromosome level to the organism level. This allows students to create and observe the organisms that grow out of fertilized zygotes. The model uses information on the genotype of organisms to display their phenotypes, such that the resulting off-spring will have certain observable characteristics (e.g., wings, horns, etc.). As a result of their exploration within these linked representations, students can come to understand the meaning of one symbolic expression in terms of its effect on the second and consequently understand the underlying scientific relation between genetic processes at the cellular level and physical characteristics at an organism level.

GenScope creates links between representations by making the actions that the student takes within one representation correspond to certain outcomes in another representation. However, linkages can be accomplished by any of a variety of symbolic conventions that would allow students to map surface features of one representation onto those of another. For example, the number and relative location of symbolic entities could be the same in both representations. In the case of GenScope, chromosomes that appear as spaghetti strands in one display at the chromosome level correspond to those in textbook diagrams that appear in the second display at this level. Another linking convention may be that the color of entities in one representation might be the same as those in another. The onset of an event in one representation could coincide with the onset of an event in another, and so on. Links can also be made through narration; a soundtrack can identify the connections between entities or events in one representation and those in another. Clearly, several of these linkage mechanisms can be used together in a reinforcing way.

The common information across representations serves several cognitive functions. First, students can use this common information to create identities across representations—that a symbol in one representation means the same thing as a symbol in another. Second, the commonality could increase the likelihood that redundant information will be stored in memory. Finally, the common information could provide a cognitively useful means for traversing the multiple representations and integrating information in one representation with that in another. That is, having used the common surface features in two representations to move from one to the other, students then encounter information in the second representation that is in some way different from that in the first, as between the cellular and organism levels in GenScope. The unique surface features of the second representation express some aspect of the phenomenon in a way that is not or cannot be expressed in the first representational system. Students can use this additional information in the second representation to elaborate the understanding formed from the first.

Multiple Linked Representations in Chemistry

We have applied design principles such as these to build a software environment that helps students understand concepts and principles in chemistry (Kozma et al., 1996; Russell et al, 1997; Russell & Kozma, 1994). Our goal with this environment is to help chemistry students become more expertlike in their understanding of chemistry and to express their understanding in various ways. The software, entitled MultiMedia and Mental Models in Chemistry, or 4M:Chem,[1] provides the professor in the lecture hall or students in the computer laboratory with a way of exploring chemical systems using multiple linked representations.

---

[1] A version of this software is soon to be released by John Wiley under the title "Synchronized multiple vizulations of chemistry," by J. Russell, R. Kozma, D. Becker, & T. Susskind.

A student might begin a typical session by selecting an experiment, say "Equilibrium," and a chemical system, "N_2O_4/NO_2" for example. The selected system would be displayed as a chemical equation in the "control window" (see Fig. 2.1). The control window allows students to manipulate certain parameters that correspond to the selected experiment (e.g., increase temperature, reduce pressure) and see the effects of their actions as they propagate through simultaneously displayed multiple dynamic representations that include a video of the reaction, dynamic graphs, displays of instrumental methods used to follow the reaction, and molecular-level animations of the reaction.

For example, the student could select the video window and in the control window he or she could change the temperature of the system. The video window would show the system as it appears on the laboratory bench, being heated and changing color as the equilibrium shifts. The students could then select the graph window and "rerun" the reaction. Simultaneous to the video replay, the dynamic graph would show changes in partial pressures that increase or decrease as the system is heated and plateau at equilibrium.

The animation window this designed such that the surface features of the representation correspond to abstract chemical entities and behaviors that students would not otherwise directly observe in the laboratory. In this window, we create symbolic objects that represent the different types of molecules moving and colliding: sometimes reactants form products, sometimes products form reactants.

We use color and the simultaneous onset of events as design conventions to link these different representations, such that objects and events in one representation correspond to those in others. For example, NO_2 is a reddish-brown gas in the video, the line of the graph labeled NO_2 is red, and the balls in the animation that represent NO_2 are also red. As the N_2O_4 dissociates when heated, the system becomes a dark red in the video window, the red partial pressure line for NO_2 increases in the graph window, and the number of red-brown NO_2 molecules increases in the animation window. As the reaction progresses, a new point of equilibrium is reached, yet this new state is represented differently in each window. The color remains constant in the video window, the partial pressures plateau in the graph window, and the molecules in the animation window continue to move and react while maintaining a constant ratio of products and reactants.

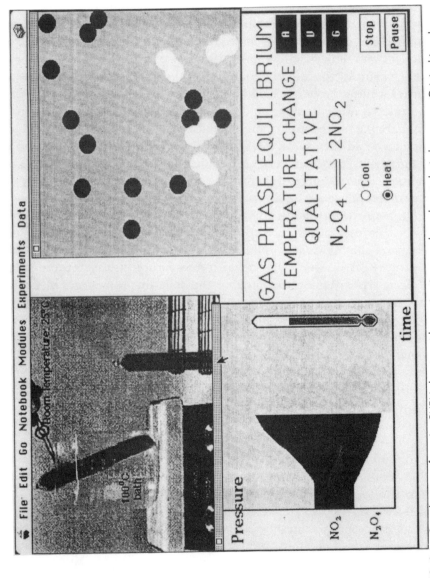

FIG. 2.1. Sample screen from 4m:CHEM showing video, animation, graph, and control windows open. Original in color.

The intended consequence of using this system is that students will come to understand equilibrium as an integration of the surface features across these multiple linked representations. That is, they will come to understand the meaning of each representation in terms of both the surface features of that representation and the surface features of other representations to which it is linked. So for example, based on the surface features of the graph (i.e., the plateau of the lines over time), a student would understand that at equilibrium the partial pressures of the species are constant. The student would take the surface features of the animation (i.e., balls continuing to collide and react) to mean that at equilibrium, reactions continue to occur in both directions. As a result of the link between the two representations—created by the common colors and simultaneous events—students would come to take the plateau of lines to mean both that the partial pressures are constant and that the reactions continue to occur. The ability to take different representations as meaning the same thing is the skill exhibited by experts (Kozma & Russell, 1997) that we are trying to instill in students.

In our early research (Russell et al., 1997), 4M:Chem was used in two sections of general chemistry at a Midwestern university. In a pre-test–posttest experiment, students significantly increased their understanding of chemical equilibrium, as measured by tests that asked them to give brief open-ended answers, calculate quantities, and draw diagrams. Also, students significantly reduced misconceptions of the sort identified by Kozma and associates (1990). In studies reported in the following section, we examine in more detail the cognitive effects of the underlying design principles.

AN EXPERIMENTAL STUDY:
THE COGNITIVE EFFECTS OF
SURFACE FEATURES

In this study, we tested two principles that underlie our design. The first principal is that the surface features designed into symbol systems and their symbolic expressions correspond in a direct way to the nature of the understanding that is achieved by using them. A corollary principle is that the use of each symbol system results in a different understanding that corresponds to its unique surface features.

For example, the primary surface feature of the video window is that the color changes when the equilibrium is effected in some way (e.g., the temperature or the pressure increases) and the color stops changing when equilibrium is reached. This surface feature would support an understanding that an increase in the temperature or the pressure results in a change in the chemical system and that after a while the system stops changing. The primary surface features in the graph window are the two lines of different colors that increase or decrease over time and then plateau. Students who use the graph window could take these surface features as meaning that the relative amounts of the two species increase or decrease and then stop changing. In the animation window, the continuous interaction of the "balls" or "molecules" represent the dynamic quality of the system such that more reactions lead to products than to reactants, but at equilibrium the relative amounts of reactants and products stay the same and the reactions between reactants and products continue at the same rate.

The second principal that we tested is that the nature of understanding derived from multiple, linked representations is additive, at least to some extent. That is, we expected that students who use videos, graphs, and animations will have an understanding of chemical equilibrium that is a combination of the understanding derived from the individual representations.

To examine the effects of the different representations in our software environment, we enlisted students enrolled in an introductory chemistry course in a community college who were randomly assigned to four different versions of 4M:Chem. Seventeen students completed the study.

Procedure

We configured the software in four different ways so we could isolate the effects of the different types of representations on student learning. Specifically, three groups of students were assigned to conditions in which they were given the chemical equations for each experiment along with one other dynamic representational form: either the Videos (V), the dynamic Graphs (G), or the Animations (A). A fourth group received video, graphs, and animations.

The content was organized around principles related to chemical equilibrium and addressed common misconceptions that college students have regarding this concept (Kozma et al., 1990). Students in all groups received a manual that structured their experience with the software. After explaining the instructional purpose of the unit and how the software operated, the manual directed the students through a series of experiments related to the concept of equilibrium, characteristics of the state of chemical equilibrium, and how equilibrium is affected by changes in temperature, pressure, and concentration—what is referred to as Le Chatelier's Principle.

Each experiment in the manual used a similar format: predict, observe, explain, and conclude. After introducing a particular experiment, the manual asked students a series of questions in which they were to predict the results of a particular experimental manipulation (e.g., increase temperature, increase pressure), make observations of the results of the experiment as displayed in the respective representational form or forms, explain the results (particularly if they disagreed with predictions), and draw conclusions about the nature of chemical equilibrium and the effects of various changes. Students were asked to write their responses to questions in the manual and to think out loud as they progressed through the materials.

Upon altering the system in some way, students would observe the effects of this change as represented by the video, graph, animation, or all three, depending on their assigned group. A voice narration directed the students' attention to key features in the representation and described what was occurring. For example, during the heating experiment for the Animation version, the narration said, "As time passes, notice that the average speed of the red and white molecules increases. Also notice that more red molecules form and only a small fraction of collisions between red molecules produce white molecules."

A group that received the full version of the software (VGA) saw the results of their actions in the following order: First, they saw the chemical equation for the reaction along with a video segment of the experiment, exactly as students in the video (V) condition. Then the experiment was rerun showing a dynamic graph (as in the G condition) and following this it was run again showing an animation (as in the A condition). Each of these was accompanied by the same narration that students heard in the single representation conditions. After watching the individual representations, students then saw all of the representations together. This was accompanied by a different narration that identified linkages across representations. For example, for the heating experiment, the narration said:

> Notice that as the tube is placed into the hot water bath, it turns a darker brown in the video, while the pressure of NO_2 increases in the graph window, and the number of red molecules increases in the animation window.

In this study, students used the materials individually. There was an experimenter in the room during the session to assist with technical problems, but if students had questions about the chemistry, they were asked to work them out on their own using the software.

Students took a pretest and a posttest. These tests consisted of items with stimuli and responses that used a variety of representations. For example, students were asked to give definitions, given a diagram of a system at equilibrium and asked to draw the diagram as it would represent the system at a new equilibrium, and were given an animation and asked to draw a graph that represented the animation. It took about two hours for students to complete the instructional materials and both tests.

Results

As a result of their experience with the software, the students as a group significantly increased their test scores from 18.8 % on the pretest to 50.0% on the posttest (t (16) = 5.49, $p < .05$). Students also significantly decreased the number of misconceptions they displayed when defining chemical equilibrium from a mean of .94 (SD = .66) to a mean of .56 (SD = .51; t (16) = 1.86, $p < .05$). These results correspond to those in previous studies using 4M:Chem (Russell et al., 1997). There were no significant differences between groups on their total scores F (3, 13) = 1.6, $p < .05$), with the V group scoring a mean of 45.0% (M = 2.5, SD = 2.12), the G group, 58.0% (M = 4.6, SD = 1.52), the A group, 48.0% (M = 3.4, SD = 2.30) and the VGA group, 42.0% (M = 1.6, SD = 2.70).

The first design principle that we tested does not predict higher aggregate scores for one group or for another, but it does predict certain qualitative differences in understanding between groups, as measured by items testing different aspects of their understanding. Specifically, the principle predicts that a student's understanding of a phenomenon will be shaped by the characteristics of the unique surface features of a given representation. In this regard, there were important differences between the understanding of students who received the Animation, the Graph, and the Video versions that corresponded to the respective surface features of these versions, as evidenced by responses to specific test items and questions in the manual.

First, students in the Animation condition (A) did significantly better on 3 of the 10 items dealing with the dynamic nature of equilibrium:

the definition of equilibrium, a similar item that asked for the meaning of an equilibrium equation, and an item regarding the effect of temperature on concentrations of a system at equilibrium. Students in the Animation group had a mean score of 2.4 (SD = 1.34) on these items, whereas students in the other groups scored .92 (SD = .79, $F(1, 15)$ = 8.25, $p < .05$).

The responses of the Animation group to these three items illustrate the impact of the animation's surface features—the motion and interaction of molecules or "balls" of different colors—on students' understanding. What distinguished the students in this group from students in the other conditions was the way they characterized equilibrium in terms of its dynamic properties. For example, in defining the concept of equilibrium, students A17 and A32 said about equilibrium "that reactions still occur but the relative numbers of the substances remain pretty stable (A17)" and that "particles are being formed and separated simultaneously (A32)." Students in other groups more often got this item wrong (e.g., G15: "When the system is balanced between reagent and product."). Or their correct answers did not include comments about the dynamic quality of equilibrium. For example, student VGA13 said, "chemical equilibrium is when the concentration of molecules remains constant over time," and V23 said, "equal or proportional amounts of reactants and products."

In describing the meaning of a given equilibrium equation, all five of the students in the Animation condition gave correct descriptions after having given incorrect responses on the pretest. Students A17, A19, and A32 all mentioned the dynamic quality of the system. As A17 put it, "N_2O_4 decomposes to $2NO_2$; $2NO_2$ combines to form N_2O_4." A19 wrote, "Dinitrogen tetroxide goes to react to give 2 mol (sic) NO_2 and vice versa, except there is only one mol (sic) of N_2O_4." Similarly, A32 said "N_2O_4 particles will be breaking into 2 NO_2 particles at the same time that the NO_2 particles will be paring to form N_2O_4." Students using other representations more often described the equation merely as an equilibrium reaction. As G24 put it, "Chemical equilibrium between N_2O_4 and 2 NO_2."

This dynamic quality was also exhibited in a question regarding the effect of temperature on systems at equilibrium. Three of the five Animation students answered this correctly on the posttest, having given incorrect responses on the pretest. None of the students in the graph or the video groups got this posttest item correct and only one of the students in the VGA group got it correct after answering it incorrectly on the pretest.

Responses to questions in the manual indicated that animation students came to understand the effect of temperature on the energy or "speed" of the molecules and the way this shifts the equilibrium. For example, after using the animations to examine the system at different temperatures, students were asked to predict what would happen to the system when it is cooled. Student A17 said, "Molecules will move slower: N_2O_4 will dominate. Reactions to NO_2 will still occur at equilibrium." Student A32 responded: "press(ure) down, particles slow movement." These responses contrasted with students in other groups who did not come to understand the effect of temperature on equilibrium. When asked to predict what would happen when a system was cooled, students in the Video treatment merely said that it would turn a lighter color. Students in the Graph group generally indicated that the pressures of N_2O_4 would increase and NO_2 would decrease. Without a sense of the mechanism or process by which temperature effects equilibrium, students in these groups more often responded incorrectly on the posttest item dealing with the effect of temperature on equilibrium.

A second finding supports the effect of surface features on understanding. Students in the Graph condition (G) did significantly better on two test items that dealt with relative proportions or concentrations of reagents: one item asked students to construct a diagram that shows the concentration of reagents at a new equilibrium and one asked for the effect of changes in pressure on equilibrium. In drawing the diagram, students in the Graph condition more often represented all of the species present at equilibrium than did students in other conditions. On the item related to pressure, Students in the Graph condition more often correctly stated the effect of pressure on a system at equilibrium. Students in the Graph conditions scored an average of 1.4 ($SD = .89$) on these two items, whereas students in the other conditions scored a mean of .33 ($SD = .49$; $F(1, 15) = 10.27$, $p < .05$).

In analyzing students' responses to questions in the manual, evidence suggests that students in the Graph condition used the shape of the curves—particularly the area under the curve and the parallel lines of the graph at equilibrium—to construct an understanding of equilibrium in terms of relative concentrations or "amounts" of the different species that are "constant" at equilibrium. In predicting the effect on equilibrium of increasing the pressure, G11 said "NO_2 will decrease more than

N_2O_4," and G12 said "Pressure increase in N_2O_4 then equal amounts of N_2O_4 & NO_2." When students were asked whether the system was in equilibrium at the end of the experiment, G11 said, "Yes, the two lines are parallel," whereas G12, G16, and G24 all responded positively because the pressures remained "constant."

Although the previously described evidence described supports our first hypothesis that surface features of individual representations can shape understanding in particular ways, the results of this study did not support our second hypothesis. This hypothesis states that the use of multiple linked representatives can have an additive effect over the use of any of the representations individually. As a group, the students in the VGA condition did no better than students in the other groups. In fact, only one of the students in the VGA condition displayed the multirepresentational characteristics that are predicted by the theory. VGA22 scored 10% on the pretest and 70% on the posttest and eliminated two misconceptions displayed on the pretest. On the pretest, VGA22 exhibited common misconceptions by defining equilibrium as "when you have two or more substances which, when mixed, are equal and stop reacting." On the posttest, however, this student correctly responded that equilibrium is "when the proportion of chemicals in a mixture remains constant."

A look at the responses of this student while using the software shows that he was able to develop his understanding by elaborating knowledge gained in one representation with that gained from others, as predicted by our theory. For example, when asked to predict what would happen to an equilibrium system when heated, VGA22 said, "I think (it would turn) more reddish-brown and the molecules will move faster and increase the pressure. The red molecules will become dominant."

In this protocol, the student displayed characteristics from all three of the representations in a linked or coordinated way—the reddish-brown color represented in the video, the motion of the molecules represented in the animation, and the increase in pressure represented in the graph. Unfortunately, this student was the exception rather than the rule for the VGA treatment. Two of the other students in the VGA condition persisted in their misconceptions on the posttest with VGA18 saying that "chemical equilibrium is a state in which a chemical reaction stops occurring." VGA20 says it is "when all the chemicals are equal."

Several questions asked students to report their observations as they conducted their experiments. The responses to these questions show the ways students in the VGA condition processed the representations. Responses to these questions show that color was the most salient feature used by these students. When asked to describe what happened when students increased the temperature on the system, four of the students in the VGA condition reported only that "the color darkened." When conducting the pressure experiment, students were asked to describe the characteristics of a system when it reached equilibrium. Again, color dominated the responses of students in the VGA condition: VGA13 said, "The color would not change." VGA18 said, "It would be darker." VGA20 said, "Color would be less." Finally, VGA27 said, "lighter color."

Discussion

As a group, the students significantly increased their understanding of equilibrium and reduced their misconceptions when they used 4M:Chem. The results of this study and those in other chapters in this volume (White & Frederiksen; Horwitz; Dede, Salzman, & Loftin; Roschelle, Kaput, & Stroup) demonstrate the potential that technology has for providing designers with a powerful new symbolic pallet that can be used to create effective instructional environments. The graphic and computation capabilities of computers can be used to design new symbol systems and symbolic representations with surface features that correspond to and behave like the abstract scientific entities and processes in the mental models of experts. These environments can provide students with access to complex scientific concepts that are otherwise inaccessible because of limitations of time, distance, size, or perception.

At the same time, the findings of this study highlight the potential limitations of these environments. The effectiveness of these environments depends heavily on the cognitive strategies that students use in response to the strategies used by designers. In 4M:Chem, symbolic elements in the various representations were referentially linked to help students make the mental connections from one representation to another that would allow them to integrate their understanding across representations. The hypothesized mechanism for the additive effect of these multiple representations is a two-step process. First, students would use the linkages, or common surface features, to establish identities between representations and thus move from one representation to another. Having done this, the students could then use the unique surface features of the second representation to elaborate or add onto an understanding gained from the first one. For example, one would expect the students in the VGA group to have displayed both an understanding of the dynamic character of equilibrium gained from the animation and the relative concentration of reagents gained from the graph. However, contrary to this prediction, the students in the VGA group did not make the expected elaborations and they did not do as well as students in the Animation group or students in the Graph group on these items.

Evidence suggests that students did engage in the first step of the hypothesized two-step process; they made links across representations. Color and simultaneity of events were the primary surface features used to create linkages across representations in 4M:Chem. For example, the reddish-brown color that appears when equilibrium shifts to NO_2 in the vessel in the video is also the color used in the graph to show the increased concentration of NO_2 and the color of the NO_2 molecules in the animation. That these common features were successful in helping students make a connection among the representations is attested to by the fact that students in the VGA group frequently referenced color and a change of color in response to a wide range of questions regarding equilibrium.

However, students in the VGA group did not engage in the second step of the process; they did not elaborate on their understanding of equilibrium beyond a change in color. Rather than building on their connection among representations and using the combination of surface features to elaborate their understanding, evidence suggests that color became the subset of surface features that students attended to most (i.e., a kind of "least common denominator"). The students in this group did not acquire the meanings for the unique features of the individual representations, such as the continuous reaction of products and reactants and the proportional changes in reagents. Because there are aspects of equilibrium that color change by itself can not explain, students in the VGA group did no better than students in other groups on the posttest.

As a result of this study, we were left to determine how we could tune the design of the environment to help students use the connections that they were making across representations to think more deeply about equilibrium and extend their understanding. We wanted students to be able to identify the unique features of the different representations and to consider their meaning as they relate to the meaning of other representations.

BUILDING ON SOCIAL DISCOURSE
FOR LEARNING

Pea (1992, 1993) and others (Brown, Collins, & Duguid, 1989; Newman, Griffin, & Cole, 1989) consider meaning to be the product not just of individual cognition but also of social interaction. From this viewpoint, social interaction is not a one-way transmission and reception of meaning, but a two-way transformative process by which meaning emerges in the space between two interlocutors.

In this space, meaning is socially constructed through processes of negotiation and appropriation by two people engaged in joint activity. That is, meaning is negotiated through a series of interleaved assertions, gestures, actions, acknowledgments, requests for clarification, explanations, elaborations, and other linguistic devices for signaling agreement and for fixing troubles in shared understanding. In the course of discussion, one party may appropriate, or express the meaning taken from another. In a reciprocal manner, the first party may come to mean more than originally thought as a reply is composed to affirm, disconfirm, or elaborate on the interpretation of the other. Through this discourse, interlocutors may converge on shared meaning that is more than either understood in the beginning. More important, they come to engage in a process of achieving expertise. From this perspective (Pea, 1992, 1993), expertise is defined dynamically as a continuing process of participation in a discourse community, rather than merely as a particular set of problem-solving skills and conceptual structures that one might have at the moment. This definition is supported by the kinds of interactions found by Amman and Knorr-Cetina (1990) in their study of scientists in a genetics laboratory and by our ethnographic study in chemistry laboratories (Kozma et al., in press).

However, as Coleman (1995) pointed out, research on argumentation and conversational analysis in schools has found that the discourse strategies students normally use while engaged in collaborative science rarely result in the extended inquiry or shared meaning that is envisioned in the previous paragraphs. Rather than refining understanding collaboratively through extended discourse, students make and defend vacuous claims and rarely produce explanations or justifications for their answers. They tend to routinely criticize or dismiss each other's ideas and, quite often, the consensus that emerges rests on the status of individuals rather than on the nature of students' discourse.

Taken together, the implication drawn from these researchers is that designers should provide students with environments that restructure the discourse in science classrooms around collaborative knowledge building and the social construction of meaning (Coleman, 1995). The intent of this restructuring is to have students actively engage in a questioning and explanation process in which they evaluate each others' queries and assertions in the effort to collaboratively revise their own theories and beliefs about the phenomena in the world that they are trying to understand.

Technology can play a significant role in structuring and augmenting these learning conversations (Pea, 1992, 1993). First, technological environments can be designed to provide students with symbolic elements that enable them to establish common attention to referents or to co-referents within their discourse; these symbols give them something specific to talk about. Second, activities in these environments can engage students in focused inquiry that involves authentic scientific tasks, such as making predictions, observations, and explanations that support their sense-making conversations.

We felt that the intersection of these two features could yield the most compelling strategies for our chemistry software environment. By providing students with inquiry activities and with symbolic representations that have surface features that correspond to and behave like abstract scientific entities and processes, we can support conversations in which students use surface features to act on and make predictions, observations, and explanations about scientific phenomena that are otherwise unavailable to them. The combination of symbolic representations and inquiry activities enables and constrains the range of meanings generated by discourse, such that students can build on each other's ideas and intentions, draw new ideas into a common frame of meaning, and repair discrepancies (Roschelle, 1992). Our prediction is that students' engagement in such conversations while using 4M:Chem will result in sustained inquiry and a more extended consideration of what the features of representations mean, as they relate to those of other representations. Ultimately, students will come to have a better understanding of the underlying science.

A Pilot Study: Students Using Multiple Representations Together

We made several changes in our software that would structure and augment the conversations of student pairs, as they collaborated on joint investigations. First, we removed the audio narrations from the software, because we felt these would compete with and reduce students' conversations during their use of the environment. In our use of 4M:Chem, we give only one manual to the two students in a pair and asked them to come to some agreement, if possible, in recording their answer. If students disagreed, they were instructed to try and convince each other of their position, using whatever evidence was available. We added questions to the manual that asked students to explicitly identify the function of certain surface features of each of the representations. For example, in the heating experiment, students were asked, "What property of the graph allows you to judge whether the amounts of N_2O_4 and NO_2 in the sample at the right are changing over time?"

All of these changes were made to engage students in extended discussions and in joint consideration of the meaning of symbolic elements and symbolic expressions.

In a pilot study, we conducted a detailed analysis of the use of this version of the software by two male university students (AR and MN) enrolled in an introductory chemistry course. During their use of the software, the students had access to all four representations, much as in the VGA condition of the experimental study. These students were guided through the experiments by the revised manual, described previously. As in the earlier study, students were asked to predict, observe, explain, conclude, and enter their responses in the manual.

We audiotaped and videotaped the students during their session and the session was transcribed. The videotape was observed by researchers and the session was coded by the type of physical references students made to each representation. Each coded reference was associated with the corresponding verbal statement in the transcript. The transcript was then analyzed to identify ways that the software enabled and constrained the social construction of meaning.

Both of the students in our pilot study began the session with significant misconceptions about chemical systems at equilibrium. AR defined equilibrium as when "the chemical reaction has taken place and at this point there is no further change." MN defined it as "the point at which a chemical reaction does not move either way." At the end of the session, AR defined equilibrium as "the point [at which] the reactions have stabilized and the changes are constant." MN defined equilibrium as "the point at which the reaction moves both ways equally. There is no net movement backward or forward." In addition, while both students drew diagrams of equilibrium reactions that showed only products on the pretest, their posttest diagrams showed that all species were present at equilibrium.

The two students interacted with each other and with the system for one hour and 23 minutes. During this time they took 307 conversational turns. They also made 115 physical references to the screen: 26 to the video, 39 to the graph window, 28 to the animation window, and 22 to the equation in the control window. The references included 91 points to a specific feature with fingers or the mouse cursor, 12 traces of the shape of a specific feature (typically following the line of a graph), and 12 waves of a more general reference. These references were fairly evenly divided between the two students, with 60 made by one student (MN) and 55 made by the other (AR).

In the following sections, we analyze the students' discourse as they engaged in activities and interacted with specific features of the various representations. In our analysis, we looked for specific instances where students came to understand equilibrium as continuous, dynamic reactions among all species in the system. We looked for the discourse moves that resulted in this understanding and for ways these moves were supported by the students' use of surface features within and across representations.

Using Surface Features
to Coconstruct Understanding

The students began their investigation by observing the NO_2/N_2O_4 system as it achieves equilibrium from two different starting states: one in which the system starts warm and then cools to room temperature, and one in which the system starts cool and then warms to room temperature. The manual directs the students to observe these phenomena using different representations—video, graphs, and animations—singularly and together, in conjunction with the equation that appears in the control window. The manual asks them to make inferences about the system at equilibrium, based on certain features or properties of the representations.

For example, after having viewed the system in the video window, the manual asks, *What observable property would allow you to judge the relative amounts of N_2O_4 and NO_2 in these two samples at the beginning of the experiment?* (In the protocol sample that follows, italics are used as indicating that the manual is being read.) In response to this question, the students write, "Color N_2O_4 is yellow at -8C, with addition of heat turns orange (NO_2)." (In the protocol, double quotation marks indicate that a portion of the discourse is being written in the manual.)

While viewing the representations and discussing the observations and responses to the manual, students made verbal and physical references to specific features of representations. For example, at one point while viewing the graph of the cooling experiment (see Fig. 2.2), AR said: "Equilibrium? Like equilibrium is right there, or something?" [Points to the intersection of the lines in the graph.] (Pointing, gestures, and other physical actions are indicated by bracketed bold words, in the protocol that follows.) Through his pointing, AR is expressing a misconception that we found in our earlier research (Kozma et. al., 1990), that at equilibrium, the partial pressures or concentrations of reactants and products are equal (what we described in our research as the "EQUALibrium" misconception).

However, as a result of their interaction, AR and MR have both come to have a correct understanding of equilibrium. In the following protocol, we examine how the students achieved this understanding through their interaction with each other and with the software. At the point where we pick up the conversation, the students have run the cooling experiment with the video window, the graph window, and the control window open (see Fig. 2.2). The students are responding to the question in the manual that reads: *Describe what you observe in the graph window.*

1. MN: The concentrations crossed at equilibrium. Actually, is that crossing at equilibrium. Or is it just ...
2. AR: Reaching it.
3. MN: Well, I mean, actually, equilibrium ...isn't it just ...is equilibrium where they reach the same concentrations or is it where they kind of have the same ...Because they don't change, like after while they level off.
4. AR: I thought it was when there's—where from the graph is when there's the same amount of N_2O_4 and NO_2, see? [AR points to the crossing lines in the graph.] They cross and that means they have the same ...the pressure was the same. The same pressure.
5. MN: So, what does that say about equilibrium?
6. AR: Well, at equilibrium they should both exchange, like go back and forth like on the animation thing at the same rate.

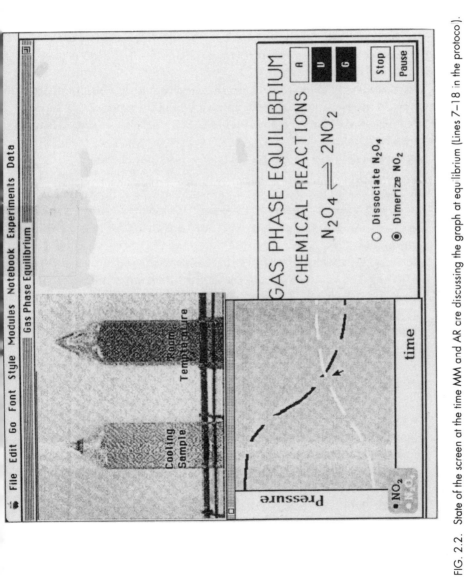

FIG. 2.2. State of the screen at the time MM and AR are discussing the graph at equilibrium (Lines 7–18 in the protocol).

7. MN: [MN reruns the cooling experiment, as it appears in Fig. 2.2.] All right. Well? Okay, so now the cooling sample already passed. [MN points to the point at which the lines cross in the graph.] It's still darker. [MN points to vial of NO_2 in the video.]

8. MN: Oh, duh, actually, it's not gonna be the same concentration, is it, because there's two of these, there's only one of these. [MN points to the subscripts of each species in the equation.] Okay.

9. AR: So, it should be darker?

10. MN: So, is this equilibrium right here then? [MN traces the plateau of the NO_2 line in the graph.] Or is this? [He points to the intersection of the lines.]

11. AR: Equilibrium should be where the pressures keep constant. [AR points to the right side of the graph where the lines plateau.]

12. MN: Okay. So it's going to be right here, then? [MN traces the plateau of the NO_2 line.]

13. AR: So maybe it's at 5 minutes and not where they cross?

14. MN: All right.

15. AR: *Describe what you observe in a concentration graph.* Um, garph [sic].

16. AR: Graph. Um ...

17. MN: Let's see. Um the pressures are just equalizing to their equilibrium for each gas.

18. AR: Actually, they're oscillating. Pressures oscillate (MN: Are they oscillating?) to equilibrium when the pressure is unchanging or the pressure is not changing much.

19. MN: Okay. *What property of the graph allows you to judge whether the amounts of N_2O_4 and NO_2 in the sample on the right are changing over time?* Well, obviously if the slope is bigger than zero.

20. AR: *What property of the graph allows you to judge whether the amounts ...*

21. MN: See, since the—I'm gonna do this again. [MN reruns the cooling experiment.] When they're—obviously, when it has a slope [MN sticks his hand out at a slant, fingers together.] it's going to be changing. When it levels off [He holds his hand parallel to the ground.], there's no change. Make sense? All right.

22. AR: *Level. No change.*

23. All right. Well, that answers our question then. It's not when they cross. All right.

24. MN: *Using this property, how can you tell when the sample is at equilibrium and when it's not?*

25. AR: When a sample ...

26. MN: *Whenever the line is—has a slope of zero.*
27. AR: When . . . yeah.
28. MN: Okay.

This brief segment of discourse shows a significant transformation in the meaning that MN and AR have assigned to specific features of the representations and in their understanding of equilibrium. At the beginning, both students had a basic misconception about equilibrium as a static state, as measured by the pretest. This misunderstanding was compounded by a misinterpretation of the graph of equilibrium, exhibited by MN in Line 1 and AR in Line 4. The students took a particular surface feature of the graph to mean that the partial pressures are equal (an accurate interpretation) and that at this point the system reaches equilibrium (a scientifically inaccurate interpretation). In Line 3, MN notices a second surface feature of the graph, the leveling off or the plateau of the lines. These two prominent surface features of the graph—the crossing point and the plateau of the lines—support the students' extended discussion of equilibrium and constrain the range of possible meanings that they have for the graph and subsequently for this concept. By the end of the segment (Lines 25–28), the students have come to take plateau to mean equilibrium, rather than the crossing point.

How does this transformation come about? First of all, in Line 3 MN interprets a particular feature of the graph, "leveling off," as meaning "not changing." This creates a dissonance between his understanding of equilibrium (expressed as "not moving" on the pretest) and the surface feature (the point where the lines cross) that both students agreed was the point of equilibrium prior to the previously mentioned segment. Is equilibrium the crossing point or the plateau? By expressing his confusion to AR in Line 1, it becomes part of their joint activity and AR becomes involved in resolving the meaning of the graph, even though he had not noticed the second surface feature and was satisfied with his original interpretation of the graph.

The source of resolution of the graph's meaning is a second representation, the video window. In Line 7, MN reruns the experiment and notices that at the crossing point of the graph, the color of the sample in the video is still changing. He uses this to restate the problem to AR in Line 10 and to ask again for an interpretation of the graph. AR resolves the issue in Line 11 by pointing to the plateau of the lines. Although MN is the person who raised the problem and noticed the feature in the video that leads to the resolution of the issue, AR—the person who was satisfied with the original interpretation—served the important function of confirming the resolution by changing his interpretation (Line 13). The students cycle through this resolution again in Lines 21 through 23, as MN links his interpretation of the graph to yet another representation, one that he generates himself—the slope and plateau formed by his hand. By Lines 25 through 28, the students have completed their new negotiated interpretation of the graph, concluding that the system is at equilibrium when the slopes of the lines are zero.

However, the students have not yet come to the understanding that at equilibrium the reactions continue to occur. At this point in the session, they are still focusing on the understanding of equilibrium as "unchanging." This understanding of equilibrium is now consonant with their interpretation of the graph. Given this alignment and the surface features that are available, there is nothing at this point that supports their further transformation to an understanding of equilibrium as dynamic and continuous. This change in the students' understanding does not occur until the students begin to use the animation.

At the point where we pick up with the following protocol, the students have rerun the heating experiment with all four windows open. The statement in the manual that they are considering is, *Describe what you observe in the animation window over time.*

29. AR: *Describe ... animation over time.* Which color is it?
30. MN: Okay. N_2O_4. [MN points to the N_2O_4 line on the graph.] Those are the double molecules. [He points to an N_2O_4 molecule.]
31. AR: What happens over time? There's more N_2O_4 than NO_2 over time. *"There is . . ."*
32. MN: Less.
33. AR: Oh, I didn't see you start. Okay. "There's less N_2O_4 and more NO_2?"
34. MN: Mm hmm.
35. AR: Okay.
36. AR: *Describe what you observe in the animation window when the sample on the right reaches equilibrium at room temperature.* Which would be pretty soon.
37. MN: Yep.
38. AR: All right.

39. MN: It's probably gonna be ... it's probably not gonna change any more. That's all. The molecules are gonna keep transferring back. I mean, they're still gonna be ...
40. AR: They're gonna go back and forth but by the same amount.
41. MN: At the same rate.
42. AR: "Molecules still change but they're amount stays close to the same."
43. MN: Okay.

By the end of this segment, both MN and AR have come to have a deeper, more scientific understanding of the unchanging yet dynamic quality of equilibrium. This understanding is supported by the dynamic surface features of the animation that show molecules moving around, colliding, and reacting to form both products and reactants. This representation is physically connected to the graph when MN points to the line for N_2O_4 and to its corresponding surface feature in the animation (Line 30). In Lines 36 through 38, the students agree on a particular point in time during the animation ("Which would be pretty soon," AR, Line 36) as being when the system is in equilibrium. They then use the surface features of this representation to extend their understanding of equilibrium, previously negotiated around the graph.

How does this extension occur? It starts with the notion of equilibrium as not changing. The "not going to change anymore" expressed by MN in Line 39 gets appropriated and reinterpreted by AR in Line 40. He then uses the surface features from the animation to interpret not changing as going "back and forth but by the same amount." In Line 41, MN reciprocates by extending the interpretation to mean at "the same rate." At this point, "unchanging" has come to mean "same amount" and "same rate" and this allows for their scientifically accurate, shared understanding of the unchanging nature of equilibrium to include the dynamic, changing notion of molecules that keep transferring (MN, Line 39) back and forth (AR, Line 40).

The results of this pilot study support the prediction that the use of a modified version of 4M:Chem in a social context will result in sustained inquiry and an extended consideration of the meaning of the surface features of multiple linked representations. Of course, these findings would need to be reproduced in future studies. Still, the students in this study were able to go beyond the surface features of the representations to develop a deep, scientifically accurate understanding of the dynamic, molecular aspects of chemical equilibrium that are not otherwise directly perceivable. These surface features supported the students' processes of appropriation, negotiation, and convergence toward their shared understanding. While engaged in these processes, the students replicated the discourse practices seen in studies of scientists interpreting the meaning of representations in their laboratories (Amman & Knorr-Cetina, 1990; Kozma et al., in press).

CONCLUSION

This chapter began by describing how important signs and symbols are to scientists and to the understanding of scientific phenomena, particularly complex phenomena that are not directly perceivable. Scientists are very skilled in using different symbol systems and symbolic expressions in a flexible way to represent these scientific phenomena and to solve problems related to them. This is sometimes an effortful activity that engages scientists in deliberation and argumentation and involves the use of representations in the making of claims and warrants. Novices are less skilled in the use of representations and rely on their surface features for meaning. Quite often, the surface features of physical phenomena and symbol systems do not correspond to the complex, underlying scientific entities and processes. Furthermore, students are unable to engage in extended inquiry and have difficulty in constructing shared meaning.

In this chapter, we examine the use of software environments to provide students with new representations that have surface features that correspond to and behave like underlying scientific entities and processes. In our experimental study, the unique surface features of different representations shaped the students' understanding of equilibrium in characteristic ways and they used the surface features shared by multiple representations to make connections across them. However, they were not able to use these connections to elaborate their understanding of the underlying scientific phenomenon. In a pilot study, we then showed how a pair of students used the system to engage in extended discourse to construct shared meaning out of surface features across multiple linked representations. In this way, they both achieved a scientific understanding of equilibrium and replicated the discourse practices of scientists.

The results of this research demonstrate the potential that technology has for providing designers with a powerful new symbolic pallet that can be used to support students' thinking and augment students' discourse. However, these new symbol systems by themselves are often insufficient to aid learning. The results of our pilot study suggest that these new symbol systems and their symbolic expressions may best be used within rich social contexts that prompt students to interact with each other and with multiple symbol systems to create meaning for scientific phenomena. These results also argue for continued research on the impact of symbolic environments on the cognitive processes and social practices of science learning.

ACKNOWLEDGMENTS

The author would like to gratefully acknowledge the support of the National Science Foundation. The project described in this chapter was performed pursuant to grant number RED-9496200 from the NSF. The opinions expressed herein do not necessarily reflect the position or policy of the National Science Foundation or the Board of Directors of SRI International.

REFERENCES

Amman, K., & Knorr-Cetina, K. (1990). The fixation of (visual) evidence. In M. Lynch & S. Wolgar (Eds.), *Representation in scientific practice* (pp. 85–122). Cambridge, MA: MIT Press.

Brock, W. (1992). *The Norton history of chemistry.* New York: Norton.

Brown, J. S., Collins, A., & Duguid, P. (1989). Situated cognition and the culture of learning. *Educational Researcher, 18,* 32–42.

Coleman, E. (1995). Learning by explaining: Fostering collaborative progressive discourse in science. In R. Beum, M. Baker, & M. Reiner (Eds.), *Dialog and instruction: Modeling interaction in intelligent tutoring systems* (pp. 123–135). New York: Springer-Verlag.

Glaser, R. (1990). The reemergence of learning theory within instructional research. *Review of Educational Research, 45*(1), 29–39.

Glaser, R., & Chi, M. (1988). Overview. In M. Chi, R. Glaser, & M. Farr (Eds). *The nature of expertise* (pp. xv–xxviii). Hillsdale, NJ: Lawrence Erlbaum Associates.

Goodman, N. (1976). *Languages of art.* Indianapolis, IN: Bobbs-Merrill.

Hoffman, R. & Lazzlo, P. (1991). Representation in chemistry. *Angewandte Chemie, 30*(1), 1–16.

Kindfield, A. (1994). Biology diagrams: Tools to think with. *Journal of the Learning Sciences, 3*(1), 1–36.

Kozma, R. (1991). Learning with media. *Review of Educational Research, 61*(2), 179–212.

Kozma, R., Chin, E., Russell, J., & Marx, N. (in press). The Roles of representations and tools in the chemistry laboratory. *Journal of the Learning Sciences.*

Kozma, R., & Russell, J. (1997). Multimedia and understanding: Expert and novice responses to different representations of chemical phenomena. *Journal of Research in Science Teaching, 43*(9), 949–968.

Kozma, R., Russell, J., Johnston, J., & Dershimer, C. (April, 1990). College students' understanding of chemical equilibrium. Paper presented at the annual meeting of the American Educational Research Association, Boston.

Kozma, R. B., Russell, J., Jones, T., Marx, N., & Davis, J. (1996). The use of multiple, linked representations to facilitate science understanding. In S. Vosniadou, R. Glaser, E. Decorte, & H. Mandl (Eds.), *International perspective on the psychological foundations of technology-supported learning environments* (pp. 41–60). Mahwah, NJ: Lawrence Erlbaum Associates.

Krajcik, J. (1991). Developing students' Understanding of chemical concepts. In S. Glynn, R. Yeany, & B. Britton (Eds.), *The Psychology of Learning Science* (pp. 117–148). Hillsdale, NJ: Lawrence Erlbaum Associates.

Latour, B. (1987). *Science in action.* Cambridge, MA: Harvard University Press.

Lemke, J. (1990). *Talking science: Language, learning, and values.* Norwood, NJ: Ablex.

Lowe, R. (1987). Drawing out ideas: A neglected role for scientific diagrams. *Research in Science Education, 17*, 56–66.

Nakhleh, M. (1992). Why some students don't learn chemistry. *Journal of Chemical Education, 69*, 191–196.

Newman, D., Griffin, P., & Cole, M. (1989). *The construction zone: Working for cognitive change in school.* New York: Cambridge University Press.

Partington, J. (1989). *A short history of chemistry.* New York: Dover.

Pea, R. (1992). Augmenting the discourse of learning with computer-based learning environments. In E. De Corte, M. Linn, & L. Verschaffel (Eds.), *Computer-based Learning Environments and Problem-solving* (Pp. 313–343). New York: Springer-verlag.

Pea, R. (1993). Learning scientific concepts through material and social activities: Conversational analysis meets conceptual change. *Educational Psychologist, 28*(3), 265–277.

Roschelle, J. (1992). Learning by collaborating: Convergent conceptual change. *Journal of the Learning Sciences, 2*(3), 235–276.

Russell, J., & Kozma, R. (1994). 4m:chem—multimedia and mental models in chemistry. *Journal of Chemical Education, 71*, 669–670.

Russell, J., Kozma, R., Jones, T., Wykoff, J., Marx, N., & Davis, J. (1997). Use of Simultaneous-synchronized macroscopic, microscopic, and symbolic representations to enhance the teaching and learning of chemical concepts. *Journal of Chemical Education, 74*(3), 330–334.

Yarroch, W. (1985). Student understanding of chemical equation balancing. *Journal of Research in Science Teaching, 22*, 449–459.

3

SimCalc: Accelerating Students' Engagement With the Mathematics of Change

Jeremy Roschelle
SRI International

James J. Kaput
University of Massachusetts, Dartmouth

Walter Stroup
University of Texas

A central phenomenon of the 21st century will be change: economic, social, and technological change. Indeed, engaging students in an analysis of change and variation is a central element of nearly every chapter in this book. Today, however, the mathematics of change and variation (MCV), despite its importance in understanding and controlling this ubiquitous phenomenon, is packed away in a course, Calculus, that sits at the end of a long series of prerequisites that filter out 90% of the population. This is especially true for students from economically poorer neighborhoods and families. Additionally, the 10% who do have nominal access to MCV in calculus courses develop mostly symbol manipulation skill but little understanding (Tucker, 1990). The traditional curriculum thus excludes most children from the concepts of rate of change, accumulation, approximation, continuity, and limit (among others). These are the very concepts children most need not only to participate in the physical, social, and life sciences of the 21st century, but also to make informed decisions in their personal and political lives. Even though MCV concepts have been at the heart of mathematics and science historically (Bochner, 1966), in education the opposite is more nearly true. Conventional curricula neglect, delay, or deny students' access to MCV.

The mission of our SimCalc project is to give ordinary children the opportunities, experiences, and resources they need to develop extraordinary understanding and skill with MCV. Using a combination of advanced technology and carefully reformulated curricula, we aim to democratize access to the mathematics of change. This chapter discusses the research findings and design principles guiding our approach, with specific attention to our first software product, MATHWORLDS. MATH-WORLDS provides dynamic, direct manipulation graphs, piecewise definable functions, and animated cartoon worlds to engage elementary, middle, and high school students in qualitative and quantitative reasoning about the relations among position, velocity, and acceleration in complex contexts. Formative evaluation experiments with diverse inner-city students (the large majority of whom were in the lowest quartile of both academic achievement and socioeconomic status) show that MATH-WORLDS, coupled with an appropriate curriculum and teaching practice, can enable students to construct viable MCV concepts.

DEMOCRATIZING ACCESS TO KNOWLEDGE

While focusing on MATHWORLDS, we explore the more general issue of democratizing access to knowledge through advanced technology (Kaput, 1994). Along with the burgeoning international excitement about the Internet and the World Wide Web (WWW) comes a temptation to substitute the problem of democratic access to knowledge and skill with the problem of network access—a superficial problem of wires, bandwidth, and transport protocols (Hardin & Ziebarth, 1996). If such a substitution were valid, our mission would be fulfilled, for soon every elementary school student will have "access" to any number of university calculus courses through the WWW. Alas, neither conduits nor conduit metaphors capture the conditions for learning (Reddy, 1979); learning requires more than delivering encoded knowledge across a wire. Indeed, the encoding of calculus in the formal algebraic language of university calculus courses creates barriers to learning that true democratic access must overcome (Kaput & Roschelle, 1996).

Similarly, the availability of multimedia on every personal computer suggests another superficial role for technology conflated with educational power—the delivery of exciting sounds and movies to motivate students and capture their interest. An inadequate analysis of video games may contribute to the confusion (Norman, 1993). Arcade and computer games do captivate young boys' attention at length, and as many have pointed out, it would be wonderful to translate such intense engagement to academic subject matter. However, as any game designer will explain, achieving a constant flow of quarters into a video kiosk is not a simple matter of choosing the right media. As with other cases of deep motivation, children play games because of the constant incremental growth of challenge, skills, and success—a condition called "optimal flow" (Csikszentmihalyi, 1990). Democratic access, thus, is not simply a matter of choosing the right media, but rather one of creating the conditions in which students experience growth in their capability to solve and understand ever more challenging problems.

LINES OF INNOVATION

Fortunately, decades of research sponsored by the National Science Foundation and others points beyond a superficial understanding of the conditions necessary for true democratic access. Real opportunity for children from diverse backgrounds to understand the difficult concepts of 21st century science requires more than the availability of a conduit to encoded knowledge, and more than pandering to their jaded media preferences. In many ways, this is not news. Indeed, the roots of SimCalc's approach can be found in Dewey's seminal analysis of the conditions for democratic access to education:

> Abandon the notion of subject-matter as something fixed and ready made in itself, outside the child's experience, cease thinking of it as also something hard and fast; see it as something fluent, embryonic, vital ... it is continuous reconstruction, moving the child's present experience out into that represented by the organized bodies of truths we call studies. (John Dewey, in McDermott, 1981, p. 427)

This quote captures two of the three lines of innovation underlying our SimCalc approach. First, democratic access requires deep inquiry into the reconstruction of subject matter. Rather than teaching a "calculus course" to middle school students, SimCalc is seeking to collaboratively define an MCV strand that is appropriate to children's development from elementary school through university-level studies (Kaput, 1994). Second, democratic access begins with a deep understanding of the genetic seeds of understanding within children's experience. Hence, with our colleagues in the mathematics education community, SimCalc seeks to ground the design of learning activities in a thorough understanding of the experiences, resources, and skills students can bring to this subject matter (Kaput, 1992). Although it is not captured in this quote, Dewey also spoke to a third line of innovation: the role of technology in mediating the process of inquiry. Inquiry allows incremental, continual growth of understanding from the child's experience to the core subject matter concepts (Hickman, 1990). SimCalc is exploiting the capability of novel dynamic graphical notations and representations (Kaput, 1992) to provide tools that engage students' conceptual resources, enable mathematical conversation (and hence exploits students' linguistic resources), and support growth toward more sophisticated understandings (including more formal notations and forms of reasoning).

These three perspectives on innovation—subject matter reconstruction, grounding in children's conceptual and linguistic resources, and technological mediation—are recurrent themes of mathematics and science educational research throughout foundational writers such as Dewey, Piaget, and Vygotsky, as well as more recent educational research (Kaput, 1992; Roschelle & Jackiw, in press). In this chapter, we present SimCalc's work with MATHWORLDS as an example of a deep interpenetration of these three perspectives. In so doing, we illustrate the kind of deep inquiry in grounded classroom context that we believe will be necessary to provide democratic access to 21st century sciences.

Children's Conceptual Resources

Exploiting the students' existing knowledge and resources can lead to major, scaleable improvements in learning as Carpenter and colleagues have shown in their research on arithmetic learning (Carpenter, Ansell, Franke, Fennema, & Weisbeck, 1993; Carpenter, Fennema, & Franke, 1996; Carpenter, Fennema, Peterson, & Carey, 1988). Activities both technology mediated and nontechnology mediated must engage the learners' best efforts, and technologies must draw on their strongest cognitive capabilities.

Colleagues at TERC have studied children's conceptual resources, and their work has influenced our design of MATHWORLDS. First, they found that children spontaneously engage in interval analysis to understand the behavior of a complex mathematical function. For example, students split a graph into intervals based on their understanding of the events that the graph represents (Monk & Nemirovsky, 1994; Nemirovsky, 1994). Operations included the construction of a graphical derivative, or an integral of a rate function, or a comparison of two functions. Students performed interval analysis without being explicitly taught and readily constructed more flexible and richer schemes as they made sense of increasingly complex situations. Within this framework, students understood curved pieces of graphs as signifying behaviors of objects or properties of events, rather than as ordered pairs of points. Moreover, they readily constructed mathematical narratives that told a story of a graph over time (Nemirovsky, 1996). The density of students' mathematical resources around interval analysis directly influenced our focus on piecewise linear functions in MATHWORLDS.

Second, research at TERC and elsewhere has uncovered the important roles of physical motion in understanding the meaning of mathematical representations (Nemirovsky, Tierney, & Wright, in press; Nemirovsky & Noble, in press; Noble, Nemirovsky, Solomon, & Cook, 1995). In examining their own movement, students confront subtle relations among their kinesthetic sense of motion, interpretations of other objects' motions, and graphical, tabular, and even algebraic notations. Moreover, in a reversal and complement to Microcomputer-based labs (MBL), TERC developed the concept of Lines Become Motion (LBM) in which graphical representations on a computer control physical devices. Their studies of functions and derivatives in MBL (with body motion, air, and water flow) led us to realize the need for students to use symbols to control phenomena, not just to interpret them. These findings support the inclusion of MBL capabilities in MATHWORLDS, and also the use of manipulable graphs to control animated motion.

Reconstructing Subject Matter

As our introduction indicates, university calculus courses based in formal algebraic symbols tacitly assume rather than actively develop students' understanding of core concepts of change and variation to which the formal symbolic calculus refers. A. G. Thompson and Thompson's (1995) research, for example, shows that most university calculus students cannot correctly answer and explain simple qualitative problems, such as this (Fig.3.1): "Two cars leave from a bridge toll gate at the same time, with speeds as shown in these curves. Which car is ahead at the end of the duration of time shown on the graphs?" Note that the text of this problem can be rephrased to be about technical, social, or economic change. For example, instead of asking about moving cars, we can invert the graphs and ask, "Congress has two plans to balance the budget, bringing the rate of deficit spending to zero over 7 years. Which plan is more desirable to the taxpayer and which one is more desirable to the politicians in power?"

Because formal symbol-based university courses fail to develop the kind of understanding that students (and adults) need, teaching simplified versions of those courses to younger students gains nothing. Furthermore, conventional curricula for introducing rates to younger students have serious problems. Most commonly, children encounter rates in the context of simple linear functions. Research suggests that simplified mathematics problems embody insufficient complexity to enable students to develop adequate generalizations (Duckworth, 1991). More specifically with respect to the rates, and the usual simplification to the linear case, Stroup (1996) wrote:

> The conjecture of this thesis is that in contrast with the richness and complexity of the earlier settings, the linear case is too simple. There is not enough there in the linear case to hang one's understanding on. More formally, the linear case is degenerate in a way that collapses the complexity. ... A major recommendation of the thesis regarding learners' developing understanding of the interaction of how much and how fast ideas, is to start with complexity. Start with graphs of situations where the slope varies and only eventually deal with the linear case as a special collapsed or degenerate case of this complexity. (p. 223–224)

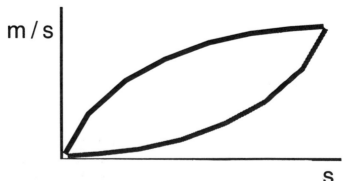

FIG. 3.1 A qualitative integration problem, "Which car travels farther?"

Thus, SimCalc seeks to construct a curricular strand that is neither a simplified symbolic calculus course nor a typical exploration of linear functions and the related notions of rate and ratio. As we discuss shortly, this strand builds on piecewise linear functions. Piecewise linear functions, like linear functions, are fairly easy for students to conceptualize, but they also allow discussion of considerably more complex (and familiar) motions. Furthermore, we will argue that piecewise linear functions bridge nicely to more abstract and general MCV concepts.

Technological Mediation of Mathematics and Science Learning

With respect to MCV subject matter, we build on extensive research on the importance of visualization in math and science reasoning (Gordin & Pea, 1995; Larkin & Simon, 1987; Rieber, 1995). The history of science demonstrates that visualization and imagery have played a key role in the development of scientific thinking (Miller, 1986), and recent sociology of science has further emphasized the importance of visual displays (e.g. Kozma, chap.1, this volume; Latour 1986; Lynch, 1985) to the everyday work of scientists. In education, simulations and animations that display conceptual objects have proven particularly valuable in advancing children's thinking (Horwitz & Barowy, 1994; Snir, Smith, & Grosslight, 1993). On one hand, artificial animations have proven exceptionally effective in provoking genuine inquiry involving difficult concepts (diSessa, 1986; White, 1993; White & Frederiksen, chap. 11, this volume). On the other hand, MBLs (Thornton, 1987; Nemirousky, Kaput, $ Roschelle, 1998) and physical output devices (Monk & Nemirovsky, in preparation) complement simulations by connecting to real phenomena. An important research topic within SimCalc is exploring the complementary advantages of cybernetic (i.e., simulated) and physical data when both are available.

Our own perspective on utilizing the power of visualization and simulation has been shaped by microgenetic studies that examine how these tools affect learning. Contrary to the popular adage that "seeing is believing," these studies show that learning is not as simple as seeing, even with the best constructed visual depictions. In particular, students do not always "register" the features of a visual depiction that an expert would see, may not interpret the features they do see as an expert would, and experience visualizations as problematic (Meira, 1991; Roschelle,

1991). Instead, the power of visualization and simulation arises from the role of computer displays as sites for interaction among students and with teachers (Roschelle, 1996; Roth, 1997). In particular, manipulable visualizations mediate students' construction of shared meanings (Laurillad, 1992; Moschovich, 1996; Roschelle, 1992). Thus, we advocate the design of visualizations and simulations specifically to leverage their role as media for collaborative inquiry (see Kaput, 1992; Roschelle, 1996):

- extending students' engagement with the aspects of concepts that they find problematic,
- supporting shared focus of attention and part–whole analysis,
- enabling gestural and physical communication to effectively supplement verbal communication,
- engaging students in actively conducting experiments, and
- providing meaningful feedback through an interface that is appropriately suggestive and constraining.

THE DESIGN OF MATHWORLDS

SimCalc's first software product, entitled MATHWORLDS, enables students to use the context of motion to explore MCV concepts such as relations among position, velocity, and acceleration and connections between variable rates and accumulation, mean values, and approximations, all in the context of motion. MathWorlds provides a collection of software components including a set of animation worlds and a variety of graphs. Actors in the worlds (such as a clown or a duck) move according to mathematical functions. Graphs display these mathematical functions and allow students to directly edit the functions. (MATH-WORLDS can be downloaded from the SimCalc Web site, http://www.simcalc.umassd.edu/, along with other articles and materials.)

MATHWORLDS provides a very rich set of tools in a flexible environment, in accordance with our component software architecture (Roschelle & Kaput, 1996). For example, we support AppleGuide for providing help, as well as drag-and-drop configuration and scripting to allow teachers and others to customize the environment and build new activities (Roschelle, Kaput, & DeLaura, 1996). Teachers and students can also draw on tools such as masking tape (which temporarily hides a portion of the screen), hiliting pens, and the ability to mark points and lines in graphs and in the world.

In this chapter, our goal is to elucidate the connection between design and democratic access to scientific and mathematical concepts. In line with this goal, we will not go into further depth about general pedagogical features of the interface, as these could apply to any kind of subject matter. Instead, we focus on aspects of our design that relate directly to MCV concept learning. We should also point out that MATHWORLDS will not be SimCalc's only software product and is not intended to implement the full extent of our vision or mission. Nonetheless, MATHWORLDS does illustrate how we interpret the principles of building on children's strengths, reconstructing subject matter, and providing technological mediation.

A central MATHWORLDS innovation is the use of piecewise linear functions to introduce and explore distance–rate–time concepts. (For brevity's sake, we will not distinguish between piecewise linear functions and the special case of piecewise constant functions, although the interface does.) In MATHWORLDS, the student or teacher can easily construct a function by concatenating segments of velocity or acceleration that are individually described as a linear rate of change over a specified duration. In a velocity graph, these functions appear as discrete steps (constant velocity) or rising or falling lines (constant acceleration). For example, Fig. 3.2 shows a motion that begins fast, gradually slows down, and then continues at a slower rate. The first and last segments have constant velocity and the middle segment exhibits constant acceleration. In the corresponding Walking World, students can run the simulation and see the clown move according to this motion.

MATHWORLDS provides a range of other function types to complement piecewise linear functions. A "sampled" function type supports continuously varying positions, velocities, or accelerations. The varying data points can be entered directly with the mouse (by sketching the desired curve, ala Stroup, 1996), from MBL data collection gear (Mokris & Tinker, 1987; Thornton, 1992), or by importing mathematical data from another software package such as FunctionProbe (Confrey, 1991). A linear or parabolic function can be constructed using a single piecewise linear segment (where, say, a velocity segment can have zero slope, yielding a linear position graph). In addition, MATHWORLDS can accept input of exponential and periodic functions.

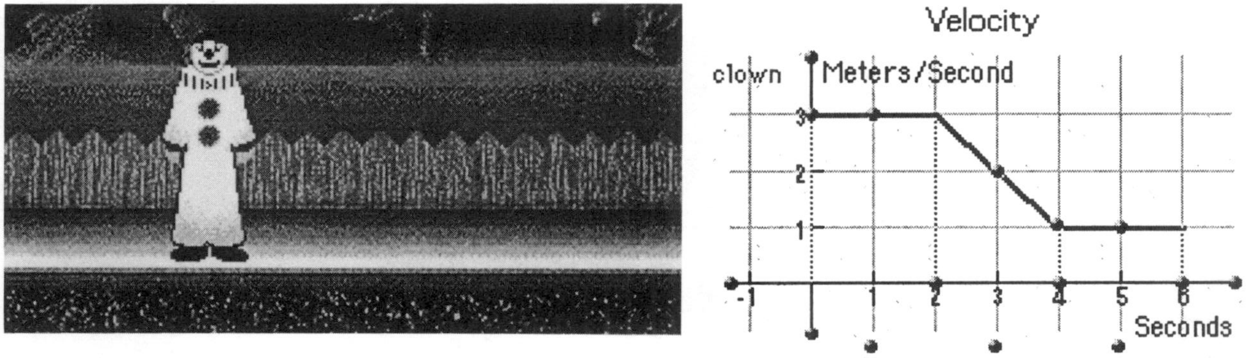

FIG. 3.2 A piecewise linear graph of the velocity of a walking clown.

In the sections that follow, we first discuss why our early design efforts converged on piecewise linear functions, and then how MATHWORLDS provides tools that enable students to learn fundamental MCV concepts by exploring piecewise linear functions. Before proceeding, we want to warn the reader that the following section is narrowly focused for rhetorical reasons. We are striving to illustrate how the design of MATHWORLDS integrates three design perspectives: children's resources, subject matter reconstruction, and technological mediation. However, due to space limitations, we cannot provide our full curricular vision, which reaches well beyond topics and skills addressable via piecewise linear functions. Thus, we restrict ourselves to an example of how design innovations can contribute to restructuring subject matter content.

Why Piecewise Linear Functions

Each of the three lines of innovation (children's resources, subject matter reconstruction, and technological mediation) informed our design perspective for piecewise linear functions in MATHWORLDS. In terms of children's resources, linear velocity segments provide a primitive object that can draw effectively on pre-existing knowledge and skills. For example, middle school students can learn to predict position from a velocity graph by using two skills that they have already developed: counting and area multiplication. The velocity graph (see Fig. 3.2) is drawn against a grid, which enables students to compute accumulated position by counting grid squares. (Note that the graph in this figure cuts across some squares. We will later present a student episode that illustrates how students readily extend their counting skills to deal with the linear velocity case by counting half squares.) Furthermore, students can integrate using the familiar area model of multiplication: height times width. Moreover, the TERC research cited earlier found that students spontaneously understand graphical representations of motions (and other phenomena) by performing interval analysis. Piecewise functions draw on this natural inclination.

Our approach differs from the traditional algebraic approach in two ways: in the way we respond to the need for computational tractability, and the greater value we place on experiencing phenomena (i.e., we put phenomena at the referential center of the learning environment). The starting point in the algebraic approach is governed by what is computationally simplest in that algebraic universe—the family of polynomial functions—that in turn leads to linear and quadratic functions as the inevitable starting point for computing derivatives and integrals symbolically. Hence, computational tractability drives the algebraic approach in the direction of simple, mathematical forms. In contrast, computational tractability in the graphically defined and manipulated universe pushes in a different direction, toward piecewise linearity that affords substantial semantic complexity without sacrificing computational tractability. This in turn allows richer relations with students' experience of motion and a more appropriate conceptual foundation on which students can build increasingly elaborate understandings of MCV ideas.

The second major difference—putting phenomena at the center of the enterprise—is partially served by the graphical approach to piecewise linear functions. Consider the problem of defining a function that represents the motion of an elevator that will pick up and drop off passengers in a building. Where as such a function is very difficult to formulate algebraically, it is relatively easy to directly drag hotspots on piecewise linear velocity segments to create an appropriate function. Similarly, defining motion functions for two characters who are dancing would be extremely cumbersome to do algebraically, and would be especially cumbersome for younger students in entirely unproductive ways. (The mathematically inclined reader might try to write out an algebraic description of the functions depicted in Fig. 3.2, or Fig. 3.3 below.)

Equally important to drawing on children's resources is providing opportunities to make necessary distinctions in places where prior knowledge may be poorly differentiated. A classic example is the distinction between slowing down and moving downward (between "going down" and "slowing down").   The graph in Fig. 3.3 shows how this distinction can be expressed in a MATHWORLDS graph that is connected to our Elevator World. In this world, the elevator moves up or down according to the specified (piecewise linear) function. The upper graph is a decreasing staircase. Many students will intuitively interpret this as "moving down" whereas a correct interpretation is "moving up with decreasing speed." The lower graph shows a function that makes the elevator car go down with constant speed. Children have great difficulty distinguishing "how much" from "how fast" (Stroup, 1996).

MATHWORLDS uses piecewise linear functions as fundamental building blocks for understanding these and other core MCV concepts. Here, we briefly trace how piecewise linear velocity segments can support a

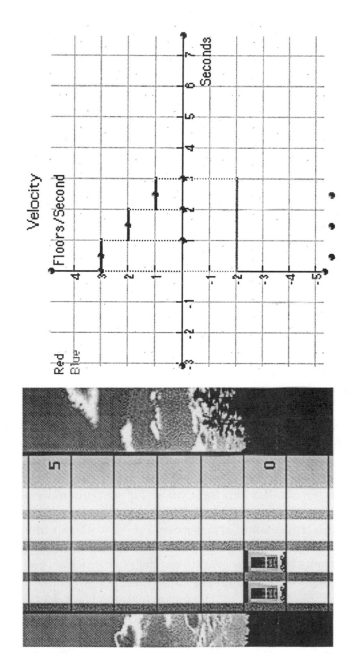

FIG. 3.3 A decreasing staircase and a constant negative velocity.

conception of mean value and how the notions of approximation and of limit can lead to a fairly classical treatment of integration as a calculation of area under a curve. (Indeed, the analysis of complex variation in terms of piecewise linear segments is a core practice in many engineering and scientific disciplines.)

In our exploratory curricula, we often introduced mean value first in a discrete case: finding a single (positive) constant velocity segment that will produce the same final position as a set of varying velocity segments occupying the same duration. In this case, students can easily compute the mean value by adding up the total area under the velocity segments and dividing by the total time. In fact, students can use counting to show that the mean velocity conserves area under the graph. For example, in Fig. 3.4, a "momma duck" swims at the mean value of the rather erratic motion of her baby duckling. Assuming they started at the same location, will they arrive at the beach at the same time? (Incidentally, the software's name, "MATHWORLDS," reflects the variety of animated "worlds" available to contextualize motion for different activities, age groups, and cultural situations.)

As mentioned earlier, MATHWORLDS also supports continuously varying motions. In particular, students can walk at a varying pace, and their body motion can be digitized (via MBL) and entered into a graph corresponding to an animated character. Students can then use a constant velocity graph to express the mean value of their motion, and compare the two motions in the animation.

Once students have gained an understanding of the mean value in the continuous variation case, they can use piecewise constant functions to find the mean value at a set of intermediate points. Figure 3.5 shows a progression in which the mean value is found once, twice, four times, and then eight times. The iterations suggest the process of finding the limit: using smaller time intervals and more segments to achieve a closer and closer approximation. Indeed, students can run the simulation to see their approximation improve; the characters will stay ever closer together throughout the motion as the number of segments increases. Moreover, the velocity graphs are each dynamically linked to the corresponding position graph so the students can see the position graph achieve a better and better approximation. The calculus teachers have noted that the student here is creating a picture found in every calculus text, that of rectangles under a varying curve. But in MATHWORLDS, the student builds this picture with deep prior understanding of the mean

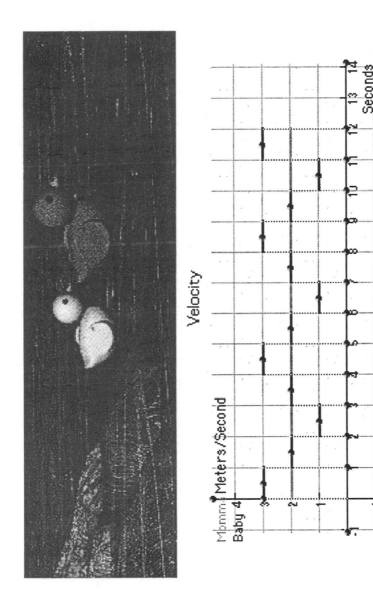

FIG. 3.4 Momma duck swims at the mean value of baby duck.

61

value theorem and the meaning of each constant velocity rectangle. (Incidentally, we have zoomed in on the position graph in Fig. 3.5 so the approximations can be seen. The dark dotted line in the position graph is the varying motion, and it is very closely approximated by the graph with eight constant velocity segments.)

MathWorlds can also support the exploration of different algorithms for approximating the area under a curve. Students can build rectangular approximations that sample the varying quantity at the beginning, midpoint, or end of each segment. Moreover, they can use constant acceleration segments to explore a trapezoidal (rather than rectangular) approximation to area. This is in strong contrast with the notation and index-laden approaches that are required when one attempts such approximations for algebraically defined functions. Hence,

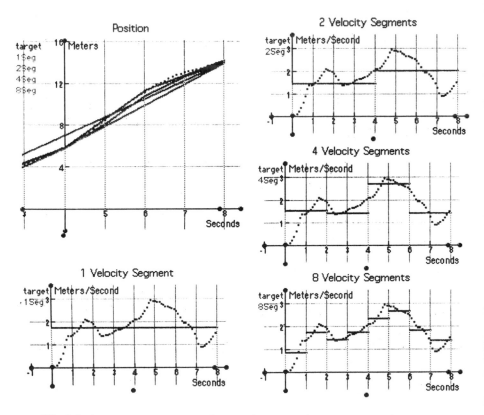

FIG. 3.5 Approximating varying velocity with more and more constant velocity segments.

MATHWORLDS readily builds from simple, comprehensible mathematical objects toward core concepts and reasoning processes in the MCV.

Finally, piecewise linear functions can be readily expressed in a format that supports technological mediation of learning. In particular, MATHWORLD's direct manipulation interface renders piecewise linear functions in a format that makes it easy for students to construct and operate on functions and to discuss their efforts with peers and with teachers.

MATHWORLD provides direct "click-and-drag" editing of any segment. For example, a user can drag the top of a rectangular velocity segment higher to make a faster velocity. Alternately, a user can drag the right edge of rectangular segment to the right to give the segment a longer duration. Students can also construct a function (or extend an existing one) by dragging additional segments into the graph. Thus, operations on the representation have clear and simple qualitative interpretations. Additionally, as students need more quantitative information, piecewise linear functions support a number of easy measurement operations, such as counting and area multiplication.

Likewise, students and their teachers share a sufficient vocabulary to permit conversing about the meaning of piecewise linear graphs. It is easy to identify a segment of the graph (the "first rectangle") or its properties ("taller" or "wider"). Similarly, corresponding motions can easily be described in a narrative such as "It goes slow, then speeds up, and then continues at a fast speed." Piecewise linear functions thus provide a convenient conversational context for talking about motion without introducing an unfamiliar technical vocabulary.

To summarize, the design of MATHWORLDS to utilize graphically editable piecewise linear functions draws on strength from each of the three perspectives. Children have ample resources to make sense of segmented graphs, and these graphs enable them to work on conceptually difficult and important distinctions. Piecewise linear functions lead naturally to core MCV concepts, such as mean value, approximation, and computing the integral via measuring the area under a curve. Furthermore, piecewise linear functions can be realized in a technological interface that supports meaningful direct manipulation operations and sense-making conversations.

Tools for Learning

Choosing suitable conceptual primitives, such as piecewise linear functions, is a necessary but not a sufficient basis for implementing learning technology. Thus, MATHWORLDS contains a number of features and tools intended to contextualize and support the mathematical learning. In the following paragraphs, we briefly describe some of the key features.

Like many modern learning technologies, MATHWORLDS supports dynamic linking among multiple representations of the same mathematical function (Goldenberg, 1995; Kozma, chap. 1, this volume). An activity document can contain any combination of position, velocity, and acceleration graphs. A mathematical object can be linked to a particular graph by dragging and dropping, and once linked, all representations are updated simultaneously. Thus, a student can adjust a constant acceleration and watch simultaneous changes to the corresponding straight line in the velocity and parabola in the position graph. Our approach to designing tools for multiple representations puts phenomena in the center. The multiple representations of MATHWORLDS always connect to simulated motion or to real-world motions, digitized via MBL hardware.

MATHWORLDS gets its name from the availability of different animated backgrounds and characters for contextualizing a motion activity (and from versions of our software under development that present water flow and other familiar phenomena that involve change over time). Each world supports different kinds of problems and challenges. For example, the elevator is used for vertical motion with a natural ordinality including both positive and negative numbers, whereas the walking characters move horizontally and invite complex motions of the sort that might occur in marching or dancing. A space world provides a UFO that can pick up rocks and drop them in a crusher, which is useful for setting up challenges that involve hitting targets in position and time. A water world provides a momma duck and baby ducks. The momma squawks if the babies get too far behind, which is useful for activities where the goal is to match a given motion or to approximate a varying motion with a mean value. MATHWORLDS also allows any (reasonable) number of moving actors, not just two or three. This makes it possible to create activities in which large numbers of actors move in patterned ways, such as a marching band (see Kaput & Roschelle, 1996 for a scenario that uses this feature).

With MATHWORLDS, SimCalc has also been exploring the relations between cybernetic (simulated) and kinesthetic (physical) experiences. For example, students can import their own body motion into MATH-WORLDS via an MBL motion probe. TERC is developing complementary hardware that generates physical motion in toy carts based on directly edited graphs; hence we can bidirectionally link the real world to graphical representations. Our conjecture is that cybernetic and kinesthetic explorations have complementary pedagogical value: cybernetics allow replay and re-examination of more controlled experiments, whereas kinesthetic explorations directly involve bodily understanding and connect directly to familiar experience. Our research is presently exploring the best ways to use these complementary qualities.

Another important set of MATHWORLDS features involves performing controlled experiments. A snap-to-grid option, shown in Fig. 3.6, constrains manipulations on graphs to integer values such as positions, times, or velocities. This can make it easier for students to produce graphs supporting direct measurement of area or of slope by counting grid squares. This constraint can easily be removed to support free exploration of any values. Similarly, a flexible "step" command allows the student to control the clock, moving it forward in fixed ("delta-t") increments, which can make it easier to examine the correspondences among multiple representations at fixed time intervals. MATHWORLDS also supports a variety of ways in which students (or the simulation) can place marks in the animated world or in a graph. "Marks" can provide a tool for making a prediction about behavior, or marks can be used to record the actor's position at uniform time intervals, thus leaving a trace of the actor's path through space that encodes velocity information.

Finally, MATHWORLDS also supports idealization by allowing a student to toggle between the visually rich world of actors and a visually bare or schematic view where the actors are replaced by dots, color-coded to their respective graphs' colors, moving along an easily scaleable one-dimensional coordinate system. This enables a move from qualitative examination of a situation to a distinctly quantitative examination. (Note, however, that a "world-ruler" can be invoked in any of the worlds to support quantitative analysis.)

STUDENTS' LEARNING WITH MATHWORLDS

In this section, we recount an episode from one of our early trial sessions with MathWorlds. The session featured a teacher, James Early, working after school with a middle school student in his inner-city mathematics classroom. It illustrates how MATHWORLDS enabled a young student to

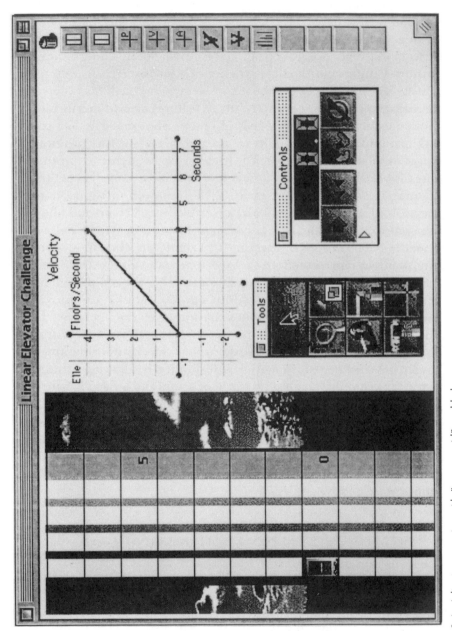

FIG. 3.6 Adjusting a motion with "snap-to-grid" enabled.

learn how to integrate a velocity graph to determine the position of an elevator, and how the same student developed considerable facility with interpreting the distance, rate, and time represented in this graph. Compared to a typical calculus classroom, a striking feature of this episode is the lack of symbolic equations. Indeed, by using MATH-WORLDS, the student and the teacher were able to explore the calculus concept of integration using only graphing and counting skills. This episode shows that students can begin tackling significant concepts in the mathematics of change before taking algebra and years before they would satisfy the prerequisites for a normal calculus course.

Of particular interest here is the student's transition from reasoning about constant velocity graphs to reasoning about linear velocity graphs (constant acceleration). It was not easy for this student to grasp the relevant features of a linear velocity graph. Nonetheless, with the teacher's help, the student was able to see that the relevant area is the area under the velocity graph. The student then was able to quickly generalize to a variety of linear velocity situations, including one in which velocity goes from positive to negative.

Prior to the beginning of the episodes recounted in the following sections, the student had developed the ability to integrate a variety of piecewise constant velocity graphs and was able to correctly distinguish time, rate, and distance. Work in class had centered on counting "blocks" of area under a velocity graph representing the vertical displacement of an elevator and on interpreting the significance of different arrangements of the blocks. The student's confidence in his abilities was evident in his phrase, "You can't stop me." He uttered this phrase as a playful taunt to his teacher. The following exchanges are excerpts from a larger series of challenges and responses the teacher and student engaged in together. After working with a few piecewise constant velocity challenges, the teacher then began setting up challenges using linear velocity segments.

Integrating by Counting

The transcript that follows begins with a linear velocity segment with a slope of 1 m/sec^2 starting at zero velocity and extended for 4 seconds (to a velocity of 4 m/sec). As the transcript shows, the student was able to correctly integrate velocity to predict position. Moreover, the student was able to predict the change in speed of the elevator over time. Finally, the end of the transcript shows that the student was able to predict the motion of the elevator with a very challenging velocity graph—a decreasing linear velocity that continues below the axis.

T: (Makes a linear velocity graph that extends over 4 seconds). What about this one?

S: It gonna go eight floors.

T: Eight floors?

S: Yeah.

T: Why?

S: There's six floors right there (points to the six whole grid squares underneath the graph). That's a floor (places one finger on the half grid square at $t = 1$, and the other finger at the grid square at $t = 2$, indicating that these two halves make a whole floor) and that's another floor (fingers on the graph at $t = 3$ and $t = 4$).

T: So it's gonna go eight floors.

S: Yep.

T: Try it and see. I don't know. Ooh, eight.

In excerpt above, we see that the student attended to area under the graph and used a counting procedure that correctly integrates the velocity function.

Identifying Changing Speed

In the following segment, the teacher next focused on the change of speed, which the student correctly described but did not explain.

T: And then what else did we notice about the elevator?

S: First it went slow and then it goes faster and then it goes to another one and goes faster.

T: Ok.

S: And then the last one it goes real fast.

T: Ok, do you have any idea why? What makes it do that?

S: No.

T: No idea.

The teacher then made another, related problem with the same area, but decreasing speed.

T: Ok, what if I did this. (Flips the existing graph so it is decreasing over 1 seconds, instead of increasing.) How about if I did that?

S: It's still at eight.

T: It's still at eight?

S: It's the same problem.

T: Huh? Same problem.

S: Yeah.

T: The elevator going to go the same way.

S: Yeah.

T: So, how does it go up?

S: No, first it's going to go fast then slow.

T: Why?

S: 'Cuz it's a different way.

T: It's a different way.

S: That's high and that's low.

T: Ok. Try it. Let's see. It still wound up at eight.

With this contrast, the student was able to correctly describe both position and rate. In particular, the student correctly identified speed with the height of the graph.

A Linear Decrease from Positive to Negative

Following this correct prediction, the teacher and student tried to make a graph that would make the elevator travel four floors. However, by accident they made a graph that instead decreased linearly from 2 floors per second to -2 two floors per second. This is a challenging graph for students to interpret because, as we noted previously, many students interpret a linearly decreasing velocity graph as a motion that continually goes down.

T: What do you think is going to happen here (a linearly decreasing graph that starts at 2 floors per second and decreases to negative 2 floors per second)? Let it go. What do you thinks gonna happen here?

S: Gonna go back to zero after it's finished.

T: You think so?

S: Yeah.

T: Try it. See. I don't know. Watch, wait, before you do that, why do you think it's going to go back to zero?

S: 'Cuz it's the same up here, it's the same right there. There both the same.

Note that here the student correctly predicted that the motion would return to its initial position. Following this episode, the student confidently began to assert "I can figure that out" as the teacher introduced additional graphical problems.

DISCUSSION

This episode demonstrates how a student, working with a teacher, can learn to correctly interpret the motion described by a velocity graph. As should be clear from the difficulties described in preceding chapters, this is not an easy concept to learn. Indeed, it would be extremely rare to find students integrating graphs outside of a physics or a calculus classroom. However, this middle school student was able to make rapid progress and eventually achieved a fairly robust and flexible interpretation of linear velocity graphs. Of course, there is much more to learn. Our point is not that this student is finished learning, but rather that is possible to begin making progress toward learning the core conceptual facets of the mathematics of change at a much younger age than traditional approaches to teaching calculus typically attempt.

We would attribute the progress evident in this episode to the interweaving of the three perspectives introduced earlier. From a student resources perspective, it is clear that this episode built upon the student's well-established skills in counting and computing with whole numbers and with simple fractions, without the need of any algebraic symbols. MATHWORLDS enable the student to build an understanding of the mathematics of change using conceptual tools that were already firmly established by the time he entered middle school. From a reconstructing subject-matter perspective, this episode moved from piecewise constant velocity segments and then introduced linear velocity segments. Because of the student's prior experience with the very simple piecewise constant cases, meanings for a single block (grid square) were already well established. Moreover, the student already understood the meaning of height in a velocity graph and the interpretation of the horizontal (time) axis. Although it was initially difficult for the student to interpret a grid square that was "cut in half," with the teacher's help the student soon overcame this difficulty and was able to interpret quite difficult graphs. Beginning with piecewise constant velocity may be a radical change to the conventional calculus curriculum, but such an approach seems to provide a powerful route into this difficult conceptual space. Finally, technological mediation clearly played a key role in allowing the rapid learning evidenced here. Directly editable graphs allowed the teacher to quickly construct and pose problem situations, and running the simulation allowed the student and the teacher jointly to ground the meaning of those graphs in observable motions. The computer screen also served as an enabling conversation space in which the student and the teacher could identify and discuss the interpretation of various features of the graph.

CONCLUSION

In choosing the title for this chapter, we drew inspiration from the concept of Accelerated Schools (Levin & Hopfenberg, 1991). Levin so clearly captured the paradox of conventional school reform: given evidence that student learning outcomes are in trouble, a typical response is to slow everything down, which only ensures that the students become further and further behind and more and more in trouble. To overcome this paradox, we must break outside the conventional wisdom and find ways to dramatically accelerate students' progress.

Without question, dramatic acceleration will be required. At the beginning of the 20th century, only 3.5% of all students needed to finish high school, and virtually no high school students took calculus. Today all students must finish high school, and 3.5% take calculus (U.S. Department of Education, 1996). We can comfortably predict that before the end of the 21st century, most students will need access to the MCV, and will acquire skill with its core concepts such as rate, accumulation, limit, approximation, etc. Furthermore, at least 3.5% of them will likely need to conquer more advanced topics such as dynamical systems modeling. Mathematics and science depend increasingly on concepts of greater complexity and abstraction, and society requires ever-greater numbers of students from diverse backgrounds to master these important and powerful concepts.

Routine applications of technology will not meet the order of magnitude of challenges we face in bringing much more mathematics learning to many more students of diverse backgrounds. The problem of access is not as simple as a wire, a transport protocol, and a university willing to publish its courses on the Internet. Nor will simply encoding the same lesson in different media radically change the rate at which students master core concepts. We need to move beyond reforming university courses and repackaging dead pedagogies in media sound bites.

Yet, we cannot achieve scientific mastery from ordinary children without technology. Visualization, simulation, and modeling are increasingly important aspects of professional mathematics and science and rely deeply on technology. As we have argued, these technologies also can draw on some of children's powerful, well-developed resources. The opportunity such innovations present is more than the chance to teach an existing course better; technological innovation opens a window to dramatically restructuring school curricula so we can accelerate students' learning. Through iterative design that is mutually sensitive to the unique affordances of technology for learning, children's resources, and the need to radically reconstruct the curriculum, we believe our society can provide democratic access for all children to the concepts most important to the next millennium. The concepts must include the power to understand and control physical phenomena through mathematical analysis of change and variation.

ACKNOWLEDGMENTS

We gratefully acknowledge the contributions of the whole SimCalc team to MathWorlds and to related research. The work reported in this article was partially supported by the National Science Foundation Applications of Advanced Technology Program (Award: REC-9619102). The University of Massachusetts, Dartmouth is a member of the National Center for Improvement of Student Learning and Achievement, University of Wisconsin–Madison, U.S. Dept. of Education Prime Grant #R305A60007 that also partially supported the work described in this paper. The opinions presented are those of the authors and may not reflect those of the funding agency.

REFERENCES

Bochner, S. (1966). *The role of mathematics in the rise of science.* Princeton, NJ: Princeton University Press.

Carpenter, T. P., Ansell, E., Franke, M. L., Fennema, E., & Weisbeck, L. (1993). Models of problem solving: A study of kindergarten children's problem-solving processes. *Journal for Research in Mathematics Education, 24*(5), 427–440.

Carpenter, T. P., Fennema, E., Peterson, P. L., & Carey, D. A. (1988). Teachers' pedagogical content knowledge of students' problems solving in elementary arithmetic. *Journal for Research in Mathematics Education, 19*(5), 385–401.

Carpenter, T., Fennema, E., & Franke, M. (1996). Cognitively guided instruction: A knowledge base for reform in primary mathematics instruction. *Elementary School Journal, 97*(1), 3–20.

Confrey, J. (1991). Function Probe [Computer software]. Ithaca, NY: Department of Education, Cornell University.

Csikszentmihalyi, M. (1990). *Flow: The psychology of optimal experience.* New York: HarperCollins.

diSessa, A. A. (1986). Artificial worlds and real experience. *Instructional Science, 14*, 207–227.

Duckworth, E. (1991). Twenty-four, forty-two, and I love you: Keeping it complex. *Harvard Educational Review, 61*(1), 1–24.

Hardin, J. & Ziebarth, J. (1996). *Digital technology and its impact on education* [Online]. Washington, DC: Department of Education. Available: http://www.ed.gov/Technology/Futures/hardin.html

Goldenberg, P. (1995). Multiple representations: A vehicle for understanding understandings. In D. N. Perkins, J. L. Schwartz, M. M. West, & M. S. Wiske (Eds.), *Software goes to school* (pp. 155–171). New York: Oxford University Press.

Gordin, D. N., & Pea, R. D. (1995). Prospects for scientific visualization as an educational technology. *Journal of the Learning Sciences, 4*(3), 249.

Hickman, L. A. (1990). *John Dewey's pragmatic technology.* Indianapolis: Indiana University Press.

Horwitz, P., & Barowy, W. (1994). Designing and using open-ended software to promote conceptual change. *Journal of Science Education and Technology, 3*, 161–185.

Kaput, J. (1992). Technology and mathematics education. In D. Grouws (Ed.), *A handbook of research on mathematics teaching and learning* (pp. 515–556). New York: Macmillan.

Kaput, J. (1994). Democratizing access to calculus: New routes using old roots. In A. Schoenfeld, (Ed.), *Mathematical thinking and problem solving* (pp. 77–155). Hillsdale, NJ: Lawrence Erlbaum Associates.

Kaput, J., & Roschelle, J. (1996). Connecting the connectivity and the component revolutions to deep curriculum reform [Online]. Washington, DC: Department of Education. Available: http://www.ed.gov/Technology/Futures/kaput.html

Larkin, J. H., & Simon, H. A. (1987). Why a diagram is (sometimes) worth 10,000 words. *Cognitive Science, 11*, 65–100.

Latour, B. (1986). Visualization and cognition: Thinking with eyes and hands. *Knowledge and Society: Studies in the Sociology of Culture, 6*, 1–40.

Laurillad, D. (1992). Learning through collaborative computer simulations. *British Journal of Educational Technology, 23*(3), 164–171.

Levin, H., & Hopfenberg, W. (1991). Don't remediate: Accelerate! *Principal, 70*(3), 11–13.

Lynch, M. (1985). Discipline and the material form of images. An analysis of scientific visibility. *Social Studies of Science, 15,* 37–66.

McDermott, J. J. (1981). *The philosophy of John Dewey.* Chicago: University of Chicago Press.

Meira, L. (1991). *Exploration of mathematical sense-making: An activity oriented account of children's use and design of material displays.* Unpublished doctoral dissertation, Berkeley: University of California.

Miller, A. I. (1986). *Imagery and scientific thought.* Cambridge, MA: MIT Press.

Mokris, J. R., & Tinker, R. F. (1987). The impact of microcomputer-based labs on children's ability to interpret graphs. *Journal of Research in Science Teaching, 24*(4), 369–383.

Monk, S., & Nemirovsky, R. (1994). The case of Dan: Student construction of a functional situation through visual attributes. *Research in Collegiate Mathematics Education, 4,* 139–168.

Moschovich, J. N. (1996). Moving up and getting steeper: Negotiating shared descriptions of linear graphs. *Journal of the Learning Sciences, 5*(3), 239–277.

Nemirovsky, R. (1994). On ways of symbolizing: The case of Laura and velocity sign. *The Journal of Mathematical Behavior, 13,* 389–422.

Nemirovsky, R. (1996). Mathematical narratives. In N. Bednarz, C. Kieran, & L. Lee (Eds.), *Approaches to algebra: Perspectives for research and teaching* (pp. 197–223). Dordrecht, The Netherlands: Kluwer Academic Publishers.

Nemirovsky, R., Kaput, J., & Roschelle, J. (1998). *Enlarging mathematical activity from modeling phenomena to generating phenomena.* Proceedings of the 22nd annual meeting of the International Group for the Psychology of Mathematics Education, A. Oliver & K. Newstead (Eds). South Africa: University of Stellenbosch.

Nemirovsky, R., & Noble, T. (in press). Mathematical visualization and the place where we live. *Educational Studies of Mathematics.*

Nemirovsky, R., Tierney, C., & Wright, T. (in press). Body motion and graphing. *Cognition and Instruction.*

Noble, T., Nemirovsky, R., Solomon, J., & Cook, J. (1995, October). *Impossible graphs.* Paper presented at the Annual Meeting of the North American Chapter of the International Group for the Psychology of Mathematics Education, Columbus, OH.

Norman, D. A. (1993). *Things that make us smart.* New York: Addison-Wesley.

Reddy, M. (1979). The conduit metaphor: A case of frame conflict in our language about language. In A. Ortony (Ed.), *Metaphor and thought* (pp. 284–310). Cambridge, England: Cambridge University Press.

Rieber, L. P. (1995). A historical review of visualization in human cognition. *Educational Technology Research and Development, 43*(1), 45–56.

Roschelle, J. (1991). *Students' construction of qualitative physics knowledge: Learning about velocity and acceleration in a computer microworld.* Unpublished doctoral dissertation, University of California, Berkeley.

Roschelle, J. (1992). Learning by collaborating: Convergent conceptual change. *Journal of the Learning Sciences, 2*(3), 235–276.

Roschelle, J. (1996). Designing for cognitive communication: Epistemic fidelity or mediating collaborating inquiry. In D. L. Day & D. K. Kovacs (Eds.), *Computers, communication & mental models* (pp. 13–25). London: Taylor & Francis.

Roschelle, J., & Kaput, J. (1996). Educational software architecture and systemic impact: The promise of component software. *Journal of Educational Computing Research, 14*(3), 217–228.

Roschelle, J., Kaput, J., & DeLaura, R. (1996). Scriptable applications: Implementing open architectures in learning technology. In P. Carlson & F. Makedon (Eds.), *Proceedings of ED-MEDIA 96–World conference on educational multimedia and hypermedia* (pp. 599–604), American Association of Computers. Charlottesville, VA: AACE.

Roschelle, J., & Jackiw, N. (in press). Technology design as educational research: Interweaving imagination, inquiry & impact. In A. Kelly & R. Lesh (Eds.), *Research design in mathematics & science education.* Amsterdam: Kluwer.

Roth, W. M. (1997, March 28). *Computers and cognition: Towards a phenomenology of learning in the presence of computers*. Paper presented at the Annual Meeting of the American Educational Research Association, Chicago, IL.

Snir, J., Smith, C., & Grosslight, L. (1993). Conceptually-enhanced simulations: A computer tool for science teaching. *Journal of Science Education and Technology, 2*(2), 373–388.

Stroup, W. (1996). *Embodying a nominalist constructivism: Making graphical sense of learning the calculus of how much and how fast*. Unpublished doctoral dissertation, Harvard University, Cambridge, MA.

Thompson, A. G., & Thompson, P. W. (1995). Talking about rates conceptually: A teacher's struggle. *Journal for Research in Mathematical Education, 27*(1), 2–24.

Thornton, R. (1987). Tools for scientific thinking: Microcomputer based laboratory for physics teaching. *Physics Education, 22,* 230–238.

Thornton, R. (1992). Enhancing and evaluating students' learning of motion concepts. In A. Tiberghien, & H. Mandl (Eds.), *Physics and learning environments* (NATO Science Series). New York: Springer-Verlag.

Tucker, T. (1990). *Priming the calculus pump: Innovations and resources*. Washington, DC: MAA.

U. S. Department of Education. (1996). *The Condition of Education* (Supplemental Table 29–6). National Center For Education Statistics, Washington, DC [Producer and Distributor. Online]. Available: http://www.ed.gov/NCES/pubs/ce/c9629d06.html

White, B. (1993). Thinkertools: Casual models, conceptual change, and science education. *Cognition and Instruction, 10,* 1–100.

4

MODEL-IT:
A Design Retrospective

Shari Jackson Metcalf
The Concord Consortium

Joseph Krajcik and Elliot Soloway
University of Michigan

We spent 4 years developing MODEL-IT, a learner-centered tool for building dynamic, qualitative-based models. From its original conception, the goal of MODEL-IT has been to support students, even those with only very basic mathematical skills, as they build dynamic models of scientific phenomena and simulations with their models to verify and analyze the results. MODEL-IT provides an easy-to-use object-oriented visual language with which students can define their models without having to use traditional programming. This allows them to construct models quickly and easily, focusing their attention on the tasks of testing, analyzing, and re-examining their models and the understanding on which these models are based.

In this paper, we review our 4 years of research with various versions of MODEL-IT. Throughout our research, we have forged a close relationship with a local high school, whose science teachers joined with us in working to design learner-centered tools for students learning science. We describe the process of taking our ideas from their original conception through several large cycles of development and testing in the classroom and its culmination in the development of a truly learner-centered software tool that promotes substantial science learning outcomes.

RATIONALE: LEARNING BY BUILDING MODELS

Scientists build models to test theories and to improve their under-standing about complex systems. In this exploratory, speculative style of modeling, Kreutzer, (1986) believed: "Simulation is used at a pro-totheoretical stage, as a vehicle for thought experiments. The purpose of a model lies in the act of its construction and exploration, and in the resultant, improved intuition about the system's behavior, essential aspects and sensitivities (p. 7)."

Students, too, can benefit from building models to develop their own understanding of natural phenomena. A number of prominent educa-tors have voiced this position. Tinker (1990) stressed that we need to support students in theory building and experimentation, because both are important activities of science. Hestenes (1992, p. 732) put it quite clearly: Students should be taught "from the beginning ...science 'mod-eling is the name of the game.'" Building models gives students oppor-tunities to use their existing knowledge, to perform thought experiments, and to gain insight into the behavior of complex systems.

The problem is that building dynamic models as it is currently practiced is very hard for students to do—requires a great deal of prior knowledge and mathematical ability. However, by redefining the mod-eling task and providing appropriate support, modeling can be made accessible to high school science students. Project 2061 advocates a high-level, qualitative approach to modeling:

> In modeling phenomena, students should encounter a variety of common kinds of relationships depicted in graphs (direct proportions, inverses, accel-erating and saturating curves, and maximums and minimums) and therefore develop the habit of entertaining these possibilities when considering how two quantities might be related. None of these terms need be used at first, however. 'It is biggest here and less on either side' or 'It keeps getting bigger, but not as quickly as before' are perfectly acceptable—especially when phenomena that behave like this can be described. (American Association for the Advance-ment of Science, 1993)

The challenges in making dynamic modeling accessible in the middle and high school science classrooms are to create a modeling environ-ment designed for the expected knowledge level of the students that is flexible enough to construct models of a wide range of complex systems. Such an environment should not only enable students to rapidly gener-ate relatively simple models but should also facilitate the learner's transition toward more expertlike modeling practices. Addressing these challenges is a central goal of Model-It.

MODEL-IT: THE DESIGN PROCESS

Learning Theory

Current educational theories emphasize the "active, reflective and social nature of learning" (Brown & Campione, 1994). Learners have come to be viewed as active constructors of knowledge, no longer being seen as passive receivers of transmitted information. We also now recognize that constructing understanding is not an isolated activity but occurs within the framework of a learning community. In this model of teaching and learning, teachers attempt to provide engaging and motivating learning opportunities for students (Blumenfeld et al., 1991). Such opportunities are fostered by situating learning in an authentic, real-world context (Brown, Collins, & Duguid, 1989; Cognition and Technology Group at Vanderbilt, 1990) and by ensuring that the activities are non-trivial and personally meaningful for the learner.

Computer applications associated with constructivist learning are typically designed as "interactive learning environments" that emphasize student-directed learning activities rather than computer-driven tutorials. Such environments may function as cognitive tools— supporting learners in representing, interpreting, and reflecting on what they know to foster the development of understanding (Lajoie, 1993; Salomon, 1990). Computer tools for constructing artifacts (e.g., databases, spreadsheets, expert systems, multimedia documents, models) can support learners in representing and thinking about their knowledge in new and powerful ways (Jonassen, 1995; Wisnudel, Stratford, Krajcik, & Soloway, 1998). For example, to learn about a stream ecosystem, a learner might build and test a dynamic model of the system, learning through the process of analyzing data, constructing relationships, and developing and testing sample hypotheses.

Learner-Centered Design

In designing software for education, we are mindfully designing for learners. In the Highly Interactive Computing (HI-C) group at the

University of Michigan, we have formulated a rationale for learner-centered design (LCD), (Jackson, Stratford, Krajcik, & Soloway, 1995; Soloway et al., 1996; Soloway, Guzdial, & Hay, 1994). Learners are also users, so the principles of user-centered design certainly apply (Norman & Draper, 1986). However, user-centered design guidelines are not sufficient to address certain unique needs of learners, such as intellectual growth, diversity of learning styles, and motivational needs. For example, learners should have software available to them that represents information in a familiar way, but that also helps introduce them to more professional or symbolic representations. By designing software to support learners' growth from apprenticeship toward mastery, we create an environment that is learner friendly.

The central claim of LCD is that software can incorporate learning supports—scaffolding—to address the learner's needs. Scaffolding is important because it enables the learner to achieve goals or accomplish processes that would not normally be possible and that are normally out of reach (Vygotsky, 1978; Wood, Bruner, & Ross, 1975). Throughout the project, we have been refining our ideas about how to design scaffolding in software. In this chapter, we discuss the scaffolding strategies that we have identified and incorporated into different versions of MODEL-IT.

MODEL-IT: STAGES OF DEVELOPMENT

Throughout the development of MODEL-IT, our goals have remained constant: to design a tool that is learnable by middle and high school students and that allows them to easily construct models of dynamic systems. We assume students learn by constructing artifacts that represent their understanding and by reflecting on those artifacts. The primary purpose of the software is therefore for students to be able to build and test models of their own design, in order to represent and explore their understanding of the phenomena being studied. We have two baseline criteria for success: (a) learnability—it must be easy for students to get started building simple models so they stay motivated and persevere in learning the tool, and (b) flexibility—the software must support diverse populations of students building models in a variety of domains and must grow with students as they develop understanding and expertise.

MODEL-IT is designed to be used within a project-based science classroom (Krajcik, Blumenfeld, Marx, & Soloway, 1994), a method of science instruction that focuses on students conducting inquiries. Throughout our research, we have been working with science teachers at a local public alternative high school who are developing a new project-based curriculum called "Foundations of Science," in which computing technologies are routinely used and the subject matter of earth science, chemistry, and biology are combined within the context of meaningful, long term projects (Heubel-Drake, 1995). The high school is "alternative" in the sense that community based and innovative instructional techniques are encouraged and that enrollment is limited, determined primarily through random selection from those applying. The students in the studies reported here were primarily middle- to upper middle-socioeconomic class, and of average to above average ability.

There have been four major versions of MODEL-IT. Table 4.1 summarizes the versions of MODEL-IT developed over the past 4 years, on which we report in this chapter.

Stage 1: Early Versions

Design

In a paper written during the time of our early MODEL-IT research (Soloway et al., 1996), we described a general framework for software-realized scaffolding and how it was applied to the design of MODEL-IT. Looking back, however, we realized that our design approach could be summarized as the application of the following three broad scaffolding strategies, which we identified as particularly appropriate for constructive tasks such as model building and testing (Jackson, Stratford, Krajcik, & Soloway, 1996):

Grounding in Experience and Prior Knowledge. The learning environment should allow learners to create models with representations that are grounded in the learner's prior experiences and knowledge (Brown et al., 1989; Cognition and Technology Group at Vanderbilt, 1990). The modeling environment, therefore, should be personally meaningful and approachable and should allow opportunities for personalization.

Bridging Representations. New representations should be connected to the learner's current understandings through examples, analo-

TABLE 4.1

Table of MODEL-IT Versions and Features Added or Changed for Each Version

Version	Date Developed	Major Features Added/Changed
1:	Spring 1994	Baseline functionality.
"Modeler 1.0"		
1.1:	Fall 1994 to Winter 1996	Object editor to create new objects.
"MODEL-IT 1.1a12"		Map view.
"MODEL-IT 1.1a17"		Run-time graphs to show change over time.
2:	Spring 1996	Interface redesign
"MODEL-IT 2.1"		Object window downplayed (exists, but not used). New Object button and Object Editor instead, for consistency with factor and relationship editors. Map view becoming focus for model designing and testing.
3:		
"MODEL-IT 3.0"	Fall 1996 to Spring 1997	Significant redesign, layers of fadeable scaffolding that hide complexity, but can fade to access advanced functionality.
"TheoryBuilder"		New windows features to scaffold learning and reflecting: Help Window and Notepad. New tasks: Planning, Evaluating. New support for testing and debugging.

gies, and multiple visual representations (Clement, Brown & Zietsman, 1989). These multiple synchronized representations act as a bridge between more expertlike model building techniques and current understandings.

Coupling Actions, Effects, and Understanding. The interactive learning environment provides a tight coupling between the learner's actions while testing the model, the visual feedback produced by the software as a result of testing actions (Mokros & Tinker, 1987), and the learner's own mental representations of the phenomenon (Draper & Swanson, 1990). Because the learner actually built the model with whom he or she is interacting, this tight coupling provides a way for the learner to "run" his or her own mental model of the phenomenon, and to perform thought experiments (Kreutzer, 1986) on an externalized representation of his or her thinking. The following is a description of the MODEL-IT v.1 program, explaining how each of the different scaffolding strategies were implemented in MODEL-IT (summarized in Table 4.2).

Grounding in Experience and Prior Knowledge

A learning environment should allow learners to work with representations that are grounded in their prior experiences and knowledge. For example, MODEL-IT begins by providing a set of familiar, predefined high-level objects with which to build a model. In developing and testing MODEL-IT, we worked with the teachers to determine an appropriate set of objects for students. In the domain of stream ecosystems, these objects might include the stream, macroinvertebrate populations, and a nearby golf course. Objects are represented visually with digitized photographs and graphics (Fig. 4.1). For our classroom studies, the background graphic is a photograph of the actual stream the students studied; this personalized representation was intended to ground learning in an authentic, meaningful context for the students.

To add objects to a model, students select objects from the object palette (at the bottom of Fig. 4.1). Factors of those objects (measurable quantities or values associated with the objects) can then be defined, such as the total phosphates measured in a stream or the count of a population of macroinvertebrates. Figure 4.2a shows the Object Editor for the stream object, and Fig. 4.2b shows the Factor Factory where the stream's phosphate factor is being defined.

TABLE 4.2

Scaffolding Strategies and Their Implementation in Model-It V.1

Scaffolding Strategy	MODEL-IT Implementation
Grounding in Experience and Prior Knowledge	Predefined high-level objects. Digitized, personalized photographs and graphics. Qualitative, verbal representation of relationships.
Bridging Representations	Textual to graphical representations of relationships. Qualitative to quantitative definition of relationships.
Coupling Actions, Effects, and Understanding	Direct manipulation of factor values while a simulation is running. Immediate, visual feedback of the effect of user's changes in factor values.

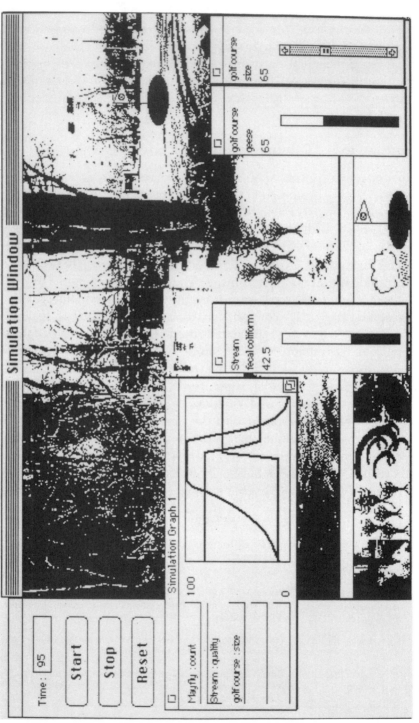

FIG. 4.1 The Simulation window, running a simulation, in MODEL-IT V1.

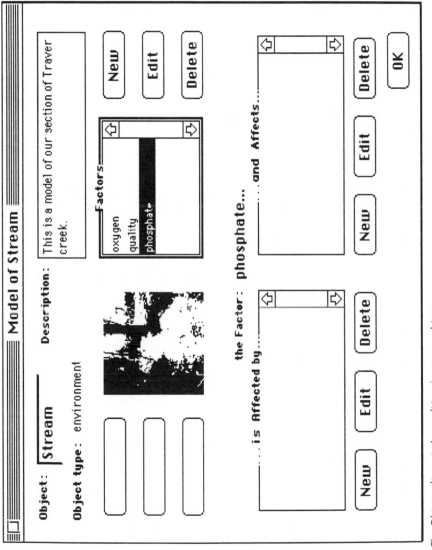

FIG. 4.2a   The Object editor window, editing the stream object.

Next, the student can define relationships between the factors (to show how the value of one factor affects the value of another). MODEL-IT supports a qualitative, verbal representation of relationships, rather than requiring formal mathematical expressions. Students can define a relationship simply by selecting descriptors in a sentence (e.g., "As stream phosphate increases, stream quality decreases by less and less," [Fig. 4.3]). This is another example of grounding on a conceptual basis—learners can create relationships simply by re-representing them on the screen as sentences. This ease of representation and scaffolding is important for learners because their knowledge structures and skills do not initially include the same quantitative command of the concepts that experts would have.

MODEL-IT also supports a qualitative definition of rate relationships in which one factor sets the rate of change of another factor over time

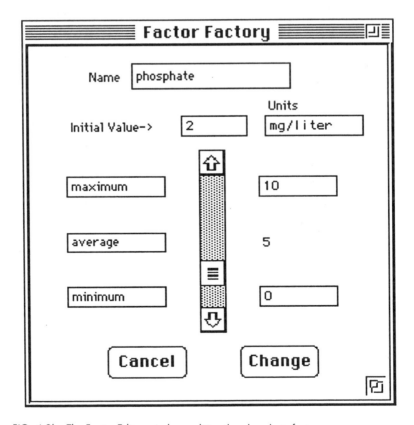

FIG. 4.2b The Factor Editor window, editing the phosphate factor.

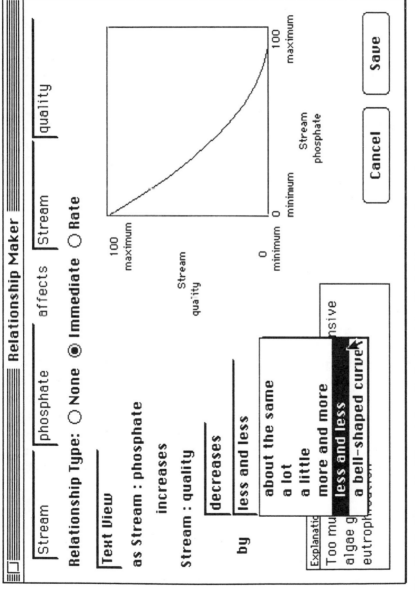

FIG. 4.3 The Relationship Editor window: Qualitative relationship definition using the text view.

(Fig. 4.4). Jackson and her colleagues (1996) provide a detailed description of the mathematics behind both types of relationships.

Bridging Representations

New representations should be connected to the learner's current understandings through examples, analogies, and multiple visual representations. Multiple synchronized representations may act as a bridge between current understandings and more expertlike techniques. MODEL-IT, therefore, provides simultaneous, linked textual-to-graphical representations of relationships. Given a qualitative, verbal definition, the software translates the text into a quantitative, visual representation (e.g. "decreases by less and less" is interpreted as shown by the graph in Fig. 4.3) These simultaneous representations can support students in learning how to read and interpret a graph. MODEL-IT provides a similar bridging link between a graph and a numerical table from which the graph can be edited to more accurately represent students' understanding of a relationship (Fig. 4.5).

Coupling Actions, Effects, and Understanding

An interactive learning environment should provide a tight coupling between the learner's actions, the visual feedback produced by the software as a result of those actions, and the learner's own mental representations of the phenomenon. MODEL-IT provides this tight coupling as students run simulations to test their models (Fig. 4.1). Students select factors to view using meters (vertical indicators) and graphs. During a simulation, meters and graphs provide immediate, visual feedback regarding the current state of the simulation. Students can directly manipulate current factor values even while the model is running and can immediately see the impact. "What if?" questions are generated and answered nearly simultaneously, hypotheses can be tested and predictions verified within moments. This interactivity provides opportunities for students to refine and revise their mental models by comparing the interactive feedback with their expectations.

Testing

MODEL-IT has been used three times with a Foundations of Science class of 22 students. Our early research all took place in the context of a project investigating the question: "How safe is our water?" Specifi-

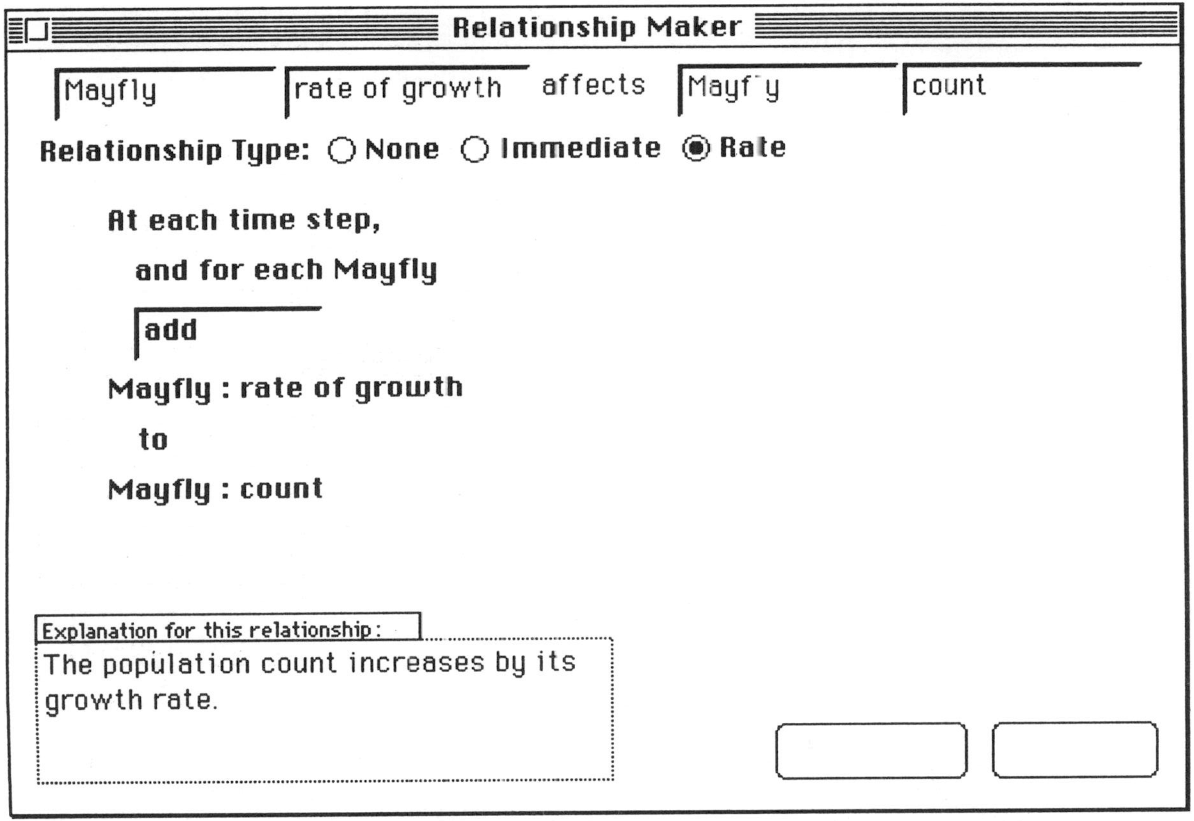

FIG. 4.4 The Relationship Editor window: Qualitative relationship definition of rate relations.

89

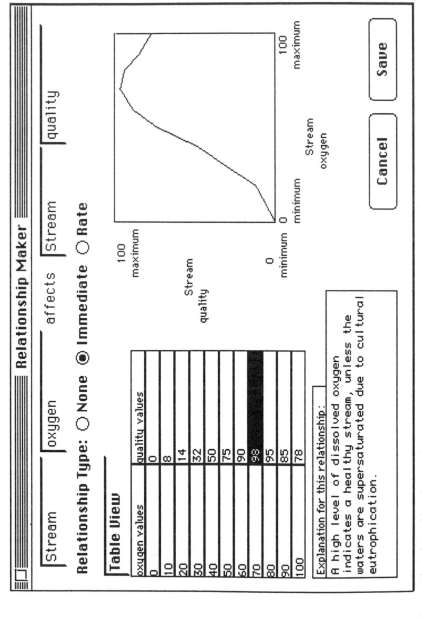

Relationship Maker

| Stream | oxygen | affects | Stream | quality |

Relationship Type: ○ None ◉ Immediate ○ Rate

Table View

oxygen values	quality values
0	0
10	8
20	14
30	32
40	50
50	75
60	90
70	98
80	95
90	85
100	78

Explanation for this relationship:

A high level of dissolved oxygen indicates a healthy stream, unless the waters are supersaturated due to cultural eutrophication.

Stream quality

100 maximum

0 minimum

Stream oxygen

0 minimum   100 maximum

Cancel   Save

FIG. 4.5 The Relationship Editor window: Quantitative relationship definition using the Table view.

cally, the students studied a tributary of a local river that flows near their school and collected a variety of data to determine the quality of the water. Because this water eventually ended up in their drinking fountains, the question was likely to be motivating and personally meaningful to the students. Their project investigations also included using various technologies to conduct and report detailed biological, physical, and chemical assessments.

First, we pilot tested the software with six ninth-grade students from the class in 1-hour sessions, and then we used the software twice in the classroom—once as the final project for a ninth-grade class, and then again by the same students early in the fall of their tenth grade. In each case, the activity covered 1 week of classroom time, about 4 hours. Students worked through a brief guide introducing them to MODEL-IT and then used the program to construct and test models of stream ecosystems. They collaborated with partners on open-ended projects in which they built models of their own design to represent their choice of particular stream phenomena (e.g., the impact of land use practices like golf courses or parking lots on stream quality). Table 4.3 summarizes these three studies.

Findings

General Findings

The findings of these studies indicate that it is possible and feasible for dynamic modeling tools to be used in real-world classrooms without

TABLE 4.3

MODEL-IT 1.0 Studies, Subjects, and Data

Dates	Students and Time Frame	Data Collected
Early spring, 1994	6 representative ninth-grade students (2 pairs, 2 individuals), 1.5 to 2 hrs. each.	Video/audiotapes of sessions; models.
Late spring, 1994	22 ninth-grade students (working in pairs) for four 50-minute class periods.	Video/audiotapes of students using MODEL-IT; models.
Early fall, 1994	22 tenth-grade students (same students as above) in pairs, for over 1 week.	Same as above, plus postinterviews.

a great deal of prior instruction (Jackson et al., 1996). Within the context of this project-based classroom, with students working on an authentic problem, they built and tested computational models, a task that has traditionally been inaccessible to learners in high school science classrooms.

Considering the processes students engaged in as they built and tested their models, we found evidence for the following: building models leads to refining and articulating understanding, building and testing leads to model extension, testing leads to the discovery of flaws in models or suggests refinements, and building their own models is motivating for students. With MODEL-IT, students appropriately focused on high-level concepts such as identifying the factors in the system and the relationships among them, running simulations with different factor values, and deciding if the results seemed valid. Once students had done the thought work of conceiving of a relationship, they were able to quickly add it to their model.

The final models typically exhibited reasonable scientific validity and significant complexity, and averaged at least 15 student-defined factors and relationships. (For further information on how the models were analyzed, readers should consult Stratford, 1996; Stratford, Krajcik & Soloway, 1997; and Stratford, Krajcik & Soloway, in press.) Furthermore, by providing a flexible tool for constructing models, we gave students the flexibility to express and explore their own understanding, often with surprising outcomes. For example, to demonstrate pollution impacts on a stream, two students chose to put a golf course object into their model, and created a new factor, geese, whose fecal matter becomes a pollution source when washed into the stream.

Findings Related to Model-It Design

The predefined high-level objects in MODEL-IT provided students with simple and accessible manipulatives. Students had little trouble learning the object-oriented environment and the high-level building blocks of objects, factors, and relationships.

Students were able to construct qualitative relationships in the MODEL-IT environment. They were comfortable expressing themselves qualitatively, and using the qualitative definition of relationships, they were able to build relationships very quickly. The options of qualitative and quantitative means of defining relationships supported students at different levels of expertise. Some students exclusively used the qualitative "text view" definition for relationships, whereas others preferred the precision afforded by using the quantitative "table view." The table view allows students to change data points to create a relationship that better matches their understanding. Often, students transitioned from one to the other during a project, switching to the table view when they realized a need to make their models more precise.

The real-time, visual feedback provided by meters and graphs allowed students to visualize the behavior of the model as it ran and aided in model testing and verification. Often, during their testing, students were able to discover errors in their model or to think of ways to expand their model. For instance, they might notice that two factors that they had defined should be related to each other. The ease with thich students could test, make changes, and test again allowed students to explore, reflect, and expand on their ideas about the systems they were representing.

Stage 2: In Depth Research

Our early research suggested that we were on the right track. Students were able to quickly learn the software and design interesting, thoughtful models to demonstrate their understanding of a complex system. Our next goals were to conduct more in-depth research with the software, to look at students' processes and products in more depth, and to gauge the effectiveness of the software supports we had designed in supporting students' learning, using, and growing with the program.

Design

For this research, two major new features were finally implemented in MODEL-IT v1.1 that we had always intended to build. The first allowed students to create their own objects and to paste in their own pictures or graphics. Using personalized images had always been part of our idea of grounding the activity in an authentic, meaningful context. We knew that students would have ideas that we had not anticipated, and they would need to create new objects to represent them. For example, in the model described previously when students created a factor for the geese whose fecal matter becomes a pollution source when washed into the stream, it would have made more sense for them to create geese as an object and have fecal matter be the factor affecting the pollution level. To create new objects, we developed the Object Editor (Fig. 4.6).

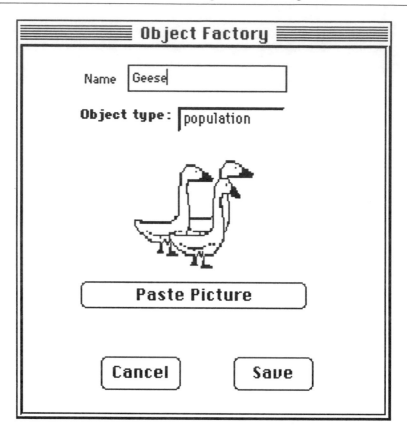

FIG. 4.6 The Object Editor window: Editing the geese object.

Students can paste in a picture by first finding or creating it with any graphics program, copying it into the Macintosh clipboard, and pasting it into MODEL-IT.

The second major change was the development of the factor map to present as a bridging representation from concrete to abstract repre-sentations of the model. The original Simulation window provides a concrete, semirealistic representation of the objects being modeled, and the new option of the factor Map presents a more structural and relational (and thus more abstract) representation of the model (Fig. 4.7).

In the factor map, factors are represented by iconized pictures of the objects, providing a bridge from the object-based Simulation window representation. The Factor map helps students understand the workings of the model by providing a means of visualizing the network of factors

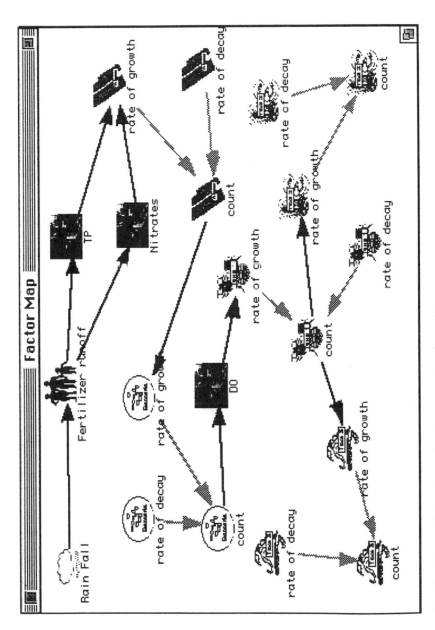

FIG. 4.7 The Map view, displaying the graphical representation of a model.

95

and their relationships. This view is interactive as students can rearrange the nodes in a visually meaningful way and can also make changes (e.g., to create a new relationship, the user simply draws an arrow from one factor to another).

Testing

With this new, more robust version of MODEL-IT implemented, a formal, detailed study was conducted with MODEL-IT during the 1994-1995 school year. Stratford, in his dissertation (Stratford, 1996; Stratford, Krajcik, & Soloway, 1998), studied the use of MODEL-IT by 4 ninth-grade classes (approximately 100 students) as the ninth-grade final project for the stream ecology unit. A longer version of the self-paced guide was developed that introduced both basic and advanced modeling concepts. Students used the guide over six 50-minute class periods. Students then spent two to three 50-minute class periods collaborating with partners on open-ended projects in which they built models of their own design to represent their choice of particular stream phenomena. They were given several general scenarios from which to choose, including the option to create their own scenario.

Stratford's research focused on of how well MODEL-IT supports learners in engaging in and developing skills in the higher level cognitive activities that the modeling task requires (Stratford, 1996). He conducted a very detailed, qualitative analysis of the thinking processes of a representative sample of eight pairs of students, as identified from their conversations and actions as they used the program. He looked for evidence of thinking strategies specifically related to modeling, such as analyzing a phenomenon, reasoning about interrelationships, synthesizing a model, and testing and debugging it, along with other more general strategies such as planning the model, asking questions, searching for information, and explaining. He also evaluated the models produced by all 50 pairs of students, focusing on the scientific content, structure, craft, and behavior of the models, and considered the relationship between the modeling processes of the students and the models they produced as final products. A brief follow-up study, 5 months later, invited four focus pairs from this study to build models of any subject that they chose.

The next year, a long-term study was conducted by Wisnudel-Spitulnik on student learning as related to artifact construction (Wisnudel-Spitulnik, 1998). As part of the study, MODEL-IT was used for several projects during the year. Notably, for one of these projects, students built models representing climate-related phenomena, marking the first time MODEL-IT had been used in the classroom in other than the stream ecosystem domain. For purposes of MODEL-IT design and evaluation, Wisnudel-Spitulnik also developed and used curriculum materials (paper-based worksheets) intended to support students engaging in high-level cognitive activities during the modeling task. For example, before building their model, students were asked to articulate their plans and design ideas. Students were encouraged to draw conceptual maps representing their models and to critique each other's ideas. After their models were built, students again returned to the worksheets to evaluate and reflect on their models and then presented their models to the class, getting feedback from the teacher and from other students. Table 4.4 summarizes the three studies conducted with Model-It v1.1.

Findings

General Findings

For the ninth-grade students in the Stratford study, this was their first experience with creating dynamic models, yet most students were able to create thoughtful, complex models that demonstrated reasonable scientific accuracy. The majority of students generally produced models with accurate content, coherent structure, and sensible, high-fidelity behavior (Stratford, Krajcik, & Soloway, 1997). Figure 4.7 shows one of these models. Students also engaged in a range of cognitive modeling strategies

TABLE 4.4

MODEL-IT 1.1 Studies, Subjects, and Data

Dates	Students and Time Frame	Data Collected
January, 1995	100 ninth-grade students (working in pairs) for nine 50-minute class periods. 8 focus pairs.	Video/audiotapes of sessions, pre- and post-interviews, of focus pairs. All models.
June, 1995	8 focus pairs from above study, for two 1.5 hour sessions.	Models
January & March, 1996	100 ninth-grade students (working in pairs) for four 50-minute class periods.	Video/audiotapes, models

(analyzing, reasoning, synthesizing, testing/debugging, and explaining) as they created their models (Stratford, Krajcik, Soloway, 1998).

We believe there were several ways MODEL-IT helped students build successful models. First, it structured the task into easily understood subtasks, such as "select an object," "create a factor," "think of relationships," and "test the model." This task breakdown seemed to provide a framework in which students were able to organize their activities. MODEL-IT made these subtasks more understandable by supporting analysis with the high-level building blocks of objects, factors, and relationships. Cognitive modeling strategies also were supported by providing simple, qualitative means for expressing relationships. In addition, the explanation boxes, which gave students the opportunity to explain the relationships they created, supported thoughtful model construction. Finally, interactive, real-time meters and graphs were useful for testing and debugging, for viewing how the model was behaving, and for looking for errors.

The new addition of the factor map seemed to help students to synthesize and unify their models. The concrete and abstract representations of their models facilitated different ways for the learners to think about their models and helped them make the transition from novice representations to more expertlike ones. Finally, the opportunity to create their own objects allowed many students to branch out even further in creating and expressing their ideas.

The second two studies clearly demonstrated that students could use MODEL-IT to build models in domains other than stream ecosystems. When students were allowed to build models exploring the causes and effects of changes in global climate, sophisticated models of the process resulted. These included a representation of the impact of factories on acid rain and global warming (Fig. 4.8); a model of how consumer demand for products like hair spray is depleting the ozone layer; and a suggestion that increased cancer rates are related to human denial of the need for cautionary measures such as wearing sunscreen.

Findings Informing MODEL-IT Design

Stratford's research showed that design features in MODEL-IT such as the basic modeling framework (objects, factors, and relationships), the Relationship maker, the Factor map, and the meters and graphs supported the analyzing, reasoning, synthesizing, and testing activities of

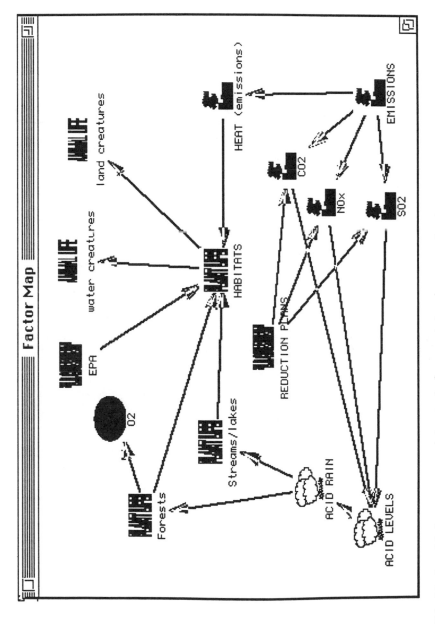

FIG. 4.8 A model of government regulations on the factory emissions that cause acic rain.

many students. However, it was also found that some students required more support to understand and engage in these activities. Table 4.5 summarizes the research findings that indicated areas where students could benefit from additional support and how they influenced software design changes for the next version of MODEL-IT.

TABLE 4.5

Changes Suggested by Research Findings

Research Outcome	Software Design Change
Students need additional support for engaging in more goal-directed, thoughtful modeling. Paper worksheets for students to plan their model on paper first helped them focus on identifying and achieving their goals.	Explicit support for planning the model (e.g., text areas in which students enter the goal, hypotheses).
Students often didn't reflect on their model, not evaluating their model in comparison with their goal, or even identifying what their goal was.	Explicit support for evaluating the model, considering how well it works, how well it meets their goals.
Students who tested their models produced better models. However, students sometimes created many relationships without testing any of them, and then had trouble figuring out why their model didn't work. An iterative build–test style tended to lead to better-crafted models.	Prompts for students to test their model after building relationships before going much further. More explicit support for testing and debugging, with visual cues, suggestions, and help.
Stating predictions helped students in evaluating their models, yet often they didn't make predictions, or understand how to evaluate the results of their testing.	Explicit support for making predictions before running a test, and for evaluating the result of a test. Debugging support.
Students had problems understanding rate relations. Students learning the program were sometimes confused about which type of relationship to use.	Provide more explicit support. Hide rate relationships at first, while students get used to the more basic relationships.
Most students seemed to be able to create unified models, enabled at least in part by the model overview provided in the Factor map.	Emphasize use of the Factor map for building and testing models. Make the Factor map more useful and interactive.
When introducing the software, it was helpful for students to structure the task into easily understood subtasks. Identifying relevant objects, then defining factors, then relationships, and testing periodically, seemed to be a useful structure.	Make subtasks more distinct and explicit. Organize the interface by subtask.
Students would have benefitted by more explicit examples of the products and processes of modeling.	Provide help and examples of how to use each part of the program.

Interlude: A Facelift

In 1996, as we were starting to show the software to a wider audience, Model-It v.2 was developed to make the interface cleaner, more colorful, and more visually appealing. (This version of Model-It was also the basis for a commercial version of Model-It, developed and published by Cogito Leaning Media, Inc., http://www.cogitomedia.com/.) A few other changes were also added: switches to go between World view and Map view; a New object button on the object palette itself instead of in the old Object window, and new tools for editing the model using the Map view, which was rapidly becoming the main interface for model building. Figure 4.9 shows the main window of this new version, displaying a model that students created to show how drugs affect the human body.

Stage 3: The Second System

Design

Model-It V3.0 was a significant redesign of the system, although still based on the same fundamental ideas. (A classic software engineering text, the Mythical Man-Month (Brooks, 1975), describes the phenomenon that the second major release of a software package often appears overstuffed with all of the features that the designers had invented after the first version and were eager to include. Being aware of this potential problem, we tried to control ourselves.) One purpose, of course, of this next phase of Model-It's design was to address the issues highlighted by our research, in identifying areas where learners needed more support to learn the task and to engage in modeling activities. Table 4.5 summarizes the major issues that came out of the research that we tried to address in version 3.0.

Our next design goal was to develop software that could grow with students as they learned and grew in expertise. Yet in a critical sense, this needed to be an inverse relation. In fact, the definition and metaphor of scaffolding—support provided for the learner to engage in activities that would otherwise be out of reach—includes the implication that the scaffolding should fade. As the learner's understanding and abilities improve, the computer, much like a human tutor, needs to back off and give the learner more autonomy, fewer hints, and so on (Collins, Brown, & Newman, 1989; Guzdial, 1995; Rogoff, 1990).

In the field of educational software research, scaffolding is a new concept that is still being explored. Many techniques have been applied

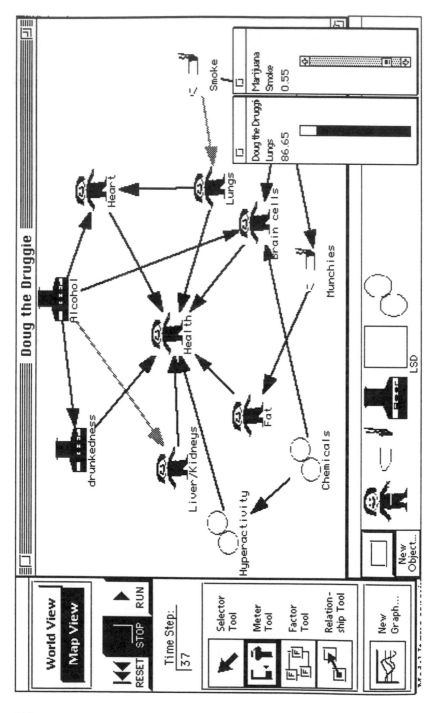

FIG. 4.9 The Model-It V2 main window showing a model of how drugs affect health.

that provide various supportive structures for learners, but typically that support does not fade within the software itself. For our new version of MODEL-IT, therefore, we decided to address the problem of "fadeable scaffolding" to support the growth of expertise. Our approach was to design Guided Learner-Adaptable Scaffolding (GLAS)—adaptability under the learner's control, with guidance and support from the software environment.

Sources disagree as to a specific definition of the teaching methods that qualify as scaffolding. Collins and associates (1989) first defined scaffolding simply as "support, in the form of reminders or help," and later added that it can also take the form of "physical supports, as with the cue cards [used to facilitate writing] ...or the short skis used to teach downhill skiing" (p. 456). Collins and associates also refer to scaffolding as one component of a broader set of teaching methods used for activity based learning: modeling, coaching, scaffolding, articulation, reflection, and exploration. Guzdial (1995) examined this list and suggested that modeling, coaching, and eliciting articulation should be considered the set of scaffolding methods, because they are all supportive strategies that can be faded.

For our research purposes, we have further expanded the definition of scaffolding by grouping modeling and coaching with other supportive strategies, retaining eliciting articulation as a special category, and adding a new category for methods that use the aforementioned "physical supports," thus defining the following three categories:

Supportive Scaffolding. Supportive scaffolding is support for performing the task. The task itself is unchanged; scaffolding is provided alongside the task, to offer advice and support (e.g., demonstrative examples, context-specific help about what to do next). Examples of supportive scaffolding are modeling, guiding, coaching, and critiquing. As supportive scaffolding fades, the task is the same as it was before, but the goal is for the learner to have internalized the procedures and concepts through which the scaffolding guided them.

Reflective Scaffolding. Reflective scaffolding is support for thinking about the task. It is similar to supportive scaffolding, in that it also does not change the task itself, but instead it makes the task of reflection explicit. A crucial part of learning is the learner's reflection about what he or she is doing, whether it is working, why he or she did it, and, he or she can generalize from what he or she did. Norman (1993) makes a distinction between two kinds of cognition, experiential and reflective, and asserts that reflective cognition, the mode of "comparison and contrast, of thought, of decision-making," is essential for learning, although it is more rarely supported by technology (p. 16).

Intrinsic Scaffolding.   Intrinsic scaffolding is our name for supports that change the task itself by reducing the complexity of the task and focusing the learner's attention (e.g., training wheels on a bicycle, outlines in coloring books) or by providing mechanisms for visualizing or thinking about a concept (e.g., finger counting to add or subtract, maps and models for visualization; Carroll & Carrithers, 1984; Collins et al., 1989). As the scaffold fades, the task is changed, but recalling the idea of "bridging representations," associations should remain so the learner can progress from simpler, more structured, or more concrete tasks to variations in which more of the underlying complexity or abstractness is introduced.

We further define software-based scaffolding as the implementation of any of the following types of support, with the requirement that it must be fadeable within the software itself. All three kinds of scaffolding have been designed into MODEL-IT 3.0 and apply to the modeling task as follows, summarized in Table 4.6. MODEL-IT 3.0 also includes other support features that make the task more accessible, but which cannot be termed "scaffolds" by our new definition because the level of support they provide is not able to change. Some of these features were present in previous versions (e.g., using photos or graphics to represent objects); others were added for this version. Figure 4.10 shows the main window of MODEL-IT 3.0 and illustrates some of the new features, which include task-switching controls (Plan, Build, Test, Evaluate) that identify and structure the subtasks and make available only those tools that are appropriate for that subtask; labels on relationship arrows that display the graph or type of relationship so it can be seen at a glance; and testing options for parts of a model by highlighting specific relationships as a debugging aid.

Supportive scaffolding guides the learner through the tasks of constructing a model (e.g., making a plan before starting to build, testing the model periodically), and makes available help and examples explaining the various modeling concepts. Supportive scaffolding is mainly displayed in the Help window (Fig. 4.11). Messages are displayed to offer

TABLE 4.6

Fadeable Scaffolding Strategies and Their Implementation in MODEL-IT v.3

Scaffolding Strategy	Model-It Implementation
Supportive Scaffolding	Guiding through subtasks (e.g., plan before building, test periodically).
	Coaching and modeling throughout the software, providing context-sensitive help and examples.
Reflective Scaffolding	Eliciting articulation with forms and prompts for:
	•Planning: stating goals of model, ideas about how system works.
	• Descriptions and explanations for objects, factors.
	•Testing: predicting before testing, comparing the outcome to the prediction.
	•Evaluating: deciding how well the model works, what could be changed.
Intrinsic Scaffolding	Multiple linked representations (from simple to advanced):
	•Factor definition (textual labels, numerical values).
	•Relationship definition (textual, graphical, table, rate).
	•Viewing model (world view, map view).
	•Viewing factor values (meters, graphs).
	Hiding complexity, but making advanced options available:
	•Weighting of relationships: option to set relative weights of relationships.
	•Delay: option to specify time over which relation should occur.
	•Combining: option to combine effects of relationships in different ways (e.g., sum).

relevant guiding, coaching, or critiquing, and buttons are available to offer extra options and fading capability (e.g., "show me an example," "stop reminding me"). Coaching and modeling scaffolds are invoked through contextual "?" buttons that appear throughout the software.

Reflective scaffolding promotes the learner's engagement in reflective activities related to modeling, for example, planning, making predictions, and evaluating. Reflective scaffolding is shown by the Notepad window (Fig. 4.12), and also by the description fields that are part of

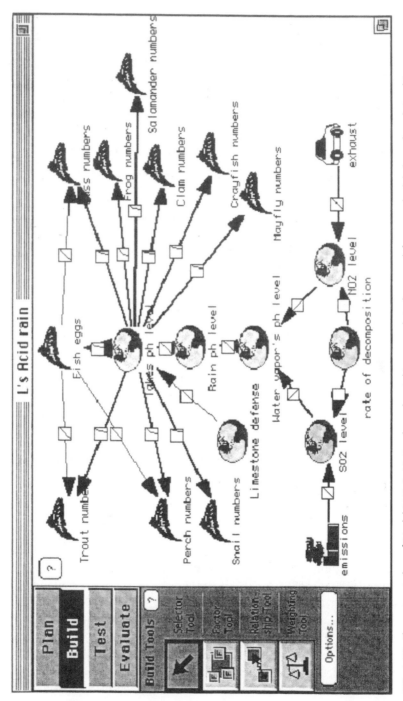

FIG. 4.10 The main window of Model-It V3.0. Notice the task-switching controls in the upper-left corner, the labels on the relationship arrows, and that some arrows are thicker than others, owing to use of the new Weighting tool.

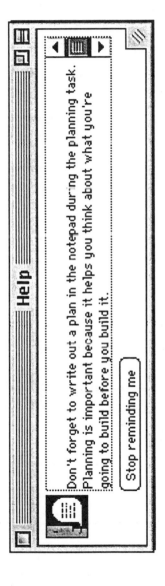

FIG. 4.11 An example of a supportive scaffold, one of several used to guide the learner between subtasks. This scaffold is faded by clicking the "Stop reminding me" button.

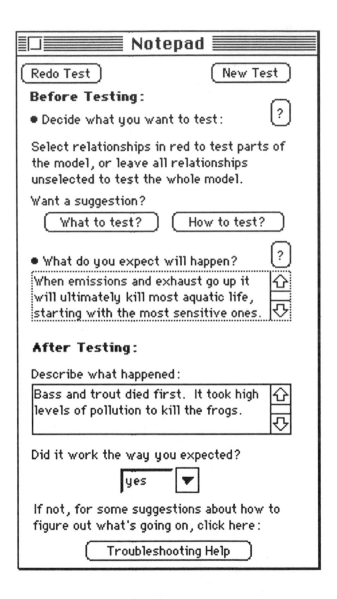

FIG. 4.12 An example of a reflective scaffold: The Notepad page for the Test subtasks. Each page of the Notepad prompts the learner to reflect on the task; here, the learner is asked to make and evaluate predictions while testing. Also note the supportive scaffolds: the "?" buttons that explain each question in further detail, and other buttons that invoke testing and debugging help.

each component's editor window. The learner is prompted to reflect by typing plans, descriptions, predictions and evaluations into the appropriate fields of the Notepad, as relevant for each subtask.

Intrinsic scaffolding sets defaults that hide all but the simplest tools from the novice learner but make advanced features available as the learner grows and develops expertise (e.g., qualitative to quantitative representations of factors and relationships). Through the main window and the editor windows used to create the model objects, factors, and relationships intrinsic scaffolding is manifested as different views and representations of the model components, or different sets of enabled controls and tools. Figure 4.13 shows the mechanism by which the learner fades intrinsic scaffolding for the Relationship editor by turning on advanced options that were previously hidden. Other advanced features accessible through Options dialogs are: the option to define an object representing a population, with rates of growth and decay, for factors, the option to use a numerical range of values (default being a qualitative range such as "low," "medium," and "high"); the option to use a new weighting tool to define the relative effect of relationships affecting the same factor; and also the option of a combining tool, to choose different combining functions such as sum, product, or difference (the default being the average).

Testing

MODEL-IT 3.0 was used by four classes of ninth graders (approximately 100 students), for three modeling projects, each project for about 1 week (about 4 hours). The projects were spaced about 2 months apart. The students, working in pairs, built models to represent their understanding of some aspect of the topic currently being studied by the class, but the specific content and structure of their models was decided by the students themselves. Tutorial materials introducing students to the software was kept to a minimum (less than 1 hour of class time).

For the first two projects, students built models of stream ecosystems. The first project focused on the physical and biological factors of the stream whereas the second was a "final exam" in which students chose their own topic relating to some aspect of the stream ecosystem (including physical, biological, and chemical factors). For the third project, the students explored global climate and used the Internet to search for information on their own chosen question that related to acid rain, global warming, or the greenhouse effect. They built models to demon-

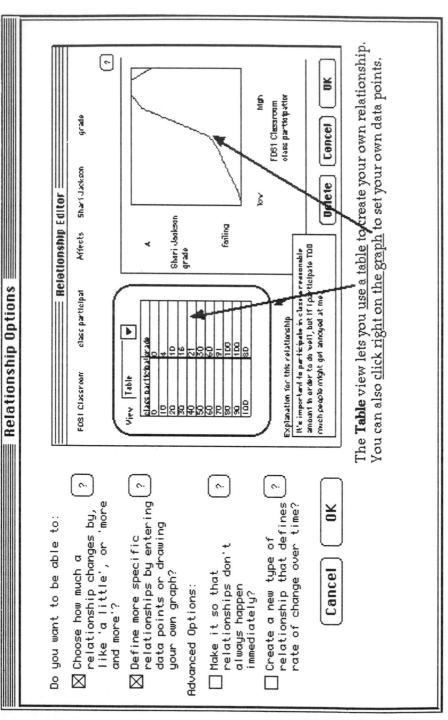

FIG. 4.13 The fading mechanism for intrinsic scaffolding for the Relationship editor. The Options button on the Relationship editor opens up this dialog that allows the user to turn options on and off, and guides the user in selecting appropriate options by showing what each option will let them do.

strate their theory or understanding about the topic they had re-searched, using data from their research where appropriate. Table 4.7 summarizes the three projects.

Findings

The data from these latest studies is currently (at the time of publication) being evaluated. The evaluation centers on an in-depth analysis of the process video data to determine the overall success of the learner-adaptable scaffolding approach in supporting students in learning the modeling task and in adapting and fading the software to meet their changing needs. We also are evaluating the effectiveness of each specific design component proposed for implementing fadeable scaffolding.

Preliminary analysis indicates that the software was quite successful. For the first project students were able to use the basic program to build useful models with only brief instruction, aided by supportive scaffolding, and shielded by the intrinsic scaffolding from the potentially confusing array of options. In successive projects, a short introduction to advanced features was sufficient for students to choose to fade selective scaffolds and build more complex and accurate models as they felt ready.

More students turned off supportive features such as guiding messages over time as they learned the task, and more students used more of the advanced features in later projects as they developed expertise.

TABLE 4.7

Model-it 3.0 Studies, Subjects, and Data

Dates	Students, Time Frame, Project	Data Collected
November, 1996	100 ninth-grade students (working in pairs) for 1 week (about 4 hours). 11 focus students. Learn Model-It, build simple model related to stream ecosystem.	Video/audiotapes of sessions, post-interviews of focus pairs. Models and log files.
January, 1997	Same students. One week. Build more complex model demonstrating in-depth understanding of stream ecosystem.	Video/audiotapes of sessions, postinterviews of focus pairs. Models and log files.
March, 1997	Same students. One week. Build complex model demonstrating understanding of climate issue, based on independent research.	Video/audiotapes of sessions, postinterviews of focus pairs. Models and log files.

For example, the only options used by any students during the first project were the most basic: 20% of the student pairs used the option of specifying the slope of a relationship, and 9% used the Table view (the first two options in Fig. 4.13). By the third project, 85% of the models used one or both of those options (37% specifically using the Table view to create more accurate relationships), and of the most advanced options, 41% used delay and 26% used rate relationships (the third and fourth options in Fig. 4.13), 28% used the weighting tool, and 11% used the combining function to calculate the product or difference of two factors' effects.

Models from the third project also tended to include more specific data that students had found in texts or on the World Wide Web. Figure 4.10 shows a third project model of acid rain and its effect on a lake ecosystem. The student who created this model used data from an EPA Web page as the basis for the relations between lake pH and each of the aquatic lifeforms.

CONCLUDING REMARKS: LOOKING AHEAD

Certainly, the work we have presented supports the claim that high school students can use MODEL-IT. But what about younger learners? What about other school settings? During the winter and spring of 1997, we used MODEL-IT in two middle schools within the Detroit Public School System with over 100 seventh-grade students. The population of these schools is primarily African American and Hispanic American. Many of the students are from low socioeconomic backgrounds and perform below grade level on state-mandated tests of achievement. Yet, even in these classrooms students were able to use Model-It efficiently to create models of weather phenomena (Roy, Singer, & Krajcik, 1997).

Although we now know MODEL-IT can be used in a variety of classrooms and with a variety of content areas, we are still faced with a number of difficult educational, technological, and research challenges. From an educational perspective, we still need to determine how to effectively distribute MODEL-IT so it is used in the manner intended. We need to further investigate the use of MODEL-IT in other science domains. We also need to explore the types of supports that might be necessary for teachers in a variety of settings to use MODEL-IT. On the technical side, we are currently exploring how we might have students share and collaborate on models over the World Wide Web and share data between MODEL-IT and other tools for data collection, visualization and analysis. Although Metcalf (1999) has collected data on students across three different uses of Model-It, we still need to explore further the learning outcomes that result when learners use MODEL-IT over sustained periods.

MODEL-IT was conceived as a tool to support students in an essential component of learning science that previously was extremely difficult to accomplish in most middle and high school audiences. Designing a tool to support students in representing, interpreting, and refining their thinking so they develop more robust understanding has been a challenging task. During the 4 years our group spent developing MODEL-IT, we struggled with how to develop computational software that embodies the principles of learner-centered design. Our goal with MODEL-IT has been to support students with a range of mathematical skills in the building of dynamic models of scientific phenomena. Encouraged by our research findings to date we now believe that we have such a computational tool.

ACKNOWLEDGMENTS

We would like to extend our great appreciation to Steven J. Stratford, Michele Wisnudel-Spitulnik, the other members of the Center for Highly Interactive Computing in Education (HI-CE), and especially the teachers and students at Community High School in Ann Arbor, for their feedback and support. This research has been supported by the National Science Foundation (RED 9353481) and the University of Michigan.

REFERENCES

American Association for the Advancement of Science. (1993). *Benchmarks for science literacy*. New York: Oxford University Press.

Blumenfeld, P. C., Soloway, E., Marx, R. W., Krajcik, J. S., Guzdial, M., & Palincsar, A. (1991). Motivating project-based learning: Sustaining the doing, supporting the learning. *Educational Psychologist, 26*(3 & 4), 369–398.

Brooks, F. P. (1975). *The mythical man-month: Essays on software engineering*. Reading, MA: Addison-Wesley.

Brown, A. L., & Campione, J. C. (1994). Guided discovery in a community of learners. In K. McGilly (Ed.), *Classroom lessons: Integrating cognitive theory and classroom practice* (pp. 229–270). Cambridge, MA: MIT Press/Bradford Books.

Brown, J., Collins, A., & Duguid, P. (1989). Situated cognition and the culture of learning. *Educational Researcher, 18*(1), 32–42.

Carroll, J. M., & Carrithers, C. (1984) Training wheels in a user interface, *Communications of the ACM, 27*(8), 800–806.

Clement, J., Brown, D. E., & Zietsman, A. (1989). Not all preconceptions are misconceptions: Finding 'anchoring conceptions' for grounding instruction in students' intuitions. *International Journal of Science Education, 11*(Special Issue), 554–565.

Cognition and Technology Group at Vanderbilt. (1990). Anchored instruction and its relationship to situated cognition. *Educational Researcher, 19*(6), 2–10.

Collins, A., Brown, J. S., & Newman, S. E. (1989) Cognitive apprenticeship: Teaching the crafts of reading, writing, and mathematics, In L. B. Resnick (Ed.), *Knowing, learning, and instruction: Essays in honor of Robert Glaser (pp. 347–361)*. Hillsdale, NJ: Lawrence Erlbaum Associates.

Draper, F., & Swanson, M. (1990). Learner-directed systems education: a successful example. *System Dynamics Review, 6*(2), 209–213.

Guzdial, M. (1995). Software-realized scaffolding to facilitate programming for science learning. *Interactive Learning Environments, 4*(1), 1–44.

Hestenes, D. (1992). Modeling games in the Newtonian world. *American Journal of Physics, 60*(8), 732–748.

Heubel-Drake, M., Finkel, L., Stern, E., & Mouradian, M. (1995). Planning a course for success. *The Science Teacher, 62*, 18–21.

Jackson, S. L., Stratford, S., Krajcik, J., & Soloway, E. (1995, March). *Model-It: a case study of learner-centered software for supporting model building*. Proceedings of the Working Conference on Technology Applications in the Science Classroom, The National Center for Science Teaching and Learning, Columbus, OH.

Jackson, S. L., Stratford, S. J., Krajcik, J. S., & Soloway, E. (1996). Making system dynamics modeling accessible to pre-college science students. *Interactive Learning Environments, 4*(3), 233–257.

Jonassen, D. H. (1995). Computers as cognitive tools: Learning with technology, not from technology. *Journal of Computing in Higher Education, 6*(2), 40–73.

Krajcik, J., Blumenfeld, P., Marx, R. W., & Soloway, E. (1994). A collaborative model for helping science teachers learn project-based instruction. *Elementary School Journal, 94*(5), 483–498.

Kreutzer, W. (1986). *Systems simulation: Programming styles and languages*. Addison-Wesley, Sydney.

Lajoie, S. P. (1993). Computer environments as cognitive tools for enhancing learning. In S. P. Lajoie & S. J. Derry (Eds.), *Computers as cognitive tools*. Hillsdale, NJ: Lawrence Erlbaum Associates.

Metcalf, S. J. (1999). *The design of guided learner-adaptable scaffolding in interactive learning environments*. Unpublished doctoral dissertation, University of Michigan, Ann Arbor.

Mokros, J. R., & Tinker, R. F. (1987). The impact of microcomputer-based labs on children's ability to interpret graphs. *Journal of Research in Science Teaching, 24*(4), 369–383.

Norman, D. (1993). *Things that make us smart: Defending human attributes in the age of the machine*. Reading, MA: Addison-Wesley.

Norman, D., & Draper, S. (Eds., 1986). *User centered system design*. Hillsdale, NJ: Lawrence Erlbaum Associates.

Rogoff, B. (1990). Apprenticeship in thinking: Cognitive development in social context. New York: Oxford University Press.

Roy, M., Singer, J., & Krajcik, J. S. (1997, August). *Model-It: Supporting urban students in the development and refinement of science understanding*. Unpublished paper, University of Michigan, Ann Arbor.

Salomon, G. (1990). Cognitive effects with and of computer technology. *Communication Research, 17*(1), 26–44.

Soloway, E., Guzdial, M., & Hay, K. E. (1994). Learner-centered design: The challenge for HCI in the 21st century. *Interactions, 1*(2), 36–48.

Soloway, E., Jackson, S. L., Klein, J., Quintana, C., Reed, J., Spitulnik, J., Stratford, S. J., Studer, S., Jul, S., Eng, J., & Scala, N. (April, 1996). *Learning theory in practice: Case studies of learner-centered design*. Proceedings from the ACM CHI '96 Human Factors in Computer Systems, Vancouver, BC.

Stratford, S. J. (1996). *Cognitive and other conceptual activities in dynamic modeling: Case studies of cognitive modeling activities in precollege classrooms*. Unpublished doctoral dissertation, University of Michigan, Ann Arbor.

Stratford, S, Krajcik, J., & Soloway, E. (March, 1997). *Technological artifacts created by secondary science students: Examining structure, content, and behavior of dynamic models*. Paper presented at the annual meeting of the National Association for Research in Science Teaching, Chicago.

Stratford, S., Krajcik, J., & Soloway, E. (1998). *Secondary students' dynamic modeling processes: analyzing, reasoning about, synthesizing, and testing models of stream ecosystems. Journal of Science Education and Technology, 7*(3), 215–234.

Tinker, R. (1990). *Teaching theory building: modeling: instructional materials and software for theory building*: The Technical Education Research Centers, Inc., Cambridge, MA.

Vygotsky, L. S. (1978). *Mind in society: The development of higher psychological processes*. Cambridge, MA: Cambridge University Press.

Wisnudel, M., Stratford, S. J., Krajcik, J., & Soloway, E. (1998). Educational technology to support students' artifact construction in science. In K. Tobin & B. J. Fraser (Eds.), *International Handbook of Science Education*. The Netherlands: Kluwer.

Wisnudel-Spitulnik, M. (1998). *Construction of technological artifacts and the teaching strategies used to promote flexible scientific understanding*. Unpublished doctoral dissertation, University of Michigan, Ann Arbor.

Wood, D., Bruner, J. S., & Ross, G. (1975). The role of tutoring in problem-solving. *Journal of Child Psychology and Psychiatry, 17*, 89–100.

5

The Knowledge Mediator Framework: Toward the Design of Hypermedia Tools for Learning

Michael J. Jacobson
Allison ~LoRue Group, L.L.C.

Anthi Archodidou
University of Illinois at Urbana–Champaign

The capabilities of hypermedia learning environments—either stand-alone or globally distributed via the World Wide Web to store, interconnect, and provide access to a wide range of knowledge represented as text, graphics, audio, and video provide significant opportunities to enrich students' learning (Baker, Niemi, & Herl, 1994; Beeman et al., 1988; Conklin, 1987; Dede, 1987; Jonassen, 1986; Jonassen & Wang, 1993; Kearsley, 1988; Landow, 1992; Lehrer, 1993; Marsh & Kumar, 1992; Nielsen, 1990; Yankelovich, Meyrowitz, & van Dam, 1988). Although research has explored educational applications of hypermedia technologies, many of these studies have primarily described features of hypermedia systems or usage patterns of these systems by students. Whereas some studies have demonstrated improved learning outcomes associated with the use of hypermedia programs, overall there has been limited empirical documentation of the educational efficacy of such systems. Factors contributing to the provisional nature of research on learning with hypermedia include preoccupation with technological functionality, methodological problems, and lack of attention to relevant cognitive learning theory and research (Jacobson, 1994). Further, there has been little systematic research into the relation between specific hypermedia design features, correlated learning activities, and cognitive learning outcomes, particularly in domains that are conceptually challenging to students (e.g., science). These criticisms, and others, are also applicable to much of the recent literature on learning with networked-distributed hypermedia such as the World Wide Web (see Slotta & Linn, chap. 7, this volume).

This chapter describes a program of research that has been investigating an approach—which we refer to as the Knowledge Mediator Framework (KMF)—for designing and using hypermedia to help students learn conceptually challenging domains. In this chapter, we describe the components of the KMF, followed by an overview of research involving this approach. We conclude with a consideration of future research directions.

KNOWLEDGE MEDIATOR FRAMEWORK AND DEVELOPING HYPERMEDIA TOOLS FOR LEARNING COMPLEX KNOWLEDGE

KMF is based on a series of hypermedia systems developed over the course of several different studies of learning with hypermedia with which members of our group have been involved. These projects include the CARDIOWORLD EXPLORER and KANE cognitive flexibility hypertexts (Spiro, Coulson, Feltovich & Anderson, 1988; Spiro, Feltovich, Jacobson, & Coulson, 1992; Spiro & Jehng, 1990), SOCIAL IMPACT of TECHNOLOGY hypertext and transfer studies (Jacobson, Maouri, Mishra, & Kolar, 1996; Jacobson & Spiro, 1991; Jacobson & Spiro, 1995), THEMATIC INVESTIGA-TOR biology case-based hypermedia learning environment (Jacobson, & Spiro, 1997; Jacobson, Sugimoto, & Archodidou, 1996), and a new web-based hypermedia tool, the EVOLUTION KNOWLEDGE MEDIATOR.

A central aspect of these varied but related hypermedia learning tools are design elements and learning activities that attempt to mediate between representations of contextualized knowledge and of abstract conceptual knowledge, and between the naive models students frequently hold and the expert models we wish for them to learn. KMF hypermedia learning tools utilize cases and problems to provide a contextual space for the knowledge to be learned while scaffolding the learner to cognitively abstract key concepts and conceptual models and to flexibly interconnect knowledge in a manner characteristic of expert ways of thinking about the domain.

Next we present the KMF design elements (DE) and learning activities (LA) and the main sociocognitive theoretical and research strands that have been informing this work (see Table 5.1). A study of conceptual change and evolutionary biology is then described in which a number of the components of the KMF were implemented.

DE-1. Representational Affordances of Technology

The first KMF design element is representational affordances of technology. In contrast to older, often linear, techniques for representing knowledge (e.g., text, instructional video), hypermedia technologies allow nodes of digitally represented symbols to be linked together in a flexible, nonlinear manner. Indeed, one might regard the two funda-

TABLE 5.1

Knowledge Mediator Framework Design Elements and Learning Activities

Design Elements
DE-1. Representational affordances of technology
DE-2. Represent knowledge-in-context
DE-3. Reify the deep structure of knowledge
DE-3A. Abstract domain concepts
DE-3B. Deep structure indexing and commentaries
DE-3C. Conceptual visualizations
DE-4. Intra- intercase hyperlinks for conceptual and representational interconnectedness

Learning Activities
LA-1. Cognitive interactivity
LA-2. Scaffolded problem solving
LA-3. Cognitive preparation
LA-3A. Thought experiments
LA-3B. Show gaps in students' solutions
LA-3C. "Seed" new concepts and models
LA-4. Preliminary learning tasks with deep structure knowledge resources
LA-5. Guided conceptual criss-crossing
LA-6. Learner centered and project-based

mental technical features of hypermedia—links and nodes—as a "metatechnology" that allows formally disparate technologies (e.g. text, images, digital video, sound, animations, simulations) to be integrated together as learning resources, whether the individual files are on a single local computer or globally distributed across the Internet and the World Wide Web. This hypermedia paradigm of links and nodes may even be extended to include emerging technologies such as virtual reality in which the learner is not just shown representations but is also cognitively and psychologically immersed in them. Fig. 5.1 shows a screen in which nodes of text, images, and digital video are linked to represent various aspects of a case about the Anglerfish.[1]

The main theoretical rationales for DE-1 are based on the general notion of affordances (i.e., opportunities for action) as articulated by Gibson (1979).[2] For example, digital video, high-resolution images, or immersive virtual reality each provide representational affordances that engage the human visual–perceptual system in significantly different ways than text alone. Another related rationale is that different types of media convey different types of symbolic information, and it is possible for media to simultaneously present certain types of symbol systems and coded information such as linguistic and visual information in television or multimedia or hypermedia (Kozma, 1991).

DE-2. Represent Knowledge-In-Context

One of the most significant changes in contemporary learning theory is that knowledge is no longer regarded as an abstract and decontextualized substance existing in the minds of an individual, but rather is a constructive process that emerges in specific situations and contexts (Brown, Collins, & Duguid, 1989; Clancey, 1993; Cognition and Technology Group at Vanderbilt, 1990; Cognition and Technology Group at Vanderbilt, 1997; Lave & Wenger, 1991). The KMF design element *DE-2. Represent Knowledge-in-context* is based on this new perspective of learning, and it advocates providing the learner with knowledge anchored or

---

[1]To illustrate KMF design elements, we use screens from the EVOLUTION KNOWLEDGE MEDIATOR, which is a web-based hypermedia learning tool developed for an ongoing series of studies into learning, conceptual change, and knowledge transfer in the domain of evolutionary biology.

[2]For an excellent overview of Gibson's views regarding ecological psychology and the notion of affordances, see Allen and Otto (1996).

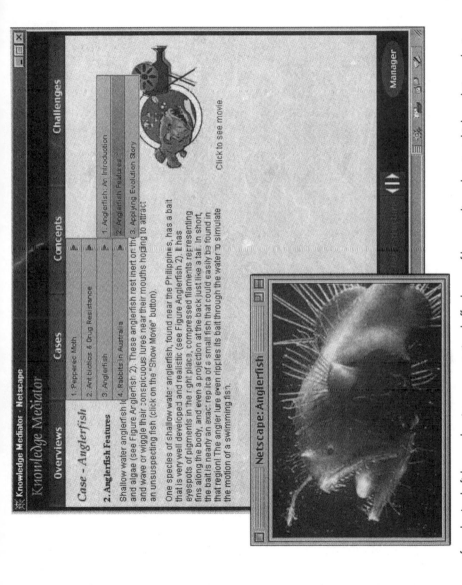

FIG. 5.1 A screen from the Anglerfish case showing representational affordances of hypermedia such as text, high-resolution color image, and access to a digital video clip.

represented in multiple contexts of application. This design element in turn forms the basis for constructive learning activities described in the following paragraphs.

In research on learning with hypermedia by our group, the *Represent Knowledge-in-context* design element has been instantiated primarily through the use of *case–and problem-based materials* (although in principle, simulations and computational models may also be used). The use of hypermedia cases and problems provides students with the opportunity to engage in contextualized activities that are cognitively manageable in order to address an unfortunate tendency in education to give students learning and problem solving activities that are abstract, or oversimplified, or both (Bransford, Franks, Vye, & Sherwood, 1989; Cognition and Technology Group at Vanderbilt, 1997; Spiro, Vispoel, Schmitz, Samarapungavan, & Boerger, 1987). In terms of developing hypermedia learning tools, this design element works in conjunction with *DE-1. Representational Affordances of Technology* so various aspects of cases and problems may be richly represented with images, figures, digital video, animations, and simulations. Figure 5.1 shows a screen from the EVOLUTION KNOWLEDGE MEDIATOR case about the Anglerfish, an unusual species–and interesting example of neo-Darwinism—that has evolved a lure from its dorsal fin now used to "fish" for other fish.

In addition to the general constructive view of learning mentioned previously, the rationale for the use of cases and problems in conjunction with this design element is based on both theory and research. A number of theorists have proposed that human memory represents experiences as cases that are indexed, searched, and used analogically when one encounters new situations and problems (Koladner, 1993; Schank, 1982; Spiro et al., 1987). By acquiring knowledge in a contextualized manner using cases and problems, students have the opportunity to understand conditions for applying knowledge related to how, why, and when (Brown et al., 1989; Cognition and Technology Group at Vanderbilt, 1997). Case-based and problem-based approaches have been used in many settings, particularly those involving professional education in the medical, business, and legal fields (Williams, 1992). However, there have been fewer systematic applications of case-based and problem-based approaches at the precollege level (Cognition and Technology Group at Vanderbilt, 1997).

Despite the potential advantages of case—and problem-based approaches, there are potential problems to be addressed. For example, research by our group suggests that students working with case-based hypermedia may be constrained by surface features of the cases, and may have difficulty learning the conceptual deep structure of knowledge related to the cases (Jacobson et al., 1996; Jacobson & Spiro, 1995). This is an issue that the following KMF elements attempt to address.

DE-3. Reify the Deep Structure of Knowledge

The third design element in the Knowledge Mediator Framework is based on research concerning expert–novice problem solving differences. This research has documented how novices often focus on surface features of a problem and fail to understand the conceptual deep structure in a manner that experts do (Chi, Glaser, & Farr, 1988). An issue in the design of technological learning tools is thus to craft ways to reify conceptual knowledge-in-context that is both accurate from an expert perspective yet accessible to less advanced learners. To this end, three KMF design subelements provide conceptual scaffolding intended to make the deep structure of knowledge explicit to the learner: *DE-3A. Abstract Domain Concepts, DE-3B. Deep Structure Indexing and Commentaries,* and *DE-3C. Conceptual Visualizations.*

DE-3A. Abstract Domain Concepts

Authoring learning materials based on the KMF requires the specification of a conceptual structure (or conceptual structures) for the knowledge in a domain (e.g., concepts, conceptual models, themes, ideas, or principles).[3] The abstract domain concepts associated with the conceptual deep structure may be determined in several ways, such as interviews with experts (i.e., knowledge engineering as used in artificial intelligence research), cognitive analysis of problem solving to ascertain

---

[3]In specifying a domain's conceptual structure, we do not claim or require that there be a single "correct" structure. Many domains may be regarded as conceptually ill-structured or ill-defined (Homa, 1984; Lakoff, 1987; Simon, 1973; Spiro et al., 1988; Voss, Greene, Post, & Penner, 1983), and thus acknowledged experts in such fields may not agree on a single conceptual structure or solution to a particular problem (e.g., economics, history, cosmological astrophysics). One advantage of hypermedia technology is that multiple conceptual structures may be represented to the learner (Jacobson & Spiro, 1995, Spiro et al., 1988; Spiro et al., 1992; Spiro & Jehng, 1990). However, because the domain of neo-Darwinian evolutionary biology is accepted in scientific circles and our pedagogical goal was to help students learn this knowledge, we have treated this as essentially a well-structured domain in the Evolution Knowledge Mediator materials described in this chapter.

expert mental representations (e.g., ethnographic analysis of experts engaged in professional practice, interviews with content experts, and content analysis of expert-written papers and books.[4] In authoring neo-Darwinian evolution cases and problems for an earlier version of the Evolution Knowledge Mediator, for example, we conducted extensive readings about the domain, referenced research papers on evolution problem-solving in refereed journals, and consulted with university biologists and high school biology teachers. As the initial learner population for this program was high school biology students who had no formal instruction in evolutionary biology, we limited the conceptual structure in these hypermedia materials to five centrally important abstract domain concepts that comprise a conceptual model of neo-Darwinism: environmental conditions, population variety, natural selection, origin of new traits, and generations and time. As shown in Fig. 5.2, the learner may link to general explanations of these abstract domain concepts from the *Concepts* top level pull-down menu option in the program.[5]

DE-3B. Deep structure indexing and commentaries

As noted earlier, novices are frequently constrained by the surface features of a problem and fail to be cognizant of the relevant conceptual deep structure (Chi et al. 1988). To address this issue, the DE-3B design subelement makes explicit how structural dimensions of knowledge (i.e., abstract domain concepts) apply in various case- or problem-specific contexts. There are two parts to this subelement. First, Knowledge Mediator case sections and problems are indexed in terms of the relevant abstract domain concepts (that is, not all abstract domain concepts necessarily apply in all case sections or problems). Second, deep structure commentaries are provided in which the abstract domain concepts are explained in terms of specific case details. In the EVOLUTION KNOWLEDGE MEDIATOR, the deep structure commentary for Population Variety in the Peppered Moth case discusses the wing coloration variations of

---

[4] Authoring may be done by a content expert such as a teacher or designer, or by students themselves as part of learner-centered activities in which they develop their own Knowledge Mediator projects (see text that follows).

[5] Note that these five abstract concepts of neo-Darwinism differ in significant ways from the naive perspectives many learners have about evolution, a critical issue further discussed in the following text.

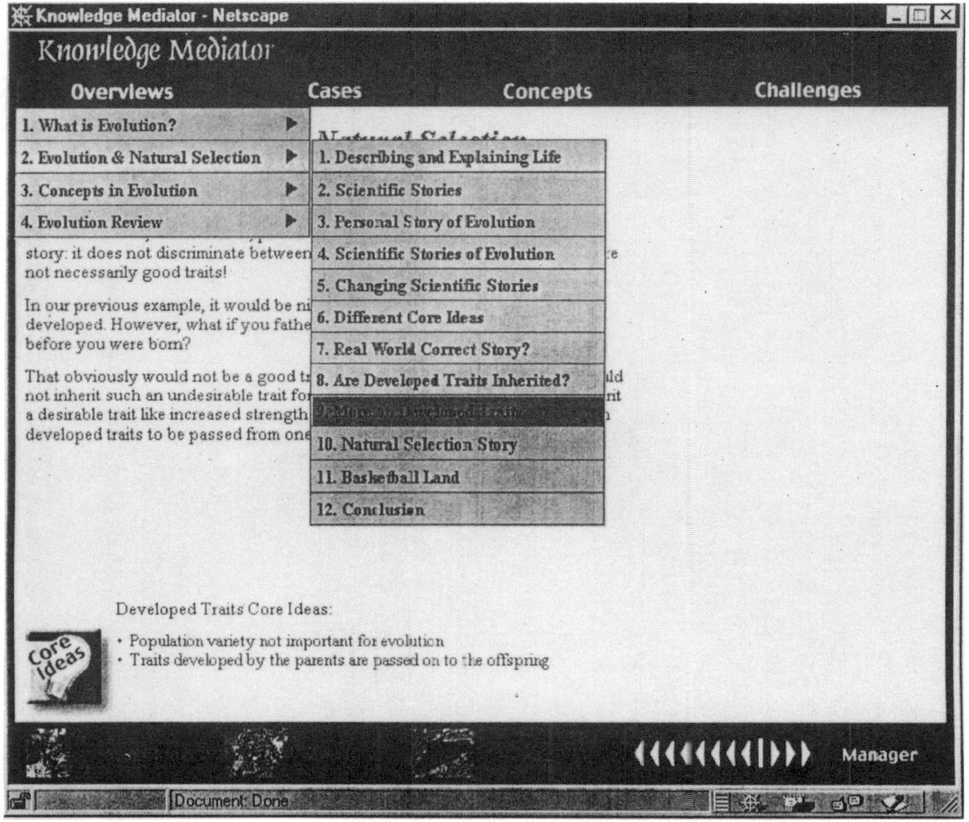

Knowledge Mediator - Netscape

Knowledge Mediator

| Overviews | Cases | Concepts | Challenges |

1. What is Evolution?
2. Evolution & Natural Selection
3. Concepts in Evolution
4. Evolution Review

Natural Selection

1. Describing and Explaining Life
2. Scientific Stories
3. Personal Story of Evolution
4. Scientific Stories of Evolution
5. Changing Scientific Stories
6. Different Core Ideas
7. Real World Correct Story?
8. Are Developed Traits Inherited?
9.
10. Natural Selection Story
11. Basketball Land
12. Conclusion

story: it does not discriminate between
not necessarily good traits!

In our previous example, it would be no
developed. However, what if you fathe
before you were born?

That obviously would not be a good ta
not inherit such an undesirable trait for
a desirable trait like increased strength
developed traits to be passed from one

Developed Traits Core Ideas:

· Population variety not important for evolution
· Traits developed by the parents are passed on to the offspring

Manager

Document: Done

FIG. 5.2 Abstract domain concepts for the Evolution Knowledge Mediator and the Population Variety general concept description.

these moths, whereas in the case of Antibiotics and Drug Resistance, the Population Variety deep structure commentary discuss the variation in bacterial resistance to antibiotics (see Fig. 5.3).

DE-3C. Conceptual Visualizations

At a technical level, the previous two design subelements employ aspects of hypermedia technologies that provide nonlinear links to nodes of text. It is also possible to provide visual representations of the conceptual deep structure of a domain in addition to textual and linguistic representations. For example, some researchers have used concept maps (i.e., diagrams that represent concepts in boxes and connections to related concepts with lines or arrows) to represent conceptual structures or to assess student understanding (Jonassen, Reeves, Hong, Harvey, & Peters, 1997). Our research has investigated another approach to reify the deep structure of knowledge through what we call *conceptual visualizations*. The intent of conceptual visualizations is to create dynamic qualitative representations or visualizations of the mental models held by experts and novice learners in a particular domain and context (Vosniadou, 1996). Conceptual visualizations may be regarded as runnable concept maps that convey facets of knowledge related to complex and dynamic phenomena such as evolution in a way that a static two dimensional representation cannot directly convey. Conceptual visualizations are also designed to be interactive, and thus serve to support *LA-1.Cognitive Interactivity*.

In the EVOLUTION KNOWLEDGE MEDIATOR, four evolution conceptual visualizations of an expert model and one of a naive model were developed. Screens from an expert neo-Darwinian conceptual visualization are shown in Fig. 5.4, whereas screens from a conceptual visualization of a naive model of evolution (based on research by Bishop & Anderson [1990]) are shown in Fig. 5.5. The learner would select an environmental condition in the conceptual visualization and would then engage in a series of screens showing evolutionary changes (i.e., change in the proportion of traits in a species) that progressed through three generations.

From a cognitive learning perspective, conceptual visualizations are provided to help students develop an understanding of the concepts and models in a domain through dynamic visual representations that complement the textual and linguistic representations in the abstract domain concepts and deep structure commentaries. Conceptual visualizations

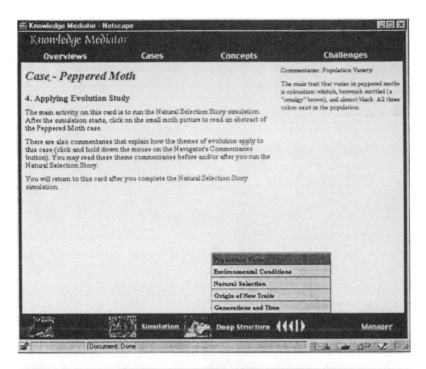

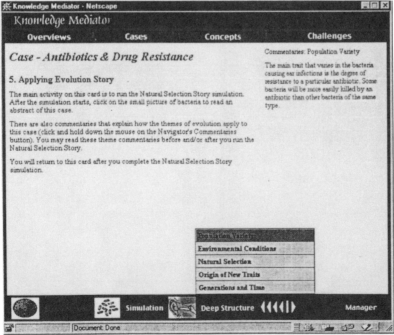

FIG. 5.3 Two contrasting deep structure commentaries, one for the Peppered Moth case and the other for the Antibiotics and Drug Resistance case.

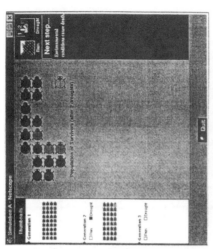
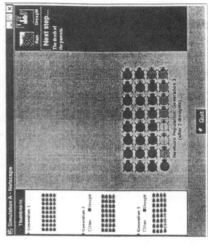
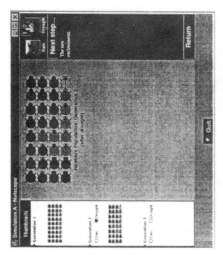
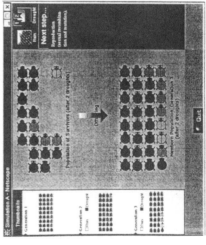

FIG. 5.4 Four screens from a conceptual visualization of an expert neo-Darwinian model of evolution from the Evolution Knowledge Mediator Overviews section.

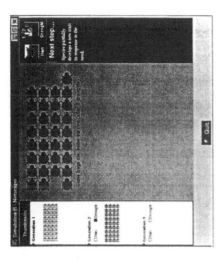

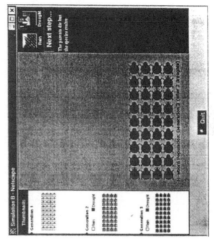

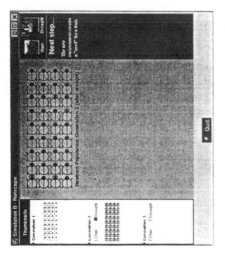

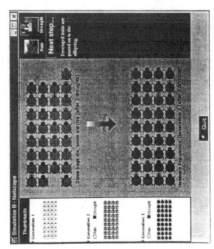

FIG. 5.5 Four screens from a conceptual visualization of a naive Lamarckian model of evolution from the Evolution Knowledge Mediator Overviews section.

may also help learning by assisting students in developing a metaconceptual awareness (Vosniadou, 1996). That is, representations of this type may increase learner awareness of the explanatory models they construct and concepts they use when dealing with problems, and how those might differ from expert perspectives.[6] It has therefore been hypothesized that increasing the learner's metaconceptual awareness may help promote conceptual change and foster representational growth (Vosniadou, 1996).

DE-4. Intra- and Intercase Hyperlinks for Conceptual and Representational Interconnectedness

The fourth KMF design element uses hyperlinks to interconnect knowledge along what might be called *intracase* and *intercase* dimensions. Both the DE-3B. Deep Structure Indexing and Commentaries and the *DE-3C. Conceptual Visualizations* design subelements provide *intracase hyperlinks* that connect surface features of a case or problem with the conceptual deep structure represented by the abstract domain concepts or the conceptual visualizations. In contrast, *intercase hyperlinks* connect different cases and problems, each with their own distinctive surface features, along structural dimensions of knowledge associated with a particular domain. In the EVOLUTION KNOWLEDGE MEDIATOR, the abstract domain concepts associated with the neo-Darwinian model are used to index cases which, in turn, forms the basis for the *LA-5. Guided Conceptual Criss-Crossing* learning activity described in the following sections.

The KMF intra- and intercase hyperlinks design subelement also has its basis in cognitive research. As is noted previously, novices are often constrained by the surface features of a problem (Chi et al., 1988). A related finding in the expert–novice literature is that novices frequently see similarities across different problems and case situations based primarily on surface features and thus may fail to notice that the deep structure of a domain provides the basis for conceptual interconnectedness across problems and cases. By providing inter- and intracase hyperlinks, this design subelement provides conceptual scaffolding for learners that may be used during initial and intermediate learning

---

[6]As can be seen in Fig. 5.4 and 5.5, the conceptual visualizations of experts and novices are quite different.

activities intended to help students construct their own understandings that are qualitatively similar to those of experts.

KMF LEARNING ACTIVITIES

Our research has also worked to identify a set of *learning activities* (LA) that utilized the particular representational affordances and conceptual scaffolding of the KMF design elements described above. The goals of these learning activities are to foster substantive learning outcomes such as deep conceptual understanding, conceptual change, and knowledge transfer. As listed in Table 5.1, six general types of KMF learning activities have been articulated to date. The nature and rationale of these learning activities are described in turn.

LA-1. Cognitive Interactivity

The importance of mindful and active engagement for cognitive processing and learning has been well documented (Bruer, 1993; Craik & Lockhart, 1972; Saolmon & Globerson, 1987). Unfortunately, as research into learning with hypermedia suggests (and as the popular expression "surf the web" implies), the very ease of traversing hypermedia environments may lead students to a mechanical or "non-mindful" exposure to knowledge resources that have minimal learning outcomes (e.g., Neuman, Marchionini, & Morrell, 1995; Tergan, 1997). To help address this concern, the KMF prescribes hypermedia learning activities intended to promote cognitive interactivity[7] and meaningful engagement with the various design elements described previously. The *LA-1. Cognitive Interactivity* learning activity is actually a general feature of most of the subsequent KMF activities, such as *LA-2. Variably Scaffolded Problem Solving* and *LA-5. Conceptual Criss-Crossing*.

LA-2. Scaffolded Problem Solving

Certainly one of the most powerful learning activities to emerge from recent sociocognitive research is the involvement of students in actively

---

[7]Our notion of *cognitive interactivity* has specific elements of depth of cognitive processing and learning engagement which differ from many "interactive" learning systems that often only require learner selection of multiple-choice items dealing with factual recall items.

solving challenging problems (e.g., Bruer, 1993; Cognition and Technology Group at Vanderbilt, 1997). However, with the exception of student-authored hypermedia projects (Barker et al., 1994; Lehrer, 1993), there have been few models of active learning and problem solving that involve stand-alone or network-mediated hypermedia.

One aspect of our research involves a model of scaffolded problem solving with a module we call *Story Maker*. In the Story Maker, the learner constructs an online explanation (i.e., story) for a problem from a series of statements on the screen (see Fig. 5.6). The learner may select from a list of statements that have been written to be consistent with naive or with expert perspectives about the problem being posed, including some neutral statements (coded "+1," "-1," and "0," respectively). A premise of this approach is that the learner will tend to select statements that are consistent with the mental representation she or he generates to solve the problem. Figure 5.6 shows a Story Maker screen in which the student was given the problem: "How did giraffes get their long necks?" She or he could then select from a pool of randomly arranged statements consistent with naive or with expert evolution models on the left side of the screen. The selected statements are then moved to the right side of the screen, where they may be rearranged in order or may be even "unselected" by being moved back to the left side of the screen. When the student is satisfied with the selected statements, the "Finished" button is selected and the program evaluates the statements on the right side of the screen. The program totals up the numeric values associated with each statement and provides feedback based on the overall score. In the EVOLUTION KNOWLEDGE MEDIATOR, Story Maker modules were developed for use in Overviews (i.e., *LA-3. Cognitive Preparation*) and in two of the cases.

The Story Maker module is a small-scale learning activity that may be selectively used by a hypermedia author to provide the learner with problem-based cognitive interactivity. This approach may be regarded as a type of "nonintelligent AI" (Nathan & Resnick, 1994) in that the Story Maker is based on research into cognitive modeling of the domain and the learner but is not implemented in a way that the system itself attempts to intelligently model the learner, domain, or pedagogy. The advantage of this approach is the relative simplicity of implementation compared to full-scale intelligent tutoring systems, whereas the disadvantage is the more focused and constrained types of problems for which Story Maker may be applied. But even with this caveat, the integration

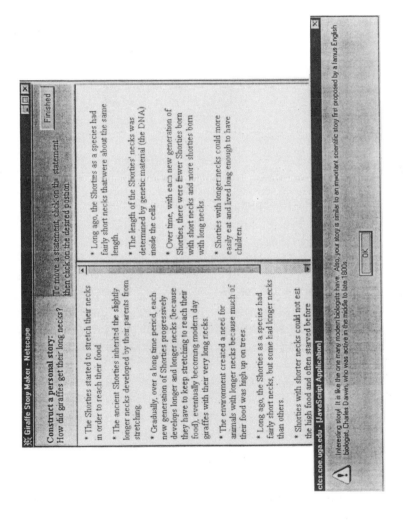

FIG. 5.6 A sample Story Maker screen with feedback on the giraffe neck evolution problem.

133

of Story Maker modules into a hypermedia learning tool provides a significant increase in cognitive interactivity beyond that of most hypermedia systems described in the literature.

LA-3. Cognitive Preparation

Cognitive and learning science research has consistently documented how novice learners typically hold a range of mental representations (e.g., beliefs, mental models, explanatory frameworks) about various phenomena that are frequently at variance with currently accepted scientific understandings (Chi, Slotta, & de Leeuw, 1994; Posner, Strike, Hewson, & Gertzog, 1982; Ram, Nersessian, & Keil, 1997; Strike & Posner, 1990; Vosniadou & Brewer, 1992; 1994; White, 1993; Wiser & Carey, 1983). Furthermore, when learners encounter information that differs from or challenges what they currently know (i.e., anomalous data), they employ a variety of assimilative strategies to respond to the anomalous data (e.g., ignore, reject, exclude; Chinn & Brewer, 1993). The reorganization of existing knowledge structures or conceptual change is a difficult process for learners.

These difficulties in fostering conceptual change have serious implications for predominately open-ended technological environments such as hypermedia in which students may be expected to learn expert perspectives that may be qualitatively different from their naive or intuitive understandings. Consistent with this view, pilot testing of an earlier version of the EVOLUTION KNOWLEDGE MEDIATOR found that students assimilated information about evolution presented in hypermedia cases of biology and did not demonstrate accommodation or conceptual change.

Given the need in many instructional domains to help students reorganize their naive models, the *LA-3. Cognitive Preparation* learning activity has been implemented with three main techniques: *thought experiments* (Horwitz, Taylor, & Hickman, 1994), *show gaps in student solutions* (Posner et al., 1982; Strike & Posner, 1990), and *"seed" new concepts and models.*[8] In the Evolution Knowledge Mediator, cognitive preparation activities and materials are accessed from the Overviews section pull-down menu (Fig. 5.7), and include expository text about

---

[8]We do not propose that these are the best or only conceptual change techniques. The *LA-3. Cognitive Preparation* learning activity may also include other approaches, such as dealing with underlying beliefs and entrenched presuppositions (Vosniadou, 1996), or with the ontological structure of knowledge (Chi et al., 1994; Ferrari & Chi, in press).

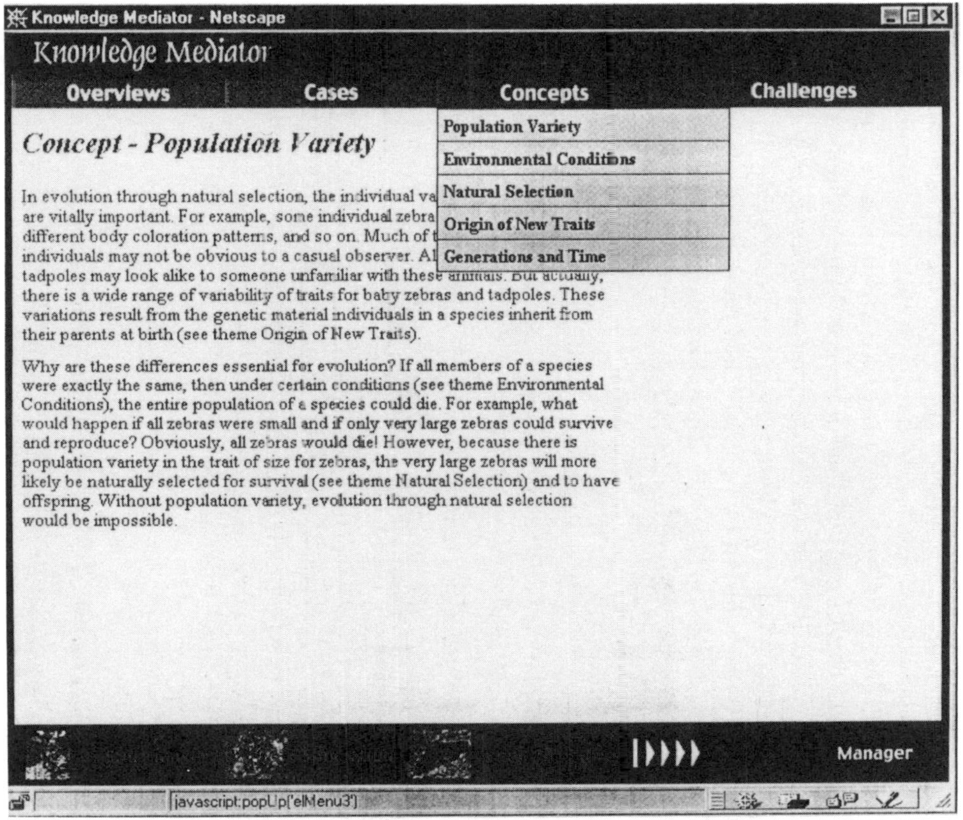

Knowledge Mediator - Netscape

Knowledge Mediator

| Overviews | Cases | Concepts | Challenges |

Concept - Population Variety

Population Variety
Environmental Conditions
Natural Selection
Origin of New Traits
Generations and Time

In evolution through natural selection, the individual va[riation] are vitally important. For example, some individual zebra different body coloration patterns, and so on. Much of individuals may not be obvious to a casual observer. Al tadpoles may look alike to someone unfamiliar with these animals But actually, there is a wide range of variability of traits for baby zebras and tadpoles. These variations result from the genetic material individuals in a species inherit from their parents at birth (see theme Origin of New Traits).

Why are these differences essential for evolution? If all members of a species were exactly the same, then under certain conditions (see theme Environmental Conditions), the entire population of a species could die. For example, what would happen if all zebras were small and if only very large zebras could survive and reproduce? Obviously, all zebras would die! However, because there is population variety in the trait of size for zebras, the very large zebras will more likely be naturally selected for survival (see theme Natural Selection) and to have offspring. Without population variety, evolution through natural selection would be impossible.

| ◄ ► ► ►

Manager

javascript:popUp('elMenu3')

FIG. 5.7 Sample screen and pull-down menus to access subsections of the cognitive preparation Overviews module of the Evolution Knowledge Mediator.

135

evolution, a brief history of science about the change from Lamarckian-ism to neo-Darwinism, conceptual visualizations (Figs. 5.4 and 5.5), and a Story Maker module (Fig. 5.6). In the Overviews section, the following thought experiment is posed to the learner: "What if your father had lost his right arm in an accident before you were born? Would that mean you would be born with no arm?" This thought experiment is intended to challenge a common naive belief that a trait acquired during the lifetime of an organism is passed on to its offspring (e.g., ancient giraffes stretched their necks, which led to the "evolution" of long necks). For some students, this thought experiment (which was adapted from Dawkins, 1986), shows gaps in their understanding that helps challenge the seductive plausibility of the Lamarckian perspective. Other sections of Overviews "seed" the main abstract domain concepts of the neo-Dar-winian theory of evolution by natural selection (e.g., the "Core Ideas" button at the bottom of Fig. 5.7), which are then elaborated on in the Concepts section and in the four Evolution Knowledge Mediator hyper-media cases.

LA-4. Preliminary Learning Tasks with Deep Structure Knowledge Resources

Two of the KMF design elements—*DE-1. Represent Knowledge-In-Context* and *DE-3. Reify the Deep Structure of Knowledge*—may be implemented as hypermedia represented cases and problems. During a student's prelimi-nary use of these resources, she or he typically will go through Overviews and the case texts, figures, Story Maker modules, digital video clips, and deep structure commentaries in a fairly linear manner. In this way, the learner gains an initial familiarity with the information represented in these resources that then serves as the foundation for other KMF learning activities.

LA-5. Guided Conceptual Criss-Crossing

There has been considerable concern about the difficulty students have with transferring knowledge acquired in instructional settings to new problems and new contexts of application, a difficulty sometimes re-ferred to as the "inert knowledge" problem (Bereiter & Scardamalia, 1985; Bransford, 1989; Cognition and Technology Group at Vanderbilt, 1997; perkins, 1992; Renkl, Mandel, & Gruber, 1996; Whitehead, 1929).

As suggested by the "periodic table" metaphor, inert knowledge does not combine or interact with other knowledge the student possesses. Thus students might accurately reproduce knowledge learned under one set of conditions (i.e., those matching the instructional or encoding context), but would be unable to apply or transfer this knowledge to new knowledge application or problem situations.

TLA-6he KMF learning activity *LA-5. Guided Conceptual Criss-Crossing*[9] has been found to promote knowledge transfer (Jacobson et al., 1996; Jacobson & Spiro, 1995). Guided Conceptual Criss-Crossing uses the intracase hyperlinks of *DE-4* (see the previous section regarding *DE-4*) to provide a scaffolded learning activity that makes explicit aspects of conceptual interconnectedness across the hypermedia library of cases and problems. To provide a learning context for Guided Conceptual Criss-Crossing, sets of hyperlinks are authored for specific "Challenge questions" (a phrase adapted from the Jasper Project) that ask students to consider various issues and problems (see Fig. 5.8). Students will typically work on challenge questions after having completed the *LA 1. Preliminary Learning Tasks.* There are multiple solutions to the challenge questions that require integrating or synthesizing information located in various Evolution Knowledge Mediator resources such as the Overviews, cases, abstract concepts, and deep structure commentaries. For example, challenge question three asks, "Do biological organisms evolve new traits because they "need" them to survive?" As shown in Fig. 5.8, three abstract domain concepts are listed as being relevant to the questions (Origin of New Traits, Population Variety, and Natural Selection). Also, in reference to this challenge question, there are seven hyperlinks to various nodes in the EVOLUTION KNOWLEDGE MEDIATOR case library that include portions of the Overviews section, different cases, and the general description of the abstract domain concept Origin of New Traits. In addition to their function as a learning activity, the challenge questions may also be used to evaluate learning. Students may be given a set of challenge questions to study with Guided Conceptual Criss-Crossing and would then be asked to write short essays on (or verbally answer) selected questions.

---

[9]In earlier papers (Jacobson & Archodidou, 1997; Jacobson et al., 1996; Jacobson & Spiro, 1995), this learning activity was referred to as "thematic criss-crossing." The phrase "conceptual criss-crossing" is preferred here as the term "concepts" is more commonly used with respect to science learning than "themes."

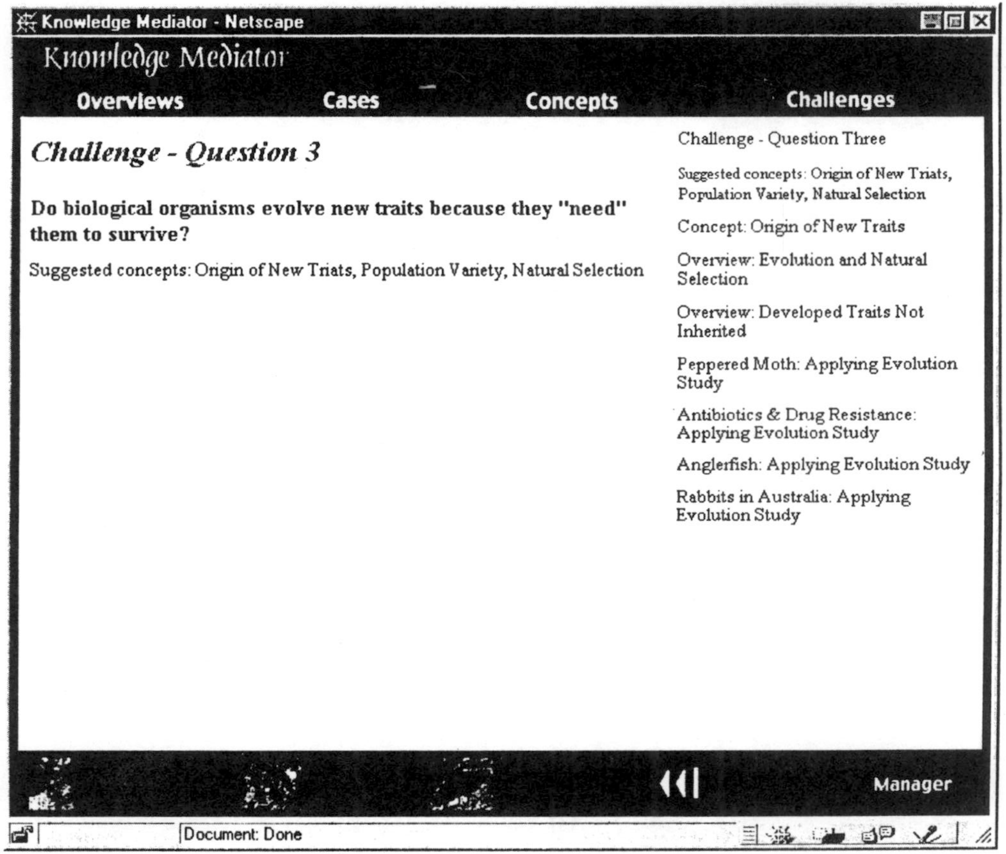

138

FIG. 5.8 Challenge Question Three from the EVOLUTION KNOWLEDGE MEDIATOR and the associated hyperlinks to case library sections based on conceptual deep structure criss-crossing.

LA-6. Advanced Learner-Centered and Project-based Learning

The previous five types of learning activities use the KMF design elements to provide the learner with cognitive and learning scaffolding that is typically lacking in hypermedia implemented on stand-alone computers or on the web.[10] Each of the previous five learning activities and related design elements has been investigated in different research projects by our group. Here we briefly mention that we are planning to explore the use of KMF tools as part of learner-centered projects and inquiries, but we defer that discussion until the "Knowledge Mediator Framework: General Issues and Future Research Directions" section.

HYPERMEDIA AND LEARNING NEO-DARWINIAN EVOLUTIONARY BIOLOGY

This section discusses research into the efficacy of the KMF approach for structuring a hypermedia tool to help high school students learn the neo-Darwinian theory evolution by natural selection.[11] The challenges of learning neo-Darwinian evolutionary biology were intended to provide a test of the strengths and limitations of this approach for designing and using a hypermedia learning tool. Also, the opportunity arose to conduct a follow-up study a year after the original study, and thus to investigate long term retention of learning. After briefly considering the nature of difficulties students have with learning evolutionary biology, the methodologies and findings of these two studies are discussed.

Learning Evolutionary Biology

The neo-Darwinian theory of evolution by natural selection is a domain of central importance to modern biology (Dawkins, 1986; Dobzhansky, 1973; Kauffman, 1993; 1995; Mayr, 1991; National Research Council,

---

[10]See Slotta and Linn (this volume) for other approaches to scaffolding learning on the Internet.

[11]The hypermedia program used in this study was originally referred to as the EVOLUTION THEMATIC INVESTIGATOR (Jacobson et al., 1996). This stand-alone experimental hypermedia system was developed on the Macintosh in HyperCard, and included the main design elements of the KMF. In this chapter, however, we refer to the older program as an "earlier version of the Knowledge Mediator" to clarify the relation between the new KMF and the features of the older program used in the study.

1996; and increasingly in other fields as well (Anderson, Arrow, & Pines, 1988; Cziko, 1995; Epstein & Axtell, 1996; Gell-Mann, 1994; Holland, 1995; Mitchell, 1996; Pagels, 1988). Unfortunately, evolution has been found to be a difficult domain for a wide range of students to learn, even those who are academically gifted (Bishop & Anderson, 1990; Bizzo, 1994; Brumby, 1984; Chan, Burtis, & Bereiter, 1997; Demastes, Good, & Peebles, 1996; Demastes, Settlage, & Good, 1995; Grene, 1990; Mintzes & Arnaudin, 1984; Settlage, 1994; Tamir, 1992).

Research has identified distinct differences between naive and expert representations about evolution (Bishop & Anderson, 1990; Brumby, 1984; Ferrari & Chi, in press; Greene, 1990; Samarapungayan & Wiers, 1997; Settlage, 1994). Students with naive beliefs about evolution tend to view evolution as a single process or event in which characteristic traits of species gradually change (e.g., necks gradually lengthen) and tend to believe the environment, use and disuse, or the species "trying to evolve" causes these traits to change (rather than random processes and natural selection). The naive view is often implicitly Lamarckian, as many learners also believe that traits acquired by an organism during its lifetime can be passed on to the offspring. Furthermore, students with a naive view of evolution do not see population variability as important in evolution and they frequently hold a teleological bias that ascribes purpose to evolutionary developments (e.g., ancient giraffes needed long necks to reach food, so they evolved longer necks). In contrast, the modern neo-Darwinian view of evolution has the following core components: Evolution is defined as the changing proportion of individuals in a population with discrete traits; the origin and survival of new traits in populations results from random changes in genetic material due to mutation or sexual recombination; the survival or disappearance of traits is due to selection associated with environmental factors (i.e., natural selection); and variation within a population is critical for evolution through natural selection. Overall, populations evolve because some individual members possess a reproductive advantage over other individual members in a particular environment.

The naive Lamarckian and expert neo-Darwinian models of evolution thus differ along a number of important conceptual dimensions. The simplicity of the naive Lamarckian model, and the surface level plausibility of the model (e.g., passing on acquired traits seems reasonable), evidently makes this a difficult model to change in conventional instructional and even in most research settings (Bishop & Anderson, 1990;

Brumby, 1984; Cumins, Demastes, & Hafner, 1994; Grene, 1990; Settlage, 1994).

Research indicates that the process of conceptual change frequently does not progress directly from a naive model to an expert model. Vosnaiadou and Brewer (1992, 1994) reported a series of cross-sectional studies that document a range of mental models about the shape of the earth and the day–night cycle generated by students in problem-solving contexts. Many elementary-age children were found to use a "flat earth" model to solve problems instead of the scientifically accepted model of a spherical earth that rotates on an axis and goes in an orbit around the sun. Other students provided explanations with synthetic models, such as models that had component ideas from the naive "flat earth" model and from the scientific model. For example, a "two earths" model was identified in which the students described a flat earth that they lived on and a round or spherical earth "up in the sky." Such a model might seem strange and is certainly not a model the students were explicitly taught. Vosniadou and Brewer proposed that synthetic models such as this are constructed by the student in an attempt to integrate information they are exposed to in school or in the culture (e.g., the earth is "round" or "spherical") with their existing mental model (e.g., the earth is "flat").

Based on the Vosniadou and Brewer research in the domain of astronomy, we hypothesized that in addition to naive models similar to those described in the literature at the time that Study One was conducted in 1993 (e.g. Bishop & Anderson, 1990), students would also construct synthetic models to solve evolutionary biology problems over the three sessions of the study. We further hypothesized that these synthetic models would have idea components from naive and expert models of evolution. The methodology and model coding framework we employed to investigate these hypotheses is described next.

Study One: Learning with Hypermedia, Problem Solving, and Mental Models of Evolution

Method

The high school students in this study were ages 14 to 16, 4 boys and 4 girls. Of the 8 students, 6 were audiotaped and 2 were videotaped. The study employed a combination of cognitive think-aloud protocols and verbal interviews of the students using the system and engaging in several learning and problem-solving activities. A pretest was administered at the beginning of Session One. The students rated on a 7-point Likert scale their personal understanding of the concept of evolution and their personal belief about whether the modern scientific view of evolution is true. These two items were asked again at the end of the third session (and in follow-up Study Two). The students then answered an evolutionary biology problem: "How did modern-day giraffes evolve long necks from ancestors with shorter necks?" As we were concerned that writing ability might constrain some students in terms of the quality of their answers, the students also solved some problems verbally as think-aloud protocols. On the pretest, verbal protocols were obtained for solving a problem dealing with the evolutionary development of the cheetah's ability to run at speeds up to 60 miles per hour.

There were several different assessment measures collected during the second and third sessions. The students used Story Maker for online scaffolded problem solving (see the previous description of Story-Maker), and log files recorded the statements they selected to solve the problems. The offline activities consisted of a series of factual acquisition questions and evolution problem-solving tasks at the end of Sessions Two and Three. Written short answer questions of factual knowledge acquisition included "Briefly explain the evolution theme of Natural Selection," or "Briefly explain the evolution theme of Environmental Conditions." To obtain a near-transfer measure, challenge question responses were written at each of the last two sessions (e.g., "Is the environment important for the evolutionary changes of the peppered moth and the antibiotic-resistant bacteria?"). Finally, the students solved far-transfer questions on evolutionary biology problems to which they had not been exposed in the evolution and hypermedia materials (e.g., "Cave salamanders are blind. Although these animals have eyes, these eyes are not functional. How did blind cave salamanders evolve from ancestors who had functioning eyes?"). The focus of the following analysis is on the representations generated by students during problem solving for the near- and far-transfer tasks.

Experimental Procedure

The study was conducted over 3 sessions lasting approximately 2 hours each, with each student working alone with an experiment monitor. After the pretest, the students began using the hypermedia program. They initially worked on the cognitive preparation lesson with the features described previously. These included

- reading general information about evolution,
- viewing two conceptual visualizations of evolution (one representing a naive model and the other the expert neo-Darwinian model),
- using the Story Maker for scaffolded problem solving to answer the cheetah evolution problem (same problem presented during pretest think-aloud),
- reading expository text dealing with a very brief history of scientific views of evolution from Lamarckism to Darwinism, and
- considering thought experiments intended to promote conceptual change (e.g., "If your father had lost his arm, would that acquired trait be passed on to you?").

During Session Two, the students completed another Story Maker problem-solving activity, read a short review of the main ideas related to a neo-Darwinian model of evolution by natural selection, went through two hypermedia cases on evolutionary biology (*Peppered Moth* and *Antibiotic Resistant Bacteria* cases), and worked on two challenge questions as part of the Guided Conceptual Criss-Crossing learning activity. The challenge questions required the students to integrate or synthesize knowledge presented in different sections of the program (e.g., "Is the environment important for the evolutionary changes of the peppered moth and the antibiotic resistant bacteria? Is it possible to explain the evolutionary changes found in the *Peppered Moth* case using the scientific story of Developed Traits? If so, how? If not, why not?"). After a short break, the students then completed the Session Two evaluation items and problem-solving tasks.

The Session Three sequence was similar to Session Two but started directly with two new evolution cases. There were two slight differences between the second and third session materials and activities. First, the second session provided the deep structure commentaries described previously that explained how each abstract theme of neo-Darwinism mapped to the specifics of the *Peppered Moth* and *Antibiotics and Drug Resistance* cases (see Table 5.1). During the third session, however, the students were instructed to verbally explain each of the neo-Darwinian themes when they read the *Anglerfish* and *Rabbits in Australia* cases to the experiment monitor. This was intended to provide a more active learning activity than reading the deep structure commentaries.

The other difference between the second and third sessions existed in the learning activities the students completed after going through the two cases. Only a single Guided Conceptual Criss-Crossing question was given during the third session. In place of a second Guided Conceptual Criss-Crossing question, the students were asked to critique two responses to one of the Guided Conceptual Criss-Crossing questions from the second session: "Is it possible to explain the evolutionary changes found in *The Peppered Moth* case using the scientific story of Developed Traits? If so, how? If not, why not?" The two critique responses had been written by high school students who participated in an earlier pilot study. One response argued that it was possible (i.e., the student employed a naive model that made assertions inconsistent with information presented in the program) whereas the other argued that is was not possible (i.e., the student employed a neo-Darwinian model). The students in this study were asked to think aloud as they went through the program to justify their critique of the responses. The Session Three test materials were then administered, after which the experiment monitor interviewed the students concerning their attitudes about using the program, ideas they felt they had trouble understanding, and so on. In addition to the written items and audio or video tapes of the students using the program and answering the think-aloud problems, computer logs were automatically collected of the students' use of the hypermedia program (e.g., time spent on each screen, recording the Story Maker responses). The Session Three test materials were then administered.

Evolution Mental Models Analytical Framework

We adapted the Vosniadou and Brewer mental model analysis methodology originally used in the domain of astronomy (Vosniadou & Brewer, 1992, 1994) to analyze the evolution problem-solving responses. An analytical framework with four evolution mental models (naive, Synthetic, Darwinian, and Neo-Darwinian) was developed for the initial analysis of the Study One data (Jacobson et al., 1996). After completing the follow-up Study Two (discussed as follows), the second author noticed that there might be evidence for multiple synthetic models of evolution (rather than a single synthetic model as the initial framework coded for). We then revised the analytical framework to include additional types of synthetic mental models and then recoded the data from both Study One and Study Two.

In the revised Evolution Mental Model Analytical Framework, four different mental model knowledge components about evolution are used as constituent parts of eight higher order types of mental models that form a continuum from novice to expert (see Table 5.2). Also, we propose that the six synthetic models (M2–M7) form two distinct classes: *C2. Synthetic Naive* that are naive models with one neo-Darwinian knowledge component (M2–M5), and *C3. Neo-Darwinian Synthetic* with two neo-Darwinian knowledge components. The other two classes of mental models are *C1. Naive* and *C4. Neo-Darwinian* (see Table 5.2). Here we briefly describe the coding rationales for the components of this framework.

Origin of New Traits.   Two main ways to characterize knowledge related to the source of new traits in a population were identified. First, the neo-Darwinian theory of evolution describes the origin of new traits as resulting from genetic mutations, with additional variability of expressed traits in certain species due to the recombination of genetic material due to meiosis. Responses consistent with modern genetics were coded as "Mutation and Genetic Recombination." Second, responses dealing with the origin of new traits that were not consistent with neo-Darwinism often described the environment as "creating a need" for a new trait, and then "causing" new traits to appear or old traits to change over time. Mechanisms the students used to explain how the environment exerted its influence included the use or disuse of certain bodily organs, physiological activities of the body, and direct influence on the genetic material of organisms. Responses of this second type were coded as "Environment 'Needs' and 'Causes' New Trait."

Inheritance.   This component was used to characterize students' knowledge related to the inheritance of different traits from one generation to the next. The neo-Darwinian theory of evolution describes inheritance in terms of genetics and thus is directly integrated with ideas concerning the origin of new traits such as mutation and genetic recombination of alleles. However, many of the students' problem-solving statements did not mention genetics. Also, many of the responses stated that traits acquired in one generation were passed to the next generation (i.e., the so-called "Lamarckian" theory of evolution). For this component, we distinguished three levels of understanding: (a) "Genetic Material," in which ideas indicated an understanding of the modern scientific view of the molecular or genetic basis of inheritance

TABLE 5.2

Evolution Mental Model Analytical Framework: Classes, Types, and Components

Classes	Types	Components			
		Origin of New Traits	Inheritance	Mechanism of Evolution	Final Causes
C1. Naive	M1. Naive	Environment "needs" and "causes" new trait	Acquired traits	Developmental "explanation"	Teleological
C2. Naive Synthetic (Naive + 1 neo-Darwinian component)	M2. Genetic naive	Environment "needs" and "causes" new trait	Genetic material	Developmental "explanation"	Teleological
	M3. Lamarckian naive	Environment "Needs" and "Causes" New Trait	Acquired traits	Natural selection	Teleological
	M4. Non-Lamarckian naive	No Specification	Acquired traits denied No genetic material	Natural selection	Teleological
	M5. Purposeful Genetic selection	Environment "needs" and "causes" new trait.	Genetic material	Natural selection	Teleological
C3. Neo-Darwinian Synthetic (Naive + 2 neo-Darwinian components)	M6. Teleological neo-Darwinian	Environment "needs" and "causes" new trait	Genetic material	Natural selection	Hidden Teleology
Synthetic (Naive + 2 neo-Darwinian components)	M7. Idealized Darwin	No Specification	Acquired Traits Denied No genetic material	Natural selection	Non-teleological
C4. Neo-Darwinian	M8. Neo-Darwinian	Mutations and genetic recombination	Genetic material	Natural selection	Non-teleological

Note: There are two additional components of evolution mental models in our framework: Environmental Conditions and Generations and Time. We expected that novices and experts would view these components in similar ways, and that was confirmed in our data analysis, and thus we do not list them in the table.

in the transmission of traits from one generation to the next; (b) "Acquired Traits," in which a response demonstrated no awareness of genetics and asserted that a trait can be passed from one generation to the next, even a trait acquired by a parent during its lifetime; and (c) "Acquired Traits Denied/No Genetic Material," in which the responses explicitly denied the inheritance of acquired traits, but no mechanism for inheritance from one generation to the next was proposed.

Mechanism of Evolution.   Two types of explanations were identified relating to the survival or disappearance of new traits in a population (i.e., the mechanism of evolution): "Natural Selection," and "Developmental Explanation." The mechanism of evolution that Charles Darwin proposed, Natural Selection, described the differential suitability of various traits to allow an organism to survive long enough to reproduce in a particular environmental niche. In contrast, many students' responses simply described the mechanism of evolution as the change in a population due to general "development" over time—what we refer to as Developmental Explanation (Sober 1984).

Final Causes.   This fourth component of evolution mental models characterized students' beliefs about evolution as a process in nature that was either predominately random (i.e., stochastic) or predominately end-determined or purposeful (i.e., teleological). We coded this component for three different levels: "Non-teleological," "Teleological," and "Hidden Teleology." A Non-teleological response, which is a central feature of neo-Darwinian theory, reflected an awareness of evolution as being fundamentally a random process (e.g., random mutations changing genetic material, random changes in the environment influencing natural selection). A Teleological response described organisms developing new traits because they "need them to survive," with the implicit assumption that new traits always improve the organism's position in the natural world (i.e., only "good traits" are passed on, such as running faster for cheetahs). Another type of Teleological response ascribed control or guidance of evolution to an external agent (e.g., the environment, a divine being) to achieve a predetermined goal or outcome, but without specifying the manner in which this "controlling" is affected. A third level is Hidden Teleology whereby a student's response initially avoided the use of teleological wording, but when the student was probed by the interviewer to explain why an organism developed a new trait, a teleological answer was given.

Scoring Procedure

The audio- and videotapes of the protocols and the students' written answers and comments were transcribed. Two trained raters independently coded each problem-solving response using a two-part scoring procedure based on the Evolution Mental Models Analytical Framework: knowledge component coding and coding of the types of mental models (M1–M8). An overall or composite mental model type for each session that was based on all of the session's responses was also assigned. The interrater reliability for coding the types of mental models was .91, and the few discrepancies were resolved by discussion. Finally, the composite types of mental models were then used to assign classes of evolution mental models based on the Evolution Mental Models Analytical Framework. For example, for Session One, a student might be analyzed as having a composite mental model type of *M1. Naive* and then would be assigned a mental model class of *C1. Naive*. At the end of Session Three, this same student might be found to have a mental model type *M3. Lamarckian Naive,* and would then be assigned a composite mental model class of *C2. Synthetic Naive*. The composite mental model classes assigned for each student are shown in Table 5.3.

Results

On the 7-point Likert scale items of the students' evaluation of their personal understanding of evolution, the pretest mean score was 4.0 (*SD* = 1.20) and the posttest mean score was 5.6 (*SD* = 0.52). This difference was significant (t_7 = 3.87, p < .05). (All reported results are two-tail *t*-tests.) This result suggests the students had a metacognitive awareness that their understanding of evolution improved after working with the evolution and hypermedia program (which our data suggests was the case; see the following description). In contrast, the mean score of the students' self-report on whether they believed the current scientific view of evolution was 4.9 (*SD* = 1.46) at the pretest and 6.0 (*SD* = 0.76) at the posttest. This was not a statistically significant difference (t_7 = 1.84, p < .05). This finding suggests that although the students assessed their personal beliefs about the validity of the current scientific view of

TABLE 5.3

Composite Classes of Evolution Mental Models for Study One and Study Two

| Participants | Study One | | | Study Two |
	Session 1	Session 2	Session 3	
357	C1. Naive	C4. Neo-Darwinian	C4. Neo-Darwinian	C4. Neo-Darwinian
425	C1. Naive	C3. Synthetic neo-Darwinian	C2. Synthetic Naive	Did not participate
454	C1. Naive	C3. Synthetic neo-Darwinian	C2. Synthetic Naive	C3. Synthetic neo-Darwinian
824	C3. Synthetic Neo-Darwinian	C4. Neo-Darwinian	C3. Synthetic neo-Darwinian	C3. Synthetic neo-Darwinian
847	C1. Naive	C4. Neo-Darwinian	C4. Neo-Darwinian	Did not participate
870 (Judy)	C1. Naive	C4. Neo-Darwinian	C4. Neo-Darwinian	C4. Neo-Darwinian
985	C3. Synthetic neo-Darwinian	C4. Neo-Darwinian	C4. Neo-Darwinian	C4. Neo-Darwinian
986	C1. Naive	C3. Synthetic neo-Darwinian	C2. Synthetic naive	C3. Synthetic neo-Darwinian
2001	–	–	–	C2. Synthetic naive
2002	–	–	–	C2. Synthetic naive
2003	–	–	–	C2. Synthetic naive
2004	–	–	–	C2. Synthetic naive
2005	–	–	–	C2. Synthetic naive
2006	–	–	–	C2. Synthetic naive
2007	–	–	–	C2. Synthetic naive

evolution as being higher by the end of the study, this was not a significant change from pretest to posttest.

In terms of the composite classes of evolution mental models (based on the students' answers to multiple evolution problem-solving tasks completed at each of the three sessions), six out of eight students initially held a *C1. Naive* model (see Table 5.3). By the Session Three posttest, five of the students demonstrated a *C4. Neo-Darwinian* model and three exhibited a *C2. Synthetic Naive* model when solving the various problem-solving tasks, with no students using the *C1. Naive model*. To statistically analyze this data, the evolution class models were coded as follows: *C1. Naive* = 1, *C2. Synthetic Naive* = 2, *C3. Neo-Darwinian Synthetic* = 3, and *C4. Neo-Darwinian* = 4. The mean evolution class model scores were as follows: Session One pretest, $M = 1.50$ ($SD = 0.93$); Session Two, $M = 3.50$ ($SD = 0.54$); and Session Three $M = 3.25$ ($SD = 1.04$). There was a significant difference between the Session One and Session Two evolution class model scores ($t_7 = 5.29$, $p < .05$), but no significant difference between Sessions Two and Three ($t_7 = 1.00$, $p < .05$). These results indicate that the students' models of evolution significantly changed from the Session One pretest to Session Two with the majority of the students acquiring a neo-Darwinian model, and that this more expert evolutionary biology problem-solving profile was maintained through the end of Session Three.

Study Two: Follow-Up Evolution Problem Solving Study

Method

The original Study One was planned as a within-subjects design with a 3 session intervention spread over a 7- to 10-day period. One year later, the opportunity arose to work with most of the original students (6 out of 8) and also to collect evolution problem-solving data from a control group of students who had taken the same biology class but had not used the evolution hypermedia program. As in the initial study, the students in the follow-up evolution problem-solving study were in high school, ages 14 to 16, 7 boys and 6 girls. All 13 students had taken a biology with the same biology teacher (an excellent teacher who had consulted with us during the development of the Thematic Investigator). The six students who participated in Study One were assigned to the experimental condition, while the remaining seven students had taken only the biology class and were assigned to the control condition. The one hour long study sessions were audio taped and each student worked alone with an experiment monitor.

Test Materials

Several of the items on the follow-up test instrument were adapted from the Study One. As before, students rated on a seven point Likert scale their personal understanding of the concept of evolution and their personal belief about whether the modern scientific view of evolution is true. Five evolutionary biology problems were then presented to the students, three as think-alouds and two as short written essays. For the initial group of students, two of the evolution problems had been used in the earlier hypermedia study and three were new problems, whereas all five of the evolution problems had not been previously presented to the control students.

Scoring Procedures

The five evolution problem responses were analyzed using the same methodology employed in Study One. The same two raters independently scored the five problem solving responses. They assigned a mental model type (i.e., M1 - M8) to each response and an overall composite session mental model type based on all of the five responses (see Table 3). As in Study One, the mental model types were then also coded in terms of the four classes of mental models (i.e., *C1. Naive, C2. Synthetic Naive, C3. Synthetic Neo-Darwinian,* and *C4. Neo-Darwinian*).

Results

Understandings, Beliefs, and Composite Group Models.
For the six evolution and hypermedia students who were available for the 1-year follow-up study, their scores on the various dependent measures at the end of the initial study and at the follow-up study were virtually the same. The means and standard deviations at the end of the initial study were as follows: understanding evolution, $M = 5.5$, $SD = 0.55$; belief in evolution, $M = 6.17$, $SD = 0.75$; and overall evolution model class, $M = 3.33$, $SD = 1.03$. At the follow-up study, the means and standard deviation scores were as follows: understanding evolution, $M = 5.43$, $SD = 0.98$; belief in evolution, $M = 5.57$, $SD = 0.79$; and overall evolution model, $M = 3.67$ $SD = 0.52$. None of these were significant differences (understanding evolution: $t_5 = 0.35$, $p < .05$; believe in evolution: $t_5 = 1.17$, $p < .05$; overall evolution model class: $t_5 = 0.79$, $p < .05$).

There were no significant differences between the experimental and control groups on their self-reports about understanding evolution (t_{12} = 0.59, p < .05, overall M = 5.15, SD = 0.99) and about believing evolution (t_{12} = 0.19, p < .05, overall M = 5.62, SD = 0.87). A significant difference was found, however, between the two groups on the overall model score assigned to the students based on their answers to the five evolutionary biology questions (t_{12} = 7.91, p < .05, experimental M = 3.67, SD = 0.52, control M = 2.00, SD = 0.00). That is, the students used the evolution hypermedia program in Study One employed models that were significantly closer to the neo-Darwinian model when solving the evolutionary biology problems than those employed by the control students.

Verbal Protocol Analysis: Judy's Evolution Problem Solving Responses.   In this section, we provide a more detailed look at selected evolution problem-solving responses by one of the students who participated in both studies. Judy participated in the follow-up study the year after she worked with the evolution hypermedia program. In the intervening time, she had finished the sophomore biology class the previous spring but indicated that she had not read any books or seen any television, videos, or movies outside of class that dealt with evolution or evolutionary topics. Judy continued to believe that the modern scientific view of evolution was true (down slightly from "7" to "6"), and she slightly downrated her understanding of evolution to from "5" to "4." Despite her somewhat critical self-evaluation of her evolutionary biology knowledge, on the five evolution problems in the follow-up test, Judy consistently used a neo-Darwinian model. Here, for example, is her think-aloud solution to the Cheetah evolution problem:

> I think the ancestors of the cheetahs developed more speed because the environment around them changed, and the cheetahs that could not keep up with the environment couldn't survive—they just died out so their genes didn't pass on to their offspring. Cheetahs that could catch up with their environment did survive and they could pass their genes to their offspring. That's why they became faster and survived.

As in her response at the end of the first study, Judy solved this problem with a neo-Darwinian model. The knowledge components of natural selection, population variety, and generations are all found in this response. However, the origin of the new trait of increased running speed due to a mutation, which was so clearly expressed the previous year, is not found in Judy's follow-up study solution to the problem. Yet despite this small omission, Judy's response to this problem is neo-Darwinian and is strikingly different than the solutions to the evolutionary biology problems by the control group of students.

Discussion

As noted previously, the overall literature on evolutionary biology education is replete with reports of the limited learning efficacy of various instructional approaches (Bishop & Anderson, 1990; Bizzo, 1994; Brumby, 1984; Greene, 1990; Settlage, 1994), although recently there have been some positive research findings concerning students' learning of evolution (Demastes et al., 1995; Ferrari & Chi, in press). Also, in terms of learning with hypermedia, rigorous research to date in this regard has been impressionistic (Jacobson, 1994; Tergan, 1997). Thus, it was encouraging that significant learning outcomes were achieved in this study, particularly given the relatively short duration of the intervention (approximately 6 hours over 3 sessions). By the end of the second session, the students in Study One solved the evolutionary biology problems with predominately synthetic Darwinian and neo-Darwinian models, which suggests that these students had acquired a reasonably deep understanding of this difficult scientific concept.

Why did the students who used this specially designed evolution and hypermedia program change their initial mental models of evolution, with the majority of the students successfully acquiring a Neo-Darwinian model? We believe there are two main reasons: *cognitive preparation* and *knowledge interconnection learning activities*. First, we had hoped that the *LA-3. Cognitive Preparation* hypermedia learning activity would elicit in the learner an awareness of the limitations of his or her current understanding of evolution and would seed ideas about the neo-Darwinian view of evolution. Given the major model shift that occurred by the end of Session Two, it may have been that students' engagement with the cognitive preparation activity in Session One in conjunction with the Session Two hypermedia cases and learning activities contributed to the observed change in models that the students used to solve the evolution problems.

Second, the combination of the four KMF design elements and the learning activities associated with *LA-4. Deep Structure Knowledge Resources* and *LA-5. Guided Conceptual Criss-Crossing* may have contributed to a process of *conceptual abstraction* from the multiple contexts of knowledge presented in the cases and problems. That is, the students in Study One may have been able to develop a reasonably coherent mental model of neo-Darwinian evolutionary biology by using features of the EVOLUTION KNOWLEDGE MEDIATOR to abstract key concepts and models that are characteristic of expert ways of thinking about the domain. In particular, the linked representations of case-specific and structural dimensions of knowledge (e.g., deep structure commentaries, conceptual visualizations) and cross-case interconnectedness (e.g., Conceptual Criss-Crossing) may have facilitated the abstraction process.

Given the relatively small sample size, these research findings must be regarded as provisional. The experimental design of this study precluded making a determination of the relative contributions of the different design features and learning activities for promoting conceptual understanding, conceptual growth and change, and transfer. Future research could attempt to control for different design features and learning activities. A different, and potentially richer, research direction could obtain process data to help establish the causal mechanisms responsible for the learning outcomes associated with the use of KMF learning tools (Kozma, 1994). Research of this type would be valuable given KMF learning tools consist of several related components, and the study of these components in isolation does not necessarily inform our understanding of their joint interaction in learning.

KMF: GENERAL ISSUES AND FUTURE RESEARCH DIRECTIONS

The KMF is intended to have applicability for the design of hypermedia learning tools in a wide range of domains (including interdisciplinary fields), not just biology or science. The KMF had in fact evolved from several precursor hypermedia systems developed in areas such as the social sciences (Jacobson et al., 1996; Jacobson & Spiro, 1995) and literary/cinematic criticism (Spiro et al., 1992; Spiro & Jehng, 1990), in addition to the sciences. Obviously, further research should investigate hypermedia learning tools based on the KMF in different domains, grade levels, and classroom situations. Given the lack of principled perspectives for developing web-based learning resources, future work could also explore the web implementation of KMF hypermedia learning tools.

Inspired in part by situated perspectives on socially mediated learning and scaffolding (Brown et al., 1989) and by the affordances of the web as a globally distributed computational and communications network, we are beginning to investigate a sixth type of learning activity for the *LA-6. Learner Centered and Project-based Learning* (see Table 5.1).[12] This sixth type of learning activity would utilize the elements and features of a KMF learning tool as part of tasks that require more learner initiative and independence. We suspect that it will be important to carefully prepare learners for more open-ended types of inquiry and project-based activities in domains that are particularly challenging cognitively and that often require a process of conceptual change and knowledge restructuring. Without cognitive preparation, there is the danger that students with naive models about a domain will assimilate new knowledge encountered during their learner-centered activities and will not undergo a process of conceptual growth leading to concepts and models that are qualitatively similar to experts in a community of practice.

We propose a pedagogical sequence as part of the KMF in which the program's conceptual scaffolding is gradually faded (Jackson, Krajcik, & Soloway, chap. 4, this volume) from the more supportive and "guided" activities associated with the first five KMF learning activities (that have been shown to help foster conceptual change) to the more learner directed approach in *LA-6*. The KMF prescribes scaffolding in the form of indexing cases and problems with abstract domain concepts and deep structure commentaries. These design elements could also be applied to selected web resources developed by others (e.g., commercial sites, research sites) that meet an author's or a teacher's standards of relevance and quality. Learners then would have a type of conceptual scaffolding that is qualitatively similar to the Knowledge Mediator materials they initially use (e.g., cognitive preparation, cases, and problems). Furthermore, KMF conceptual scaffolding would be further faded as students engaged in problem-based and project-based learning activities in which they would access web resources on their own, but which would obviously not have the abstract conceptual indexing and deep structure commentaries.

Another learner-centered activity would involve students using a KMF authoring tool to create their own "Knowledge Mediators" on a particular topic of their choice (e.g., global warming, extinction of dinosaurs). Students would gather their own information through research or

---

[12] Actually, this might more accurately be described as a set of learning activities that are more generally learner centered and directed.

scholarly work (e.g., web resources, books, journals, interviews, experiments) and then use KMF authoring "templates" to develop their own cases, abstract domain concepts, deep-structure commentaries, challenge questions, and so on. Although students would have considerable flexibility in terms of the specific content they authored for Knowledge Mediator projects, KMF authoring "templates" would provide a form of metaconceptual scaffolding to the learners. Carey (1995) has observed that children often lack a metaconceptual awareness of their mental representations and inferential processes. Furthermore, the lack of a metaconceptual awareness may negatively impact the learner's ability to conceptually reorganize her or his knowledge (Vosniadou, 1996). It may be that Knowledge Mediator projects could metaconceptually scaffold students to be aware of their representations in ways that are expertlike in at least four main ways: (a) awareness of *surface features* of case-specific facts and information, (b) awareness of a *deep structure* of knowledge reflected in the abstract concepts they analyze or index the cases with, (c) awareness of contextual interactions of their proposed conceptual deep structure with the cases and problems, and (d) awareness of interconnected knowledge relations across diverse cases and problems. It would also be possible to explore the use of KMF projects as part of computer-supported collaborative learning (CSCL) activities in which students work together collaboratively (in person or mediated by electronic communication), and "publish" their projects on a class web server. We are in the process of planning research involving KMF learning tools in ways such as these, and how such CSCL interactions might enhance the process of learning of conceptually challenging knowledge.

CONCLUSION

This chapter provides a perspective for designing hypermedia tools for learning based on the KMF. The framework is composed of design elements and learning activities that have theoretical and research rationales. Proof-of-concept research using an experimental hypermedia system with the main features of the KMF was found to foster conceptual change and to help students learn neo-Darwinian evolutionary biology. Long-term retention of the acquired knowledge was also documented in this research. There is a need for future research to explore the applicability and viability of the KMF for the development of web-based hypermedia tools for learning in other domains and other grade levels. The use of Knowledge Mediator learning tools as part of learner-centered projects was also considered in this chapter.

As we enter the 21st century, the increasing power and availability of technologies such as globally distributed hypermedia, computational modeling tools, and virtual reality environments will provide significant opportunities to enhance the educational process. However, in order to realize these opportunities, it is vital that these technologies be appropriately developed and used in ways informed by current learning theory and research. There is, therefore, a great need to identify and validate design and pedagogical principles for technological learning tools that actually help students construct deep, thoughtful, and useful understandings of difficult conceptual domains. It is hoped that the framework and research outlined in this chapter might provide useful perspectives to address this need.

ACKNOWLEDGMENTS

This research was supported in part by a grant to the first author from the National Science Foundation under Grant No. RED-9253157. The U.S. government has certain rights in this material. Any opinions, findings, and conclusions or recommendations expressed in this material are those of the authors and do not necessarily reflect the views of the funding agencies. Additional support for this research was provided by the University of Georgia College of Education in a grant to the first author. The authors gratefully acknowledge the ideas and contributions of Rand J. Spiro, Punyashloke Mishra, Susan Ravlin, Chrystalla Maouri, Brian Levine, and Akiko Sugimoto to this research. Also, the insightful comments of an anonymous reviewer on an earlier version of this chapter are acknowledged. The lead designer for the web-based Evolution Knowledge Mediator was Phoebe C. Jacobson, who was assisted by JavaScript programmers Ricardo Serrano, Besim Atalay, and Chih-Hsiu Peng. Finally, Alex J. Angulo provided valuable editing assistance on this manuscript.

REFERENCES

Allen, B. S., & Otto, R. G. (1996). Media as lived environments: The ecological psychology of educational technology. In D. H. Jonassen (Ed.), *Handbook of research for educational communications and technology* (pp. 199–225). New York: Simon & Schuster Macmillian.

Anderson, P. W., Arrow, K. J., & Pines, D. (Eds.), (1988). *The economy as an evolving complex system: The proceedings of the evolutionary paths of the global economy workshop* (Santa Fe Institute Studies in the Sciences of Complexity, Vol. 5). Reading, MA: Addison-Wesley.

Baker, E. L., Niemi, D., & Herl, H. (1994). Using HyperCard technology to measure understanding. In E. L. Baker & H. F. O'Neil, Jr. (Eds.), *Technology assessment in education and training* (pp. 133–152). Hillsdale, NJ: Lawrence Erlbaum Associates.

Beeman, W. O., Anderson, K. T., Bader, G., Larkin, J., McClard, A. P., McQuillan, P. J., & Shields, M. (1988). *Intermedia: A case study of innovation in higher education (Final report to the Annenberg/CPB Project)*. Providence, RI: Brown University, Office of Program Analysis, Institute for Research in Information and Scholarship.

Bereiter, C., & Scardamalia, M. (1985). Cognitive coping strategies and the problem of "inert knowldege." In S. F. Chipman, J. W. Segal, & R. Glaser (Eds.), *Thinking and learning skills: Current research and open questions* (vol. 2, pp. 65–80). Hillsdale, NJ: Lawrence Erlbaum Associates.

Bishop, B. A., & Anderson, C. W. (1990). Student conceptions of natural selection and its role in evolution. *Journal of Research in Science Teaching, 27*(5), 415–427.

Bizzo, N. M. V. (1994). From down house landlord to Brazilian high school students: What has happened to evolutionary knowledge on the way? *Journal of Research in Science Teaching, 31*(5), 537–556.

Bransford, J. D., Franks, J. J., Vye, N. J., & Sherwood, R. D. (1989). New approaches to instruction: Because wisdom can't be told. In S. Vosniadou & A. Ortony (Eds.), *Similarity and analogical reasoning* (pp. 470–497). Cambridge, NY: Cambridge University Press.

Brown, J. S., Collins, A., & Duguid, P. (1989). Situated cognition and the culture of learning. *Educational Researcher, 18*(1), 32–42.

Bruer, J. T. (1993). *Schools for thought: A science of learning in the classroom.* Cambridge, MA: MIT Press.

Brumby, M. N. (1984). Misconceptions about the concept of natural selection by medical biology students. *Science Education, 68*(4), 493–503.

Carey, S. (1995). Are children fundamentally different kinds of thinkers and learners than adults? In S. F. Chipman, J. W. Segal, & R. Glaser (Eds.), *Thinking and learning skills* (vol. 2, pp. 485–517). Hillsdale, NJ: Lawrence Erlbaum Associates.

Chan, C., Burtis, J., & Bereiter, C. (1997). Knowledge building as a mediator of conflict in conceptual change. *Cognition and Instruction, 15*(1), 1–40.

Chi, M. T. H., Feltovich, P. J. & Glaser, R. (1981). Categorization and representation of physics problem by experts and novices. *Cognitive Science, 5,* 121–152.

Chi, M. T. H., Glaser, R., & Farr, M. J. (Eds., 1988). *The nature of expertise.* Hillsdale, NJ: Lawrence Erlbaum Associates.

Chi, M. T. H, Slotta, J. D., & de Leeuw, N. (1994). From things to processes: A theory of conceptual change for learning science concepts. *Learning and Instruction, 4,* 27–43.

Chinn, C. A., & Brewer, W. F. (1993). The role of anomalous data in knowledge acquisition: A theoretical framework and implications for science instruction. *Review of Education Research, 63*(1), 1–49.

Clancey, W. J. (1993). Situated action: A neuropsychological interpretation response to Vera and Simon. *Cognitive Science, 17,* 87–116.

Cognition and Technology Group at Vanderbilt. (1990). Anchored instruction and its relationship to situated cognition. *Educational Researcher, 19*(6), 2–10.

Cognition and Technology Group at Vanderbilt. (1997). *The Jasper project: Lessons in curriculum, instruction, assessment, and professional development.* Mahwah, NJ: Lawrence Erlbaum Associates.

Conklin, J. (1987). Hypertext: An introduction and survey. *IEEE Computer, 20*(9), 17–41.

Craik, F. I. M. & Lockhart, R. S., (1972). Levels of processing: A framework for memory research. *Journal of Verbal Learning and Verbal Behavior, 11,* 671–684.

Cummins, C. L., Demastes, S. S., & Hafner, M. S. (1994). Evolution: Biological education's under-researched unifying theme. *Journal of Research in Science Teaching, 31*(5), 445–448.

Cziko, G. (1995). *Without miracles: Universal selection theory and the second Darwinian revolution.* Cambridge, MA: MIT Press.

Dawkins, R. (1986). *Blind watchmaker.* New York: Norton.

Dede, C. J., (1987). Empowering environments, hypermedia and microworlds. *The Computing Teacher, 15*(3), 20–24, 61.

Demastes, S. S., Good, R. G., & Peebles, P. (1996). Patterns of conceptual change in evolution. *Journal of Research in Science Teaching, 33,* 407–431.

Demastes, S. S., Settlage, J., & Good, R. (1995). Students' conception of natural selection and its role in evolution: Cases of replication and comparison. *Journal of Research in Science Teaching, 32*(5), 535–550.

Dobzhansky, T. (1973). Nothing in biology makes sense except in the light of evolution. *Journal of Biological Education, 35,* 125–129.

Epstein, J. M., & Axtell, R. (1996). *Growing artificial societies: Social science from the bottom up.* Washington, DC: The Brookings Institution.

Ericsson, K. A., & Simon, H. A. (1993). *Protocol analysis: Verbal reports as data* (rev. ed.). Cambridge, MA: MIT Press.

Ferrari, M., & Chi, M. T. H. (in press). The nature of naïve explanations of natural selection. *International Journal of Science Education.*

Gell-Mann, M. (1994). *The quark and the jaguar: Adventures in the simple and the complex.* New York: Freeman and Company.

Gibson, J. J. (1979). *The ecological approach to visual perception.* New York: Berkeley Publications Group.

Greene, E. D. (1990). The logic of university students' misunderstanding of natural selection. *Journal of Research in Science Teaching, 27*(9), 875–885.

Holland, J. H. (1995). *Hidden order: How adaptation builds complexity.* Reading, MA: Addison-Wesley.

Homa, D. (1984). On the nature of categories. In G. H. Bower (Ed.), *The psychology of learning and motivation* (vol. 18, pp. 49–94). New York: Academic Press.

Horwitz, P. Taylor, E. F. T., & Hickman, P. (1994). "Relativity readiness" using the RelLab program. *Physics Teacher, 32*(2), 81–86.

Jacobson, M. J. (1994). Issues in hypertext and hypermedia research: Toward a framework for linking theory-to-design. *Journal of Educational Multimedia and Hypermedia, 3*(2), 141–154.

Jacobson, M. J., & Archodidou. A. (1997, March). *Case-based hypermedia learning environments and conceptual change: The evolution of understandings about evolution of understandings about evolution.* Paper presented at the annual conference of the American Educational Research Association, Chicago, IL.

Jacobson, M. J., & Maouri, C., Mishra, P., & Kolar, C. (1996). Learning with hypertext learning environments: Theory, design, and research. *Journal of Educational Multimedia and Hypermedia, 5*(3 to 4), 239–281.

Jacobson, M. J.m & Spiro, R. J. (1991). Hypertext learning environments and cognitive flexibility: Characteristics promoting the transfer of complex knowledge. In L. Birnbaum (Ed.), *The International Conference on the Learning Sciences: Proceedings of the 1991 Conference* (pp. 240–248). Charlottesville, VA: Association for the Advancement of Computing in Education.

Jacobson, M. J., & Spiro, R. J. (1995). Hypertext learning environments, cognitive flexibility, and the transfer of complex knowledge: An empirical investigation. *Journal of Educational Computing Research, 12*(5), 301–333.

Jacobson, M. J., & Spiro, R. S. (1997). *Learning and applying difficult science knowledge: Research into the application of hypermedia learning environments (Final report to the National Science Foundation Applications of Advance Technologies program).* The University of Georgia, Learning and Performance Support Laboratory.

Jacobson, M. J., & Sugimoto, A., & Archodidou, A. (1996). Evolution, hypermedia learning environments, and conceptual change: A preliminary report. In C. C. Edelson & E. A. Domeshek (Eds.), *International Conference on the Learning Sciences, 1996: Proceedings of ICLS 96* (pp. 151–158). Charlottesville, VA: Association for the Advancement of Computing in Education.

Jonassen, D. H. (1986). Hypertext principles for text and courseware design. *Educational Psychologist, 21*(4), 269–292.

Johassen, D. H., Reeves, T. C., Hong, N., Harvey, D., & Peters, K. (1997). Concept mapping as cognitive learning and assessment tools. *Journal of Interactive Learning Research, 8*(3 to 4), 289–308.

Jonassen, D. H., & Wang, S. (1993). Acquiring structural knowledge from semantically structured hypertext. *Journal of Computer-based Instruction, 20*(1), 1–8.

Kauffman, S. (1993). *The origins of order: Self-organization and selection in evolution.* New York: Oxford University Press.

Kauffman, S. (1995). *At home in the universe: The search for laws of self-organization and complexity.* New York: Oxford University Press.

Kearsley, G. (1988). Authoring considerations for hypertext. *Educational Technology, 28*(11), 21–24.

Kolander, J. (1993). *Case-based reasoning.* San Mateo, CA: Morgan Kaufmann.

Kozma, R. B. (1991). Learning with media. *Review of Educational Research, 61*(2), 179–211.

Kozma, R. B. (1994). Will media influence learning? Reframing the debate. *Educational Technology, Research and Development, 42*(2), 7–19.

Lakoff, G. (1987). *Women, fire, and dangerous things: What categories reveal about the mind.* Chicago: University of Chicago Press.

Landow, G. P. (1992). *Hypertext: The convergence of contemporary critical theory and technology.* Balitmore, MD: Johns Hopkins University Press.

Lave, J., & Wenger, E. (1991). *Situated learning: Legitimate peripheral participation.* Cambridge University Press.

Lehrer, R. (1993). Authors of knowledge: Patterns of hypermedia design. In S. P. Lajoie & S. J. Derry (Eds.), *Computers as cognitive tools* (pp. 197–227). Hillsdale, NJ: Lawrence Erlbaum Associates.

Marsh, E. J., & Kumar, D. D. (1992). Hypermedia: A conceptual framework for science education and review of recent findings. *Journal of Educational Multimedia and Hypermedia, 1*, 25–37.

Mayr, E. (1991). *One long argument: Charles Darwin and the genesis of modern evolutionary thought.* Cambridge, MA: Harvard University Press.

Mintzes, J. J., & Arnaudin, M.W. (1984). *Children's biology: A review of research on conceptual development in the life sciences.* Wilmington, NC: North Carolina University, Department of Biological Sciences. (ERIC Document Reproduction Service No. ED 249 044).

Mitchell, M. (1996). *An introduction to genetic algorithms.* Cambridge, MA: MIT Press.

Nathan, M. J., & Resnick, L. B. (1994). Less can be more: Unintelligent tutoring based on psychological theories and experimentation. In S. Vosniadou, E. DeCorte, & H. Mandl (Eds.), *Technology-based learning environments.* Berlin: Springer-Verlag.

National Research council. (1996). *National Science Education Standards.* Washington, DC: National Academy Press.

Neuman, D., Marchionini, G., & Morrell, K. (1995). Evaluating Perseus 1.0: Methods and final results. *Journal of Educational Multimedia and Hypertext, 4*(4), 365–382.

Nielsen, J. (1990). *Hypertext and hypermedia.* San Diego: CA: Academic Press.

Pagels, H. R. (1988). *The dreams of reason: The computer and the rise of the sciences of complexity.* New York: Simon & Schuster.

Perkins, D. N. (1992). Technology meedts constructivism: Do they make a marriage? In T. M. Duffy & D. H. Jonassen (Eds.), *Constructivism and the technology of instruction: A conversation* (pp. 45–55). Hillsdale, NJ: Lawrence Erlbaum Associates.

Posner, G. J., Strike, K. A., Hewson, P. W., & Gertzog, W. A. (1982). Accommodation of a scientific conception: Toward a theory of conceptual change. *Science Education, 66*(2), 211–227.

Ram, A., Nersessian, N. J. & Keil, F. C. (1997). Special issue: Conceptual change, guest editors' introduction. *The Journal of the Learning Sciences, 6*(1), 1–2.

Renkl, A., Mandl, H., & Gruber, H. (1996). Inert knowledge: Analyses and remedies. *Educational Psychologist, 3*(2), 115–121.

Salomon, G. T., & Globerson, T. (1987). Skill may not be enough: The role of mindfulness in learning and transfer. *International Journal of Educational Research, 11*, 623–637.

Samarapungayan, A., & Wiers, R.. W. (1997). Children's thought on the origin of species: A study of explanatory coherence. *Cognitive Science, 21*(2), 147–177.

Schank, R. C. (1982). *Dynamic memory.* Cambridge, NY: Cambridge University Press.
Settlage, J. (1994). Conceptions of natural selection: A snapshot of the sense-making process. *Journal of Research in Science Teaching, 31*(5), 448–457.
Simon, H. A. (1973). The structure of ill-structured problem. *Artificial Intelligence, 4,* 181–210.
Sober, E. (1984). *The nature of selection.* Chicago, IL: University of Chicago Press.
Spiro, R. J., Coulson, R. L., Feltovich, P. J., & Anderson, D. K. (1988). Cognitive flexibility theory: Advanced knowledge acquisition in ill-structured domains. In *Tenth annual conference of the Cognitive Science Society* (pp. 375–383). Hillsdale, NJ: Lawrence Erlbaum Associates.
Spiro, R. J., Feltovich, P. J., Jacobson, M. J., & Coulson, R. L. (1992). Cognitive flexibility, constructivism, and hypertext: Random access instruction for advanced knowledge acquisition in ill-structured domains. In T. M. Duffy & D. H. Jonassen (Eds.), *Constructivism and the technology of instruction: A conversation* (pp. 57–75). Hillsdale, NJ: Lawrence Erlbaum Associates.
Spiro, R. J., & Jehng. J. C. (1990). Cognitive flexibility and hypertext: Theory and technology for the nonlinear and multidimensional traversal and complex subject matter. In D. Nix & R. Spiro (Eds.), *Cognition, education, and multimedia* (pp. 163–205). Hillsdale, NJ: Lawrence Erlbaum Associates.
Spiro, R. J., Vispoel, W. P., Schmitz, J. G., Samarapungavan, S., & Boerger, A. E. (1987). Knowledge acquisition for application: Cognitive flexibility and transfer in complex content domains. In B. K. Britton & S. M. Glynn (Eds.), *Executive control processes in reading* (pp. 177–199). Hillsdale, NJ: Lawrence Erlbaum Associates.
Strike, K., & Posner, G. (1990). A revisionist theory of conceptual change. In R. Duschl & R. Hamilton (Eds.), *Philosophy of science, cognitive science, and educational theory and practice.* Albany, NY: Sunny Press.
Tamir, P. (1992). *Dealing with misconceptions in preservice education of biology teachers.* Unpublished manuscript, Hebrew University, Jerusalem.
Tergan, S. O. (1997). Conceptual and methodological shortcomings in hypertext/hypermedia design and research. *Journal of Educational Computing Research, 16*(3), 209–235.
Vosniadou, S. (1996). Learning environments for representational growth and cognitive flexibility. In S. Vosniadou, E. DeCorte, R. Glaser, & H. Mandl (Eds.), *International perspective on the design of technology-supported learning environments* (pp. 13–24). Mahwah, NJ: Lawrence Erlbaum Associates.
Vosniadou, S., & Brewer, W. F. (1992). Mental models of the earth: A study of conceptual change in childhood. *Cognitive Psychology, 24,* 535–585.
Vosniadou, S., & Brewer, W. F. (1994). Mental models of the day/nigh cycle. *Cognitive Science, 18*(1), 123–183.
Voss, J. F., Greene, T. R., Post, T. A., & Penner, B. C. (1983). Problem-solving skill in the social science. In G. H, Bower (Eds.), *The psychology of learning and motivation: Advance in research theory* (vol. 17, pp. 165–213). New York: Academic Press.
White, B. Y. (1993). ThinkerTools: Causal models, conceptual change, and science education. *Cognition and Instruction, 10*(1), 1–100.
Whitehead, A. N. (1929). *The aims of education and other essays.* New York: Macmillan.
Williams, S. M. (1992). Putting case-based instruction in context: Examples from legal and medical education. *The Journal of the Leaning Sciences, 2*(4), 367–427.
Wiser, M., & Carey, S. (1983). When heat and temperature were one. In D. Gentner, & A. L. Stevens (Eds.), *Mental models.* Hillsdale, NJ: Lawrence Erlbaum Associates.
Yankelvoich, N., Meyrowitz, N., & van Dam, A. (1988). Intermedia: The concept and the construction of a seamless information environment. *IEEE Computer, 21,* 81–96.

6

Computer-Based Manipulatives for Teaching Scientific Reasoning: An Example

Paul Horwitz and Mary Ann Christie
The Concord Consortium

This chapter describes the design and use of an exploratory software environment—GENSCOPE—that is designed to help students learn to reason and solve problems in the domain of genetics. Our goals for GEN-SCOPE are largely cognitive. We want our students to grasp not only scientific explanations of phenomena, but also the nature of the scientific process itself. In short, we want to teach them how to think like scientists.

GENSCOPE is one of a class of applications we call "computer-based manipulatives" (CBMs). CBMs are designed to guide students to an understanding of science by enabling them to observe and manipulate graphic objects whose behavior is determined by an implicit model. By experimenting with the objects on the screen, students gain an intuitive understanding of the scientific concepts underlying the domain. Neither simulations nor modeling tools, CBMs are intended to provide students with relatively open-ended exploratory environments that teach both by the constraints they place on students' activities and by the actions they allow.

After a brief exposition of some of the barriers to science learning arising from traditional instruction, we use GENSCOPE as an exemplar for investigating the potential of CBM technology to help teachers and learners overcome these barriers. In describing the software we emphasize the educational philosophy that informed its design, as well as our observations of how its use alters classroom practices and students' learning. It should be understood, however, that what we are presenting is very much a work in progress. At the time of this writing (December, 1997), we can offer little more than interesting snapshots from our classroom-based research over the last year, primarily in urban high schools.

SCIENCE EDUCATION, INSTRUCTION, AND COGNITION

A gradual change is emerging in science education (National Research Council [NRC], 1996), characterized by a shift from the teaching of mechanical information and "science facts" to an effort to impart a deeper comprehension of the subject matter and its reasoning processes. This change in emphasis has been made feasible, in part, by recent advances in applied cognitive science that provide us with general accounts of what it is to understand. Detailed studies of how students come to "understand" abstract concepts in science have documented the importance of moving beyond the linguistic labels that represent these concepts to a deeper comprehension of their significance and interconnections (Carey, 1986; Johnstone, 1991). If they are to learn to reason scientifically, students' performance must encompass much more than the recall of facts or the application of procedural knowledge. The barriers they face are both linguistic and pedagogical.

Linguistic Barriers to Understanding

Cognitive research has shown that to understand text or spoken language, one must relate it to pre-existing knowledge schemata for understanding the world (Carey, 1986). To understand a science textbook, for instance, students must relate what they are reading to what they already know. However, introductory science students often do not have existing schemata with which to form a basis for understanding. Moreover, the scientific vocabulary used to describe the concepts under study is itself a formidable barrier. As Carey has pointed out, high school science texts often introduce more new vocabulary per page than foreign language texts. This is even more remarkable when one considers that the concepts denoted by new words in the foreign language text are presumably already known to the student, whereas the scientific terms have no cognates in prior experience. Thus, the terminology used to describe scientific concepts may pose as formidable a barrier to understanding as do misconceptions (Kindfield, 1994) or the need for specialized problem-solving skills (Carey, 1986; Johnstone, 1991).

Pedagogical Barriers to Understanding

Research on scientific reasoning, and in particular on classical genetics problem solving, has shown that scientists reason and learn inductively and from effect to cause (Johnston-Slack & Stewart, 1990). In contrast, the traditional textbook approach to science learning gives students information and challenges them to think deductively by reasoning from cause to effect.

Novice science students without appropriate mental schemata or relevant conceptual frameworks find it difficult to think abstractly or to reason about phenomena at multiple levels (Johnstone, 1991). Lacking a conceptual map of the domain, they find it difficult to think about how the phenomena they can see (effects) connect with those they cannot see (causes). Traditional activities to promote acquisition of schemata via problem solving involve the student, pencil, paper, and text (Stewart & Hafner, 1994). Progression in self-practice sets involves some degree of memorization, both for the categorization of the problem and for the instantiation and subsequent application of the solution (Dufresne, Gerace, Hardiman, & Mestre, 1992). Students practice similar problems, learn to recognize similarities, and apply a solution strategy that has been ingrained as a result of this extensive practice.

However, as Stewart and Hafner (1994) have pointed out, producing a correct answer does not necessarily mean that the student understands the underlying concepts. Both correct and incorrect answers can be obtained by the application of algorithms without such understanding. All that is required is "procedural" knowledge. The reverse often happens as well. Due to incorrect information at the onset, students may create appropriate mental models through traditional instruction, yet obtain incorrect answers to problems. Such students are not likely to be recognized as competent in abstract modeling. As Stewart and Hafner have suggested, although the ability to solve problems is widely used as a measure of whether learning has taken place, problem solving as a means of learning is often ignored. It is all too common for bemused science teachers to find that recent students—students who received good grades—are unable to apply basic principles shortly after the completion of a course (Carey, 1986; Johnstone, 1991).

A DESCRIPTION OF GenScope SOFTWARE

Genetics is the study of how the physical characteristics of an organism are inherited from its ancestors and passed on to its descendants. The mechanism by which this happens must account, among other things, for the fact that living things somehow contrive to attain a wide degree of variation within very strict constraints. Although no two humans look exactly alike, they all resemble each other more than they do, say, an elephant. The details of how this happens are only just now being worked out, but the basic mechanism was guessed at in the 19th century by Gregor Mendel (1866), who postulated a set of rules by which each organism receives at birth the instructions that determine how it will grow. In an abstract sense, then, genetics is the study of information flow in biological systems, and it is probably no coincidence that this discipline should flourish at precisely the moment in history when the advent of computers has revolutionized the way we ourselves handle information.

One of the major barriers students face when they attempt to learn genetics stems from the fact that the phenomena they are studying occur at many different levels of description. In devising software to help students with this difficulty, we have considered six such levels, dealing respectively with *molecules, chromosomes, cells, organisms, pedigrees,* and *populations*. At each of these we have devised representations of the information we wish to present to students, as well as tools for manipulating that information. The information then flows between the levels, linking them in such a way that the effects of manipulations made at any one level may immediately be observed at each of the others. The levels thus combine to form the seamless computer-based manipulative we call GenScope.

The *organism level* is the simplest to describe. It deals with the observable traits of living things and emphasizes what we see around us every day: that each organism of a species is different from all the others. The set of physical traits that differentiate a poodle, say, from a Great Dane, is called its *phenotype*, which is, in turn, a direct consequence of the *genotype* of the animal—the set of genes that contain the information required for its development.

"Gene" is the name given to a unit of information that codes for a particular physical trait. (This definition of a gene, by Mendel, is actually a bit simplistic in light of what we know today, but its technical difficulties will not materially affect the discussion.) The existence of genes was postulated long before anyone had any idea about what they actually are, but we now know that they are portions (often noncontiguous) of a very long molecule called DNA, the main function of which is to aid in the production of other molecules, called proteins, that in turn perform important functions within and between the cells of living organisms. The DNA in a cell (technically, in a eukaryotic cell) is not a single continuous molecule, but rather is divided into substructures called *chromosomes*, which migrate as individual entities when cells from a male and a female organism combine to produce offspring. Thus, genetics involves *molecular-*, *chromosomal-*, and *cellular-level* events whose effects are evident at the organism level.

If we mate a poodle and a Great Dane (and such matings take place all the time—often to the dismay of the owners), the resulting litter of puppies will combine the parents' traits in various ways. Some of the pups may have the curly hair of their poodle father while retaining the coloring of the mother. Some may combine the long legs of a Great Dane with a poodle head and ears. If the puppies grow up and have puppies of their own, the genes they carry will mix some more, and it may become harder to perceive the original poodle and Great Dane traits in the offspring. Those traits were produced in the first place, of course, by the controlled breeding of dogs over many generations. Humans have used such selective breeding for thousands of years to produce desired traits in farm animals, food plants, and other organisms. In fact, insights gained from such activities were the precursors to many of the early discoveries in genetics, and they form an important part of what we refer to in GENSCOPE as the *pedigree* level of description.

Poodles and Great Danes are in a sense artificial organisms—varieties of dog brought into the world by human beings for their own purposes. However, nature has its own way of selecting for certain traits, and the study of how this happens over many generations in response to changing conditions is the central subject of population genetics. It is a remarkable fact—and one of the triumphs of modern genetics—that the complex and often surprising adaptations of plants and animals that are observed at the population level can now be understood and modeled as the consequences of countless unseen processes that take place at the molecular and cellular levels within each organism.

Because the goal of GENSCOPE is to help students learn to think like geneticists, its design consciously models such thinking. At the heart of the program is a simplified but realistic model of genetics. This model comprises representations of many biological structures and processes as well as tools for examining and altering them. The combination of representations and tools leads to a rich environment for exploration and discovery.

A representative GENSCOPE screen, showing the introductory dragon species, is presented in Fig. 6.1. Three windows are open. The organism window shows two dragons: a gold female named Juliet, and an azure male named Romeo. The chromosome window shows Romeo's pair of number 2 chromosomes, each of which carries genes that code for the presence or absence of wings, number of legs, and shape of tail. The wing gene comes in two varieties or alleles: W and w. Romeo's wings genes are both w, which is why he has wings (which are a recessive trait in dragons). If we were to open her chromosome window, we would see that Juliet has one w and one W allele. The labels for all genes are pull-down menus that enable students to change them from one allele to the other. When they do this the effect, if any, on the dragons is immediately visible. Students can also view and alter alleles at the DNA level, with similar results. Partially visible at the bottom of the screen is the cell window, where we see one of Juliet's cells undergoing meiosis (division into four gametes, each of which has only half the chromosomal content of the original cell). This simulation is not a canned movie, but a random process in which the outcome (i.e., which chromosome will segregate with which) is not predictable in advance.

For example, at the molecular level of GENSCOPE, students may alter a DNA molecule to create a mutation. Moving up to the chromosomal level, they may examine the particular chromosome within which the altered DNA resides and verify that they have created a new variant of a particular gene. They can observe he effect of this mutation, if any, on the organism and its progeny. If the new allele happens to confer a selective advantage on to individuals possessing it, it will multiply and after many generations may come to dominate the genome of a population of interbreeding organisms. Using the population level of GENSCOPE, students can observe and quantify this effect as well, by defining a "fitness function" that models the effect of the environment.

PEDAGOGICAL APPROACH

We introduce GENSCOPE in the classroom by focusing on the connections between only two levels, the organism and chromosome levels, and

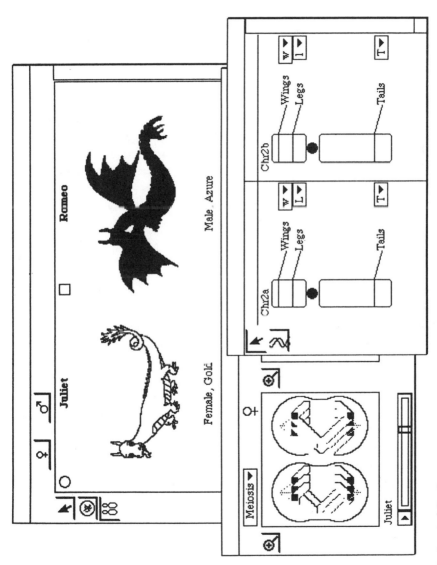

FIG. 6.1 A typical GenScope screen.

169

gradually introduce other levels in a logical progression. Also, we begin with a fictitious and simple species—dragons—introducing students only later to the complications (both scientific and ethical) of real species. (We generally introduce real species—dogs, horses and humans—by the third week of classes.)

In an ideal classroom, which we seldom encounter, the computers should be placed far enough apart so that students may work in pairs with plenty of room to read handouts and take notes, yet close enough so conversations between pairs may take place easily. After they have familiarized themselves with the GENSCOPE interface (which generally takes about 15 minutes), we challenge the students to create dragons with specified traits (e.g., a fire-breathing green one, with horns, wings, no legs, and a fancy tail). Because it is quite unlikely that anyone will create such a beast entirely by luck, the students must alter genes in a purposeful fashion (at the chromosome level) to achieve the desired aim (at the organism level). Once they have done this (and everyone succeeds without assistance at this simple task), we switch to a paper and pencil exercise that presents screen shots of chromosomes and asks the students to describe the dragon that possesses those genes. When they have completed this exercise they are encouraged to use GENSCOPE to verify, and if necessary to correct, their answers.

All these activities deal with the rules built into GENSCOPE that specify how a dragon's phenotype depends on its genotype. However, rules of this kind are foreign to many students, for whom rules are prescriptive and optional (e.g., wash your hands before coming to supper), rather than descriptive and compulsory (e.g., a dragon with one or more dominant alleles for horns will necessarily have horns). It is not surprising, then, that students often have trouble articulating their newly forming knowledge in the language of universal "scientific" rules. We introduce the topic, typically on the day after the introductory dragon activities described previously, by giving the students a handout that challenges them to write, using their own notation, the rules for each of the six dragon traits (presence or absence of horns and wings, number of legs, type of tail, color, and whether or not it breathes fire). The students are encouraged to develop these rules using GENSCOPE (rather than having to remember them). This activity, which may appear quite straightforward, has proven quite challenging and instructive for students to whom the central concept of a descriptive rule is strange.

After the students have developed and verified their "rule sheets" for dragons, they are given pictures of various dragons and asked to specify the allelic combinations that match the phenotypes. This phenotype-to-genotype reasoning is significantly more difficult than figuring out the phenotype from the genotype—primarily, we postulate, because the mapping is not one-to-one as more than one genotype may correspond to the same phenotype.[1] After each group has filled out its worksheet we hold a class discussion to compare results. Ideally, this discussion should be facilitated by projecting GENSCOPE on a screen and having individual groups come to the front of the class to demonstrate their answers to the others. However, in many schools suitable projection equipment is not available, and we generally have to resort to a blackboard.

The activities described so far have all involved reasoning at just two levels: organisms and chromosomes. We introduce a third level, the DNA level, by connecting it to the chromosome level (see Fig. 6.2). We do this by taking away the students' ability to alter the genes in the way to which they have become accustomed. We tell the students to load a particular file into GENSCOPE. When they do this, they get a dragon named "Susie," who is wingless. Their task is to give Susie wings by altering her genes. (Note that wings, in dragons, are a recessive trait. In other words, Susie would have to possess two lowercase w alleles to have wings.) Yet, when the students use the chromosome tool, they discover that although they are still allowed to view the genes on the chromosomes, they can no longer alter them. However, a new tool has appeared—a DNA tool—with which they can both view and alter the molecular structure that under-lies the genes. Figure 6.2 shows what happens when the students use the DNA tool to "zoom into" Susie's two wings genes.

Luckily for the students, Susie is *heterozygous* for wings—in other words, she has the dominant W allele on one chromosome and the recessive w on the other. In terms of these alleles, the students' task is to change the W to a w. They can do this by operating on the DNA in much the same way they would alter a line of text in a word processor. After they have identified the difference between the two alleles (see the caption to Fig. 6.2), they simply place their cursor to the right of the "A–T" pair in

---

[1] "Many-to-one" mappings (i.e., mappings that do not have a unique inverse) are common in elementary mathematics but are not usually examined carefully until college-level courses. It is intriguing to speculate whether introducing this important concept earlier in the mathematics curriculum would have a beneficial effect on students' ability to master pheno-type-to-genotype reasoning.

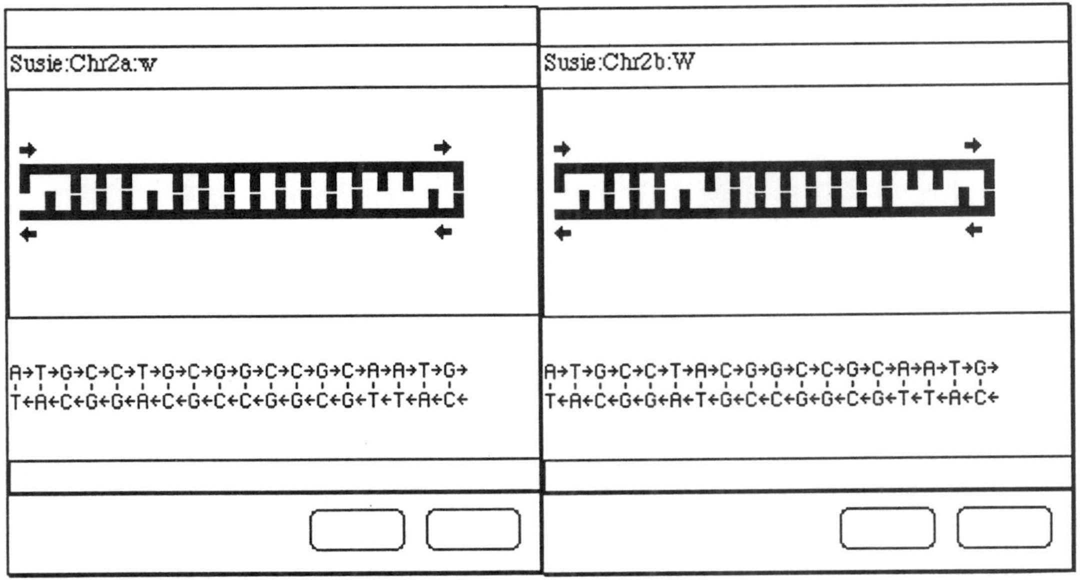

FIG. 6.2 A DNA window in GenScope showing two genes for wings. Note that the w and W alleles differ by a single point mutation in the seventh position—the replacement of a "G–C" (Guanine–Cytosine) base pair in the w allele by an "A–T" (Adenine–Thymine) pair in the W allele.

the W allele, hit the delete key, and type "G" in its place. When they click on the "Apply" button, the W changes to w in both the DNA and the chromosome window, and Susie sprouts wings!

However, what if the students had done something entirely different to the DNA? For example, what if they had typed "GAG" right in the middle of the gene? If they did this, and hit Apply, they would create a mutation.[2] In the case of the wings gene (and most of the others), we have prepared for this eventuality and have assigned a phenotype and a graphic to this (or any other) mutation of the wings gene (see Fig. 6.3).

The new allele, denoted WW, when paired with the w gives rise to an organism with a double set of wings. Paired to the W (which normally results in no wings), it gives a single (normal) set of wings. Two WW alleles are lethal to the organism.

All the genes in the dragon genome can be mutated in a similar way. In most cases such mutations will give rise to dragons with new traits (e.g., "unicorns," albinos, dragons that breathe green fire). The rules for how the mutated allele pairs up with itself and the original ones to produce the different phenotypes differ in each case and students are challenged to determine and describe them.

Up to this point in the curriculum, students have had to think only about a single organism, albeit at more than one level. Genetics, however, is fundamentally about how offspring inherit traits from their parents. Such intergenerational reasoning is neatly introduced at GEN-SCOPE's cell level.

The cell window can show up to two cells—one from each parent—and enables students to create gametes (eggs and sperm), examine their chromosomes, and select one of each for fertilization. By controlling gamete selection in this way, a student may ensure that the resulting offspring will have a particular trait, and this provides the basis for the set of problems that we have created. After outfitting our students with a particular set of dragon parents (with unalterable genes and DNA), we challenge them to mate them and create the following:

1. Make a baby with no horns. This "monohybrid" problem requires the student to select an egg and a sperm that each have the recessive h allele.

---

[2]For the technically inclined, the mutation will only have an effect if it alters the amino acid sequence coded for by the altered gene. So-called "silent" mutations, which code for the same amino acids, have no effect in GENSCOPE, just as they have no effect in real life.

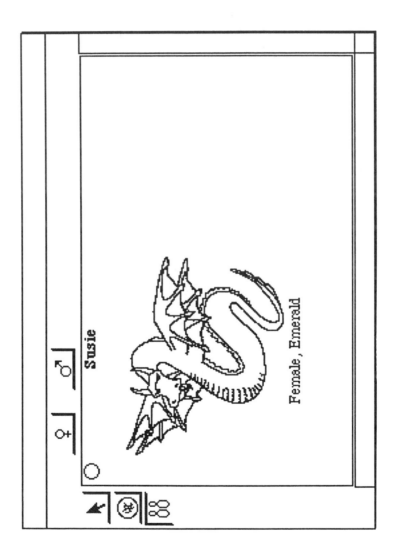

FIG. 6.3 This figure shows the effect of a mutation in the wing gene. Any alteration in the DNA sequence that also changes the resulting protein will result in a new allele automatically designated *WW*. When this allele is paired with the *w* allele the result is a dragon with two sets of wings.

2. Make a male baby. Male dragons have two X-chromosomes and females have an X and a Y so the sex of the offspring is entirely determined by which egg is selected. (A technical side note: In mammals, females are XX and males are XY. Dragons, however, are closely related to birds, most of which are the reverse.)

3. Make a female baby with wings and no horns. This problem involves not only selecting appropriate gametes but also involves controlling the formation of those gametes during meiosis. For this purpose we momentarily give students the ability to control chromosomal alignment and segregation. (We later take this control away from them to impress on them, now that they have understood its significance, that the process is random in nature.)

4. Make a baby with four legs, a plain tail, and wings. Because the legs, tail, and wings genes are all located on Chromosome 2, this problem involves modifying the assortment of alleles between the homologous pairs of Number 2 chromosomes—a process called *crossover*. Again, we give students the ability to control this process, and then take away that control so they can observe how it occurs randomly in nature.

5. Make a fire-breathing female. Because the gene for fire breathing is on the X chromosome, this problem introduces sex linkage.

6. Make an azure dragon. Two genes, both on the X chromosome, control color in dragons. This activity thus combines sex linkage and polygenicity.

The particular sequence of activities we have described is not crucial. What is important is that students be forced to think at three levels at once: organisms (both the parents and the baby-to-be), chromosomes and genes (and the fact that one cannot tell what the baby will be like without considering the genes from both parents), and cells (after all, it is purely cellular processes that determine which chromosomes end up in any particular offspring).

At the cellular level, all the problems lead to "forward inferencing"—from parents to offspring. The reverse reasoning pattern—moving from observed traits of offspring to inferred genotypes of parents—is the domain of the pedigree level of GenScope .

The parent dragons in Fig. 6.4 do not have wings (wingless females are represented as unfilled circles in a pedigree, wingless males as an unfilled square). However, their offspring does (the filled square denotes a winged male). How is such a thing is possible? This is the

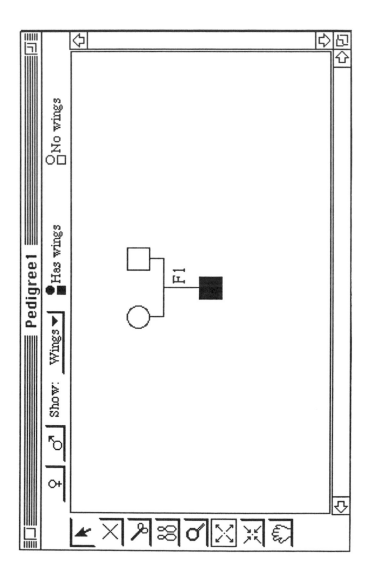

FIG. 6.4 This figure shows the pedigree level of GenScope. The window is set to show the "Wings" trait and here neither parent has wings (their symbols are unfilled), though their offspring does (filled square at the bottom). The explanation for this puzzle requires that one reason from phenotype to genotype (the baby has wings, wings are recessive, the baby must have two w alleles), and from offspring to parents (the baby must have gotten its w from its parents, neither of whom has wings. Thus, each parent must be heterozygous, its w allele being "overruled" by its W allele. By setting an option, a student can create a very large number of offspring all at once—a useful feature for examining the statistical distribution of traits.

challenge we give the students, along with its complement: "Is it possible for such a thing to happen in reverse? In other words, is it possible for two wingless parents to have a baby who has wings?"

A more challenging pedigree-level puzzle is one that requires the student to infer not only the genotype of an organism but also the mode of inheritance of a trait. We give students a pedigree similar to that of Fig. 6.4 but involving a new trait that the students have never observed (e.g., scaly skin). The trait is genetically inherited, but the gene that controls it has been hidden. The challenge for the students is to determine whether the trait is dominant, recessive, or incompletely dominant and to identify which chromosome carries the gene. Because they cannot observe the gene for the trait directly, much less manipulate it, the problem can only be solved by the students as it would be by scientists in the real world—by breeding the scaly dragon with others whose genotype is itself known because they are the outcome of a series of careful breeding experiments. Such a procedure exactly matches the research program of a professional geneticist and introduces students to what is loosely termed "the scientific method" at a very high level.

The pedigree level also provides an ideal setting in which to introduce the difference between the inherent probability of an event, as determined by combinatorial analysis, and the statistically determined outcomes of multiple trials. We have seen how at the cellular level one can introduce the notion of independent assortment of chromosomes and the corresponding uncertainty inherent in allele formation. The cell level, with its emphasis on meiosis and fertilization, tends to focus students' attention on the combinatorial problem of enumerating all possible outcomes of these two processes. (The Punnett square, familiar to generations of biology students, is a tabular representation aimed at facilitating this calculation.) At the pedigree level, in contrast, the relative ease of creating multiple offspring naturally leads students to consider patterns of inheritance across generations—the approach that led Mendel to the discovery of genes in the first place.

Before leaving the pedigree level, we return briefly to the problem enunciated previously—the fact that the offspring of parents each of whom exhibits a dominant trait need not themselves exhibit that trait. The reverse is not true recessive traits "breed true," in the sense that all the offspring of recessive parents are recessive. These rules, first discovered in breeding experiments, actually follow from the mechanism of inheritance itself. The pedigree level of GENSCOPE enables students to discover them by straightforward experimentation, and many students do this. More important, however, they can also use GENSCOPE to figure out why the rules apply, or more precisely, why they follow from processes that take place at lower levels. In the previous example, the students can examine the chromosomes of the parents and observe that each has one copy of the recessive *w* allele that causes wings. Because the offspring have a 50% chance of inheriting this allele from each parent, there is a 25% probability that two such heterozygous parents will have a winged offspring. In contrast, two winged parents are of necessity homozygous recessive (they must have two *w* alleles) and there is no chance of either of them passing along the dominant allele to their baby. Thus, all their offspring will have wings.

The kinds of problems that arise naturally at the population level tend to focus attention on alleles, rather than organisms—a mode of thinking characteristic of population geneticists. Here is an example: Color in dragons is a *polygenic* trait—in other words, it is caused by the combined action of two genes, named, appropriately, *col1* and *col2*. One of these genes, *col2*, has a recessive lethal allele. Since the gene is located on the X chromosome, a female receiving a single copy of this allele is born dead; a male, who has two X chromosomes, can survive as long as he has at least one wild type, dominant allele. Males who have one wild type and one lethal *col2* allele can be either bronze or azure, depending on the state of their *col1* genes. Homozygote males (who have two wild type alleles for *col2*) are topaz and amethyst.

If one starts off a population of dragons with approximately equal numbers of all six colors (in addition to the four mentioned previously for males, females may be emerald or gold), after half a dozen generations or so one finds that azure and bronze dragons are becoming quite rare, even though they are as fit and thus as able to survive and procreate as any other color. The reason lies in the fact that they carry that lethal *col2* allele. The allele does not affect the father dragon in any way, but it does decrease that father's fertility by ensuring that on average half of his daughters will die before they can procreate. Thus, although the allele is in no way harmful to the organisms that possess it, it nevertheless shows a strong tendency to die out of the population because of its harmful effect on the female offspring of its carriers.

EVALUATION OF GenScope's EFFECTIVENESS IN THE CLASSROOM

Those of us who advocate the use of learning technologies for education are obligated to address the question, "How do computers teach?"—or, if we do not believe they teach, exactly, then how is it that students learn from them? We know that students can learn in many different ways: from books, lectures, laboratory experiments, field trips, homework, tests, watching a videotape, and so on. How does learning from a computer differ from those other ways of learning?

Project Goals and Protocol

Our original hypothesis was that students using GenScope would be better able to demonstrate multilevel reasoning than students not using it would. Given that GenScope provides students with affordances not available through textbook-mediated science learning, we surmised that they might develop more powerful problem-solving strategies and skills. Our pedagogical approach was to challenge the students with problems to solve in GenScope and then leave them alone to solve them by experimentation. Our initial research plan was to compare a group of students who used GenScope in this way to another group, taught by the same teacher but without the use of the computer. Assessment was to be done in both cases by means of specially constructed paper-and-pencil tests designed to probe for multilevel reasoning.

Inevitably, the method of instructional delivery had an impact on the instructional content. The linear nature of the textbook and the multi-level nature of GenScope made it infeasible to expose students in the two classes to the same content each day. For example, using the textbook, students learn first about genes and chromosomes before they learn anything about meiosis. With GenScope, in contrast, students move back and forth at will between levels: chromosomes, genes, cell, organism, and pedigree. The amount of material, or cognitive load, that the GenScope group was exposed to on any given day was thus more complex than that to which the non-GenScope group was exposed via the textbook. However, it was precisely the students' ability to deal with this kind of exposure, and to develop multilevel thinking and problem-solving ability as a result, that we wished to evaluate.

Working in the Classroom

The classroom-based trials lasted approximately 6 weeks. After a brief period of student-directed activity on the first day, to provide initial exposure to the software, learning goals were largely set by the teacher via handouts that described a sequence of genetics problems to be solved both on and off the computer. Actual computer activity remained student directed as students worked in pairs with little or no direction. After several weeks, students in both groups were given a written assessment that included surface knowledge questions regarding rules and attributes, as well as more complex questions regarding backward inferencing. Here is an example of a surface knowledge question:

> Imagine that there is a trait in dragons that has to do with skin type. Dragons that have two copies of one allele have large scales. Dragons that have two copies of a second allele have no scales. What kind of skin would dragons that have one of each allele of the skin type gene have? (Check only one.)
>
> _____   Large scales
>
> _____   No scales
>
> _____   Small scales
>
> _____   It's impossible to tell.
>
> Please explain your choice (even if you chose "It's impossible to tell").

Given the statement of the problem, the correct answer is that it is "impossible to tell" because there is no mention in the problem of the mode of inheritance for scales. One student correctly explained his answer: "because I don't know which copy is dominant to the other." Another student who answered the question correctly explained: "because it never happened and I see nothing in the question to make it do any of them." However, the set of possible answers resembles the codominant pattern in dragons for legs. Some students appeared to recognize the similarity. One selected "Small scales" and explained: "If the Dragon with _one_ allele has _large_ scales. And if the _second_ allele has no scales, then if the dragon has one of each it should be in the middle which is small scales." Another student who selected "Small scales" explained: "because just like with legs (LL) four legs, (Ll) two legs (ll) no legs so it will be small scales."

Here is an example of a more complex question involving backward inferencing and multilevel thinking (see Fig. 6.5). It is possible that

5) Tongue rolling is a dominant trait. Two parents who are able to roll their tongues have six kids. Ernest, one of the six kids, cannot roll his tongue. His friends make fun of him and say he is adopted because all of his brothers and sisters, as well as his parents, are able to roll their tongues. Are they wrong? That is, is it possible that Ernest is not adopted? Look at the diagram below before answering the question.

Hint : You can use a Punnett square to help explain your answer.

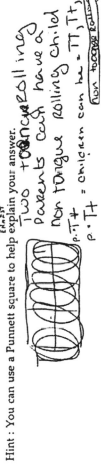

Two +Onguerolling
Parents ccú have a
non Tongue Rolling Child.
p · T̄+
p · T+ = children can be . TT, Tt, tt
                                    non toccoge Rolling

FIG. 6.5 This figure shows an example of a complex genetics question involving backward inferencing and multilevel thinking that students were asked to complete on a posttest. Many students did not use or complete the Punnett square as suggested in the problem's text but some invented their own notation as a tool to demonstrate their reasoning.

181

Ernest is not adopted, though one cannot tell for sure. He could have inherited one recessive allele from his mother and one from his father. As one student explained: "Yes, because the parents could have had a recessive gene in their makeup." Another student correctly pointed out that "Two tongue-rolling parents can have a non-tongue-rolling child." Although many students did not use the Punnett Square or make any notes, some invented their own notation as a tool to demonstrate their reasoning (see Fig. 6.5).

Student Outcomes

Based on our qualitative observations of students working with GEN-SCOPE, we believe that students not only learn basic concepts of genetics and their corresponding linguistic labels but are also able to use this knowledge and reason with it. Their interactions on the computer appear to bear this out. However, when we assessed students' knowledge and understanding via performance on paper-and-pencil tests, we found that the mean differences on test scores between GENSCOPE and non-GENSCOPE classes were not significant. In fact, performance at the computer and on tests appeared to differ significantly—students who evince an understanding of genetic principles while working with GEN-SCOPE often do not appear to use that understanding in attempting to answer questions posed to them in writing. Our experience, which is consistent with the findings of other research groups (Cognition and Technology Group at Vanderbilt, 1997), is that traditional paper-and-pencil assessment methods alone do not tell the whole story about students' learning and understanding.

Currently, we are evaluating the impact of GENSCOPE on students' science learning through a triangulation of research methodologies. In addition to quantitative student outcomes in the form of scores on paper-and-pencil assessments, we are beginning to analyze the more qualitative aspects of the learning process and the classroom environment. Specifically, we are analyzing videotaped transactions of students interacting with GENSCOPE in the classroom and transcripts of students' reflection on this experience. The data we have collected by means of interviews and observations describe the behavior of individual students in social contexts. This approach is consistent with the theory that learning occurs between individuals (Vygotsky, 1978) and with theories of *social cognition* that support the idea that any analysis of thinking and learning must be contextualized within an analysis of socially organized work (Rogoff & Lave, 1983; Wertsch, 1985). Just as the context of thinking and learning is socially organized (Levine, 1990), we believe that the interactions between the computer and students' thinking and learning in context must be observed before we can fully understand and characterize the effects of the computer in a classroom (Sheingold, Kane, & Endreweit, 1983).

The analysis of these observational data does not follow systematic models of sociolinguistic analysis for classroom discourse (Green & Wallat, 1981; Kelly & Crawford, 1996). Rather, ethnographic perspectives (Goldman-Segall, 1998) provide preliminary evidence for why achievement outcomes in the form of paper-and-pencil test results do not constitute complete data for the analysis of these students' learning. These observational data of students at the computer provides preliminary evidence that students were able to demonstrate critical thinking *in situ* though they failed to demonstrate the same knowledge on paper-and-pencil assessments. The qualitative data on *process* offer a rebuttal of the quantitative findings on achievement outcomes as well as an extension of the GENSCOPE group's learning experience. "The Horns Dilemma" is one example out of many in our data.

In this problem, students are asked to predict and then construct the genotype of two horned parent organisms that can produce hornless offspring. As we have seen previously, horns are a dominant trait in the dragon species. Therefore, both parents must be heterozygous (i.e., possessing one dominant and one recessive allele for horns) to display the trait, yet be capable (by each supplying the recessive allele) of producing an offspring that does not.

Although this exercise involves a simple dominant–recessive trait, it forces students to reason at multiple levels and from effect to cause. To solve the problem correctly, the students must

- understand the phenotype-genotype relation,
- know the genotypes corresponding to horns and to no horns,
- understand that offspring get half of their genes from each parent,
- understand that both parents can either be homozygous or heterozygous for horns to display the trait,
- recognize that both parents must be heterozygous to display the horns trait and have an offspring that does not, and
- understand that the hornless offspring must inherit the recessive allele from each parent.

Students must also know how to use the software to make a male and female organism, examine the genes to make sure they are appropriate and alter them if they are not, take a cell from each parent organism, perform meiosis on both cells, identify sperm and egg, examine gametes to find a pair that will produce a hornless baby, and then fertilize them to produce a homozygous recessive zygote.

On the same day that students worked on the Horns Dilemma, they were given an isomorphic activity, the Sickle-Cell Anemia Problem posed as a paper-and-pencil quiz item. This problem challenges students to employ critical thinking around an understanding of Mendel's law of dominance, rules of inheritance, and transfer of understanding from the GenScope computer activity. It was designed to "test" for the same domain-specific knowledge as the Horns Dilemma but involves a different trait and is represented using written language.[3]

If a baby dragon has sickle-cell anemia disease and neither of the parent dragons have it, what can you say about the parent dragons? Circle all responses that apply:

(a) Mom is homozygous dominant.

(b) Mom is homozygous recessive.

(c) Mom is heterozygous.

(d) Dad is homozygous dominant.

(e) Dad is homozygous recessive.

(f) Dad is heterozygous.

(g) This cannot happen.

To solve this problem correctly, the students must

- be familiar with specific genetics vocabulary and its relation to concepts,
- understand that offspring get half of their genes from each parent,
- understand that both parents can either be homozygous or heterozygous to carry the sickle cell trait,

---

[3]Prior to this session and approximately 2 weeks into the trial, the teacher introduced the requisite genetics vocabulary. By this time, students had manipulated many, if not all, of the abstract concepts represented by the linguistic labels in the form of vocabulary words and definitions.

- recognize that both parents must be heterozygous to carry the trait but not express it, and
- understand that the baby with sickle cell disease must inherit the recessive allele from each parent.

In the transcript of the videotape, one of the students, F, not only displays the ability to solve the Horns Dilemma *in situ*, but also recognizes its correspondence to the Sickle-Cell Anemia task, an isomorphic problem. A few minutes later, however, F is unable to solve the isomorphic problem when it is presented as part of a paper-and-pencil assessment:

> F and R, two students in an urban high school first-year biology class, usually work as a pair when solving genetics problems on GenScope. F is a quiet and withdrawn student who has very little interaction with his classmates or his teacher. In fact, he rarely speaks at all except to R, a classmate and friend. R is a bright and interested student, but he has a low attendance record. In the classroom, F sits with his head down most of the time; he does not participate. In the computer lab, there are days when F does not work, but quite often (more than half the time) he does. In this transcript, F has just completed the Horns Dilemma problem. R has come in late to class and sits near F. R is asking the teacher about the Sickle Cell Anemia Problem. F is trying to help the teacher explain how babies can express traits that their parents do not express.
>
> R: (to Teacher) If your parents don't have something, how can you get it? (Teacher turns to blackboard near R's seat and begins to draw a Punnett square)
>
> F: (gestures his hand over toward Teacher and R. He yells out to Teacher by last name) James! James! Lookit ...It's like this (pointing to the computer screen where he has created horned parents who have hornless offspring in GenScope). The parents have horns and they don't ...

Note that F's gestures and words are a demonstration of his understanding of inheritance outcomes and of the similarity between these isomorphic problems. Furthermore, he reaches his hand out and desperately tries to get the teacher's attention to help the teacher explain it. The teacher either ignores F or doesn't hear him, so we do not know what F would have explained if he had been recognized. We do see that R does not understand how "you can get somethin' if your parents don't have it" whereas F does. When F hears R pose a question to the teacher that reflects what he himself has already learned, he tries to explain what he knows. F appears to recognize the similarity in the solution space of the two problems, transfer his knowledge, and explain this similarity in his understanding through speech.

Later the same day, however, neither R nor F were able to demonstrate this knowledge in written form. From their written responses, therefore, it is not clear that F has a different level of understanding than R has, nor is it demonstrable that either has grasped the concept.

Reflections

We have argued in this chapter for a unique niche for the computer in education, a niche whose value we are just beginning to explore. Focusing on a particular paradigm—the computer-based manipulative—we have tried to show how it can be used in science education to help students acquire the "habits of mind" of the professional scientist, learning to reason about the world around them in terms of abstract concepts that are not directly perceptible. We hasten to add that the ability to reason in this way is not new—all of us use mental concepts every day to make sense of our world. What is different in science is that the concepts involved are unfamiliar and often counterintuitive to the learner. In one sense, then, the designer of a CBM, by offering students a carefully selected set of affordances and constraints, in effect creates for them a world that fosters the creation of particular scientific concepts—concepts that do not arise naturally in the everyday world.

In preliminary classroom trials, primarily in urban classrooms, we have verified that students are capable of solving quite difficult problems with a minimum of assistance when working directly on the computer. More unexpected, perhaps, is the fact that the overwhelming majority of students greatly enjoyed the process, even though (or more likely, because) they found it difficult. Here are some representative quotes, taken from "exit interviews" conducted with ninth-grade students in the spring of 1997:

> I liked it when we were makin' the babies and stuff and we had to try to figure out how one of them gets one disease and how the other one didn't and stuff like that. ...it showed us more and we understood it more 'cause we were doin' it ourself.

> Other classes are boring. No fun. All we do is work, work, work. They don't try to make it interesting or nothin'. Here we had time, we could talk about it yet we were still learnin', we had class discussions. Other classes they just sit there and teach. And we just write uuuhhhhhh! It's aggravatin'! (sighs).

I like the genetics better because it was working on the computers? But now we're back in books it's like I hate—I like readin' books but them books are just boring. They're boring! It's like nnnnnnn ain't nothin' interestin' in here—could I go back down to the computer room?

Sometimes it was frustrating because I was like ugghhh! I couldn't get it!

It is good to have another person with you 'cause they could help you if you are havin' ... trouble? But if you are not, you could put your mind into it, you could say 'OK I wanna see what I could do without no help'. You see it's like a challenge you doin'. Some people like havin' challenge, some people don't.

I listened, I started lookin' at the papers, tryin' to put everything together, try to use the computer to see what I thought was right or was it wrong and that's how I learned.

However, what did they learn? That question, it turns out, is harder to answer than we had anticipated for reasons that we have alluded to previously. Students' performance on the computer and in classroom discussions is not reflected in their scores on written assessments that have been expressly designed to probe for multilevel reasoning. Students exposed to GENSCOPE do not perform measurably better on such tests than those who have been taught in a conventional classroom.

We do not yet understand the reasons for the disparity between students' solid achievements in the computer-based learning environment and their disappointing scores on written tests. One theory considers the notion that their developing knowledge is so fragile that any change in the learning environment negatively impacts performance. Four distinct types of change suggest themselves:

Language Barrier. GENSCOPE uses very little specialized language. Representations of abstract concepts are very concrete in this learning environment. Whereas GENSCOPE does not require the student to assign linguistic labels to genetic concepts, subsequent paper-and-pencil tests of that student's understanding are entirely dependent on the use of language. We surmise that there may be a mismatch between students' hands-on, inarticulate knowledge acquired through interaction with GENSCOPE only, and the linguistically encoded knowledge required to respond to written assessments.

Shift In Modality. There is a fundamental difference between using a mouse and using a pencil. It is possible that students who have constructed knowledge with the former cannot easily demonstrate that knowledge with the latter.

Examination Effect.   It is likely that the psychological conditions involved in the nature of test-taking itself has a negative impact on the performance of students, regardless of modality. Students faced with the stress of trying to answer questions in the context of a "final exam" may perform significantly more poorly than students who think they are "just solving problems."

New Understanding.   It may be that understanding *in situ* is qualitatively different from understanding gained through interactions with the written word. Traditional expectations about the ways in which knowledge is encoded may not apply to learning that takes place through the use of computer-based manipulatives.

It is important to bear in mind the students' own perception of the classroom environment and of learning in general. Each student brings to the classroom certain beliefs about learning as well as a set of expectations surrounding the academic experience. The pedagogical changes entailed by the introduction of a new technology such as GenScope are as unfamiliar to students as they are to teachers, and neither may be able to adapt adequately to them, especially in a relatively short period. It may be naive to expect major benefits from changes in the learning environment that last only a few weeks.

During 1998 (subsequent to the preparation of this chapter) we will implement an experiment designed to investigate in detail students' understanding and performance in multiple modalities. We are design- ing an experiment to observe the situation modeled by F and R, as described previously. (This incident was discovered quite by accident in an analysis of videotaped sessions performed long after the students had completed their written exams.) We will provide students with isomor- phic pairs of activities to be completed both on and off the computer. Some paper-and-pencil items will be presented as non-exam items. We will compare student performances on and off the computer and in and out of exam conditions. We will also interview students using a "think- aloud" protocol designed to probe their reasoning during problem solving. We hope to trace the evolution of understanding regarding particular knowledge and whether and how that understanding differs under different conditions. We will pay particular attention to students' perspectives of their learning experiences with varied tasks.

CONCLUSION

Although we are at an early stage in understanding exactly what is happening in the GenScope classrooms and the relation of these activities and experiences on students' learning, our preliminary research suggests that there are demonstrable effects on students and on teachers. The GenScope curriculum is a challenging one. Students are offered very little assistance and are required to "think on their feet" in a way that most of them are quite unused to doing in school. With very few exceptions, we have observed our students rise to this challenge, and we have witnessed the pride they take in doing so. Our greatest challenge, at this point, is to help the students translate their newfound knowledge and skills to better performance on traditional paper-and-pencil tests, as tests of this type will no doubt continue to be used for large-scale assessment purposes in the foreseeable future. However, to do this we must develop more complex instruments to support investigation into the processes and products of learning. We are obliged to address not only the question of "How do computers teach?" but also, "How do students learn with computers?" and "How do we evaluate learning situated at the computer?"

The verb "to learn" means something very different depending on the different modalities of learning. Thus, learning to ride a bicycle is not the same as learning the capitals of the states, which in turn differs from learning genetics. Just as one cannot evaluate someone's ability to ride a bike with a paper-and-pencil test, so it may be difficult to test GenScope-acquired knowledge via the written word. This may be especially true with the inner-city population, whose reading and writing skills are below grade level. Thus, our carefully designed assessments may not be measuring what the students know. To test this hypothesis, we are modifying our software so as to make it possible to assess the students on items similar to those we have developed, but situated directly on the computer. The use of such so-called "embedded assessments" may improve students' scores. More important, it may help us to understand, explain, and affect the process of learning, the impact of technology, and the complex interaction between the two.

ACKNOWLEDGMENTS

The work described herein was performed under two grants from the Applications of Advanced Technology Program of the National Science Foundation, most recently grant number REC-9553438. The support of the Foundation is gratefully acknowledged. The authors have also benefitted enormously from discussions with many colleagues, among whom they would like to mention Joyce Schwartz, Eric Neumann, Ann Kindfield, and Daniel Hickey. Finally, the authors would like to acknowledge the students and teachers who have participated in this work. Their continued support allows us to merge theoretical views with practical findings in support of educational reform.

REFERENCES

Carey, S. (1986). Cognitive science and science education. *American Psychologist, 41*(10), 1123–1130.

Cognition and Technology Group at Vanderbilt. (1997). *The Jasper project: Lessons in curriculum, instruction, assessment, and professional development.* Mahwah, NJ: Lawrence Erlbaum Associates.

Dufresne, R. J., Gerace, W. J, Hardiman, P. T., & Mestre, J. P. (1992). Constraining novices to perform expertlike problem analyses: Effects on schema acquisition. *Journal of the Learning Sciences, 2*(3), 307–331.

Goldman-Segall, R. (1998). *Points of viewing children's thinking: A digital ethnographer's journey.* Mahwah, NJ: Lawrence Erlbaum Associates.

Green, J., & Wallat, C. (1981). Mapping instructional conversations: A sociolinguistic ethnography. In J. Green & C. Wallat (Eds.), *Ethnography and language in educational settings* (pp. 161–205). Norwood, NJ: Ablex.

Johnstone, A. H. (1991). Why is science difficult to learn? Things are seldom what they seem. *Journal of Computer Assisted Learning, 7*(20), 75–83.

Johnston-Slack, S., & Stewart, J. (1990). High school students' problem-solving performance on realistic genetics problems. *Journal of Research in Science Teaching, 27*(1), 55–67.

Kelly, G. J., & Crawford, T. (1996). Students' interactions with computer representations: Analysis of discourse in laboratory groups. *Journal of Research in Science Teaching, 33*(7), 693–707.

Kindfield, A. C. H. (1994). Understanding a basic biological process: Expert and novice models of meiosis. *Science Education, 78*(3), 255–283.

Levine, H. G. (1990). Models of qualitative data use in the assessment of classroom-based microcomputer education programs. *Journal of Educational Computing Research, 6*(4), 461–477.

Mendel, G. (1866). "Versuche uber Pflanzen-Hybriden," Verhandlungen des Naturforschenden Vereines Abhandlungen, Brunn, Vol. 4, pp. 3–47.

National Research Council. (1996). *National science education standards.* Washington, DC: National Academy Press.

Rogoff, B., & Lave, J. (Eds., 1983). *Everyday cognition: Its development in social context.* Cambridge, MA: Harvard University Press.

Sheingold, K., Kane, J. H., & Endreweit, M. E. (1983). Microcomputer use in schools: Developing a research agenda. *Harvard Educational Review, 53*(4), 412–432.

Stewart, J., & Hafner, R. (1994). Research on problem solving: Genetics. In D. Gabel (Ed.), *Handbook of research on science teaching and learning* (pp. 284–300). New York: Macmillan.

Vygotsky, L. (1978). *Mind in society: The development of higher psychological processes*. Cambridge, MA: Harvard University Press.

Wertsch, J. V. (1985). *Vygotsky and the social formation of mind*. Cambridge, MA: Harvard University Press.

7

The Knowledge Integration Environment: Helping Students Use the Internet Effectively

James D. Slotta and Marcia C. Linn
University of California at Berkeley

How can we prepare students to make the Internet a lifelong learning resource as many envision? Because of its scope, flexibility, and accessibility, the Internet has clear promise for science instruction. However, students require new kinds of support in making sense of information from the World Wide Web, as they must recognize and interpret "evidence" from a wide range of new sources. Much of the information on the Internet is written by amateur authors with the purpose of convincing readers, but they might be interpreted by students as established fact. Additionally, many Web sites are long and complex, so relevant science content is often difficult to discern. How can we help students recognize the valid information from the invalid, or the credible sources from the noncredible ones? In this paper, we explore how students learn to ask critical questions that reveal the strengths and weaknesses of incomplete or conjectural information.

We have developed the Knowledge Integration Environment (KIE) to engage students in sustained investigation, providing them with cognitive and procedural supports as they make use of the Internet in their science classroom. Students work collaboratively in KIE, performing design, critique, or theory–comparison projects that involve scientific "evidence" from the World Wide Web. Students working within the KIE environment can take advantage of cognitive, social, and procedural supports, including checklists to help monitor progress and tools to help organize thoughts about evidence. These software elements allow for the design of curriculum projects that support knowledge, although project designers must incorporate them appropriately to guarantee success. The KIE software and curriculum are complementary tools that work together to support students as they use the Internet in constructive, autonomous science learning. In this paper, we focus on those aspects of KIE that support students in critiquing Internet evidence.

To illustrate how KIE supports and guides students, we describe research where students in an eighth-grade science class performed a KIE project relating to passive solar architecture. In their class, KIE projects are used to supplement an existing physical science curriculum that deals with topics of light, heat, and sound energy. Several KIE projects are used during the semester to help students integrate the ideas they have learned in other classroom activities (e.g., labs and lectures). This paper is concerned with one such activity, known as "Sunlight, SunHEAT!"

In the Sunlight, SunHEAT! project, students are asked to survey six different Web sites that deal with passive solar energy. These Web sites, selected deliberately by the project designer on the basis of their good science content, still vary in terms of how much science they include, their purpose (e.g., sophisticated advertisement for a home design vs. carefully prepared educational resource), their target audience, their overall length and complexity, and their overall relevance to the topic of passive solar energy. KIE helps students to successfully critique such evidence from the web and to ask productive questions to help them apply its content in a design or debate project.

KIE includes cognitive guidance to help students understand and interpret evidence, procedural guidance for using the KIE software effectively, and social supports to encourage discourse and sharing of ideas. For example, KIE prompts students to ask questions, such as: Who authored this evidence? What is their profession? Is this evidence useful to you? How trustworthy is it? In the Sunlight, SunHEAT! activity, the diverse set of evidence allows students to practice these valuable critiquing skills. For each piece of evidence, students formulate two "critical questions" that address specific gaps in their own science knowledge. This project allows students to think actively about how evidence impacts their understanding. Students using a KIE project like Sunlight, SunHEAT! connect and link their ideas through personally meaningful activities.

We describe the kind of learning supported by KIE as *knowledge integration*. The overarching pedagogical framework which guides the development of the KIE software and curriculum is known as *Scaffolded Knowledge Integration*. This chapter begins with a discussion of the principles of Scaffolded Knowledge Integration, offers a brief review of the various components of the KIE software, and then describes research on the design of cognitive guidance for the Sunlight, SunHEAT! project. We explore the nature of students' critiques and questions and identify ways to scaffold such knowledge integration activities.

HOW DOES KNOWLEDGE INTEGRATION WORK?

Since 1985, we have worked in a middle school classroom developing the Computer as Learning Partner curriculum, where students work collaboratively to understand science topics relating to light, heat, and sound (Linn, 1992; Linn & Songer, 1991). Through this ongoing effort of principled refinement, we have formulated a theory of learning as *knowledge integration*. This theory views learning as a dynamic process where students build connections between their existing knowledge and the curriculum content.

In our view, students come to science class with a repertoire of models of scientific phenomena as suggested by work of Piaget (1970), diSessa (1988, 1993), and others. We use the term *model* loosely to refer to ideas, conjectures, principles, visualizations, and examples from everyday life. All of these mental constructs are drawn upon by students in support of their reasoning, and we refer to their totality as a *repertoire of models*.

Students engage in knowledge integration when they add new models to this repertoire, refine existing models, and restructure their knowledge. Our theory guides the design of science projects where students are enabled to develop the autonomous learning skills they will need for a lifetime of knowledge integration. Thus, a curriculum should help students add accessible models, scaffold critical knowledge integration skills, and provide social supports for learning.

Our view suggests new goals for science education to emphasize knowledge integration rather than the transmission of science content. Students should learn how to add new ideas to their existing repertoire, select appropriate models for use in solving their problems, identify good explanations, and make sense of new ideas and evidence. Finally, science instruction should help every student become a lifelong learner.

Knowledge integration can often go awry, as an extensive body of research demonstrates. Reif and Larkin (1991) showed that students often connect physics ideas superficially to formulas rather than concepts. Soloway (1985) has shown that students connect programming ideas to syntax rather than to processes or patterns. Chi, Feltovitch, and Glaser (1981) found that students organize knowledge around apparatus rather than around principles in introductory physics courses. How can we guide the learning process so students develop fruitful ideas rather than superficial ones that are not connected to their repertoire of existing models? What models can we add to the mix of ideas that students already possess so they engage in fruitful knowledge integration, and what activities can we provide to enable students to organize their existing ideas productively?

Our work on the Computer as Learning Partner (CLP) project has validated our approach for providing cognitive, procedural, and social supports for knowledge integration. Open-ended science exploration environments often fail to provide adequate scaffolding for knowledge integration. For example, "discovery learning" does not provide the supports available in most real-world scientific investigations (Eylon and Linn, 1988).

In our own research community, we provide extensive resources for project work. Individuals start by undertaking projects in supportive research groups with experienced collaborators or in classes where regular guidance is provided. We have an agreed-on vocabulary, criteria for evaluating progress, and a professional practice of critiquing. Generally, investigators draw on a wealth of knowledge of related work to design a project of their own, with much research consisting of replication and extension of existing findings. Finally, there exists an established set of methodologies that support research efforts, as well as reward structures for successful work. In unscaffolded exploration, many students fail to make real progress toward knowledge integration because they lack these valuable supports.

Based on our research in the CLP project, we have formulated a set of design principles in what we call the Scaffolded Knowledge Integration framework. The CLP research demonstrated that students approach the study of heat and temperature with a wide array of loosely connected ideas and language, sometimes suggesting that they view heat and temperature as being one and the same (e.g., "turn up the heat; turn up the temperature"), whereas at other times maintaining their difference (e.g., "The baby has a temperature so heat the bottle."). They may connect insulation with physical barriers and distinguish heating from cooling. They may have fruitful expectations about whether a metal or a wood stick would prevent burned hands when roasting marshmallows, but harbor less helpful views about the insulating properties of aluminum foil (e.g., students in our CLP classroom often suggest that aluminum foil is a good insulator for wrapping cold cokes or hot potatoes!).

In the CLP work, we sought to foster knowledge integration by engaging students in sorting out these ideas and coming up with a predictive set of models. We helped students to develop personal criteria for linking ideas and expectations about what it means to explain and what it means to understand. Knowledge integration is a complex cognitive and social process that is influenced by many factors (e.g., the student's knowledge of domain material; the nature of the instruction provided; the student's values and attitudes about school and learning; social interactions within the classroom). We have articulated four major principles of our theory that include cognitive, social, and epistemological components. We have drawn heavily on these principles in designing the Knowledge Integration Environment software and curriculum.

1. New Goals for Science Learning

We believe that new science learning goals are required to shift students (and teachers) away from their traditional focus on memorizing content material and performing well on standardized tests. We advocate a curriculum that emphasizes opportunities for students to evaluate scientific evidence according to their own personal understanding, to articulate their own theories and explanations, and to participate actively in principled design. In this way, students gain valuable lifelong learning skills that will serve them in all future endeavors. We also propose starting in middle school or earlier to establish a habit of distinguishing among ideas and reconciling diverse perspectives.

The Scaffolded Knowledge Integration framework recommends that any models introduced by instructors should connect to students' everyday life (Linn & Muilenberg, 1996). Many researchers have called for explicit instruction in connecting ideas with everyday experiences. Reif and Heller (1982) in physics, Anderson, Boyle, & Reiser (1985) in tutoring, and others have reinforced the notion of using such connections. Other approaches involve the modeling of ideas in the form of case studies (Guzdial, Rappin, & Carlson, 1995; Jacobson & Archodidou, chap. 5, this volume; Linn & Clancy, 1990), visualization tools (White & Frederiksen, 1989), or employing spontaneous "think-aloud" problem solving in class (Schoenfeld, 1985). Students also need to develop autonomy in evaluating connections and seeking out disconnected information. Thus, we find this process of connecting ideas most valuable when combined with efforts to encourage students to emulate it autonomously. Schoenfeld stressed this in his work on learning mathematics. He modeled the process of solving complex problems and encouraged students to emulate his approach, often asking whether or not they have yet completed a problem to encourage them to find more connections and to test the connections they have made. In the Scaffolded Knowledge Integration framework, connecting ideas is an extremely important element, and is captured by our principle of "making thinking visible."

2. Make Thinking Visible

An important aspect of helping students work within their own repertoire of models is to help students make their own thinking visible, as suggested by many authors (e.g., Collins, Brown and Holum, 1991; see also Jacobson, Angulo, & Kozma, chap. 1, this volume). We provide students with tools and opportunities to represent their own thinking. This includes providing students with feedback about their current models. We also scaffold students in acquiring more sophisticated models, as well as more diverse models. Several types of scaffolding help, including cognitive, procedural, and metacognitive supports. In the CLP curriculum, we designed accessible models of new or difficult concepts. These models might be "intermediate causal models" (e.g., White & Frederiksen, 1989; Slotta & Chi, 1996) or qualitative models (e.g., Linn & Songer, 1991). For example, in thermodynamics, a "heat flow" rather than a sophisticated molecular account might be more accessible to students who hold the intuitive conception of heat as a caloric-like substance (see Linn & Songer, 1991; Slotta, Chi, & Joram, 1995; Linn & Muilenberg, 1996).

3. Autonomous Student Activities

We emphasize activities that connect to students' concerns and engage students in sustained reasoning. Design or critique projects that require students to form opinions or explanations about evidence or to make principled design decisions encourage autonomy. To make such projects authentic, we draw on students' existing knowledge and incorporate scientific evidence that students find personally relevant.

4. Social Supports for Learning

The use of social supports for learning can help students learn valuable skills of collaboration and gain insights from their peers. Science learning is rarely performed in isolation from one's peers; rather, peer exchange is often vital to learning (e.g., Brown & Campione, 1990; Vygotsky, 1987). Science projects should be designed to foster collaborative work, both because this will be an important skill for students throughout their lives, and also because it is an efficient means of learning how others connect ideas. Designing an effective social context for learning involves guiding the process of social interaction. Dewey (1920) called for taking advantage of the social context of learning at the turn of the century. Recent environments such as CSILE (Computer Supported Interactive Learning Environment; Scardamalia & Bereiter, 1991, 1992), KGS (Kids as Global Scientists; Songer, 1993, 1996), Community of Learners (Brown & Campione, 1994), CaMILE (Collaborative and Multimedia Learning Environment; Guzdial & Turns, chap. 8, this volume; Guzdial et al., 1995), and the Multi-Forum Kiosk (Hoadley & Hsi, 1993) demonstrate the advantages of having students discuss their efforts at knowledge integration with peers.

Hearing ideas in the words of peers, validating each others' ideas, and asking questions of peers can all foster links and connections among ideas. Yet, these efforts can fail if students lack important ideas, copy paragraphs from texts without reflection, or reinforce unfruitful ideas held by others. Opportunities for class discourse succeed when structured into the curriculum, so students share opinions, offer feedback to others, and reflect on the mix of ideas. In this area, we seek ways to support all students in their learning of science and to actively work against social status or gender stereotypes that discourage some groups from participating in science discourse.

To make a learning environment productive involves principled design and redesign. In developing the Knowledge Integration Environment we have closely adhered to the principles of Scaffolded Knowledge Integration, and have refined our KIE software and curriculum after each semester of classroom trials. We now describe the KIE software, illustrating how it incorporates the principles of Scaffolded Knowledge Integration, including the constraints involved in building effective curriculum units.

THE KNOWLEDGE INTEGRATION ENVIRONMENT

The KIE software implements the Scaffolded Knowledge Integration framework, providing an instructional shell that is suitable for any science domain and for students in Grades 4 to 14. We conceive of KIE as a platform to scaffold students as they work on projects that rely on scientific "evidence" from the web, as well as on other evidence from their classwork. Our ultimate goal is to scaffold autonomous learning, which includes the abilities to integrate diverse sources of information and to critique their credibility. Clearly, the World Wide Web is an ideal domain for such learning, especially given its breadth of content and convenient location (right on the student's desktop!). We are challenged to take advantage of the ambiguous credibility of web resources, which has a clear application to the fostering of critiquing skills.

KIE consists of both custom and commercial software components, all working together to support collaborative work as students use web evidence, compose scientific arguments, or design artifacts. KIE provides students with access to relevant Internet evidence, online guidance of three varieties (procedural, cognitive, and social), organizational tools to scaffold project completion, argument-building tools to assist in sorting and interpreting evidence, an online discussion tool that supports meaningful peer interactions, and web-based search tools to scaffold collaborative search. The KIE software runs on the student's personal computer, helps keep track of students' work and helps manage the project flow, and interacts with various web-based tools. KIE includes several major software components: KIE Evidence Database, Mildred the Cow Guide, the KIE Tool Palette, Activities Checklist, SenseMaker, and SpeakEasy.

The KIE Evidence Database is a structured database of web resources that can be used in KIE projects. These are Web sites that have been selected by a KIE curriculum designer because they are relevant to the project or are sometimes created specifically for the project. Each of these items is added to a database of evidence, where it is annotated with conceptual keywords (e.g., "light," "heat," "evolution"), target age level, and estimated time required for reading. In addition, evidence-specific guidance is attached to each item in the database.

Designing evidence and guidance to help students develop integrated understanding is a primary focus of the research reported in this chapter. Web sites often consist of many linked pages, which could quickly lead students into confusion or wasted effort. We avoid selecting highly complicated sites and help students navigate and use selected evidence by providing each evidence item with an "Evidence cover page." The Evidence cover page contains guidance to be read by the student in advance of exploring the evidence. We refer to this guidance as "Advance Organization" information. Figure 7.1 shows an example of the Evidence cover page for a lengthy Web site whose topic is passive solar architecture. Because the content of the site is so relevant to the project topic of passive solar energy, we chose to include the site as evidence. The Evidence cover page provides students with advance guidance about the overall structure of the Web site, how to use it effectively, and some things to keep in mind while surveying its content. In the following passages, we describe research on the design of such Advance Organization information to help students critique and ask questions about web materials.

To provide additional guidance while students are actually viewing the evidence, we have written a custom piece of software, known as *Mildred the Cow Guide*. This interactive guidance tool allows students to receive cognitive guidance on demand about any piece of evidence they are reviewing. Figure 7.2 shows Mildred providing hints about the piece of evidence whose Evidence Cover page appears in Fig. 7.1. Students consult Mildred when they are confused by the evidence or when they are struggling with the project activities. Mildred does not provide students with any answers. Rather, her "hints" come in the form of questions that focus students on important "science content" within the evidence. The question of how to design guidance for students is an ongoing part of the KIE research program (Bell, Davis, & Linn, 1995; Davis, 1997).

The KIE Tool Palette, seen at the right of Fig. 7.3, provides links to all the components of the KIE. By clicking on buttons for one of these

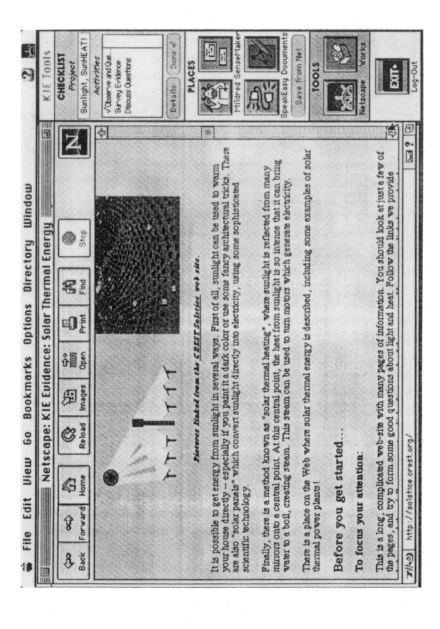

FIG. 7.1. The Evidence cover page for one piece of evidence from the Sunlight, SunHEAT project. Note, some additional text occurs "below" what is visible in the figure.

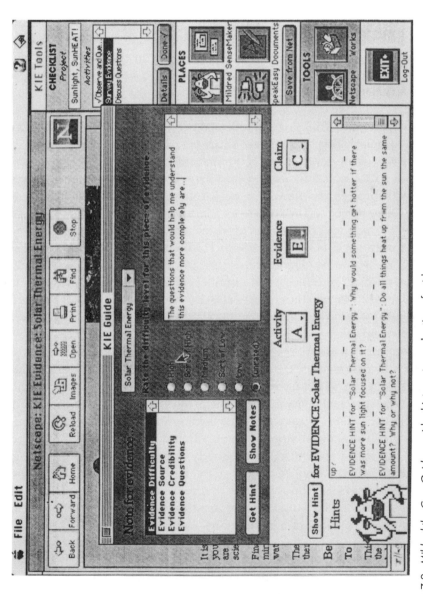

FIG. 7.2 *Mildred the Cow Guide provides hints, notes and rating of evidence.*

tools (or the Activities Checklist, described in the following paragraph), students bring the chosen software to the foreground of the screen. This might be Mildred, the "Netbook" (a tool for organizing project documents, visible in Fig. 7.3 behind the Details window), Netscape (the web browser employed by KIE), the SpeakEasy (an electronic discussion tool, described in the following paragraph), or SenseMaker (an evidence sorting and argument creation tool, also discussed in the following paragraph). The Tool Palette is one constant in the KIE's otherwise dynamic appearance, providing students with continuous access to all KIE functionality.

The Activities Checklist, visible above the Tool Palette in Fig. 7.3, guides students through a sequence of project activities, such as "State your opinion about a debate," "Survey evidence from the web," or "Revise your design." When students enter the KIE, they log in and choose a project from a menu of options. Typically, students engage in one KIE project at a time, but we foresee contexts in which students would have more than one project underway. The KIE software manages students' work, and keeps track of which activities have been completed. This information is made visible to students in the "activity checklist" that is always visible to students as they work on a project. The checklist displays which activities have been checked off, and it provides an interface with which students can check (or uncheck) activities that they have completed. The "current activity" is the first one on the list that is not checked off.

Students can always request detailed procedural guidance about an activity by clicking the "Details" button that appears below the checklist. This brings up the Details window (also shown in Fig. 7.3) with guidance about the current activity or about the project as a whole (known as "The Big Picture"). The Details window provides students with explicit instructions about exactly what to do (e.g., "Survey three pieces of evidence from the list of evidence") and equally important, how to do it (e.g., "Click on Mildred, choose a piece of evidence from the list of evidence there, then perform the rating for that piece of evidence and fill in the Notes section"). This kind of procedural scaffolding relieves the instructor of what is otherwise a standard component of using computer technology in the classroom: running around from student to student, answering questions, and helping them figure out what to click on next. We continue to refine our guidance software, providing the teacher with more time to focus on students' conceptual concerns. Overall, students

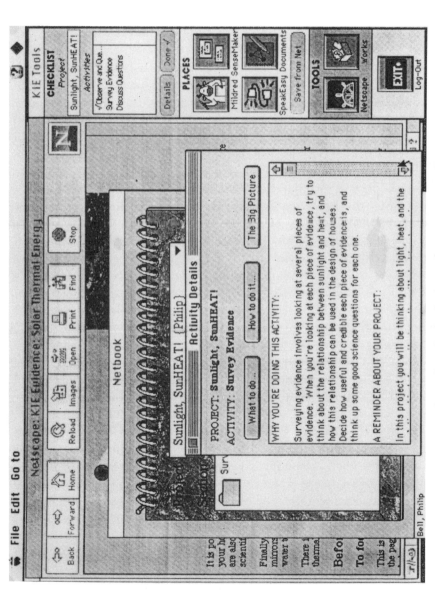

FIG. 7.3 *The KIE Tool Palette and Details window with* Netbook *in background.*

who use KIE become quickly familiar with the various tools and guidance structures, and rarely get confused about "what to do next."

The SenseMaker provides students with an effective way of "making thinking visible," as shown in Fig. 7.4. Developed by Philip Bell (Linn, Bell, & Hsi, in press), this unique argument editor allows students to create argument "frames" (represented by the nested boxes) and sort evidence into similarity based groupings to support their argument. For example, as shown in Fig. 7.4, when students are asked to compare two theories of "How far does light go," they are provided with initial SenseMaker, frames labeled, "Light goes forever" and "Light dies out." Students review the evidence on the web, take notes on each item in Mildred, return to SenseMaker and "sort" each item into a relevant frame. New frames can be created, either within the higher level frames, or in parallel to them. In this way, students are scaffolded to make use of the evidence in forming their own argument about a topic. Students can "follow" the Evidence links from SenseMaker directly to the evidence (which opens up the relevant web site in Netscape), and then return to SenseMaker in a cyclical fashion. It is also possible to make new evidence items in the SenseMaker corresponding to personally relevant experiences or insights. When students have completed such a sorting task, they are left with a visible representation of their interpretation of all the evidence, which allows them to reflect and make connections between the evidence and their existing repertoire of models.

The SpeakEasy provides an online asynchronous discussion tool for students. When first joining a SpeakEasy discussion, students log in and respond to a seed "topic statement" that was provided by the instructor. By requiring this initial opinion, each student is enabled to take some position before reading other students' comments. The student then proceeds to the conversation area (displayed in Fig. 7.5) to read and respond to other students' statements, as well as to offer new topics for conversation. Each comment is represented with social information, including a small image of the contributor's face and first name, as well as an indication of whether the comment is a statement, an addition to a statement, a rebuttal of a statement, a question, or a response to a question.

Social discourse is an intrinsic part of knowledge integration, and a lifelong learning skill that should be an important goal of all education (Hsi, 1996; Scardamalia, Bereiter, McLean, Swallow, & Woodrull, 1989). Traditionally, teachers have only a limited amount of time to allow for

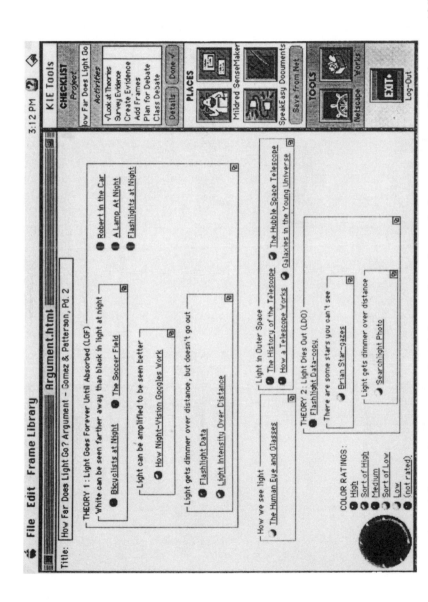

FIG. 7.4 The *Sensemaker* tool allows students to "sort" evidence links into relevant frames. Students can create new links or frames, and follow links to view evidence in Netscape.

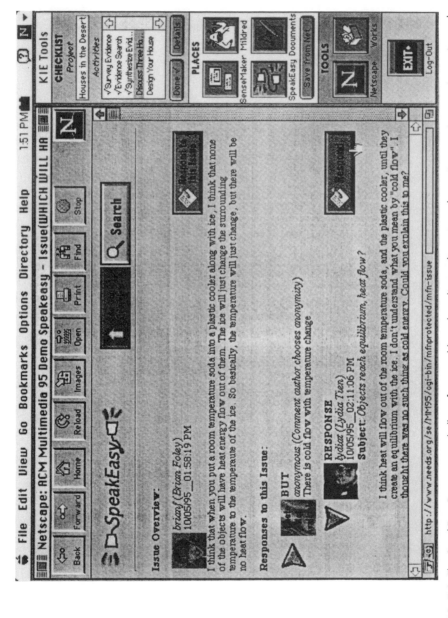

FIG. 7.5 The SpeakEasy Discussion tool allows for equitable and productive discussions about science topics, peer interaction and exchange of ideas.

classroom discussion, and management of productive discourse is a very difficult task. Typically, few students are able to voice an opinion in response to a teacher's comments, with even less exchange occurring between students (Wellesley College Center for Research on Women, 1992).

In contrast, electronic discussions can occur asynchronously, extending throughout the duration of the project or even the semester. Hsi and Hoadley (1997) found that electronic discussions enable equitable participation in scientific discourse. Their studies compared gender differences in participation between class discussion and electronic discussion. All electronic discussions are characterized by high levels of conceptual content, elaborations, and question asking. Overall, students generate a repertoire of models for phenomena, ask content-focusing questions, and provided causal explanations. We continue to research the domain of electronic discussion, both in terms of matters of equity in the classroom (Hsi, 1997), as well as in understanding issues of social representations (Hoadley et. al, 1997).

In addition to the software components outlined previously, we are working in partnership with scientists and teachers to create KIE projects for our growing library of activities (Fig. 7.6 shows the Project Manager tool that can be used for this purpose). In all of this work, we continue to research important issues surrounding pedagogical approaches, as well as issues with the use of Internet materials. In the sections below, we present an overview of this work and discuss in detail one strand of our classroom research relating to how KIE projects can foster vital critiquing skills. (For more details about the software, curriculum, and partnership opportunities, see our KIE Web site: http:\\www.kie.berkeley.edu.)

The KIE software provides many important tools and opportunities for knowledge integration activities. However, the design of curriculum projects and related materials remains equally central. Table 7.1 presents a list of the kinds of activities that characterize successful KIE projects. A growing library of KIE projects is currently available, providing teachers with access to a curriculum that meets these criteria.

Designing Guidance for Sunlight, SunHEAT!

How can we design KIE activities to help students critique web evidence by scrutinizing its authorship and assessing its relevance to the project topic (in this case, passive solar energy)? How can we help students focus

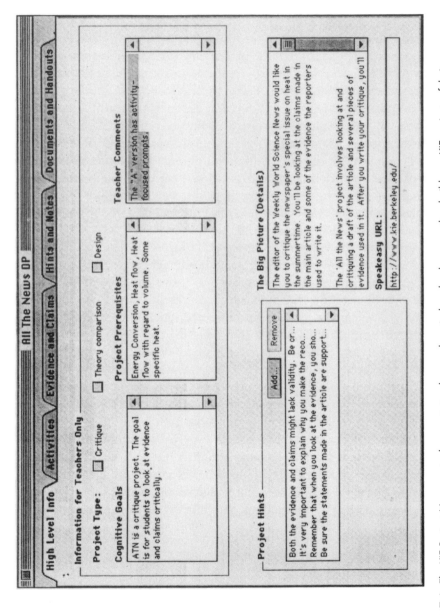

FIG. 7.6 The KIE Project Manager tool supports teachers and curriculum developers as they build new KIE projects of their own.

TABLE 7.1

Kie Projects Emphasize Scaffolded Knowledge Integration

KIE projects do emphasize...	KIE projects do not emphasize...
Depth of knowledge	Breadth of knowledge
Learning a repertoire of models and when to apply them	Learning isolated "right" answers
Subject matter applicable to real life	Esoteric subject matter
Student responsible for learning	Teacher responsible for learning
Teacher as coach/facilitator	Teacher as transmitter of knowledge
Constructivist teaching methods	Didactic teaching methods
Student critique of evidence sources	Unquestioning acceptance of authority
Using the web productively	Surfing the web randomly
Reflection on progress	Blindly following steps

their attention on the relevant science content within the evidence? Critiquing and asking questions about science evidence is an essential knowledge integration skill, and one that we must support in any learning environment that makes use of web resources (Collins, Brown, & Newman, 1990; Palinscar & Brown, 1984). (For a thorough review of the research on student questions, see Rosenshine, Meister, & Chapman, 1996.)

As mentioned previously, successful KIE projects rely on cognitive and procedural guidance included in the KIE Evidence cover page accompanying each evidence item in the project. The present study contrasts different levels of cognitive and procedural guidance provided to students on the Evidence cover pages. One group of students encountered a brief overview of the evidence; the second group received specific advice about how to make good use of each evidence item; and third group of students received the same advice, together with some model questions obtained from students' work in a previous semester. This comparison study suggests ways to design procedural and cognitive guidance to support students in the lifelong learning skills of critiquing and questioning evidence.

Materials: The Sunlight, SunHEAT! Project

The Sunlight, SunHEAT! project supports students as they critique web evidence and gain understanding of passive solar energy. The topic connects to students' interests in solar energy (many of whom live in homes or apartments with some solar architecture–such as solar water heaters or insulated window coverings), and it contributes to a subsequent project where students design a house for the desert. In the three consecutive semesters during which we have studied this project, students have been excited by its content and often refer back to its evidence during subsequent projects.

The "Sunlight, SunHEAT!" KIE project includes several activities: a preliminary class discussion about "good science questions"; a small group hands-on activity; teacher-led discussion of evidence and the Internet; small group Evidence Critique and questioning; and a final class discussion.

In the preliminary class discussion about effective questions, students focus on three criteria for useful science questions: they are specific (e.g., "Is the car battery drained?" as opposed to "Why won't my car start?"); they are relevant to gaps in understanding; and they are productive in the sense of suggesting an experiment. In the hands-on activity, students spend one class period exploring a mysterious object called a radiometer,[1] and formulate questions that will lead them to a better understanding of how it works.

In the "Evidence and the Internet" discussion, the class establishes definitions of evidence, including evidence from the web, and considers the importance of critiquing evidence source and content. The classroom targets several specific concerns about web evidence (e.g., authorship, bias, validity, etc).

In the Evidence Critique activity, students are guided by the instructor through the review and critique of the first evidence item (which is an educational Web site concerning the history of passive solar energy, the science of solar energy, and some applications). Students then choose three of the remaining five evidence items to critique on their own. For each piece of evidence, students respond to four questions: "How difficult was it for you to understand this evidence?" (1 = *not difficult*, 3 = *very difficult*). Who do you think wrote this evidence (check all that apply: scientist, advertiser, journalist, regular adult, student).

---

[1]The radiometer consists of a horizontally oriented pinwheel that sits on a small pin in the center of a partially evacuated glass globe. The pinwheel has four fins, each of which is painted black on one side and white on the other. When a light bulb is placed in the vicinity of the radiometer, the pinwheel begins to spin around rapidly. Explanations for why the pinwheel spins is left for the reader as the same mystery encountered by students running this project!

How credible or trustworthy was the evidence (1 = *low credibility*; 3 = *high credibility*). Write two questions about the science in this evidence that would help you understand it more completely.

In the final class discussion, students shared their questions about the evidence and discussed their critiques. Students in this study had never encountered the KIE software before, and many had never experienced the World Wide Web. However, they appeared to easily understand and complete all activities in the project, as reflected by the high quality of their questions and critiques across all instructional conditions.

The six different Web sites used as evidence in this project varied in their credibility and relevance to the topic. The first site was designed for educational purposes in the domain of alternative energy, but was very long and convoluted, consisting of more than 100 distinct pages all linked together by an esoteric navigational system provided at the bottom of each page. Apparently, this was an effort at bringing "textbooklike" material to the web, as the navigation system consisted mainly of "Next" and "Previous" arrows that would lead the reader serially through its content. The next site was commercial in nature, dedicated to a specific brand of energy efficient home. Despite the marketing angle of this site, it contained high-quality discussions of the science of passive solar energy geared toward explaining the design of the home. Three other sites were also of this nature, in that they provided examples of interesting solar homes with supporting scientific content. A final site was authored by a private individual to document his own solar house and included a broad range of interesting discussions.

Instructional Conditions

We designed three different versions of the Evidence cover page to provide alternate forms of advance guidance, as well as a link to the actual evidence site on the web. KIE provides cognitive and procedural guidance to students in advance of their exposure to the web evidence to focus their attention on useful parts of the evidence, connect its content to their existing ideas, and use it productively in the course of project activities. In this study, we assess the effectiveness of different levels of guidance for evidence on the Sunlight, SunHEAT! project.

For each piece of evidence, three different versions of the Evidence cover page were constructed and delivered to different groups of students. The Overview version of the cover page included only limited statements about the basic theme of the Web site, followed by a link to the site. The Advance Guidance version included Focusing information to help students identify the critical concepts in the site, Challenging information to bring difficult or hidden questions or issues to light, and Logistic information to suggest effective approaches to reading and evaluating the site. The third version of the cover page was referred to as Advance Guidance plus Model Questions, and included the Advance Guidance information plus model questions that were drawn from the best of students' questions from a previous semester. The central research question concerned the effect of these different types of guidance on the quality of students' questions as they critiqued ordinary Web sites.

Participants

A total of 345 eighth-grade students participated in the project: 177 in one semester, and 168 in the following semester. These students had never used the KIE environment before, and they varied widely in their prior experience with computers and with the World Wide Web.

Procedure

The project was conducted within the first month of the semester, and it was embedded in a broader physical science curriculum relating to topics of light, heat, and sound energy. All students worked collaboratively in pairs to complete the activities over 5 class days as part of their curriculum in their eighth-grade science class. All activities were coordinated by their usual science teacher. Students spent the first day in the hands-on exploration activity and the second day in a class discussion of evidence and the Internet. They then spent 3 class periods critiquing the KIE Sunlight, SunHEAT! evidence, with a final wrap-up discussion at the end of the last period. (Occasionally, this discussion was held during the beginning of a sixth class period.)

Analysis of Critiques and Questions

To assess the impact of the different forms of guidance, we looked deeply into the content of our various measures (i.e., the critique ratings and the questions generated). As students' work was performed collaboratively, outcomes represent contributions from both members of the pair in an unknown mixture. Our claims thus apply to pairs of students: If pairs of students working in one condition reliably outperform pairs of students working in another, we reasonably infer that the measured differences reflect cognitive effects.

Although students could choose which of the five KIE evidence items to critique, two of the five items were selected by a large majority of the student groups. Students rarely selected the item relating to the energy design and performance of a privately owned solar home (which was produced by the homeowner) or the commercial advertisement for a solar design company (which consisted primarily of text). Thus, allowing students to choose among evidence items resulted in less variety than expected. We plan to replace the unpopular items in future versions of this project.

Here, we analyze the two most popular evidence items: the first was a colorful description of one company's passive solar house design, including many attractive graphics, as well as some very difficult science content; the second was an alternative house design, which was popular for its catchy name, and the fact that it included recycled materials such as empty aluminum cans and old tires. Restricting our discussion to those students who critiqued both of these items reduces our sample from 174 pairs of students to 129 pairs: 30 pairs in the Overview condition, 56 pairs in the Advance Guidance condition, and 43 pairs in the Advance Guidance plus Modeling condition. Each pair of students performed three critique ratings and formulated two questions for each of the two evidence items. We assess the effect of the different instructional conditions on student critiques, as well as the overall effectiveness of KIE in supporting student critique activities.

Analysis of Evidence Critiques

Students in all three instructional conditions critiqued the evidence items by performing ratings of the authorship, the usefulness of the evidence for their understanding of passive solar energy, and the validity ("trustworthiness") of the evidence content. These ratings were contrasted between the groups of students, as well as with "expert ratings" obtained from two members of the research team.[2] We can

---

[2]Agreement on these ratings was nearly 100% between the two independent raters (performed over all 6 original evidence items), with any disagreements resolved by discussion to result in a reliable set of "standard ratings"). The ratings for usefulness were obtained according to the query: "How useful would this evidence item be for an eighth-grade science student's understanding of passive solar energy?"

interpret differences between ratings from the three groups to be a consequence of the different guidance provided to those groups on their respective Evidence cover pages.

Analysis of Student Questions

Students were required to formulate two questions about each piece of evidence. From class discussion, as well as from Mildred prompts, students understood that their goal was to ask questions that would help them understand the science content of the evidence more completely. Because both pieces of evidence were advertising house designs, much of their content consisted of images of houses, discussion of ethical matters, and even pricing scales. Thus, students were challenged to locate and focus on the fraction of the evidence offering science content. In earlier project activities, students had identified criteria for effective questions, which therefore provided us with a means of assessing students' questions. Each question was scored (on a scale of 1–3) for the following three criteria:

Specificity: Does The Question Focus On A Specific Part Of The Evidence?   For example, a nonspecific question might be "Why should we have solar homes?" In contrast, a question that targets a specific feature of a house design from the evidence (e.g., the circulation of an "air envelope") might be "How can the cold air manage to rise, when I thought it was hot air that rises?"

Relevance: Does The Question Target a Gap in The Student's Knowledge?   It is possible to have a highly specific question whose answer would not contribute much to any scientific understanding. For example, the house designs reviewed in one of the evidence items make use of passive solar energy stored in thick exterior walls made of recycled tires filled with dirt. One student asked of this evidence, "What happens to the tire walls in an earthquake?" This is a very specific and even interesting question. However, it is somewhat peripheral to the task, which was to generate questions about the science of heating these homes. Furthermore, its answer (they do not stand any more of a chance of collapse than conventional walls) would not contribute much to the student's understanding of that science. Rather, a question such as,

"Why are the tire walls filled with dirt?" would result in some direct increase in understanding the thermal physics of the house design.

Productivity: Is The Question "Productive," In The Sense Of Possibly Spawning An Experiment Or Activity That Would Address The Gap In The Student's Knowledge? There was considerable focus placed on this issue in the class discussion of evidence, as well as in the Explore and Question (radiometer) exercise. The classroom teacher would contrast a question such as "Why are the tire walls filled with dirt?" (i.e., requests the entire answer from some authority) with a question such as: "Would the tire walls be as good if they weren't filled with dirt?" (i.e., suggests a possible experiment) or "Why does the dirt help the tire walls retain heat?" (i.e., casts at a more precise level of causal inquiry).

These three measures comprise a progressive scale. That is, questions that have a specific focus might not be relevant or productive (e.g., the "appeal to authority" type of question); questions that are relevant to a student's understanding are probably specific, but not necessarily productive; and questions that are productive are probably both specific and relevant. We employed these three measures in exploring differences between the three instructional groups, as well as to gain some overall insight into how the KIE is able to support students in this important knowledge integration activity.

RESULTS

Students' Critiques of Authorship

Students were completely successful in judging the authorship of these two evidence items. There was virtually no difference between authorship judgments of the three instructional groups and those of the expert ratings, consistent with findings reported by Clark and Slotta (1997). These evidence items may not have provided the best test of the effect of advance guidance on authorship judgments, because they were both obviously advertisements. Nearly every student who participated in the project judged the authors of these sites to be advertisers. Although in this particular project the effect of advance guidance on students' ability to judge authorship was at ceiling, the task of judging authorship—however easy to perform—may have helped to support students as they began their critique of the evidence by drawing their attention to the advertisement nature of the evidence.

Students' Critiques of Credibility

Students in different instructional groups were found to differ in their ratings of the credibility of the evidence. When asked to judge how "trustworthy" the information in the evidence was, students who received Cognitive Guidance were in closer agreement with the expert ratings than their peers in the Brief Introduction condition. Table 7.2 provides means and standard deviations for all students' and experts' ratings of credibility. It is important to note that the experts' ratings differed for the two items. Evidence Item One consisted of a sophisticated account of the energy properties of a specific house design, which was clearly presented with compelling graphics and supporting theory. The two "expert raters" judged this evidence to be "highly credible" (a score of 3), and students in the three groups were seen to progressively agree with this rating with increased levels of advance guidance. Similar results are seen for credibility judgments of Evidence Item Two, which was judged by the expert raters as "moderately credible" (a score of 2). The Overview group was seen to rate the credibility of this item more highly than the other two groups, who drew progressively nearer to the expert judgment. This difference is significant, with $F(2, 126) = 3.52$, $p < .05$.

TABLE 7.2

Mean Credibility and Usefulness Ratings for two Evidence Items (with standard deviations)

Evidence Item + Rating Category	Expert Rating	Overview	Cognitive Guidance	Cognitive Guidance + Modeling
House #1 Usefulness	3	2.50 (0.64)	2.68 0.47)	2.71 (0.46)
House #1 Credibility	3	2.32 (0.67)	2.51 (0.50)	2.61 (0.54)
House #2 Usefulness	2	2.28 (0.66)	2.46 0.54)	2.57 (0.50)
House #2 Credibility	2	2.61 (0.50)	2.32 (0.58)	2.27 (0.54)

Students' Usefulness Judgments

Usefulness judgments are perhaps the most interesting of all of the critiquing measures, as they do not agree with the expert ratings yet still vary systematically. Table 7.2 displays the usefulness ratings of students in the three instructional groups, as well as those of the expert raters. Once again, the two "expert raters" of the evidence agreed that Evidence Item One was more sophisticated than Evidence Item Two, as the latter provided only a qualitative description of the science involved in their house design. The expert rating of usefulness was thus agreed to be "very useful" for Item One (a score of 3), and "somewhat useful" for Item Two (a score of 2). Student ratings across all three groups agreed with these expert ratings, with evidence item number one being rated more useful overall than evidence item number two: $F(1, 125) = 7.54, p < .001$. Still, a curious effect is observed in the group differences, with those students in the Advance Guidance groups tending to rate both evidence items as being more useful than did students in the Overview group. Combined across the two evidence items, this effect is significant, with $F(2, 125) = 3.60, p < .05$. Apparently, having one's attention focused on the relevant science in a piece of evidence leads to heightened estimations of its inherent usefulness. This is an encouraging result, because it demonstrates that the advance guidance affected the character of students' critiques of the science content of the evidence.

Students' Relevant Science Questions

Figure 7.7 shows that students' questions improved significantly along all three of our measures (specificity, relevance, and productivity) as a result of advance guidance. The difference between the three conditions was significant: $F(2, 121) = 15.01; p < .05$. Table 7.3 provides the mean values of students' questions for the two evidence items. All apparent differences in the table are significant, and even the Advance Guidance + Modeling condition showed a significant increase over the Advance Guidance condition: $F(1, 90) = 3.96; p < .05$.

The results shown in Fig. 7.7 and Table 7.3 suggest that our approach in designing guidance for the Sunlight, SunHEAT! evidence was successful in scaffolding students to ask critical questions of evidence. In all three measures, students who received cognitive guidance consistent with the Scaffolded Knowledge Integration framework were able to ask

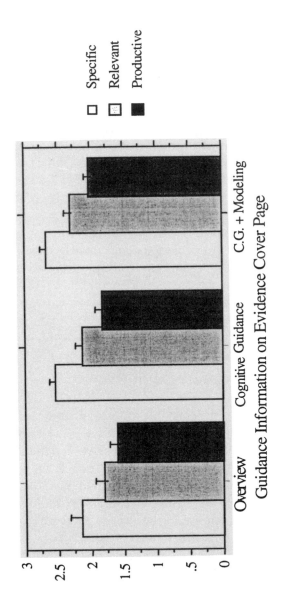

FIG. 7.7 Students with increasing level of scaffolding asked questions of the evidence that were increasingly more specific, more relevant, and more productive.

TABLE 7.3

Mean Values of Student Questions as Rated on Scales of Specificity,
Relevance, and Productivity (with standard deviations)

Evidence Item + Question Type	Overview	Cognitive Guidance	Cognitive Guidance + Modeling
House #1 Specificity	2.43 (0.78)	2.77 (0.42)	2.78 (0.41)
House #1 Relevance	2.02 (0.80)	2.43 (0.55)	2.39 (0.54)
House #1 Productivity	1.82 (0.64)	2.17 (0.55)	2.23 (0.58)
House #2 Specificity	1.88 (0.72)	2.29 (0.73)	2.58 (0.55)
House #2 Relevance	1.50 (0.63)	1.75 (0.61)	2.01 (0.80)
House #2 Productivity	1.33 (0.47)	1.36 (0.60)	1.56 (0.64)

questions that were rated nearly a 1 SD deviation better than those of students receiving the Overview information.

The power of advance guidance is clear in these results. This effect can only derive from differences in the advance guidance information, for once the students left the Evidence cover pages (where the advance guidance and modeling information was supplied) and went out to the actual Web sites, they all viewed exactly the same information. That is, students in all three groups received exactly the same evidence, in the form of existing Web sites. Thus, KIE was able to influence students' critiques as well as their ability to ask critical questions, simply by providing students with guidance in advance of their seeing the evidence.

DISCUSSION

This chapter describes the KIE software and details the careful design process we follow to create effective activities for the KIE. Our overall progress involves basic research, development, testing, and refinement of the KIE software and curriculum, as well as ongoing partnerships with teachers and scientists to create new KIE projects. Cognitive guidance can help overcome some of the dangers and challenges of incorporating Internet materials into science curriculum. Carefully designed guidance can help students use Internet materials effectively in spite of variable characteristics such as authorship, organizational complexity, content validity, rhetorical purpose, and age appropriateness.

We have developed the KIE to take advantage of the opportunities afforded by Internet evidence. Like all citizens, students in today's world must become lifelong learners on the Internet, using the web to answer their questions and to solve their problems. Cognitive guidance can help students learn to actively critique the source and content of materials from the web and to ask questions that foster their own knowledge integration. Our future research will pursue the question of whether such critiquing abilities can be sustained by students, even when they are using the Internet in the absence of KIE guidance.

The research described here provides an example of the manner in which we have refined the KIE software and curriculum based on principles of Scaffolded Knowledge Integration. By manipulating the guidance on the KIE Evidence cover pages, we can improve the effect of this information on students' success in critiquing the evidence. Our discussion of the Sunlight, SunHEAT! project illustrates the way in which specific KIE curriculum projects evolve through successive refinement according to the principles of knowledge integration. This marriage of software and curriculum is no coincidence, as the rapidly developing Internet technology commands a synergistic approach to development. Changes in the software are motivated by research on the effects of various curriculum elements, all of which rely on the function and affordances of an emerging technology. Thus, we pursue a flexible and responsive approach to development to capitalize on this inherent synergy.

Refining the KIE Software

We have illustrated our basic approach to refining the KIE software by describing how we study the design of cognitive guidance for Internet evidence. The KIE software can scaffold students' use of evidence, increasing their ability to connect the evidence content to their existing ideas about science. This clarifies forms of cognitive guidance that help students critically evaluate web evidence: Focusing information helps students identify critical science concepts; Challenging information, which brings difficult or hidden issues to the student's attention; and Logistic information suggests strategies for approaching the Web site (e.g., "you may want to follow the link at the bottom of the page, which will lead you to a helpful table of facts").

For every component or function of the KIE software, we have employed this strategy of comparing various designs in a tailored curriculum project. This has allowed us to inform our design decisions by testing ideas and gaining new insights for subsequent revisions. Just as we are confident that the advance guidance we provide on our Evidence cover pages will support students as they learn to critique evidence, we have a similar research basis for other components of KIE: the nature and content of Mildred's guidance; the most effective representations for SpeakEasy conversations; and what information is most helpful to students on the Tool Palette, to name a few.

Refining the KIE Curriculum

A design goal for KIE is to support students as they learn to critique web materials. In the "Sunlight, SunHEAT" project, these supports took the form of Advance Organization guidance from the Evidence cover page, as well as Mildred notes that prompted students to rate the author, credibility, and usefulness of the evidence. In this way, students' attention was guided to the most important elements of critique for their purposes. Without these vital supports, students could develop inappropriate or inconsistent critiquing strategies, or could fail to attend to some important features as they make use of Internet evidence.

The Scaffolded Knowledge Integration framework has suggested a focus on critiquing skills, and we have designed both curriculum and software in this light. Students learn from critiquing, because this is an activity that they find personally relevant and comprehensible. Through critiquing, they also gain a valuable lifelong learning skill. Furthermore, critiquing is particularly relevant to activities that use the World Wide Web, because evidence from the web is often of questionable origin and intent. Thus, most KIE curriculum projects support students in critiquing the evidence used within the project.

A second knowledge integration activity addressed by this research is that of generating questions. By articulating their own questions about the evidence, students are able to target gaps in their understanding. We have seen from the results mentioned previously that students' questions become more relevant and productive when they are provided with advance cognitive guidance as to which aspects of the evidence are the most salient. To support students in asking effective questions of evidence, we provided modeling questions that were drawn from students' work in a previous semester.

A Synergy of Technology, Software, and Curriculum

The KIE software and curriculum has been through many cycles of refinement, with major revisions occurring in each of the past 3 years. During this time, students have used the KIE in a variety of different classroom contexts, ranging from middle school, to high school, to university engineering courses. Because KIE was developed to support a process of knowledge integration, rather than any specific conceptual content or domain, it has emerged as a highly powerful and flexible learning environment. The Scaffolded Knowledge Integration framework guides KIE design decisions, and research findings such as those reported here allow us to refine our understanding of Scaffolded Knowledge Integration.

Our research program has led us naturally to embrace the Internet as an essential resource for knowledge integration in the science classroom. In combination with tools and resources offered by KIE, the diversity and accessibility of the web helps students become lifelong science learners. In web-based activities, they can connect science instruction with their existing ideas, gain valuable lifelong learning skills, and discover personally relevant science evidence. Additionally, the uncertainty of web authoring and validity of information can serve as an important opportunity for students to gain prowess in looking at evidence with a critical eye. The cognitive scaffolding offered by KIE enables students to critique web evidence and to recognize its potential strengths and weaknesses.

REFERENCES

Anderson, J. R., Boyle, C. F., & Reiser, B. J. (1985). Intelligent tutoring systems, *Science, 228,* 456–496.

Bell, P., Davis, E. A., & Linn, M. C. (1995). The knowledge integration environment: Theory and design. *Proceedings of the Computer Supported Collaborative Learning Conference (CSCL '95: Bloomington, IN,* pp. 14–21). Hillsdale, NJ: Lawrence Erlbaum Associates.

Brown, A. L., & Campione, J. C. (1994). Guided discovery in a community of learners. In K. McGilly (Ed.), *Classroom lessons: Integrating cognitive theory and classroom practice.* Cambridge, MA: MIT Press/Bradford Books.

Brown, J. S., Collins, A., & Duguid, P. (1988). *Situated cognition and the culture of learning.* (Institute for Research on Learning report no. IRL 88-0006)

Chi, M. T. H., Feltovitch, P., & Glaser, R. (1981). Categorization and representation of physics problems by experts and novices. *Cognitive Science, 5*(2), 121–152.

Clark, D. B., & Slotta, J. D. (1997). *Interpreting evidence on the Internet: Sex, lies, and multimedia.* Paper presented at the annual meeting of the American Educational Research Association, Chicago, IL.

Collins, A., Brown, J. S., & Holum, A. (1991). Cognitive apprenticeship: Making thinking visible. *American Educator, 15*(3), 6–11, 38

Collins, A., Brown, J. S., & Newman, S. E. (1990). Cognitive apprenticeship: Teaching the crafts or reading, writing and mathematics. In L. Resnick (Ed.), *Knowing, learning and instruction: Essays in honor of Bob Glaser* (pp. 453–494). Hillsdale, NJ: Lawrence Erlbaum Associates.

Davis, E. A. (1997, March). Students beliefs about science and learning. Paper presented at the *Annual meeting of the American Educational Research Association.* Chicago, IL.

Dewey, J. (1920). *The child and the curriculum.* Chicago, IL: University of Chicago Press.

diSessa, A. A. (1988). Knowledge in pieces. In G. Forman & P. Pufal (Eds.), *Constructivism in the computer age.* Hillsdale, NJ: Lawrence Erlbaum Associates.

diSessa, A. A. (1993). Toward an epistemology of physics. *Cognition and Instruction, 10,* 1–196.

Eylon, B. S., & Linn, M. C. (1988). Learning and instruction: An examination of four research perspectives in science education. *Review of Educational Research, 58*(3), 251–301.

Guzdial, M., Rappin, N., & Carlson, D. (1995). Collaborative and multimedia interactive learning environment for engineering education. In *Proceedings of the ACM Symposium on Applied Computing 1995* (pp. 5–9). Nashville, TN: ACM Press.

Hoadley, C. M., Fishman, B., Harasim, L., Hsi, S., Levin, J., Pea, R., Scardamalia, M., & Linn, M. C. (1007, April). *Collaboration, communication, and computers: What do we think we know about networks and learning?* Panel presented at the Annual Meeting of the American Educational Research Association, Chicago, IL.

Hoadley, C. M., & Hsi, S. (1993). A multimedia interface for knowledge building and collaborative learning. *The adjunct proceedings of InterCHI '93, (International Computer-Human Interaction Conference,* pp. 103–104). Amsterdam, The Netherlands: Association for Computing Machinery.

Hsi, S., & Hoadley, C. M. (1997). Productive discussion in science: Gender equity through electronic discourse. *Journal of Science Education and Technology, 6*(1), 23–36.

Linn, M. C. (1992). The computer as learning partner: Can computer tools teach science? In K. Sheingold, L. G. Roberts, & S. M. Malcolm (Eds.), *Technology for teaching and learning.* Washington, DC: American Association for the Advancement of Science.

Linn, M. C., Bell, P., & Hsi, S. (in press). Lifelong science learning on the Internet: The knowledge integration environment. *Interactive Learning Environments.*

Linn, M. C., & Clancy, M. J. (1990, April). Designing instruction to take advantage of recent advances in understanding cognition. *Academic Computing, 4*(7), 20–41.

Linn, M. C., & Muilenberg, L. (1996). Creating lifelong science learners: What models form a firm foundation? *Educational Researcher, 25*(5), 18–24.

Linn, M. C., & Songer, N. B. (1991). Cognitive and conceptual change in adolescence. *American Journal of Education, 99*(4), 379–417.

Palinscar, A. S., & Brown, A. L. (1984). Reciprocal teaching of comprehension-monitoring and comprehension-fostering activities. *Cognition and Instruction, 2,* 117–175.

Piaget, J. (1970). *Science, Education and the Psychology of the Child.* New York: Orion Press.

Reif, F., & Heller, J. I. (1982). Knowledge structure and problem solving in physics. *Educational Psychologist, 17,* 102–127.

Reif, F., & Larkin, J. H. (1991). Cognition in scientific and everyday domains: Comparison and learning implications. *Journal of Research in Science Teaching, 28*(9), 733–760.

Rosenshine, B., Meister, C., & Chapman, S. (1996). Teaching students to generate questions: A review of the intervention studies. *Review of Educational Research, 66*(2), 181–221.

Scardamalia, M., & Bereiter, C. (1991). Higher levels of agency for children in knowledge building: A challenge for the design of new knowledge media. *The Journal of the Learning Sciences, 1,* 37–68.

Scardamalia, M., & Bereiter, C. (1992). A knowledge building architecture for computer supported learning. In E. DeCorte, M. C. Linn, H. Mandl, & L. Verschaffel (Eds.), *Computer-based learning environments and problem solving*. Berlin: Springer-Verlag.

Scardamalia, M., Bereiter, C., McLean, R., Swallow, J., & Woodrull, E. (1989). Computer supported intentional learning environments. *Journal of Educational Computing Research, 5*(1), 51–68.

Schoenfeld, A. H. (1985). *Mathematical problem solving*. Orlando, FL: Academic Press.

Slotta, J. D., & Chi, M. T. H. (1996, July). *Understanding constraint-based processes: A precursor to conceptual change in physics*. Paper presented at the *Eighteenth Annual Cognitive Science Society Conference*, San Diego, CA.

Slotta, J. D., Chi, M. T. H., & Joram, E. (1995). Assessing the ontological nature of conceptual physics: A contrast of experts and novices. *Cognition and Instruction, 13*(3), 373–400.

Soloway, E. (1985). From problems to programs via plans: The content and structure of knowledge for introductory LISP programming. *Journal of Educational Computing Research, 1*(2), 157–172.

Songer, N. B. (1993). Learning science with a child-focused resource: A case study of Kids as Global Scientists. *Proceedings of the Fifteenth Annual Meeting of the Cognitive Science Society* (pp. 935–940). Hillsdale, NJ: Lawrence Erlbaum Associates.

Songer, N. B. (1996). Exploring learning opportunities in coordinated network-enhanced classrooms: A case of kids as global scientists. *The Journal of the Learning Sciences, 5*(4), 297–327.

Vygotsky, L. S. (1987). *The collected works of L. S. Vygotsky: Volume 1, problems of general psychology* (R. W. Rieber & A. S. Carton, Series Eds.). New York: Plenum.

Wellesley College Center for Research on Women. (1992). *How schools shortchange girls* (Executive Summary). American Association of University Women Educational Foundation.

White, B. Y., & Frederiksen, J. R. (1989). Causal model progressions as a foundation for intelligent learning environments. *Artificial Intelligence, 24*, 99–157.

8

Computer-Supported Collaborative Learning in Engineering: The Challenge of Scaling-Up Assessment

Mark Guzdial and Jennifer Turns
Georgia Institute of Technology

Computer-supported collaborative learning (CSCL) is a term for a broad range of activities and goals that have become increasingly popular for science and engineering education. CSCL is a technology based educational practice that encourages students to communicate and work together as a means for fostering learning. Collaborative activity, such as teamwork on engineering design projects or collaboration in scientific inquiry, has been found to enhance student learning as measured by standardized test scores (e.g., Bereiter & Scardamalia, 1989). Positive learning outcomes in CSCL may be attributable to many features of the collaborative environment including enhanced students' motivation (Blumenfeld et al., 1991), increased student immersion in problem complexity (Lehrer, 1992), and increased quantity and quality of student dialogue (Roschelle, 1992).

The nature of this dialogue has been the focus of much of the work in the CSCL research community. Indeed, much of the research has been focused on understanding how dialogue about subject matter contributes to a process of conceptual change (Jeong & Chi, 1997). Dialogue activities that might contribute to conceptual change include the articulation of personal conceptualizations, the challenging of the conceptualizations of others, and the subsequent development of new shared conceptualizations (Roschelle, 1992). Other research has focused on how dialogue provides an opportunity for students to practice important metacognitive skills such as monitoring personal knowledge, identifying the type of evidence one has for personal theories, and constructively critiquing personal and peer theories (Scardamalia & Bereiter, 1991).

Studies like these show that collaborative activity can lead to enhanced learning and how dialogue contributes to such outcomes. Studies of conceptual change and collaboration typically focus extensive effort on fine-grained analysis of the dialogue structure and content, typically involving a substantial effort (Ericsson & Simon, 1980). In a real classroom, teachers need feedback on the efficacy of their activities with much less effort. The classroom contexts of this paper, undergraduate engineering classes, are typically large, ranging from 50 to 300 students per class. How does a teacher in such a classroom determine whether CSCL is working in his or her classroom? An open challenge is to determine what types of evidence and evaluation methods are appropriate for judging when students' dialogue might be promoting learning in an environment with hundreds of participants and their contributions.

To better understand the nature of this issue, consider a scenario in which an introductory engineering class of 50 students uses a CSCL tool, over a 10-week university term, with students contributing an average of 3 notes per week. The teacher, in overseeing the CSCL tool, has to review approximately 150 notes per week (1500 notes across the term), not including notes contributed by himself or herself and others who may be moderating the discussion. The volume of material becomes even larger when such a tool is being used in multiple classes. Although it will still be valuable to carefully analyze selected student contributions for evidence of learning and conditions that contribute to learning, real teachers in real classrooms need measures that allow one to quickly gauge whether conditions conducive to learning exist.

Additionally, such analyses, focused on a different level of description than the detailed analyses, might lead to unanticipated patterns in the data that contribute to the CSCL research community. Although careful analysis of students' dialogues can inform our understanding of collaborative learning in individuals or in small groups, it is less effective at drawing a picture of how the class as a whole is engaging in the discussion in the CSCL forum (that is, the set of students' contributions for a given class using a CSCL tool). Which students participate, and which ones do not? What is the ecology of the flow of information in the CSCL forum (Pitkow, 1997)? Analyses of large numbers of students can present new results and perhaps introduce new questions to the CSCL community.

This chapter discusses our efforts to address the challenge of large-scale analysis. Others have begun to explore higher levels of description for computer-based classroom dialogue (e.g., Taylor, 1996), but these other descriptions have not always been anchored in research about learning via dialogue. In this chapter, we analyze the use of a tool, in real classroom contexts, from the dialogue level up through large numbers of students in multiple classes.

Specifically, we report on a set of studies surrounding a specific CSCL tool, CaMILE (Collaborative and Multimedia Interactive Learning Environment, Guzdial et al., 1995; Turns et al., 1995). In these studies, the focus of the evaluation scales from microanalysis of individual contributions within a single dialogue to macroanalyses of activity in groups of discussions with thousands of notes and tens to hundreds of participants. At this macroanalytic level, we use the ideas of the CSCL community to identify properties of the discussions that suggest conditions indicative of learning without requiring a detailed analysis of each note.

We begin by describing CaMILE, a tool we have developed and introduced into a variety of engineering classes. In our baseline analysis, we look at a single discussion, and at a single dialogue within that discussion, and point out some features that suggest the dialogue to be a productive one for learning. We then ask, "What is the nature of this dialogue?" and "Who is participating?" In answer to these questions, we describe two approaches to macroanalysis. In Section Three we use measures of the extent and focus of the discussion to compare two CSCL classes, one using CaMILE and one using a newsgroup. In Section Four we use measures of the level and type of discussion participation to compare a group of classes using CaMILE with a group of classes using newsgroups. In these latter two analyses, we cannot be certain that conditions supportive of learning are present. We can only say that properties of the discussions suggest effective learning. However, the findings then help us to answer important questions about CSCL environments and lead to new open questions for the CSCL research community.

AN INTRODUCTION TO CaMILE

CaMILE is a web-based CSCL tool designed to support students' discussion. CaMILE development has been iterative, evolving as we have gained a better understanding of students' needs when participating in computer-based discussion that supports classroom goals. Features in our current version of CAMILE make it possible for us to provide students with support for writing notes, support for tracking and monitoring discussion activity, and support for understanding the purpose and context of the discussion.

CAMILE operates much like an Internet newsgroup. Students using CaMILE create notes (see Fig. 8.1) that are organized into *threads* (see Fig. 8.2). Notes are typically text, but can actually contain any kind of media that can exist on a Web page. Any text that students write into a note is treated as HTML code. A thread of notes is the collection of notes

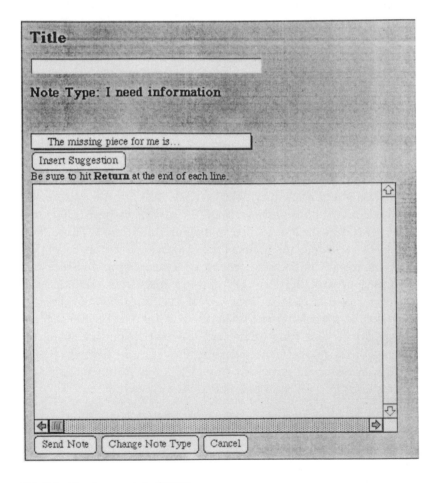

FIG. 8.1 Creating a note in CAMILE.

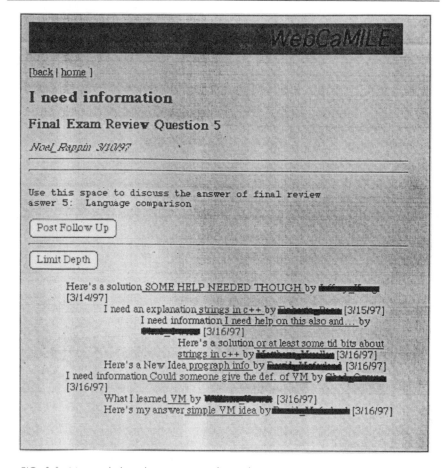

FIG. 8.2 Note with threading represented as indentation.

that are created in response to some initial note, both direct responses and indirect responses (those that respond to intermediate level responses). Figure 8.2 shows the appearance of a note with the thread of responses

CaMILE provides students with two kinds of support for note writing: metacognitive and topical. Before a student can create a CaMILE note, the student must first think at a metacognitive level and identify the function of the note within the discussion. Will it agree with a previous note? Present a new idea? Provide an alternative resolution to an issue? When actually typing the text of the note, a menu of suggested phrases and topics is available to support students in composing the note text.

The two types of support are based on the procedural facilitation of Scardamalia, Bereiter, and Steinbach (1984).

Features of the CAMILE interface and implementation help students with tracking and monitoring the state of the discussion (see Fig. 8.3). The threaded display of the discussion reifies the nature of the exchange and contributions up to the present time, so a student can "see" and understand what has taken place. Because CAMILE stores all notes on the server (not on the user's computer) and does not track what a user has and has not seen, all notes are available at all times. Note persistence ensures that a reader, attempting to understand the history of the discussion, can find and read all notes that have been posted to the discussion. Because the number of notes can get large, CAMILE provides interface features that permit users to control the visibility of portions of the discussion space.

Features of CAMILE allow us to support students in understanding the purpose and the context of the discussion. Generally, people do not discuss a topic for the sake of discussion, but rather discuss it to accomplish a goal (e.g., negotiate an issue, achieve a better understanding of some topic, etc.). To facilitate making the context or goal of a CAMILE discussion more apparent, we have designed CAMILE discussions so they can be embedded in other activities. Specifically, each note in CAMILE has a unique web address. This makes it possible for us to easily embed a CAMILE discussion within Web pages that present something of interest to students (e.g., an assignment page, a design to critique). We call discussions embedded in other activities anchored collaborations and we are currently exploring the implications of this arrangement on students' discussion activity and learning (Guzdial & Turns, 1997).

STEP ONE: EVALUATING A DISCUSSION
FOR MEANINGFUL CONTRIBUTIONS

Much of the evaluation focus in CSCL research is at the level of individual students' contributions and the dialogues in which these contributions reside. CSCL research has identified how both dialogue on subject content and dialogue providing opportunities for practice of metacognitive skills can enhance learning. Thus, studying the details of dialogue among students is a natural place to look for evidence of learning and learning opportunities in CSCL settings.

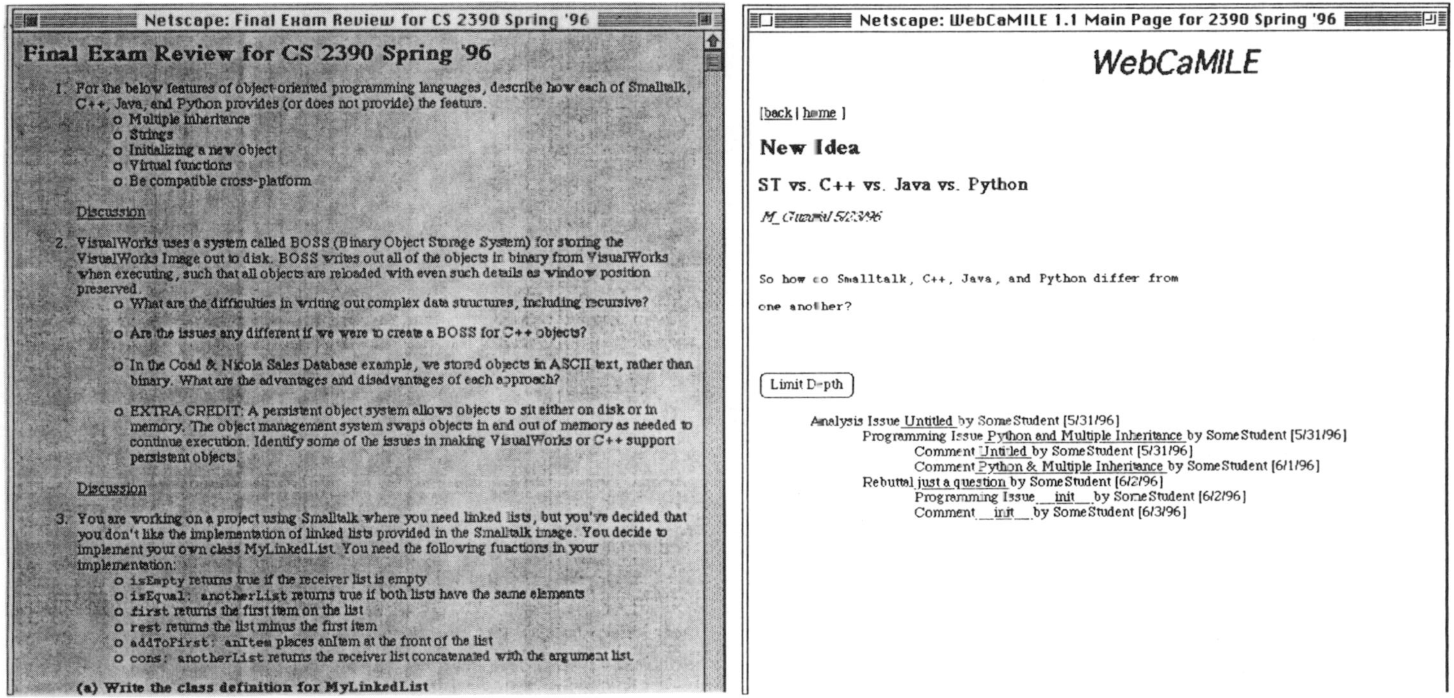

FIG. 8.3 Discussion context (final exam review on left) with link into CaMILE discussion space (on right).

233

In this section, we perform a detailed analysis of a portion of a CaMILE dialogue. Our examples in this section are taken from a collaborative computer-supported midterm exam review, conducted for a computer science course on object-oriented analysis, design, and programming and orchestrated with CaMILE. The midterm exam review consisted of a set of eight sample exam questions that were posted outside of CaMILE but contained links into a CaMILE discussion space.

In the example transcript that follows, students are discussing one of these questions. The question asks them to identify a set of classes necessary to model an engine, specifically a clog in an engine (see Table 8.1). This process of identifying the set of object classes appropriate for modeling a system is a basic step in object-oriented software engineering and one which requires a firm understanding of the nature of classes and of objects. In our analysis, we first discuss the nature of the interactions as a whole and then look at specific details of student-written notes within that discussion.

The trace of the discussion in response to the question is provided in Table 8.2. In this trace, each note is given a separate number for easier identification. Indentation indicates threading. The total discussion contains 24 notes written by 19 different authors (18 students and the instructor). One student wrote three notes, two students and the instructor authored two notes each, and the remaining authors created only one note each. The course instructor created the discussion space on the 17th of January, but the first student note was not posted until 7 days later. The discussion continued for 5 more days, although most of the notes were posted in a 3-day period between the 24th and the 26th of January. The timing of the notes is important because it indicates that the students' responses were not driven by the appearance of the note,

TABLE 8.1

Anchor Provided to Students in the Midterm Exam Review

Midterm Review Q2: You are creating a simulation of an engine with a particular emphasis on modeling the flow of fuel through the engine (e.g., if we were to cause a clogged fuel line, our model would show a lack of fuel to the carburetor and pistons).

Identify at least FOUR classes that you would need to (a) create the Problem Domain component and (b) create the Human Interface component. Identify which are which (this does NOT have to be ALL the classes you would need, but it must be SOME of them). Using the graphical notation used in Coad and Nicola, show how your classes would relate.

TABLE 8.2

Threading of the CaMILE Midterm Review Discussion

1. Question Midterm Review Q2 by teacher [1/17/96]

2. Analysis Issue Composing the engine and a clog class by student 1 [1/24/96]

3. Question: Hmm, what's a clog? By student 2 [1/25/96]

4. Revision by student 1 [1/28/96]

5. Analysis Issue A clog is ...by student 3 [1/29/96]

6. Analysis Issue Clog classes by student 4 [1/26/96]

7. Revision More on density model ...by student 1 [1/29/96]

8. Question engines??? By student 5 [1/24/96]

9. Comment by student 6 [1/25/96]

10. New Idea Posting drawings by student 7 [1/28/96]

11. New Idea Re-posting drawing by student 7 [1/29/96]

12. Comment Design question by student 8 [1/24/96]

13. Comment Fuel Flowing by student 9 [1/24/96]

14. Analysis Issue by student 10 [1/24/96]

15. Analysis Issue Is Fuel Line an object or method by student 11 [1/24/96]

16. Comment It depends? By student 12 [1/24/96]

17. Comment Fuel Line a Method? By student 13 [1/24/96]

18. Comment Fuel Lines by student 14 [1/24/96]

19. Comment Re: Question 2 Bias by student15 [1/24/96]

20. Analysis Issue Hear, Hear! By teacher [1/25/96]

21. Comment simple fuel lines by student 4 [1/26/96]

22. Design Issue by student 16 [1/25/96]

23. Rebuttal Comparer? By student 17 [1/26/96]

24. Comment engine thing by student 18 [1/31/96]

but by their need for the information; the actual midterm examination was on the 27th.

Most of the discussion is a serious effort to address the question. The students start the discussion by immediately proposing sets of objects that together provide an answer to the question (Notes 2, 9, 22, and later, 24). Other students choose to critique the proposed models by offering criticisms or by asking questions (Notes 3, 6, 14, 15, and 23). In some cases the author of the model being critiqued responds to the criticism by proposing a revised model (Notes 4 and 7). In other cases, students suggest possible resolutions to the issues raised (Notes 5, 16, and 21). In still other cases, the result is an even deeper debate referring to the specific definitions about the nature of objects and classes, and about heuristics for their identification, using the textbook as a reference (Notes 17 and 18). The one intervention of the teacher occurs when students begin to worry that the exam review question would be too difficult for them to complete on the exam. Specifically, there are four notes in which students propose the idea that the modeling of an engine requires them to have knowledge about how an engine functions, knowledge that they claim not to have (Notes 8, 12, 13, and 19). The instructor replies in Note 20. In the note, the instructor agrees that the problem is difficult, states that is why the problem has never before appeared on an exam, but asserts that the problem is representative of the type of problem that will appear on the exam.

Even without looking further into the details of the discussion, we can see evidence of a successful exchange that supports learning. The students' contributions are clearly focused on the design of a set of classes for modeling the engine, the topic at hand. Furthermore, the students are readily taking on the responsibility of monitoring and questioning the responses of their peers. Through this monitoring and questioning, the students begin to abstractly discuss the main issues in the computer science course (e.g., What exactly is the object-oriented programming construct of class? How should a class be defined?) and to reason with this knowledge.

This descriptive analysis has been performed without looking at the contents of individual notes. To verify that the description is accurate, we must look at the individual notes. We look at three individual student postings from a separate question on the exam review, as presented in Table 8.3. The concepts in this exchange are not the critical matter, but rather the important feature is the nature of the discussion about the concepts.[1]

---

[1] The *Model–View–Controller* paradigm is an approach to building user interfaces. Models are computational objects that represent real-world data (PDC or Problem Domain Components). Views are visible representations. Controller objects translate user interface events into actions on the models and the views.

TABLE 8.3

Excerpts From a Discussion of Computer Science Concepts

Student 1	Model–View–Controller: In class, we've talked a little already about the whole model–view–controller thing (would one call that a "design schema"?) and it seems cool. I understand that Models are used mostly for PDC stuff and takes care to note when any of its data "changes ", so that the corresponding view(s) can update themselves appropriately. But what of Controllers? What are they?
Student 2	Controllers? Good thing this is the review section....What exactly is the relationship between models and views? And how does that interaction affect controllers? Please explain.
Student 3	Models, Views, and Controllers: Well, this is my understanding of the whole thing.
	The MODEL in the Counting thing would actually be the Count that we create. It knows how to do what a count should do. All of the algorithmic details of a count are provided here.
	The VIEW in the Counting problem is the actual window that was created. Literally, a Count View Container, which contained a few buttons plus a value window. All of this is part of the HIC, which from my understanding the VIEW always takes care of.
	And I think that the CONTROLLER is something I remember in class as being the "pluggable adapter." Someone correct me on this if I'm wrong, but the Controller has to deal with hardware i/o and the like.

In this example, we see students engaged in the metacognitive skills of monitoring their own understanding, elaborating on the ideas of others, and explaining conceptual issues. The first student explains what he is aware of knowing ("I understand models are used to ..."), and what he thinks he does not know ("What are controllers?"). Monitoring one's personal knowledge state is an important learning strategy (Bruer, 1993), therefore having students demonstrate and practice such strategies is useful.

A second student recognizes a similar problem in his own understanding, and speaks up with an elaboration on the other student's question ("What is the relationship ..."; "How does the interaction affect controllers?"). Together, these two students are collaboratively forming a complex and focused question about a critical course concept. Questioning of this variety has been found to be an important metacognitive comprehension strategy (Palincsar, 1986).

A third student then offers his own examples to address the questions of the first two. The third student's contribution is important, not as an authoritative answer to the first two, but as a peer contributing his understanding for others to accept or to critique. In this case, the student is not rotely regurgitating a definition for a test, but is rather having the opportunity to learn through explaining to others, and to himself, and from having to articulate this explanation. The activity of self-explanation has been found to be common among better learners (Chi, Bassok, Lewis, Reimman, & Glaser, 1990).

In a cursory analysis of other CaMILE discussion forums, we have seen the presence of these types of productive interactions. Specifically, we have seen evidence of these patterns of interaction in a diverse set of classes crossing both domain (e.g., mechanical engineering design, computer science, psychology) and developmental (e.g., sophomore, junior, and senior) boundaries.

Although these tentative results reassured us that we are on the right track, we continued to be concerned by some open issues. Consider the emergent structure of the discussion given the exam review anchor question. Although the previously mentioned midterm review question could have led to a series of separate and isolated answers from students, this is not what we had hoped to see nor what theories of collaborative learning suggest will be helpful to students. In fact, we were encouraged by the extent to which students responded not only to the original anchor by the instructor but also to the issues raised by other students. This feature showed up clearly in the threading of the discussion (represented by the hierarchical structure of Table 8.2). This suggests another question: How often are notes in response to others in CaMILE, as opposed to being a statement outside of a discussion context?

The second issue relates to students' participation levels. Although there were 60 students enrolled in the class, only 18 contributed notes to this dialogue. What characterizes the group of students that chose to contribute? Additionally, what happened to the other 40 + students in the class? Are the nonauthors learning, too (presumably from reading the discussion), or are only the authors learning?

The third issue is the general issue of this chapter, the performance of these analyses in real time, with entire classes of students. The analyses described previously can be time consuming and can require extensive manual effort. As CSCL discussion tools move from research environments to full-scale classroom environments without the support of research staff, and as participation in these forums increases, we need to develop sets of indicators to quickly assess the state of the discussion. Teachers may not be able to read every note in a discussion, but they need to know about the discussion to decide whether or not to intervene. To make such decisions, a teacher needs a way to quickly assess the state of the CaMILE discussion and get a sense of whether the discussion is being successful in creating opportunities for learning. Designers of CSCL tools would also benefit from aggregate measures if these measures were to indicate properties of the tool that could be, or needed to be, changed.

To address these issues, we need to develop and evaluate appropriate assessment techniques. We need to know what measures can be used, what can be learned from different measures, and what issues go unaddressed by using such measures. The next two sections explore two alternative sets of measures, measures that characterize discussions themselves, and measures that characterize overall participation within that discussion.

STEPPING UP A LEVEL: CHARACTERIZING DISCUSSIONS

Discussions may be characterized by their duration and by their topic, where a discussion involves many students across many dialogues. In the case of students' discussions, we are interested in whether students engage in sustained discussions on course topics. A sustained on-topic discussion, we suggest, is the kind of dialogue that promotes and facilitates learning. The extent to which the discussion is sustained can be operationalized by looking at thread length—the number of notes created in a CSCL tool in response to an initial note. The extent to which the discussion is on topic can be operationalized by quickly coding the subject of the notes and then looking at the percentages of notes that are coded as being about the course subject.

We have used this type of analysis to compare and contrast the use of different CSCL tools in a computer science course taught during successive terms. In one term, students used an Internet newsgroup, which is a common collaboration tool that has thousands of users and is frequently used to support classes in undergraduate science and engineering (Taylor, 1996). During the following term, students used CaMILE. The instructors differed in the two terms, but the topics, the assignments, and even many of the lecturers' slides were identical.

A comparison of discussion activity in the two forums could be used to explain differences in learning in the two classes. Differences between the learning outcomes in the two settings certainly could be due to uncontrolled factors (e.g., the instructor, when the class was offered, the personalities of the individuals in the two classes), but they could also be due to features of the tool. Furthermore, similarities between the two classes could point at important issues of collaborative learning that bridged tools, and in particular, may not be apparent when looking at the details of individual notes and discussions. In the following two subsections, we first present a brief overview of newsgroups as an alternative CSCL tool, describe the results of our comparison of the use of these two tools, and point out some interesting questions raised by this type of analysis.

Newsgroups

Newsgroups, an old form of asynchronous collaboration support on the Internet, are an alternative CSCL discussion technology. They have been used for years to discuss everything from TV shows to the latest computer operating system. Most users know them through Usenet news groups, such as comp.lang.basic and alt.tv. Several important differences and similarities between CAMILE and newsgroups are summarized in Table 8.4.

In our university, all college of computing classes have automatically generated class newsgroups for use by students to discuss the class, ask and answer questions, and perhaps interact with the class teacher or teaching assistants. The use of Internet newsgroups is also popular in other academic units. Newsgroup use varies dramatically between classes. Participation is rarely a requirement but may be encouraged.

Like CAMILE, newsgroups support asynchronous, threaded discussion. Notes in a Newsgroup are threaded—the newsgroup protocol tracks that notes were composed in response to other notes. Also, both tools support asynchronous activity. Users do not need to be online at the same time to communicate with one another.

Unlike CAMILE, which requires a username in order to participate in a discussion, anyone with access to the Internet can participate in newsgroup discussions. Although this results in CAMILE being more restrictive for participation, the username makes it possible for CAMILE to keep better track of the participation of individuals. Such records are useful for research purposes. Other important differences between newsgroups and CAMILE can be described based on the three function

TABLE 8.4

Describing and Contrasting Newsgroup and CaMILE Collaboration Tools

Feature	Newsgroups	CaMILE
Prevalence in engineering education	Common	New
General Structure	Threaded notes in an asynchronous forum	Threaded notes in an asynchronous forum
Who can participate?	Anyone	Requires a username
Use of multiple media	Newsreader dependent, but not typical	In anchors and notes
Writing facilitation	None	Both metacognitive and topical support provided
Searching	Newsreader dependent	None
Note persistence	Newsreader dependent, default is not persistent	Persistent
Location of notes	Distributed	Centralized
Note addressing	None	Each note has a unique web address

issues CaMILE attempts to address: support for writing of notes, support for monitoring discussion activity, and support for understanding the purpose and context of the discussion.

Newsgroup support for note writing and discussion monitoring is based primarily on which newsgroup reader a user adopts. For example, newer newsgroup readers permit the composition and reading of newsgroup notes combining multiple media, but individual participants with a text-only newsgroup reader do not see the additional media. No Newsgroup readers provide users with facilitation for note writing.

Like CaMILE most recent newsgroup readers show notes presented as hierarchical threads that reify the structure of the discussion. Newsgroups, unlike CaMILE often provide searching mechanisms that help users locate notes of interest. Also unlike CaMILE most newsgroup readers typically show a note only once. Unless the participant makes an explicit effort, a viewed note will not be shown again. The lack of persistence may make a difference in a user being able to keep track of the state of the discussion. For example, if a user does not comment on a note immediately, it may be difficult to retrieve for later comment or review. Additionally, newsgroup notes are stored, and purged, in a distributed manner. The result is that access to notes is sometimes improved (because even if one news server is down, another news server may be able to provide access to the newsgroup interaction), and sometimes access is made impossible because a note of interest has been deleted. As described in the CAMILE section of the chapter, CAMILE does not delete notes and shows all notes in each discussion.

A final key difference between newsgroups and CAMILE is that unlike CAMILE notes, notes are not uniquely addressable from Web pages. Although some newsgroup tools used by students do support unique reference to newsgroup notes, it is not at all common. Therefore, Newsgroup discussions cannot be embedded within student activity as CAMILE discussions can.

Comparison of a CAMILE and a Newsgroup-Using Class

We have hypothesized that uses of CAMILE and newsgroups would have different characteristics because of the different features of the two tools. Specifically, we hypothesized that the CAMILE features lead to higher levels of sustained discussion on course topics. We compared uses of these two CSCL tools accordingly.

We carried out the analysis using a two-step process. First, we determined the length of the discussion threads in each CSCL tool (using automated programs) and then calculated the required descriptive statistics. Second, we read each note out of context and coded whether the note was ontopic.

Table 8.5 summarizes the results of the thread length analysis. The CAMILE-using class (with 50% more students) had many almost five times as many notes as the newsgroup-using class (493 vs. 119), but had essentially the same number of threads (the CAMILE class had 68, whereas the newsgroup class had 64). The average length of a thread was much longer in CAMILE (M = 7.2 notes) than in a newsgroup (M = 1.9 notes), significant on a two-tailed t-test with p < 0.05. These results suggest that discussions in CAMILE were more sustained in newsgroups.

Not all CAMILE discussions were equally as long, as evidenced by the high standard deviation and thread length. One reason for this is that anchored threads (those indexed from an external Web page) were very long, with an average of 56 notes in these threads (Guzdial & Turns,

TABLE 8.5

Measuring Thread Length in Two Class Forums

Statistic	CaMILE-Using Class	Newsgroup-Using Class
Number of Notes	493	119
Number of Threads	68	64
Average Length of Threads	7.2 (SD 21.2)	1.9 (SD 1.3)
Students	75	49
Student Authors	59 (79%)	23 (47%)

1997). Beyond the anchoring of the threads, we are not certain of the extent to which other features of a CaMILE forum, such as note persistence and note writing support, contribute to the duration of the discussion.

For the topical analysis, each note in each forum was categorized by content, based on a set of issues determined to be pertinent to the class. Table 8.6 shows these content categories and summarizes the results of the content coding. In neither class was the discussion offtopic. However, students using CaMILE were much more likely to talk about course learning topics, rather than simply how to get their homework done. The majority of the notes on class learning topics occurred during two special CaMILE anchored threads, a midterm review and a final exam review, where it was quite natural to identify issues pertaining to the course learning objectives that were confusing or misunderstood.

From our analysis, we learned that sustained discussion seems to be more prevalent in CaMILE, whereas on-topic discussion is prevalent in both forums. We also learned that the unique note addressing feature of CaMILE seems to make it more flexible for classroom use. In our example, students responded to the midterm exam anchors by participating in a discussion very focused on class learning topics. We are interested in the properties of such anchors that will reliably lead to high levels of sustained, on-topic discussion. As for the discussion measures, we learned that the thread length analysis can be automated but the topic analysis can be quite time consuming. It may be possible, though, to use spot-checking approaches for note content analysis to get a sense of whether the discussion is on topic.

TABLE 8.6

Categorizing Notes by Content

Content Code	Newsgroup-Using Class	CᴀMILE-Using Class
Class learning topic	2 (2%)	219 (44%)
How to use the programming environment	41 (34%)	99 (20%)
Help on homework	72 (61%)	171 (35%)
Use of tool (CᴀMILE or newsgroup)	0 (0%)	49 (10%)
Infrastructure: Quality of lecture, curriculum, etc.	13 (11%)	26 (5%)
Off-Topic	0 (0%)	12 (2%)

STEPPING UP TO A DIFFERENT LEVEL: CHARACTERIZING PARTICIPATION

Participation in a discussion is another way of characterizing the discussion. We have focused on participation operationalized as authoring notes in the CSCL forum, since our theory of collaborative learning emphasizes the role of active dialogue, not that of passive reading (Jeong & Chi, 1997; Roschelle, 1992). It is an open question as to how much reading notes in a CSCL forum influences learning. Most studies have shown an enormous variance in reading patterns that are not yet well understood (Hsi & Hoadley, 1997).

Our earlier studies suggested that people focused on class topics when they participated. At the same time, we had noticed low to medium levels of participation in both our detailed analysis and our discussion analysis. We had become interested in the extent to which students participated in the discussions, and the extent to which different levels of classroom reform, different teachers, different class subjects, and different CSCL tools might contribute to the level of participation. In the study reported in this section, we began to explore these issues by looking at the level of students' note-writing participation, based on an information ecology metaphor, across many CᴀMILE and newsgroup forums.

We apply an information ecology perspective to our study of patterns of participation in CSCL (Pitkow, 1997). Collaboration forums are a kind of information space where information is being produced (written) and consumed (read). An understanding of students' reading and writing behaviors from an information ecologies perspective may make it possible for us to generalize results from other domains (such as the World Wide Web) to better understand and design CSCL environments. Furthermore, papers that present new CSCL tools, and discussion tools in general, often present information ecology statistics in describing use of the tools (e.g., *MFK/Speakeasy* [Hsi & Hoadley, 1994], *CoNote* [Davis & Huttenlocher, 1995], the *CoVis Collaboratory Notebook* [O'Neill, Edelson, Gomez, & D'Amico, 1995]). In this section, we look at the information production patterns in CaMILE and in newsgroups, relate these to the patterns that we believe indicate successful learning conditions, and then contrast these results to others in the literature.

The study in this section of the chapter analyzes 27 computer-supported collaborative learning forums in science and engineering classrooms. Together, these forums contain a total of 6800 notes written by over 1100 students, teachers, and teaching assistants. These forums are split almost equally between CaMILE and Newsgroups. The results provide a picture of what is common behavior at a high-level of aggregation and how the difference in tools affects the information ecology of CSCL forums.

Selection of Datasets

In this study, we focused on larger classes (where more forum activity may occur) and on a predominantly undergraduate engineering population (the user population on which we focus in our research). Summary statistics for the two resulting datasets appear in Table 8.6. Overall, there were 6800 notes analyzed, with 1157 authors. There were 2735 CaMILE notes by 441 authors, and 4065 newsgroup notes by 716 authors.

The CaMILE uses listed in Table 8.6 represent a sampling from the past 2 years of CaMILE experimentation. We selected 13 CaMILE undergraduate class forums from computer science (CS) and from chemical engineering (CHE), because these units have had the most experience in testing CaMILE.

A brief survey of the CaMILE use summaries in Table 8.7 reveals that there were some unusual uses. For example, in one instance, a single author composed all 13 notes in the CaMILE forum. These forums were still included in the analysis, as part of the broad range of use that might be expected with a new tool. There are also instances where the number

TABLE 8.7

Summary Statistics for CAMILE and for Newsgroup-Using Dataset Classes

CAMILE Classes	# of Notes	# of Authors	# In Class	Newsgroup Classes	# of Notes	# of Authors	# In Class
CS2390 f96	409	61	81	CS2360 Sp	446	59	81
CS2390 sp96	464	65	79	CS2360 Wi	1110	103	75
CS2390 w96	487	57	79	CS2430 Sp	587	83	92
CS2390 w97	503	60	80	CS2430 Wi	536	98	89
CS2390 sp97	452	109	92	CS2760 Sp	159	45	61
CS4345 w97	35	15	30	CS2760 Wi	108	54	57
CS6397 w97	141	23	32	CS3156 Sp	40	20	51
CS6398 sp96	15	7	16	CS3302 Wi	88	27	47
CHE2208 sp97	13	1	31	CS3361 Sp	186	37	49
CHE2210 s96	71	16	40	CS3361 Wi	233	45	47
CHE2210 w97	103	18	66	CS3411 Sp	214	43	49
HE4803 w96	42	9	20	CS3411 Wi	204	44	50
CS3431 Sp	79	28	60	CS3431 Wi	4	3	45

of authors is greater than the number of students in the class. Outsiders do occasionally visit a class forum and participate. This is much more likely to occur in newsgroups (in which anyone can participate) than in CAMILE (which requires a username and password to enter, but where entrance into one CAMILE forum provides access to all).

For the comparison group, we chose 14 computer science undergraduate course newsgroups bove the freshman level. The justification for this choice is multifaceted. We select only classes above the freshman level because we wanted to be certain that the audience was familiar with newsgroups. Freshman CS students learn to use newsgroups in their first-year courses. We also wanted to ensure that the user population was at the same academic level (if not same unit) as theCAMILE user population. We chose required courses, to be sure of larger numbers of users. We chose 7 courses from each of 2 quarters (winter and spring of 1997).

From discussions with teachers in these classes and a brief review of the forum activity, we can make a small number of observations about how the forums were used. Participation was not required in any of these classes, although some students may have perceived use as being required. The main purpose was question asking and answering. CaMILE-using teachers were encouraged to, and did, make use of anchored collaborations (see the previous section). We might also assume that CaMILE-using teachers, because they sought out use of a new tool, were more interested in collaboration in the classes and may have encouraged its use more, perhaps subtly or implicitly.

Analysis Methods

Analysis focused on writing (information-producing) behavior across the entire dataset. Three questions about writing behavior were addressed:

1. How much do individual students contribute over time? Each forum was scanned, and individual author's contributions were tabulated.
2. How broad is participation (operationally defined as writing, not reading) in the forum? We simply divided the number of authors by the number of registered students in the class.
3. How many of the notes are in response to the notes of others (i.e., threaded)? This final question focuses on detecting interactivity within the discussion.

How Much Do Individual Students Write Over Time?

On average, a student using either tool wrote 5.7 notes ($SD = 14.7$). Newsgroup authors wrote slightly fewer notes ($M = 5.5$, $SD = 15.9$) and CaMILE authors wrote slightly more notes ($M = 6.1$, $SD = 12.5$). The difference is not significant. Overall, this is about a half a note per student per week of the course.

The number of notes written per student is heavily weighted toward those students who write few notes (i.e., "low-contribution" authors). Of

248

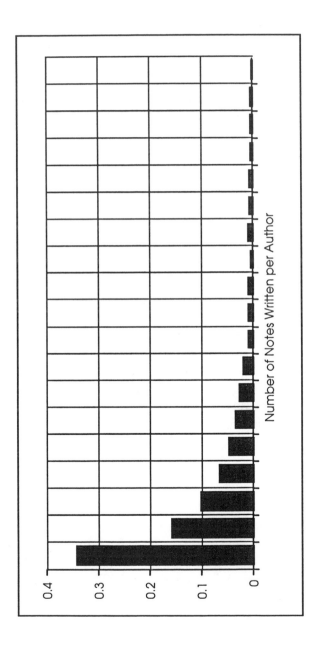

FIG. 8.4 Percentage of authors (horizontal axis) writing a specified number of notes. Vertical axis represents authors writing only one note, then two notes, and so on.

the authors, 34% wrote only a single note, 84% of all authors wrote between 1 to 10 notes in the 10-week quarter, and 89% wrote between 1 and 20 notes. Less than 2% of authors wrote more than 50 notes; that is, more than 5 notes per week. The results are graphically depicted in Fig. 8.4.

About half of the notes in the forum were written by low-contribution authors. The 34% of authors who write only a single note wrote 6% of all notes. Authors who wrote 1 to 10 notes produced 26% of all notes in a forum, authors who wrote 1 to 20 produced 55% of the notes. The high-end authors (writing 50 or more notes in a quarter) accounted for 26% of all the notes in a forum. These results are graphically depicted in Fig. 8.5. These findings suggest that, although prolific authors wrote approximately 1 out of 4 notes, over half of the notes are written by the more common "low-contribution" author.

An additional result is that in most forums, it was not found that a handful of students dominated the conversation. Rather, it was the teacher or a TA who was the most prolific author. Table 8.8 lists the most prolific two authors in each forum. Almost always, it was a teacher or a TA who was the biggest contributor, and the second most prolific author was a much smaller contributor. Overall, students' involvement in most class forums was fairly egalitarian, without a handful of students dominating the conversation. Note, however, that the teacher was much more often a prolific author in CaMILE than in newsgroups. This may be one of the ways that CaMILE-using teachers encourage participation

How Broad is Participation in the Forum?

Overall, the average participation ratio, the ratio of authors to students registered for a course, is 68% (SD = 29%). In calculating this value, we recoded to 100% all values greater than 100% resulting from outsiders participating in the forum. The average CaMILE participation ratio in each class was slightly lower (57%, SD = 27%), and the average newsgroup participation ratio was slightly higher (76.5%, SD 27%). The difference was significant at p 0.10 (p = 0.07, two-tailed t-test). This may indicate that fewer students participated in CaMILE than in newsgroups, but it may also mean that more outsiders participated in newsgroups (because 5 newsgroups had ratios over 1.00 (before correction) whereas only 1 forum did).

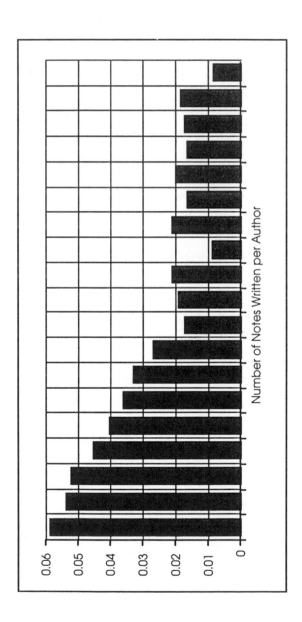

FIG. 8.5 Percentage of total notes (horizontal axis) written by authors who contributed a specified number of notes (vertical axis).

TABLE 8.8

Top Two Most Prolific Authors in Each Forum in the Dataset

Class	Top Author	Number of Notes	% of Notes	Second Author	Number of Notes	% of Notes
CaMILE						
CS2390 f96	Teacher	108	26%	TA	17	4%
CS2390 w96	Teacher	94	19%	Student	28	6%
CS2390 sp96	Teacher	100	21%	Student	39	8%
CS2390 w97	Teacher	76	15%	Student	44	9%
CS2390 sp97	Teacher	116	26%	Student	16	4%
CS4345 w97	Student	5	14%	Student	5	14%
CS6397 w97	Student	33	23%	Student	17	12%
CS6398 sp96	Teacher	5	30%	Student	2	13%
CHE2208 sp97	Teacher	13	100%			
CHE2210sum96	Teacher	42	25%	Student	4	6%
CHE2210 w97	Teacher	38	37%	Student	26	25%
CHE4803 w96	Teacher	23	55%	Student	4	10%
Newsgroups						
CS2360 Sp	TA	83	19%	TA	53	12%
CS2360 Wi	TA	296	27%	TA	69	6%
CS2430 Sp	TA	152	26%	Student	30	5%
CS2430 Wi	Student	104	19%	Student	20	4%
CS2760 Wi	Student	17	11%	Student	17	11%
CS2760 Sp	Student	11	10%	Student	6	6%
CS3156 Wi	TA	50	31%	Student	18	11%
CS3156 Sp	Student	5	13%	Student	3	8%
CS3361 Sp	Student	16	9%	TA	14	8%
CS3361 Wi	TA	55	24%	Student	31	13%
CS3411 Sp	Student	19	9%	Student	18	8%
CS3411 Wi	TA	89	44%	Student	15	7%
CS3431 Sp	Teacher	10	13%	Student	7	9%
CS3431 Wi	Student	2	50%	Student	1	25%

How Many of the Notes Are
in Response to the Notes of Others?

Overall, 55% of notes posted in a forum were in response to the notes of others. In CaMILE, the percentage was slightly higher at 60%. In newsgroups, it was slightly lower at 50%.

The locus of this interactivity, embedded in sustained discussions or simply answers to straightforward questions, seems to depend on both the forum as well as on the individual thread. The average length of a thread across all forums was 2.8 notes (SD = 6.5), which suggests that most notes get a response and many get a third note in the thread. Newsgroup threads were shorter: the average length was 2.2 notes (SD = 2.1). This implies that most threads in a newsgroup are simply a note (perhaps a question) and a response (perhaps an answer). In CaMILE, the average thread length was significantly higher at 4.4 notes (SD = 11.6, $p < .05$, two-tailed t-test). In other words, an initial note leads, on average, to 3 replies. Interestingly, the maximum thread length in any newsgroup was 56 notes, whereas the maximum in a CaMILE forum was 176 notes. In these cases, there was extensive interactivity in the forum but with the more extensive interactivity occurring in a CaMILE forum than in a newsgroup forum.

Discussion Including a Comparison
With Results From the Literature

A positive finding in our results was that participation is relatively representative of the students. Most students participated, and the average student author (in terms of number of notes written) created the majority of the notes. It was not true in these results that a small number of highly prolific student authors were dominating the discussion—at least, in terms of percentage of notes in the entire forum. Through force of ideas or language, a small percentage of authors may have actually been controlling the discussion, but that is not possible to determine from this type of analysis.

As a percentage of students registered, the number of authors in CaMILE was lower than that in newsgroups. Although disappointing, this was not unexpected. Accessing CaMILE is more difficult than accessing newsgroups. There are many newsgroup readers, any student account on any computer on-campus can access a newsgroup, and newsgroup access is distributed. CaMILE requires a special username and password and must be accessed via the web. For some computer science students, being required to access the discussion tool via the web is a disincentive for use. Some CS students complain in surveys and via e-mail that they do not like using graphical web browsers and do not want to be forced to use the web to engage in class discussions. Although a minority, this "hacker" culture insists on use of text-only tools and revolts against graphical user interfaces as used in CaMILE.

What is more disturbing is that few authors are writing much. Although there is evidence that conceptual change is not correlated with the amount of notes written (Hoadley, 1997), all of our existing theory of collaborative learning points to the need for dialogue (Jeong & Chi, 1997; Roschelle, 1992). A total of 4 or 5 notes (the average writing by an author with either kind of tool) over the course of 10 weeks is not what one might call a dialogue where individuals are presenting their views and responding to the views of others. However, in contrast with literature on similar tools, these are not surprising findings.

CaMILE and newsgroups are two of a large number of CSCL tools that are currently under development and evaluation (see Table 8.9). Other CSCL tools used in science and engineering classrooms have reported participation data. By exploring the results, we can get a better picture of common patterns of behavior in the use of CSCL tools.

Participation data available for these other tools resembles the data resulting from our analysis. In one use of CoNote, 65 students wrote 428 notes over 8 weeks, resulting in an average of 0.80 notes per student per week. In AnswerGarden, 59 students and researchers wrote 121 messages over 20 weeks, for an average of only 1 message for every 10 students per week (0.10 messages per student per week). Results with Belevedere, CoVis Collaboratory Notebook, and Clare are more promising, but with more carefully structured activities that required students' use. The end result is a tension or inconsistency in the current CSCL community. Evidence suggests that existing CSCL environments are not being used for the broad-based dialog that is thought to be critical for learning. However, learning still seems to be occurring. Does learning within a CSCL paradigm not actually rely on contributing to the discussion? If not, what is the learning mechanism? This tension needs to be resolved by either improving our tools and our practice with these tools or by improving our theory for explaining more specifically the mechanisms by which learning occurs through dialogue.

TABLE 8.9

CSCL Tools With Similarity to CaMILE

CoNote (Davis & Huttenlocher, 1995)	An asynchronous collaboration tool through which computer science students annotated WWW pages as part of a studying activity for a quiz.
AnswerGarden (Ackerman, 1994)	An e-mail-based system for tracking questions and answers that was used with computer science graduate students and researchers.
Belvedere (Suthers & Weiner, 1995)	A collaboration tool for recording argumentation and evidence, that was used in testing by middle school students trying to understand evolution.
CoVis Collaboratory Notebook O'Neill et al., 1995)	A collaborative visualization tool that allows high school students and researchers to interact synchronously (with live video and audio) while jointly viewing visualizations on atmospheric conditions. The Collaboratory Notebook is an asynchronous collaboration component for sharing results and constructing scientific arguments.
CLARE (Wan & Johnson, 1994)	A web-based collaborative learning environment that computer science students used in reviewing papers.

CONCLUSIONS ON SCALING-UP OF ASSESSMENT IN CSCL

In this chapter, we have explored various levels of assessment of a CSCL tool. We initially report on a detailed analysis of participation in CaMILE and the characteristics of the resulting discussion, pointing out features of students' participation and features of the discussion suggestive of supportive learning conditions. Because this type of detailed analysis would be difficult for a teacher in a real class environment, we explore measures that work on a higher level of aggregation yet capture important features of the discussion. We describe analyses based on features of the discussion and on students' participation in the discussion forums. By using these higher level, more aggregate measures, we were able to compare and contrast CSCL tool use in multiple classes with hundreds of students and thousands of notes, leading to important questions for the CSCL community.

With the later analyses, we lost a level of certainty but gained a broader view. In the first analysis, we could be most certain that the conditions for learning existed, but we did not know how widespread these conditions were. In the latter two analyses, we tried to develop measures that captured critical features associated with conditions for learning but additionally could be applied to large populations of users and notes and could be applied quickly. Although certainty about learning was reduced in the scale-up, certainty about widespread practice grew.

The tension between knowledge of the individual and knowledge of the community of practice is clearly an issue when scaling up the level of assessment in any educational intervention, not just CSCL tools. Learning occurs, for the most part, at the level of the individual (Kolodner & Guzdial, 1996), and any movement away from the individual lessens our certainty about learning. At the same time, the practice of education occurs across many classes with many teachers and many students. The relation between practice and learning is a complicated one, and that relation is what scaling-up assessment is really all about. Overall, we hope that our multilevel view of learning with technology in real classroom settings may contribute to a better understanding of how we may improve student education.

ACKNOWLEDGMENTS

Research on CAMILE has been funded by the EduTech Institute at Georgia Tech through a grant from the Woodruff Foundation, by the GE Foundation, and by the National Science Foundation (RED-9550458, CDA-9414227). Macintosh-based CAMILE was designed by Mark Guzdial with the help of Jorge Vanegas and Janet Kolodner and was implemented with the help of David Carlson and Noel Rappin. WebCAMILE was designed with the help of Cindy Hmelo and was implemented primarily by David Carlson with help from Mark Guzdial and Brad Fortenberry. Cindy Hmelo and Jennifer Turns introduced the term *anchored collaboration* into our understanding of CAMILE usage patterns, based in part on the ethnographic research of Wendy Newstetter. Thanks to the ME3110 faculty who first used both versions of CAMILE and aided in their design: Farrokh Mistree, Janet Allen, and David Rosen. Thanks also to Gregory Abowd who was very supportive in the CS2390 research.

REFERENCES

Ackerman, M. S. (1994). *Augmenting the organizational memory: A field study of Answer Garden.* In R. Furuta & C. Neuwirth (Eds.), Proceedings of CSCW'94 (pp. 243–252). Chapel Hill, NC: ACM.

Bereiter, C., & Scardamalia, M. (1989). *Intentional learning as a goal of instruction.* In L. B. Resnick (Ed.), Knowing, learning, and instruction: Essays in honor of Robert Glaser (pp. 361–392). Hillsdale, NJ: Lawrence Erlbaum Associates.

Blumenfeld, P. C., Soloway, E., Marx, R. W., Krajcik, J. S., Guzdial, M., & Palincsar, A. (1991). Motivating project-based learning: Sustaining the doing, supporting the learning. *Educational Psychologist, 26*(3 & 4), 369–398.

Bruer, J. T. (1993). *Schools for thought: A science of learning in the classroom.* Cambridge, MA: MIT Press.

Chi, M. T. H., Bassok, M., Lewis, M., Reimman, P., & Glaser, R. (1990). Self-explanations: How students study and use examples in learning to solve problems. *Cognitive Science, 13,* 145–182.

Davis, J. R., & Huttenlocher, D. P. (1995). *Shared annotation for cooperative learning.* In J. L. Schnase & E. L. Cunnius (Eds.), CSCL'95 Proceedings (pp. 84–88). Hillsdale, NJ: Lawrence Erlbaum Associates.

Ericsson, K. A., & Simon, H. (1980). Verbal reports as data. *Psychological Review, 87,* 215–251.

Guzdial, M., & Turns, J. (1997). *Supporting sustained discussion in computer-supported collaborative learning: The role of anchored collaboration.* Manuscript submitted for publication.

Guzdial, M., Vanegas, J., Mistree, F., Rosen, D., Allen, J., Turns, J., & Carlson, D. (1995, January). *Supporting collaboration and reflection on problem-solving in a project-based classroom.* Paper presented at the Second Congress on Computing in Civil Engineering, Atlanta, GA.

Hoadley, C. (1997, December). *Comment at CSCL'97 Plenary Talk.* Toronto, Canada

Hsi, S., & Hoadley, C. M. (1994). *An interactive multimedia kiosk as a tool for collaborative discourse, reflection, and assessment: Unpublished manuscript.*

Hsi, S., & Hoadley, C. M. (1997). Productive discussion in science: Gender equity through electronic discourse. *Journal of Science Education and Technology, 6*(1), 23–36.

Jeong, H., & Chi, M. T. H. (1997). *Construction of shared knowledge during collaborative learning.* In R. Hall, N. Miyake, & N. Enyedy (Eds.), Proceedings of Computer-Supported collaborative Learning '97 (pp. 124–128). Toronto, Ontario, Canada.

Klodner, J., & Guzdial, M. (1996). *Effects with and of CSCL: Tracking learning in a new paradigm.* In T. Koschmann (Ed.), CSCL: Theory and practices of an emerging paradigm (pp. 307–320). Hillsdale, NJ: Lawrence Erlbaum Associates.

Lehrer, R. (1992). *Authors of knowledge: Patterns of hypermedia design.* In S. Lajoie & S. Derry (Eds.), Computers as Cognitive Tools (pp. 197–227). Hillsdale, NJ: Lawrence Erlbaum Associates.

O'Neill, D. K., Edelson, D. C., Gomez, L. M., & D'Amico, L. (1995). *Learning to weave collaborative hypermedia into classroom practice.* In J. L. Schanse & E. L. Cunnius (Eds.), CSCL '96 Proceedings (pp. 255–258). Hillsdale, NJ: Lawrence Erlbaum Associates.

Palincsar, A. S. (1986). The role of dialogue in providing scaffolded *instruction. Educational Psychologist, 21*(1'2), 73–98.

Pitkow, J. (1997). *Characterizing WWW ecologies.* Unpublished dissertation in the College of · Computing. Georgia Institute of Technology. Available as GVU Technical report 97–16 at: http://www.cc.gatech.edu/gvu/reports/techreports97.html

Roschelle, J. (1992). Learning by collaborating: Convergent conceptual change. *Journal of the Learning Sciences, 2*(3), 235–276.

Scardamalia, M., & Bereiter, C. (1991). Higher levels of agency for children in knowledge building: A challenge for the design of new knowledge media. *Journal of the Learning Sciences, 1*(1), 37–68.

Scardamalia, M., Bereiter, C., & Steinbach, R. (1984). Teachability of reflective processes in written composition. *Cognitive Science, 8,* 173–190.

Suthers, D., & Weiner, A. (1995). *Groupware for developing critical discussion skills.* In J. L. Schnase & E. L. Cunnius (Eds.), CSCL'95 Proceedings (pp. 341–348). Hillsdale, NJ: Lawrence Erlbaum Associates.

Taylor, D. (1996). *Process metrics for asynchronous concurrent engineering:* Communication in an Internet newsgroup. Proceedings of the 1996 ASME Design Engineering Technical Conferences and Computers in Engineering Conference. Irvine, CA: ASME.

Turns, J., Mistree, F., Rosen, D., Allen, J., Guzdial, M., & Carlson, D. (1995, June). *A collaborative multimedia design learning simulator*. Paper presented at the ED-Media 95: World Conference on Educational Multimedia and HyperMedia, Graz, Austria.

Wan, D., & Johnson, P. M. (1994). *Computer supported collaborative learning using CLARE: The approach and experimental findings*. In R. Furuta & C. Neuwirth (Eds.), Proceedings of CSCW '94 (pp. 187–198). Chapel Hill, NC: ACM.

9

Astronomical Experiences Using Internet-Accessible Remote Instrumentation

Philip M. Sadler
Harvard University

Roy Gould
Smithsonian Astrophysical Observatory

Kenneth Brecher
Boston University

Beth Hoffman
Education Development Center, Inc.

The majority of high school students have little opportunity to engage in science in the way that most scientific research is actually conducted. Most of their time is spent reading or listening to their teachers lecture. Even in the laboratory, they engage in the oft-repeated search for the single, correct answer. The possibility of learning science by conducting original research with state-of-the-art instruments has been virtually nonexistent for students at introductory levels. However, the Internet offers opportunities for students to initiate their own astronomy investigations. Using many of the same advances that have made it possible to build a new generation of powerful research telescopes, small, high quality, low-maintenance telescopes have been developed that allow high school students to carry out a variety of research activities. Moreover, students' use of the MICROOBSERVATORY network of telescopes can reproduce activities of research scientists, from the writing of a proposal to secure time on the telescope for observation to collaborating with other users who have either taken images or want to help analyze them.

259

Students work collaboratively, collecting data to reveal the secrets of some of natures wonders, from the Sun's changing face, to the ever circling Galilean Jovian moons, to the brightening and dimming of distant stars.

The MICROOBSERVATORY telescope network is the first generation of remote instruments that have found their place on the Internet. Because instrumentation can be shared and used efficiently online, availability of scientific tools will quickly take hold in this medium. Already, networks of seismometers gather earthquake data and scanning electron microscopes take pictures of hundreds of specimens. It is likely that soon remote cameras will monitor coral reefs and Geiger counters will measure the decay of hazardous isotopes. This technology has the potential to revolutionize the teaching of science and to attract a new and larger generation of youngsters to become lifelong "fans" of the scientific enterprise.

THE NEED FOR REMOTE INSTRUMENTS

Research in the Science Classroom

" ... there is little student satisfaction with science classes. Students generally see science class as dull, no fun, and a place where they do not wish to be. Students do not like the typical or traditional science class" (Holdzkom & Lutz, 1985).

School science does not have to be dull; real science rarely is. In school, students rarely have the opportunity to engage in the enterprise of science. Instead, they learn science through reading and lectures or by doing experiments that have been done by others for years (Stake & Easley, 1978). Learning science does not have to be such a rote activity.

The best teachers have always taught by engaging in activities that have a high intrinsic interest to their students, where students can apply their science knowledge and skills to real problems or situations (Murnane & Raizen, 1988). Earth science teachers take their classes on field trips to collect and study rocks. Physics teachers study acceleration from roller coaster seats. Biology teachers slog through the biomes of local habitats. These are all effective means to helping students to use their knowledge to gain fresh insights into the world around them. To such students, their studies are relevant. They may well be rediscovering what is already known to scientists, but this fact does not diminish their sense of discovery and of feeling like scientists (Welch, 1985). When students have the option to exercise their own discretion concerning decisions about their science activities, their engagement in the activity increases (Cavena & Leonard, 1985). Choosing their own area of investigation, having the potential of a new contribution to science, is very empowering for students.

There have been several attempts at school science activities that qualify as original research and contribute to the front-line work of professional scientists.

- In 1971, a simple kit developed by the Advisory Centre for Education (Cambridge, England) was used by some 8,000 students to estimate water pollution in rivers and streams in Britain. This program helped researchers identify the sources of pollution of rivers (Mellanby, 1974).
- In 1972, 13 and 14-year-old students conducted a survey of air pollution in the British Isles. Using simple observational techniques, 2,000 reports allowed for identification of 6 areas with elevated SO_2, areas unaffected by pollution, and the first pollution map of Scotland (Gilbert, 1974).
- Since 1987, U.S. schools have participated in a national survey of acid rain through KidNetwork, an NSF-sponsored project run by the Technical Education Research Center (Cambridge, Massachusetts) and the National Geographic Society. Data were provided to the NOAA (National Oceanic and Atmospheric Administration) to augment their data collection network. KidNetwork expanded to 7,000 sites over the last several years (Julyan, 1988, 1991).

In each of these programs, students were very enthusiastic about their participation. The two British programs showed a roughly equal level of involvement by boys and girls. Astronomy traditionally has encouraged skilled amateurs to contribute to the field. There are too few professionals to study all of the objects in the heavens. In particular, certain types of observation are best performed by amateurs and require continual scanning for discovery (comets, novae, asteroids), continual monitoring for changes (variable stars, novae, supernovae), and observations in regions where there is no permanent telescope occultations; Stebbins, 1987). In comparison to secondary school students, college and university students have more opportunity to contribute to research because their professors may be researchers. Students can join a research team, and depending on their skill, can make some real contribution to ongoing work. However, opportunities for the involvement by students in introductory science courses are small and in many junior or community colleges there are few faculty members with research programs. Even at 4-year colleges, too few faculty members are able to engage students in their activities.

The Potential of Astronomy for Classroom Research

Astronomy is an ideal discipline for engaging the interest of students. It is a visual science dealing with phenomena that are experienced every day. The rising and setting of the Sun, the changes in the seasons, and the nightly movement of the Moon and its changing appearance all provoke curiosity. Astronomy provides observable, macroscopic experiences, as compared to more abstract microscopic phenomena that are hidden from plain view. Astronomy is also on the frontier of scientific discovery, yet many of its basic concepts lie within reach of most students.

Astronomy appeals to students at every level. It is popular in elementary school science curricula; in eighth and ninth grades, 1,450,000 students learn about astronomy each year as a part of earth science (Welch, Harris, & Anderson, 1984). More than 1,200 public and private U.S. high schools (of an 11,100 total) presently offer astronomy as an elective, enrolling 46,000 students each year (Weiss, 1987). In college, astronomy's estimated national enrollment exceeds 300,000 students annually (Hoff, 1982). Newspapers regularly report on astronomical discoveries. Meteor showers, eclipses, lunar phases and planetary alignments, and the parade of the constellations engage large numbers of adults. For these reasons, astronomy is a powerful entre into general science literacy.

Astronomy remains interesting to many people long after their formal education is completed, as evidenced by the popularity of the 117 planetaria in U.S. science museums (International Planetarium Society [1990]); 700,000 annual subscriptions to astronomy and space-related magazines; and the sale of roughly 1,000,000 small telescopes each year (U.S. Department of Commerce, 1986).

A substantial fraction of high schools already have their own telescopes. Reports indicate that 29% of U.S. high schools have purchased telescopes that were available to teachers for use with students in their school (Weiss, 1978, 1987). However, our own interviews with science teachers have uncovered many difficulties encountered by teachers in using telescopes with students, such as the following:

- Students are usually unable or unwilling to return to school at night.
- Considerable skill is required to align the telescope.
- The instrument needs constant adjustment over an observing session.
- Celestial objects are difficult to find in narrow field-of-view telescopes.
- Interesting objects are often faint. They do not look like the long-exposure, enhanced photographs students have seen.
- Permanent records of observed objects are difficult to produce.
- Only one person at a time can view an object.
- Light pollution often obscures objects.
- It can get cold.
- It does get late.

Fortunately, recent advances in the technology of astronomy can overcome these barriers that have severely limited the use of conventional telescopes by high school science students.

Advances in Telescope Technology

Much of the progress in astronomy since the late 1980s has been the result of advances in three technologies: solid-state detectors that surpass photographic film and even the human eye in their ability to detect light (Buil, 1991); computer processing of images of the sky stored in digital form; and the computer control used to automatically point and guide telescopes (Huchra, 1988). These three technologies have revolutionized the ability of large- and medium-sized telescopes to carry on front-line research. As an example, the Center for Astrophysics' Redshift Survey, which resulted in the astonishing discovery of great bubblelike voids in the universe, was conducted for the most part on a mere 1.5m diameter telescope equipped with state-of-the-art detectors.

Inexpensive charge coupled devices (CCDs) that have found their way into consumer video cameras and integrated, single-chip cameras will eventually cost less than $40 each (Scott, 1991). The requirements of CCDs for astronomy are quite different than for ordinary video uses. They must have very low noise, a high signal-to-noise ratio, and square pixels with no "dead space" between them (Aikens, 1990). Even with these special requirements, the price of these devices is dropping rapidly, mainly because these same specifications describe the needs of the electronic still cameras currently being developed and marketed. Kodak, Thompson, and several Japanese companies are pummeling costs into a lower and lower range. It is not unreasonable to expect that 500 X 500 pixel chips that cost as much as an automobile in 1980 will, by the year 2000, cost less than 1% of that.

Low-cost image processing software has recently made an appearance, so microcomputers are now capable of image processing techniques that were reserved for mainframes in the past (Freiher, 1991). Computation costs have been dropping at a rate of approximately a factor of 10 every 10 years (Tessler, 1991). The future equivalent of the Macintosh IIX, which cost $6,000 in 1990, may cost one tenth of that by 2000. Not only are detectors and imaging technology improving, but recent developments in automating research telescopes have proven very cost-effective. The Smithsonian Astrophysical Observatory (SAO) in conjunction with the Fairborn Observatory operates several automatic photometer telescopes for observing variable stars (Baliunas et al., 1987). These telescopes are completely computer driven. They check weather conditions and, if they are acceptable, observe selected stars using a variety of automatically selected filters. An astronomer can request observations by modem and have the data transmitted back electronically. Virtually every minute of useful observing time can be exploited, even in remote locations, without the need for human operators (Hayes, Gienet, Boyd, & Crawford, 1987).

To these innovations, we must add three more advances that only in the last few years have increased the potential for affecting astronomical research at the school level.

Image Compression.   Whereas digital images of the sky had to be previously stored and shipped on magnetic tape, fractal techniques show promise in compression rates as high as 100:1. Such processes which took more than 200 hours on special computer systems in the mid-1990s can now be accomplished on microcomputers in seconds (Zorpette, 1988).

Internet.   Transmitting uncompressed images over computer networks is very expensive. The combination of new high-speed networks and image compression techniques means that images can be sent quickly and cheaply. Our network of MicroObservatories is held together with the "glue" of a computer network. Observing requests can be transmitted, telescopes can be controlled directly, images can be distributed, and students can communicate with scientists over these networks at a low cost.

CD-ROM. Inexpensive storage media allow the publication of collections of students' observations, professional images from terrestrial, orbiting telescopes, and spacecraft (Freiher, 1991). Students can compare their own observations with reference images to look for changes or to find objects for further investigation.

In the coming years, research-grade instruments and access to networks to connect them will be common for high schools throughout the country. The capability will exist for students just beginning to study the skies to participate in astronomical research.

The unique characteristic of the MICROOBSERVATORY is its allowance for astronomical observation within the classroom as opposed to on inaccessible rooftops or in mountain observatories. This makes the experience of observing available to those students who are physically unable to gain access to conventional observatories or manipulate conventional telescopes. It also opens observational activities to students in urban areas, where light pollution obscures the heavens.

In 1987, Project STAR conducted a census that identified 1,500 astronomy teachers in U.S. high schools. Most of these teachers considered astronomy to be a hobby—many own telescopes and subscribe to popular astronomy hobbyist magazines. The average astronomy teacher has taught the subject for 8 years. Of these high school astronomy teachers, 36% are members of astronomy societies or organizations. A subset of these teachers has served as a test bed for the MICROOBSERVATORY.

THE MICROOBSERVATORY

The MICROOBSERVATORY is a collection of five identical instruments connected through the Internet and based at the Harvard Smithsonian Center for Astrophysics. The system is composed of hardware, control software, and a Web site. These elements are seamlessly connected to provide the user with an astronomical telescope control label from his or her desktop. The MicroObservatory is designed to be used in three modes:

- *Dedicated instrument.* It is utilized by project engineers on site or by modem for testing and calibration. The telescope is controlled directly by its attached computer.
- *For real-time use.* Time can be scheduled for exclusive use by teachers for their classes. Often this takes the form of one class period per week reserved for the proper time when the telescope is in darkness.
- *Delayed observing.* The telescope takes a picture at a later time, often when viewing conditions are best for the object, and an e-mail is sent to the observer informing him or her that the image is resident at the MICROOBSERVATORY Web site.

Hardware

The MICROOBSERVATORY instrument is a small, weatherproof telescope approximately 1m tall. Because it is sealed to the weather elements, the telescope does not require a separate enclosure or dome. Constructing such buildings usually exceeds the cost of the instrument they protect. This lack of a necessary enclosure makes the MICROOBSERVATORY completely portable. It can be disassembled in minutes and transported in 3 pieces weighing less than 30 kg each. Unlike most professional telescopes, it does not require a pier. It can be aligned with the north celestial pole remotely and requires no special placement other than a clear view of the sky. The compact telescope is designed to be shipped by common carrier between sites. When unpacked, it is easily set up. It can remain outside in snow and in rain. These telescopes have survived Boston winters and Arizona summers without any difficulties. The telescope electronics are rated to -40° C. Its mechanical parts are designed for conditions to -60° C. The telescope includes two optical systems or cameras. The largest (labeled "Aperture" in Fig. 9.1) is a 560 mm focal length Maksutov design with a 133 mm aperture (5.25"). A 6-position filter wheel allows for photometric observations. This main telescope has a rather wide field of view of 1° with a 2.5 arcsecond resolution on its 1,000 X 1,400 pixel Kodak CCD. The smaller camera (labeled "Finder" in Fig. 9.1) is independent of the main optics, but is enclosed in the same instrument and gives a 10° field of view through a Minolta camera lens. The CCD imagers are maintained by thermoelectric coolers at a constant 0° C independent of ambient conditions.

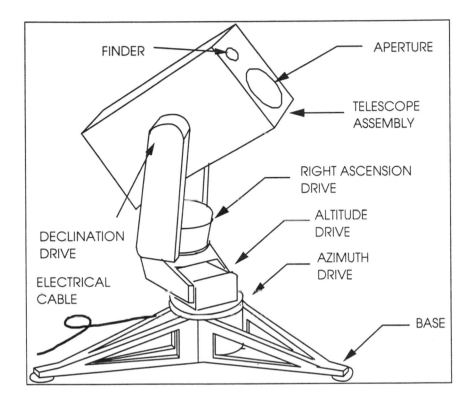

FIG. 9.1   The MicroObservatory instrument.

The telescope uses a four-axis mount. It moves in altitude and azimuth to align itself to the north celestial pole, while it drives in declination and hour angle to point to and track celestial objects. The telescope has an on-board computer, custom designed using an Intel 80C196KC microcontroller. All telescope functions are handled through this device using the telescope's local coordinates. These functions include communication and six motor drives (altitude, azimuth, hour angle, declination, filter wheel, and focus). Solenoids control shutters and extra filters. The microcontroller senses the state of the telescope though optical encoders on each of its axes and through four temperature sensors. The telescope is connected to its power supply and to a Macintosh computer with a single umbilical cable, providing power and communication functions.

The telescopes have proven to be very rugged and highly dependable. Rather than having to repair them onsite, as is the case with larger instruments, these devices have been shipped back to our facility on the rare occasions that they have needed repairs. Parts are interchangeable allowing for quick turnaround. Whereas conventional telescopes often need nightly adjustments and changes in instruments, the MICROOBSERVATORY has been design for low maintenance and ease of use. All functions are automated.

Attention has been paid to making the instrument as safe as possible. Power that is run to the telescope is a low 24 V with ground fault interruption. All motorized axes are clutched to prevent mechanical failure or to slip when forced by human hands.

Software

Each MICROOBSERVATORY instrument is controlled by a Macintosh computer through an Ethernet communications protocol. The software that controls the telescope was originally designed to let local users, especially engineers, participate in testing and troubleshooting the instrument. The local user can have direct control of the instrument or can access the telescope through a telephone modem connection.

The Macintosh transmits commands to the instrument in its local coordinate system of encoder position. This is not a dependable method to acquire celestial objects because every mechanical system manufactured always has measurable differences. For the telescopes, optical and mechanical alignments are not identical; each has its own set of physical characteristics determined through extensive testing using hundreds of observations. These parameters affect pointing and tracking accuracy if they are not corrected. These measured parameters are used by each local computer to bring pointing accuracy to below 5' of arc. Students do not have to worry about which telescope they are using. They all point identically because the appropriate correction parameters are automatically used. The local telescope also has knowledge of its geographic position and time, and it corrects for these differences as well, never attempting to observe objects that are below the horizon or that are hidden by obstructions. For daytime observations, it assiduously avoids pointing at the sun and exposing its more sensitive parts to sunlight. (However, the telescopes can be manually fitted with an optional external solar filter for observing sunspots and other solar active regions.)

When the local weather is bad or when the instrument is done with its observing run, it points downward to protect the optical window.

The Macintosh and the local MICROOBSERVATORY software can be thought of as the instrument's babysitter, keeping track of the telescope's state, needs, and complaints. The Macintosh organizes all of the queues of observations that it receives from the web. It generates report and error files (e.g., if one of the motors fails to reach its destination, which signifies a loosening of a clutch). It coordinates observations, downloading information quickly so the instrument can move on to another observation. Should the Internet have its own problems, the telescope will merrily continue to make observations and store its images, transmitting when the web comes back online. The software also sends e-mail back to our project whenever there is a problem, with a full description of the difficulty (see Fig. 9.2).

The local software makes decisions regarding how to best present the images it collects. Twelve-bit images usually look quite flat and contrastless. Excellent for quantitative analysis, they often appear bloodless. The software adjusts the mapping to an 8-bit dynamic range based on the type of image it takes. This allows students to quickly determine whether the object is the one they wanted or to "surf" other people's images and see a fascinating array of objects without performing any additional image processing.

Web Site

The MICROOBSERVATORY Web site permits the user to control the telescope from a distant location. Students can check the weather at a particular location and then select the telescope they wish to use. Dark skies require a rural location. Some objects can only be seen below certain latitudes. Daylight may preclude observation in certain time zones. Observations can be delayed until the most opportune time for observing. Users can check the waiting list; observation queues are maintained for each instrument in real time. Password protection gives priority to different levels of users. The Web site maintains a database of images, usually culled on a weekly basis. Interesting images may be moved to an archive. All images are available to all users.

Help is provided to users though a tutorial. Examples of problematic images and how to make them better are also available. Links are provided to other astronomical sites and to free sources of image

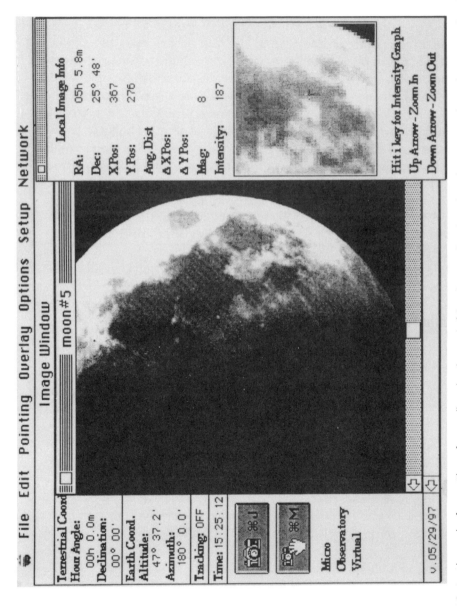

FIG. 9.2 Local control software. This software allows local control of the telescope directly and is a forerunner to the Web site. It is still useful for troubleshooting and monitoring each of the telescopes.

processing software. We are planning to locate our telescopes globally so objects can be followed throughout the 24-hour day at regular time intervals (see Fig. 9.3).

HOW THE MICROOBSERVATORY IS USED

The MICROOBSERVATORY has been used remotely in several high school, middle school, and elementary school classrooms throughout the United States. We have also extended MICROOBSERVATORY use to the college classroom, experimenting with its use in introductory astronomy courses, physics classes, and schools of education. We have seen students pass through various stages in their use of this unusual telescope. We report on each in order of increasing sophistication.

Imaging Objects That Are Visible To The Naked Eye

Objects very familiar to students seem to be the most common starting point for student investigations. The Sun, the Moon, visible planets, and stars are objects of great interest because they help to place the power of the MICROOBSERVATORY in context. By imaging familiar objects, students begin to identify ways in which this telescope is similar to and different from their normal vision. For example, the MICROOBSERVATORY sees with much greater resolution than the human eye and with much greater sensitivity. A picture of the Moon becomes brighter, clearer, and perhaps more important, permanent. Students can see features in the Moon's surface that are not apparent to the naked eye (see Fig. 9.4). Moreover, the telescope provides raw material for the computer's image processing capability. Students can easily improve the appearance of an image they have acquired. As one team of students reported,

> While working with the MICROOBSERVATORY we got a total learning experience. With this program we got to be in control of a telescope ... The images we received would often need work ... Through NIH [National Institutes of Health Image Process Program] we learned hands-on how to process and maximize the clarity of our images ...If you look closely at the surface you can also see the man on the moon. (Christina M. & Rebecca B., ninth-grade earth science students).

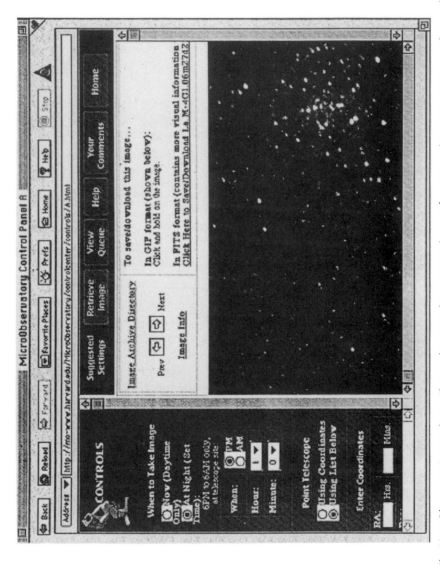

FIG. 9.3 The MicroObservatoryNet Web site. The user has control over many telescope functions and can view images simultaneously. The URL is http://mo-www.harvard.edu/MicroObservatory

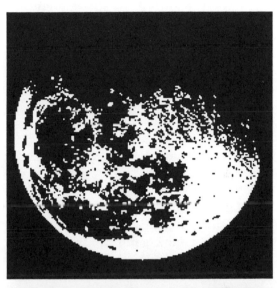

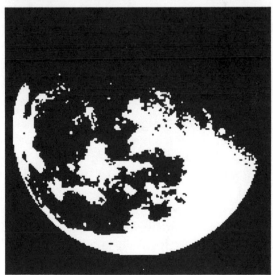

FIG. 9.4 Students' images of the moon. The raw data is on the left. The image processed for increased clarity and contrast is on the right.

We find that teachers often assign projects which are normally carried out as paper-and-pencil activities using previously acquired images, such as plotting the position of Jupiter against the background of stars or calculating heights of mountains on the moon (Cain & Welch, 1980; Gibbs, 1989; Hoff, Kelsey, & Neff, 1984; Snydle & Koser, 1973; Sunal & Demchik, 1985; Watson, 1981). Students collect original data using the MicroObservatory to carry out these projects. We have found that their ownership and enthusiasm for such projects is enhanced by carrying out these conventional activities using their own images.

Imaging Invisible Objects

Students often extend their searches to objects of which they have heard or have seen pictures in their textbooks. Often these objects are too faint for observation with the naked eye. Searching out these "invisible" objects is an important stage in understanding astronomy. Objects of interest must be identified using the celestial coordinate system of right ascension and declination. Many exposures must be made to find the proper length of time for the telescope to acquire a bright, but not overly exposed image. Searching out these objects demands a more sophisticated notion of the cosmos in which objects exist but appear much differently through the telescope than to the observer's eye (see Fig. 9.5 for examples of invisible objects).

Original Students' Research

After carrying out a teacher-assigned project, classes undertake an original research project in which teams of students work cooperatively. As an example, comet Hale-Bopp was an exciting subject to follow during the spring of 1997. Its changing shape and brightness was recorded by several groups of students. One team pooled images from other classes nationwide (from students as young as the fifth grade) to produce a computer-based movie of the comet's changing position. Figure 9.6 contains two images from this movie. One can clearly see that it is moving in a direction that is quite different from the way its tail is pointed. Using multiple images, students were able to estimate the comet's distance from Earth.

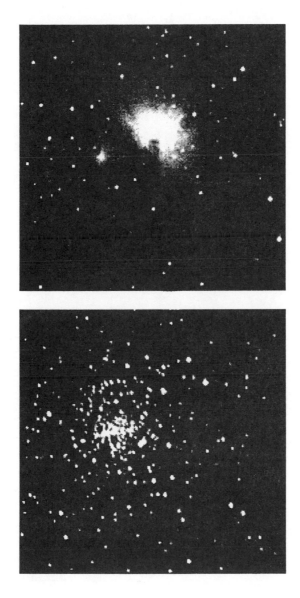

FIG. 9.5 Students' image of M-4, a globular cluster in Scorpius and of M-42, the Orion Nebula. These objects show detail that is not visible to the naked eye.

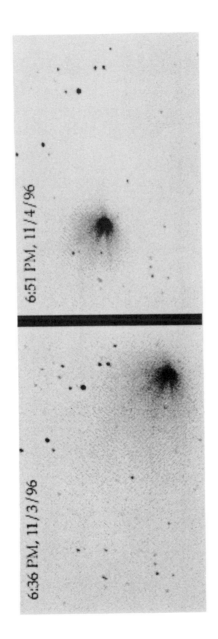

6:36 PM, 11/3/96

6:51 PM, 11/4/96

FIG. 9.6 Images of comet Hale-Bopp (in negative). These were taken one day apart by 12th grade students from the Brooks School, North Andover, Massachusetts. Note that the comet is moving against the background of stars in the direction of its tail.

Teachers' Development of
MICROOBSERVATORY Activities

Teachers often use demonstrations as part of their lessons (Miller, 1990). Daytime observations of sunspots, planets, and the Moon have been presented during class periods and integrated into lectures and activities by teachers. Teachers have used the MICROOBSERVATORY to prepare images that they project in class to illustrate certain astronomical concepts. For example, the discovery of the moons of Jupiter by Galileo in 1610 changed forever our view of the universe by displacing the earth from the center of the heavens. Successive images of Jupiter and its entourage allow for discussion of the period of the moons' revolution and the calculation of Jupiter's mass in the same way that we measure masses throughout the universe (see Fig. 9.7).

Teachers have invented a variety of imaginative ways, in addition to demonstrations, for using MICROOBSERVATORY. Many of the online activities have been created by teachers themselves and are accessible to anyone who uses the site. Activities range in detail and in difficulty and vary according to the grade level to which they are targeted.

Students from fifth grade to graduate school use the telescopes. The site is used to study not only astronomy, but also physics, chemistry, earth science, geology, and history. Graduate students in education have used the site to model ways of teaching students how to conduct research and to track the course of their own understanding while learning about astronomy.

A total of 14 teachers from across the country participated in a 3-week MICROOBSERVATORY workshop during July of 1997. Workshop sessions, which took place entirely online, were designed to expose educators to MICROOBSERVATORY and to create a forum for discussion of the ways they could use the site in their classrooms. Teachers found the most appropriate ways to integrate MICROOBSERVATORY into their lessons by matching activities with curriculum projects they were planning to undertake in the coming year. Several teachers worked individually to design activities. Others formed groups that communicated via e-mail, via online (real-time) discussion through a special MICROOBSERVATORY chat room, and by posting messages to the workshop participants on the MICROOBSERVATORY bulletin board.

The workshop created a cohesive MICROOBSERVATORY "educator team" with which the MICROOBSERVATORY staff works to test all aspects of the site for its educational impact, practicality, and usefulness. Mem-

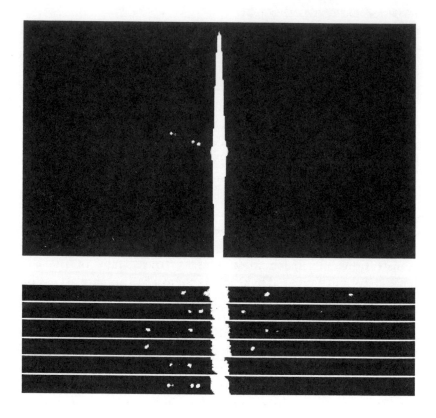

FIG. 9.7 Successive images of Jupiter and its moons. The planet has been intentionally overexposed to bring up the brightness of its moons. The photo was taken by Professor Linda M. French, Wheelock College, Boston, Massachusetts, over a 6-day period.

bers of this team provide valuable input that continues to enable effective use of the MICROOBSERVATORY in classrooms nationwide. In addition, it has given teachers and students a foundation for building collaborative environments for understanding the value of studying astronomy through imaging the sky with online telescopes.

MICROOBSERVATORY In Conjunction With Other Resources

Educational uses of MICROOBSERVATORY are not limited to the Web site. By using additional Web sites and software, such as sky information programs and information processing programs, in conjunction with the MICROOBSERVATORY site, students are made aware of the rich array of resources available for studying astronomy. In addition, activities may involve the participation of students in more than one classroom or school, further increasing students' understanding of how to conduct research with colleagues and improving their collaboration skills. Two MICROOBSERVATORY workshop teachers developed such an activity, which they currently use in their respective classrooms. This pair, comprised of one high school teacher from Massachusetts and one from Alaska, designed an activity they now use to teach students how to locate, image and understand the history and properties of asteroids.[1] In this activity, "Pursuit of Asteroids," students work together, sharing their findings, results, and questions with their colleagues on the other side of the country.

Students use MICROOBSERVATORY telescopes in conjunction with the dynamic sky simulation software, Voyager II (Voyager II. V 2.0. Carina Software: San Ramon, California, 1994). Before they can make their observations, students must conduct research on the nature and history of asteroids to determine where in the sky they would most likely locate one.

The exercise includes an exploration of the sky through which the students become familiar with the concept of right ascension (RA) and declination (Dec), the coordinate system used to locate objects in the sky. Using Voyager II, they determine the rising and setting times of the asteroid's orbit relative to Earth's and then model these orbits to understand the context within which their observations will be made.

Once they have simulated the orbits, teams of students create a plan for conducting their asteroid investigation. Using the MICROOBSERVA-TORY Control Center page, they enter the coordinates that will give them an image of the sky within which they hope to find their asteroid. After taking two images of the same region, students import their data into the image processing program NIH Image (NIH Image. National Institute of Health Image Processing Program), where they can improve the quality of their images, eliminate some of the noise, and magnify the region in which they hope to find the asteroid. They use the technique of *blinking*, or shifting back and forth between the two consecutive images, to detect the asteroid. The asteroid is distinguished from the stars around it by changing its position from one blink to the next (see Fig. 9.8).

---

[1]Larry Weatherwax teaches astronomy, geology, and biology at West Anchorage High School in Anchorage, Alaska. Bruce Mellin teaches astronomy, geology, meteorology, and oceanography at the Brooks School in North Andover, Massachusetts.

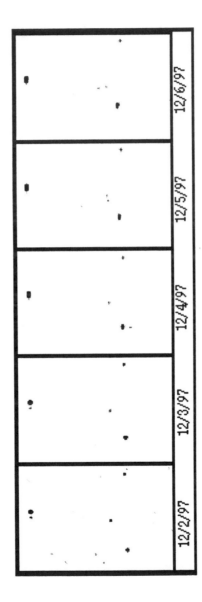

FIG. 9.8 Blinking asteroid. Five images of asteroid Lutetia (lower left) on five consecutive nights. When blinked, the image appears to move upward and toward the right. Courtesy, Brooks School, North Andover, Massachusetts.

While investigations are going on simultaneously in Massachusetts and Alaska, students communicate with their counterparts via e-mail and through the MICROOBSERVATORY bulletin board. By sharing their experiences of asteroid exploration, the students become part of the larger MICROOBSERVATORY research team.

Teachers have found that students are often more motivated and enthusiastic about conducting their MICROOBSERVATORY investigations with colleagues, rather than in isolation. Two workshop teachers are planning to establish a partnership between one group of college students in Massachusetts and a group of fifth graders in New York. The respective groups will work together, providing the younger students with mentors who can help answer their questions, and giving the college students the opportunity to learn by assisting others.

INVESTIGATIVE RESEARCH

Although students can use other Web sites for obtaining more colorful and vivid images of objects, the advantage of MICROOBSERVATORY is rather in its ability to give students control and potential mastery of a remote telescope with sharp images that are highly efficient for sophisticated astronomical research. At a high school in Weymouth, Massachusetts, teams of students conduct semester-long research studies of the Moon, which require that they first submit a proposal to their teacher, complete with timeline and the details of their investigation.[2]

The emphasis of the activity is on learning how to operate the telescope, and on developing an understanding of the value of efficient data collection and an appreciation of the complexity of the research process. It is designed to be consistent with problem-based learning, an instructional approach intended to develop students' problem-solving strategies by placing students in the active role of problem solvers confronted with real-world problems.[3]

---

[2]Michael Richard teaches astronomy, geology, and earth science at Weymouth High School in Weymouth, Massachusetts.

[3]The Center for Problem-Based Learning (CPBL) was established by the Illinois Mathematics and Science Academy to engage in PBL research, information exchange, teacher training and curriculum development in K–16 educational settings. See http://www.imsa.edu/team/cpbl/cpbl.html.

In this activity, students are required to make and keep complete records of their work in a team log book. The log book contains the dates of their observations, telescope settings, information on the images they produce, and any other notes the team thinks will help them complete the project. After they acquire images of the Moon in its various phases, students hone their image processing skills by using NIH Image to improve the quality of their images and make them more efficient for the investigation. Using a variety of resources in addition to MICROOB-SERVATORY, including various NASA Web sites, students explore the geology of the lunar surface. Once they compile their results, teams use powerful multimedia presentation software, such as PowerPoint (Microsoft PowerPoint 97: Microsoft, 1997) to present their findings to the rest of the class.

This activity has produced a highly positive response from students, who claim that it is among the most unique activity they have ever accomplished. "Working with the MICROOBSERVATORY has been the most interesting and involved project so far," commented one student. "It wasn't something you could understand just from reading a book," said another, "the only way you really could grasp what was needed to be done was to do it yourself." Although the students reported that their investigations required hard work, their remarks gave evidence that their efforts yielded highly rewarding results.

POTENTIAL FOR WIDESPREAD IMPACT

It is impossible to predict with certainty the potential impact of a low-cost student observatory on the teaching of earth science, physics, and astronomy in the nation's schools. If adopted by a large number of schools, this project could help to popularize and increase the role of student-centered investigations, encourage the future development of joint efforts between scientists and students, engage students in activities that would increase news coverage of students' investigations, and provide a seed for 24-hour observation through the expansion to international sites.

In addition, many research projects cannot be attempted by professionals because they lack a sufficient number of telescopes and adequate manpower. Students can fill that gap. A few examples of possible research projects follow:

- *Comets.* New comets appear unexpectedly in the night sky. They are detected by observing faint objects and by looking for those that have moved from a previous night. The use of image processing to subtract sky brightness and to blink between images of the sky taken at different times will allow for comet-hunting by students. Students' observations of known comets could help to refine their orbits and more accurately predict their paths (A'Hearn, 1983). New comets are named for their discoverer.

- *Asteroids.* Many asteroids do not have their size, shape, or position known very accurately. However, measurements of their varying brightness (photometry) can allow the measurement of tumbling rates. Students can also find "missing" asteroids, those that are perturbed by close passes to Earth or to other planets. Observations over time allow distances and other orbital elements to be determined. More than 100 asteroids are discovered each year and the discoverer gets to propose a name for the asteroid (Binzel, 1983).

- *Variable Stars.* There are thousands of variable stars that can be monitored for their change in brightness. Many have unpredictable, explosive brightening, but astronomers cannot monitor even a small fraction of them. Students can monitor brightness changes of some of 3,600 variable stars and can contribute their data to the American Association of Variable Star Observers (AAVSO), who forward data to scientists working on variable stars (Chromey, Hunt, Edelstein, & Bonar, 1991; Genet, Boyd, & Hall, 1985; Shore, 1989; Walker, 1991). The AAVSO is located in Cambridge, Massachusetts, and maintains a close association with the Center for Astrophysics.

The professional community is interested in the development of the MICROOBSERVATORY instrumentation. It fits in a logical niche, not just for high schools or museums, but also for the professional astronomer.

CONCLUSION

Astronomy is a very popular science among the nation's youth and is followed by millions of the nation's adults. Taught as a part of general science, earth science, and physics, astronomy has an almost universal fascination. Although many schools own telescopes, they are difficult and inconvenient to use. The MICROOBSERVATORY's five telescopes show promise in making astronomy more of a hands-on experience for students. Using this instrument can be both frustrating and rewarding.

Other tools for collecting data have been used on a national level, but none with the sophistication of these telescopes. Built on the developments of automated telescopes for professional astronomers, and incorporating the innovations of amateurs, easy-to-use software makes these instruments accessible to students, even at primary school levels.

The MicroObservatoryNet consists of several specially designed telescopes that can be used by anyone with an Internet connection. Which telescope to use can be determined based on weather conditions or on the visibility of celestial objects. The telescopes can be controlled as dedicated instruments in real time or can be programmed for later observations. All of the images taken by the telescope are assessable to all visitors to the Web site. Unusual or especially useful images are stored in an archive for later use by students or teachers.

Students utilize the MicroObservatory in increasingly sophisticated ways over time. Most start by imaging easily identifiable objects with which they are familiar, such as bright stars, constellations, the Moon, and the planets. By becoming familiar with the capabilities of the telescope, students then move on to imaging more exotic or faint objects. Finally, many students engage in research projects where they examine a particular object as it changes position, brightness, or appearance using different exposures or telescope filters. These more in-depth studies have been undertaken as class projects or as a part of national competitions sponsored by the MicroObservatory project.

The MicroObservatory marks a new generation of remote instrumentation available over the Internet. Its existence has spurred unusual collaborations between students thousands of miles apart or years apart in age. "Virtual teams" have emerged to study particular problems that members have a common interest in studying. Several time-lapse videos have been created with images taken by many contributors and have been used by thousands more for illustrating the changes in the appearance of the Moon, Sun, planets, and comets.

The future will see more such instruments, too expensive or exotic for purchase or full-time use by single institutions, being shared using the Internet. Shared use is more cost-effective, and it opens the window of opportunity for students to collaborate and experience the thrill of scientific inquiry. Virtual communities of like-minded students will grow in response to the opportunity of engaging in activities that model the scientific enterprise and have the potential of making substantial contributions to the research efforts of professional scientists.

ACKNOWLEDGMENTS

The authors wish to thank Paul Antonucci, Freeman Deutsch, and Steve Leiker of the MicroObservatory project staff for assistance in the preparation of this article. The MicroObservatory is indebted to Robert Kimberk for many of the innovations embedded in the telescope and to Center for Astrophysics scientists Nat Carlton, John Geary, Sallie Baliunas, Irwin Shapiro, Bruce Gregory, Sam Palmer, and Josh Grindlay. Teachers and professors worked for many years on the project including Mark Petricone, Mike Richards, Bruce Mellin, Linda French, and Clark Neilly. This project has been supported by the National Science Foundation (RED-9454767), Kodak, Inc., and Apple Computer, Inc. We thank Nora Sabelli and Andrew Molnar of the NSF for their advice and support.

REFERENCES

A'Hearn, M. F. (1983). Photometry of comets. In R. M. Genet (Ed.), *Solar system photometry handbook* (3-1 to 3-33). Richmond, VA: Willmann-Bell.

Aikens, R. S. (1990). Watch out photography, here come cooled HCCD cameras. *Photonics Spectra, 24*(11), 95-106.

Baliunas, S. L., Donahue, R. A., Loeser, J. G., Guinan, E. F., Genet, R. M., & Boyd, L. J. (1987). Broadband photometry of bright stars: The first year of APTS at the F. L. Whipple observatory. In D. S. Hayes, R. M. Genet, & D. R. Genet (Eds.), *New generation small telescopes* (pp. 97-116). Mesa, AZ: Fairborn Observatory.

Binzel, R. P. (1983). Photometry of asteroids. In R. M. Genet (Ed.), *Solar system handbook*, (1-1 to 1-17). Richmond, VA: Willmann-Bell.

Buil, C. (1991). *CCD astronomy*. Richmond, VA: Willmann-Bell.

Cain, P. W., & Welch, D. W. (1980). *Astronomy activities for the classroom*. (Teaching Guide). South Carolina State Department of Education. (ERIC Document Reproduction Service No. ED199062)

Cavena, G. R., & Leonard, W. H. (1985). Extending discretion in high school science curricula. *Science Education, 69*(5), 593-603.

Chromey, F. R., Hunt, M. E., Edelstein, M., & Bonar, E. (1991). A CCD photometer for the Vassar College observatory. In A. G. Davis Philip & F. R. Chromey (Eds.), *Precision photometry astrophysics of the galaxy* (386, pp. 293-297). Schenectady, NY: L. Davis Press.

Freiher, G. (1991). Rediscovering the outer planets. *Computer Graphics World, 14*(7), 36-42.

Genet, R. M., Boyd, L. J., & Hall, D. S. (1985). Variable star observations with automatic telescopes. In J. B. Hearnshaw & P. L. Cottrell (Eds.), *Instrumentation and research programmes for small telescopes* (482, pp. 47-55). Dordrecht, Holland: D. Reidel.

Gibbs, R. E. (1989). *Observing the sky*. Ellensburg, WA: Eastern Washington University, Department of Physics.

Gilbert, O. L. (1974). An air pollution survey by school children. *Environmental Pollution*, (6), 175.

Hayes, D. S., Genet, R. M., Boyd, L. J., & Crawford, D. L. (1987). Remote-access automatic photometry. In D. S. Hayes, R. M. Genet, & D. R. Genet (Eds.), *New generation small telescopes* (pp. 19-25). Mesa, AZ: Fairborn Observatory.

Hoff, D. (1982, March). Astronomy for the non-science student—A status report. *The Physics Teacher*, 175.

Hoff, D. B., Kelsey, L. J., & Neff, J. S. (1984). *Activities in astronomy* (2nd ed.). Dubuque, IA: Kendall/Hunt.

Huchra, J. (1988). Silicon eyes. *Technology Window. A Publication of the Office for Information Technology. Harvard University, 2*(April), 1–3.

International Planetarium Society. (1990). *IPS membership directory*.

Julyan, C. (1988). *Conversation with kid network*. Cambridge, MA: Technical Education Research Center.

Julyan, C. (1991). *Conversation with kid network*. Cambridge, MA: Technical Education Research Center.

Mellanby, K. (1974). A water pollution survey, mainly by British school children. *Environmental Pollution*, (6), 161.

Miller, I. A., & Haracz, R. D. (1990). Macintosh demonstrations for introductory physics. In E. F. Redish & J. S. Risley (Eds.), Computers in physics instruction (pp. 109–110). Raleigh, NC: Addison-Wesley.

Murnane, R. J., & Raizen, S.A. (1988). *Improving indicators of the quality of science and mathematics education in grades k–12*. Washington, DC: National Academy Press.

Scott, D. (1991, September). Video image on a chip. *Popular Science*, 50.

Shore, S. N. (1989). Variable stars. In R.A. Meyers, (Ed.), *Encyclopedia of Astronomy and Astrophysics*, San Diego, CA: Academic Press.

Snydle, R. W., & Koser, J. F. (1973). An activity oriented astronomy course. *Science Activities, 10*(3), 16–18.

Stake, R. E., & Easley, J. A., Jr. (1978). *Case studies in science education*. Urbana, IL: University of Illinois, Center for Instruction Research and Curriculum Evaluation.

Stebbins, R. A. (1987). Amateurs and their place in professional science. In D. S. Hayes, R. G. Genet, & D. R. Genet (Eds.), *New generation small telescopes*. (pp. 217–225). Mesa, AZ: Fairborn Observatory.

Sunal, D. W., & Demchik, V. C. (1985). *Astronomy education materials resource guide* (3rd ed.). Morgantown, WV: West Virginia University Bookstore.

Tessler, L. G. (1991). Networked computing in the 1990s. *Scientific American, 265*(3), 86–93.

U.S. Department of Commerce. (1986). *U.S. imports for consumption and general imports*. (#FT 246, pp. 18–38).

Walker, A. R. (1991). CCD photometry with small telescopes. In A. G. Davis Philip & F. R. Chromey (Eds.), *Precision photometry astrophysics of the galaxy*. Schenectady, NY: L. Davis Press.

Watson, F. G. (1981, November). Tracking the visible planets. *The Science Teacher*, 53–55.

Weiss, I. (1978). *Report of the 1977 National Survey of Science, Mathematics, and Social Studies Education*.

Weiss, I. (1987). *Report of the 1985-86 National Survey of Science, Mathematics, and Social Studies Education*.

Welch, W. W. (1985). A science based approach to science learning. In D. Holdzkom & P. B. Lutz (Eds.), *Research within reach: Science education* (pp. 161–170). Washington: National Science Teachers Association.

Welch, W. W., Harris, L. J., & Anderson, R. E. (1984). How many are enrolled in science? *The Science Teacher, 51*, 16.

Zorpette, G. (1988). Fractals: Not just another pretty picture. *IEEE Spectrum, 25*(11), 29–31.

10

Technology Supports for Student Participation in Science Investigations

Barbara Means and Elaine Coleman
SRI International

"Use school teachers and their students to monitor the entire earth"
(Gore, 1992).

In his book, *Earth in the Balance: Ecology and the Human Spirit*, then-Senator Al Gore outlined his concept for an international partnership between scientists and students who would monitor and study earth systems, with students acting as a worldwide system of "sensors," collecting data on the condition of their local environments and sharing and discussing their data through the Internet. Three years later, the Global Learning and Observations to Benefit the Environment (GLOBE) program was established to bring Gore's vision to fruition.

GLOBE seeks to promote elementary and secondary school students' learning of science by involving them in real scientific investigations following detailed data collection protocols for measuring the characteristics of their local atmosphere, soil, and vegetation. Students then use data entry forms on the World Wide Web to submit data to a central archive, where it is combined with data from other schools to develop visualizations that can be viewed on the Web. Other than requiring careful adherence to the data collection protocols, GLOBE gives schools complete latitude in determining the (K–12) grade levels and classes in which to implement the program, the educational activities to provide, and and the way in which the program will fit into the local curriculum.

Although the involvement of students in the collection of environmental data, interchanges with practicing scientists, international telecommunication, and the sharing of data through the Internet have been features of previous education programs such as Kids Network and Global Lab, GLOBE is unique in terms of its scale (with more than 7,500 schools in 84 countries signed on) and in the weight it gives to science, with students involved in real, ongoing research investigations by earth scientists. GLOBE seeks to strike a balance between its scientific objectives—to obtain accurate and reliable data to enhance our scientific understanding of earth systems—and its educational goals—to promote science and mathematics learning and environmental awareness.

The GLOBE program can be viewed as an example of "anchored instruction" (CTGV, 1997; Goldman et al., 1996). During anchored instruction, rather than being told about a body of facts (instructed directly), students are placed in situations where inquiry and problem solving can occur. The GLOBE program seeks to help students become actively engaged in learning about their environment by anchoring instruction in realistic problem-solving situations. GLOBE educational and data collection activities are intended to enable teachers and students to experience the kinds of problems that experts (in this case, environmental scientists) continuously encounter. The assumption behind this approach is that when students immerse themselves in genuine scientific activities, they experience what it is like to be a real scientist, begin to make connections among concepts and principles that are relevant to their areas of study, and undergo changes in their own thinking and understanding.

An important design feature of anchored instruction is that students are provided with authentic materials. In the GLOBE program, students use technology and follow procedures for taking measurements and analyzing data that are isomorphic with those used by scientists. The program seeks to facilitate collaboration between student and scientist while encouraging students to become more aware of their local and global environments. The expectation is that students learn from collecting data, from the guidance that they receive from the scientists and from their teachers, and most important from the analyses and inferences drawn from the data.

A BRIEF PROGRAM HISTORY

The GLOBE program's history provides a case study of the level of commitment and resources required to launch a major Internet-based international science education program. On Earth Day (April 22) 1994, Vice President Al Gore enunciated the concept for the GLOBE program and invited the participation of countries from around the world. The program enjoyed a level of support and visibility that is unusual for science education programs. An interagency team, including the National Oceanic and Atmospheric Administration (NOAA), the National Aeronautics and Space Administration (NASA), the National Science Foundation (NSF), the Environmental Protection Agency (EPA), and the Departments of Education and State worked together to set up and staff the new program. Programmer teams at both NOAA and NASA were given the task of developing software for students' data reporting and archiving as well as for creating visualizations from the students' data.

A workshop of scientists and educators was held in Aspen, Colorado, in September of 1994 to identify the minimum set of areas in which students would need to make measurements to advance both their own understanding of the earth as a dynamic system and the scientific database about our globe. The three broad areas for scientific measurement that emerged from the workshop were atmosphere and climate, hydrology and water chemistry, and biology and geology. Scientists worked with the GLOBE program staff to develop data collection protocols for each investigation and to identify reasonably low-cost equipment that students could use to make the measurements with an acceptable degree of accuracy and reliability. Materials from existing environmental education programs were combed to identify educational activities related to the measurement protocols.

The Early Days

The Federal Register published a notice in November of 1994 inviting U.S. schools to apply to become GLOBE participants. Requirements for participation included an Internet connection and a computer capable of running a web browser and data visualization software. Schools interested in participating in GLOBE but lacking the needed equipment or Internet connection were invited to apply for federal assistance if they could demonstrate financial need. (Subsequent announcements did not include the option for federal subsidy.) Schools applying to join GLOBE had to commit to the schedule of data collection (which included weekends and school vacations) and to participation for a 3-year period.

By March of 1995, the 400-page first edition of the *GLOBE Teacher's Guide* was ready and soon after GLOBE began training teachers. The

GLOBE training model in the United States was one of GLOBE-arranged training for one teacher from each GLOBE school. Three-day training sessions were hosted by Space Grant programs at roughly a dozen university sites across the country. Training was conducted by teams composed of a facilitator plus two scientists, one technology specialist, and two educators. (By the summer of 1995, GLOBE teachers trained earlier were able to fill this role.) Training sessions began in March of 1995 and continued throughout the year. In total, nearly 1,700 U.S. teachers received GLOBE training during 1995.

Internationally, GLOBE provides the program infrastructure, and international partners manage their own implementation, acquiring the resources necessary to equip their own schools. Each country selects its own country coordinator, decides how many and what schools to sponsor, and determines how GLOBE will be implemented in its schools. The only requirement is that participating schools conduct the measurements in accordance with the GLOBE data collection protocols, using equipment that meets GLOBE specifications, under the supervision of teachers trained by individuals who have completed GLOBE-provided training.

International workshops for country coordinators were held in four locations around the world during the summer and fall of 1995. The country coordinators then set up and conducted their own teacher training programs. The program's official launch was on Earth Day of 1995. Two years later, in April of 1997, the program was able to boast of participation by 3,500 schools in 50 countries from around the world.

The Second Phase

During the spring of 1995, as the GLOBE program was gearing up for its first year of training using the initial set of data collection protocols and first edition *Teacher's Guide*, it was also laying the groundwork for a second phase to involve a larger collection of scientific investigations, original educational activities, and curriculum integration and evaluation activities. In November of 1994, the NSF issued an announcement inviting applications from teams of earth scientists and educators interested in shaping the GLOBE Phase II investigations. Teams were sought to design scientific investigations in the areas of atmosphere and climate, trace gases, water chemistry (e.g., water temperature, pH, and oxygen content), hydrology (e.g., water cycle), and land cover, and in the use of global positioning systems (GPSs). Each scientific investigation team was to be headed up by a scientist acting as a principal investigator (PI) who was committed to using GLOBE data in his or her research. In addition, they were to collaborate with an education co-PI who would help develop educational activities that would put the data collection into a meaningful context. After selection of the grantees, work on the Phase II materials began in May of 1995 and continued through July of the next year, when the first draft of the substantially rewritten second edition of the *Teacher's Guide* became available for training teachers in the summer of 1996.

Research on the GLOBE Program

In May of 1995, SRI International was selected in the NSF grants competition as the GLOBE evaluation partner. SRI is responsible for designing and implementing data collection efforts that assist the program in determining how well its various elements are functioning and in identifying directions for improvement. We are also seeking evidence concerning the program's impact in the three areas set forth as program goals: to enhance environmental awareness, to increase scientific understanding of the earth, and to improve achievement in science and mathematics education.

The empirical data reported in this chapter were collected during school years 1995–1996 and 1996–1997, the first two full academic years of program implementation. Both a random sample of 400 teachers trained by GLOBE in 1995 and the 250 GLOBE teachers most active in reporting data during school year 1996–1997 were surveyed concerning their GLOBE experiences that school year in the spring of 1996. Responses were received from 310 of the 400 teachers in the random sample (for a response rate of 78%) and from 229 of the 250 most active teachers (response rate of 92%). Those active teachers whose GLOBE students were in the fourth, seventh, or tenth grades were asked to administer a student survey to their classes.

In the spring of 1997 another sample of 441 active GLOBE teachers was surveyed. Responses were received from 344 of the 441 teachers for a response rate of 78%. In addition, student surveys and assessments were given to students in 44 GLOBE classes and in 27 classes of teachers who had signed up for GLOBE training but had not yet taken the training or implemented the program.

During the first two years of the evaluation, SRI researchers conducted site visits to 15 GLOBE schools, where GLOBE activities were observed and teachers and students were interviewed. Additional sources of data included observations of teacher training sessions, analyses of the teacher training database and the archive of students' GLOBE data, and e-mail interchanges with selected classes.

GLOBE USES OF TECHNOLOGY

From the beginning, Vice President Gore and GLOBE's framers wanted the program to demonstrate the power of the Internet as an infrastructure for sharing data. At some level, scientific data can be collected and reported through other means (e.g., telefacsimile), as some countries without reasonable access to the Internet are doing. But to a major extent, reporting data through the Internet and accessing the GLOBE Web site to find the data they submitted earlier in the week are important parts of what makes the program "real" for students and for teachers. The importance of the Internet within the project may be felt most keenly by those without access to it. As the country coordinator for Benin put it, "Without Internet access we [Benin participants] feel as if we are on the periphery ... not in the center of things." The fast turn around and flexible access to a rich array of resources provided through the World Wide Web appear to be important elements in creating a sense of program identity and community.

GLOBE Web Site

The GLOBE program has used its Web site as a central tool for communicating with GLOBE schools, creating a tangible "presence" for the project, and fostering a sense of community among project participants. The Web site, the current version of which can be viewed at http://www.globe.gov, began with a project introduction, data reporting forms, the Student Data Archive, a Scientist's Corner, and the GLOBE Stars page.

Data Reporting Forms and Data Archive. Web-based forms were developed for students to use in reporting their GLOBE data. Fig. 10.1 shows an example of the form for reporting surface water tempera-

ome
earn about GLOBE
LOBE Schools Login

cience and Education
Teacher's Guide
Student Investigations
Scientists' Corner
LOBE Data
Data Entry
Visualizations
Data Archive
LOBE Exchange
School Search
School To School
Educators' Forum
Partner Countries
U.S. Franchises
ews and Events
Special Events
GLOBE Stars
GLOBE Bulletins
Teacher Workshops
Newsletters
ibrary
Resource Room
Image Gallery
nfo and Help
Help on this page
GLOBE Help Desk
FAQs

Not a registered GLOBE School

All measurements should be taken within one hour of <u>Local Solar Noon</u> and at the same Study Site Location.

Measurement Time:
Year: [Select ⬍] **Month:** [Select ⬍] **Day:** [   ] **Hour:** [   ] <u>UT</u>
Current Time: 1999 March 30, 18 UT
Local Solar Noon at your school location : 12 UT

Study Site Location: [Atmosphere Study Site   ⬍]
<u>Please remember to **define and/or update your study site!**</u>

Cloud Observations:

Cloud Type(s):

☐ **No clouds present**
High : ☐ Cirrus ☐ Cirrocumulus ☐ Cirrostratus
Middle: ☐ Altostratus ☐ Altocumulus
Low : ☐ Cumulus ☐ Nimbostratus ☐ Stratus ☐ Stratocumulus
☐ Cumulonimbus

Cloud Cover:

○ Clear ○ Scattered ○ Broken ○ Overcast

Metadata (Comments): [

Precipitation:

Enter **T** for a trace amount or **M** for missing data.

RAINFALL:

Enter the amount of rain in your rain gauge and choose the number of days since you last checked the rain gauge.

Rain Amount : [   ] mm **over** [1 ⬍] day(s)
* pH of Rain: [   ] **measured with** [Select ⬍]
Metadata (Comments): [

SNOWFALL:
Total Snow Accumulation: [   ] mm
Daily Snow Accumulation: [   ] mm **over** [1 ⬍] day(s)
Daily Liquid Equivalent: [   ] mm
* pH of Snow: [   ] **measured with**
Metadata (Comments): [

Air Temperature:

Current Air Temperature: [   ] degrees Celsius

FIG. 10.1   GLOBE I data input form for water temperature and pH.

ture data. The GLOBE Web site provides links to these forms as well as to the archive of all GLOBE student data. Different types of data are collected on different schedules. For example, temperature and precipitation data are collected daily whereas the measurement of vegetation within the study site occurs just twice a year. When entering data, students indicate their school code and the date and time when the data were collected as well as entering the data. The data reporting form incorporates checks for out-of-range values and some common reporting errors. A "smiley face" signals students that their data report has been received by the archive. (Some of the youngest GLOBE students imagine that the GLOBE scientists themselves are bestowing these tokens of appreciation in real time.)

The GLOBE Student Data Archive is available for inspection and downloading by GLOBE students, scientists, or anyone else with an interest in the data. Students can find the data that their class contributed, look for the data contributed by any other GLOBE school, or search for a selected type of data reported on a specific date. As will be discussed in the following sections, the data archive becomes an important resource for students' investigations and for analyses of data quality and reasonableness, as well as providing the databases that will be used by GLOBE scientists and other members of the scientific community.

Data Visualizations.   Data visualizations were developed to help students see their data in a geophysical context. NASA programmers developed software that generates visualizations of the GLOBE minimum and maximum temperatures, precipitation, and cloud cover data on a daily basis (see de La Beaujardiere et al., 1997 for a detailed description). Students can view visualizations of the prior day's GLOBE data for a variable of their choice or can view visualizations of two selected variables side-by-side. In addition, visualizations of reference data sets from the National Weather Service and the Environmental Modeling Center are posted on the Web site. Figure 10.2 shows a visualization of students' minimum temperature data.

GLOBE Stars.   The GLOBE Stars section of the Web site was intended as a form of reinforcement and encouragement for participating classes. The number of pieces of data reported by each GLOBE school was tabulated automatically on a continuous basis. The Stars section highlights those schools that have attained various reporting

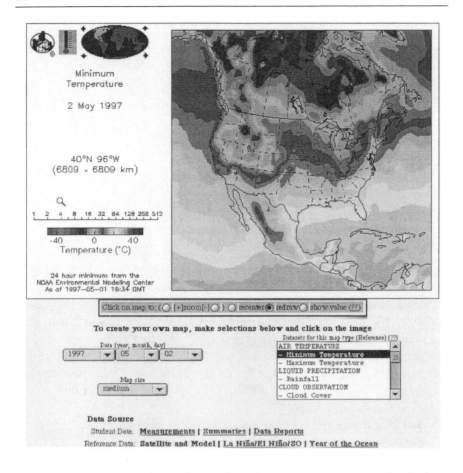

FIG. 10.2 An Example of a visualization for students' minimum temperature data for the United States.

levels (500–599 pieces of data, 400–499 pieces, and so on). Students are generally quite excited the first time they find their school's name on the GLOBE Web site; such recognition makes them feel that their efforts are integral to the project and fosters a sense of achievement.

Scientist's Corner. To provide students and teachers with more contexts for their GLOBE investigations and a sense of relationship to the scientists (principal investigators), a Scientists' Corner was developed for the Web site. This section contains rotating messages from individual scientists comprised of a personal message about why the data the students are collecting is important and one or more digitized photographs of the scientists. (Photos of the scientist as a child are big hits.) A sample of the scientists' messages is shown in Fig. 10.3.

GLOBEMail.   The GLOBEMail feature of the GLOBE Web site enables GLOBE schools to send messages to other GLOBE schools. Users can easily identify GLOBE schools on the Web site on the basis of their location or on the amount of data they have contributed. Messages can then be sent to the desired school over the Web. Students are able to share information about their schools and their local environments with other students around the world.

GPS, Satellite Images, And MultiSpec

In addition to extensive, multiple uses of the World Wide Web, GLOBE makes significant use of technologies that support remote sensing. The GLOBE program seeks to help students and teachers relate the knowledge they gain from taking measurements on their local environments to images of their area captured by satellite and to a global view of earth systems. Each GLOBE school selects a 15 km X 15 km plot as its study site and receives a Landsat image of the local area that includes their study site. The size of the study site corresponds approximately to one pixel in the satellite image.

As schools join the GLOBE program, they borrow a GPS receiver to determine the latitude and longitude of their study site. The GPS receiver is a handheld device that receives signals from satellites orbiting the earth. Originally used in military applications, GPS receivers are now widely used in recreational applications such as boating and hiking.

The GLOBE GPS protocol provides a nice introduction to the concept of data accuracy. The receiver needs to obtain readings from at least four satellites to produce an accurate latitude and longitude reading. Given this many satellite signals, the receiver generates a reading that is accurate to within 100 m. The GLOBE GPS protocol has students take 15 successive readings at one-minute intervals and average them, thus obtaining a reading with accuracy within less than 30 m (the size of a Landsat pixel). The average latitude and longitude readings are submitted to the GLOBE database where they are linked to all of the observations the school reports thereafter.

The GPS, satellite imagery, and associated software are intended to introduce students to the concept of remote sensing and to the idea that

e
n about GLOBE
BE Schools Login

ace and Education
cher's Guide
dent Investigations
entists' Corner
BE Data
a Entry
ualizations
a Archive
BE Exchange
ool Search
ool To School
cators' Forum
tner Countries
. Franchises
and Events
cial Events
OBE Stars
OBE Bulletins
cher Workshops
sletters
ary
ource Room
ge Gallery
and Help
p on this page
OBE Help Desk
Qs

Land Cover Assessment Report

Dr. Russell Congalton, Land Cover Scientist

Hello everyone!

My name is Russ Congalton and I am excited to be working together with you on the GLOBE Program. In fact, what excited me most about GLOBE was the opportunity to work with you students and your teachers to collect environmental measurements and analyze them to learn more about our planet. I work as a professor of remote sensing and geographic information systems (GIS) in the Department of Natural Resources at the University of New Hampshire. This means that I teach courses and conduct research on how to use tools like aerial photographs, satellite images, and maps from many sources to solve natural resource problems. Most recently I have been studying black bear habitat in New Hampshire; I have also used GIS to map potential locations of a rare and endangered plant; finally, I have spent a lot of time working on GLOBE. My work takes me to lots of interesting places to meet with many fascinating people. This picture of me (43 kbytes) was taken in August of 1994 just hours before a scheduled shuttle launch. Because of my work with NASA I was able to get so close to the shuttle. It was very thrilling for me. I would really love to go for a ride. Maybe someday you will.

One subject that I have been researching for about 17 years is the accuracy and/or usefulness of land cover maps created from remotely sensed data. These land cover maps can be used for a great many reasons including evaluating change, identifying potential habitat, reducing environmental risk such as fires or landslides, or predicting forest biomass or agricultural crop production. For any land cover map, it is important to know its correctness because this accuracy will affect the confidence we have in the decisions that are based upon the map. Many, many land cover maps of all regions of the Earth have been created from remotely sensed data. However, very few have ever been assessed to see how good they are. Testing the accuracy requires having sufficient field data to compare to the map. It is this comparison that allows us to see how good a job we did of making the land cover map using the remotely sensed data.

In the GLOBE Program, you will be able to make your own land cover map of the area surrounding your school and then collect the necessary ground validation data to see how good a job you did. Also, I will be able to use the validation data that you collect to check out many other land cover maps to see how good they are. You and I will be doing the same science, and together we can learn some new things about our ability to map the Earth. It is absolutely incredible to me what you as students can now learn in school. When I was in college in the early 1980's, a computer and software to perform the land cover mapping cost at least half a million dollars. Now your school has the technology for just a few thousand dollars. It is really amazing. I look forward to seeing your maps and getting your validation data. You are really making a difference when you learn more about our environment. Thank you for being a member of the GLOBE team.

FIG. 10.3 Example of a GLOBE scientist's message.

the data they gather locally can be used to validate or provide "ground truthing" for images gathered from space. GLOBE has arranged to have 9.3 mile by 9.3 mile five-band subsets of Landsat images (the amount of data that fits on a 3.5" high-density floppy disk) purchased by universities and research institutions for educational purposes made available to GLOBE schools. In addition to the Landsat image for its own area, each school receives a diskette of Beverly, Massachusetts, which is used as the data set for the educational activities designed to teach students how to classify land cover and use remote image manipulation software.

Software called MultiSpec, developed by David Landgrebe at the Purdue Research Foundation under a NASA grant, provides GLOBE teachers and students with the ability to manipulate their Landsat images. MultiSpec allows students to zoom in on the region they wish to investigate, to choose the three channels (or sections of the radiation spectrum) they wish to view, and to develop and compare histograms of the reflectance values at various wavelengths. (Different wavelengths highlight different physical features. For example, green visible light and infrared energy are useful in determining types of plants and plant health.)

The MultiSpec software will support highly sophisticated investigations of the sort practicing scientists perform. One activity suggested in the *Teacher's Guide* is to use MultiSpec to graph reflectance values of one's school's study site and to find another pixel in the data set with values as close as possible to those of the study site. Students can then physically visit the second area and compare its vegetation and other features to those in the study site.

Technology Use in GLOBE's First Year

GLOBE's use of technology was a draw for many teachers entering the program. Some were at schools receiving new Internet connections and were eager to launch a worthwhile educational program using the technology. Some used the lure of the program as an argument for obtaining computers or Internet connections for their classrooms. Many teachers felt that GLOBE satisfied their need for an academically rich use of the Internet. The following quote provides an example: "Thank you for allowing us to use the Internet. We have participated in many others science activities including NASA Space Shuttle flights and Comet sightings ... GLOBE was my introduction into the Internet and from there everything is available. More than the program itself, it has provided a vehicle to get Internet computer technology into my classroom. I have the only "online" computer in the school.... My classroom is one of the more popular and busiest in the school."

However, assembling the required hardware and software and arranging for Internet connections was a barrier that slowed many teachers' implementation of the program. The problem was exacerbated during the first part of the year because many of the technology tools were in a state of flux. Some teachers became frustrated, for example, when a planned CD-ROM-based approach to data submission and viewing was abandoned in view of the rapid growth of World Wide Web connectivity.

Of those teachers trained by GLOBE during 1995 who had not started to implement the program by April of 1996, lack of Internet access was the most frequently cited barrier (by 46%) on our teacher survey. For teachers with little technology background or support within their schools, the technical requirements of GLOBE can be daunting. For those who had implemented the program, getting access to adequate computers and getting computer technical support were experienced as "major challenges" by 25% and 24%, respectively. To put these figures in perspective, other issues were cited as major challenges by larger proportions of program implementers: collecting data on weekends and holidays, 50%; having time to complete GLOBE activities within the school schedule, 45%; finding time to prepare for implementing GLOBE activities, 40%; getting to the data collection site, 30%.

The typical GLOBE classroom contains only a single computer with an Internet connection. Teachers with such limited access to Internet-capable computers find it difficult to incorporate GLOBE technology based activities into their classroom management structure. The following quotes provide examples of these difficulties. "I haven't figured out ways to use the graphics and the data available to us from GLOBE via the Internet since I have just one computer in my room." "Having one computer for a class of 20 forces me to choose only a few students at a time to get on line and manipulate data. By the time I get online, the class is over!" "People really need more computers to implement this ... GLOBE's potential is enormous, but teachers can't do it without computers.""Getting online through Prodigy during the day sometimes takes so long that we don't take the time to look at any data other than ours."

Despite the challenges posed by technology, its use was clearly a major attraction for students. Of the various components of GLOBE, using computers to work with GLOBE data was the one in which teachers reported their students had the most interest (86% of teachers reporting that their students were "very interested") in the spring, 1996 survey. Students confirmed the teachers' observations in responses to their own survey: As shown in Table 10.1, technology use was the aspect of GLOBE receiving the highest student approval rating with 81% of fourth graders, 58% of seventh, and 56% of tenth graders reporting they "like it a lot."

The widespread general popularity of technology use within GLOBE should not mask the fact that in this program, as in others, the available technology is not always employed to its full potential. Table 10.2 displays the proportion of teachers reporting that none of their students performed various technology based GLOBE activities during a typical week (in school year 1995–1996). Even among the classes that were most active in reporting data, 50% did not have any students using telecommunications (GLOBEMail) and 40% did not have anyone using data visualizations in a typical week.

TABLE 10.1

Extent to Which Students Like Various Aspects of GLOBE (%)

Aspect of GLOBE	Fourth graders			Seventh graders			Tenth graders		
	Like a Lot	Like a Little	Do Not Like	Like a Lot	Like a Little	Do Not Like	Like a Lot	Like a Little	Do Not Like
Putting GLOBE data on computer	81	15	4	58	33	10	56	27	17
Looking at satellite pictures	73	24	3	57	27	16	55	33	12
Taking measurements	70	25	5	52	41	7	46	41	13
Looking at GLOBE data collected by students in other places	56	38	7	27	51	22	35	41	23
Talking about weather, the earth, and water	55	42	3	29	63	9	34	56	10

Note. Sample sizes: 4th grade, 499 < n < 758; 7th grade, 138 < n < 223; and 10th grade, 82 < n < 107.

TABLE 10.2

Active Data Provider Reports of Students' Participation in GLOBE Activities
in a Typical Week, 1995–1996 (%)

GLOBE Activity	Percent Reporting			
	No Students	1–4 Students	5–10 But Not Whole Class	Whole Class or >10
Enter data on computer	3	48	32	17
Use visualization software	40	31	17	13
Telecommunicate with other GLOBE schools	50	33	11	7

Note. Sample sizes: 216 < n > 225

The case of GLOBEMail was illustrative. Students were excited by the prospect of having an easy way to telecommunicate with other GLOBE students around the world. As more international schools came online, some interesting dialogues emerged concerning issues such as ground-level ozone or extreme weather events. However, many GLOBE classrooms had only limited access to an Internet-capable computer, and GLOBEMail messages to other schools often went unanswered. Students were discouraged when their messages did not evoke replies. Moreover, students were sometimes unprepared to deal with a school they had selected whose GLOBE students were at a very different grade level or level of sophistication regarding earth science issues. Figure 10.4 provides an example. Mismatches in students' sophistication concerning science concepts were particularly likely in international exchanges because whereas U.S. GLOBE students are most frequently in Grades 4 through 6, those in other countries are more likely to be 14 to 16 years of age. Like other telecommunications-supported education projects, GLOBE found that simply providing the technical facility was not enough.

The exchange of data or other joint activities with distant schools was not part of the data collection and educational activities supported by the GLOBE teacher training and instructional materials in the program's first year. The GLOBE program concluded that an infrastructure (i.e., a teacher's guide and training experiences) that includes suggestions for interesting cross-school activities and some help in finding appropriate partners is needed. (Many network-based education programs provide a moderator for online discussions.) In GLOBE's second

GLOBEMail for: Belton Junior High School, Belton, TX, United States

From School: Mountain View School, Ontario, CA US
Subject: Re: Ground level Ozone
To: 4TH PERIOD 8TH GRADERS
From: 4TH GRADERS

Hello to all of you Texans,

We received your message just last week because our Internet connection was down for 7 days. Sorry you have had to wait so long for a reply. Your questions are interesting, but as 4th graders we have no clue about ozone alerts. Our air quality is monitored by the South Coast Air Quality Management District. They have a new office located only 15 miles from our school. We found them on the WWW and have contacted their Education Liason person. We have sent them your message and are hoping for an answer that is scientifically based.

We do have smog alerts several times a year – particularly in the summer and fall. We didn't know they came from "gound level ozone." To be truthful, we don't even know what that is. Can you explain that in terms 4th graders can understand? When we have smog alerts, they come in different stages. When it is a serious smog alert, we are not allowed to take jump ropes or other equipment to recess. In fact, we are not allowed to run. We do know smog is especially hazardous to children and the elderly.

We will get back to you as soon as we hear from the SCAQMD. Thanks for waiting.

Sincerely,

The 31 GLOBE students in Room 7
and their teacher, Mrs. Carteen,
at Mountain View School

FIG. 10.4 Example of GLOBEMail between two schools.

year, several joint activities with other schools were developed and recommended as educational activities. In addition, a "matchmaking" function for GLOBE schools seeking partner schools for e-mail exchanges was set up.

Enhancements to GLOBE's Use of Technology

Strengthening Supports for Technology Use.   As illustrated by the GLOBEMail example, the GLOBE program leadership has taken steps to promote more effective use of its technologies as the program has continued to evolve. Greater time was carved out for demonstrating and training technology use within the GLOBE training sessions. As the science–education investigation teams continued to design data collection protocols and associated educational activities, they were instructed to develop activities that make use of the GLOBE data visualizations and to stress the analysis and interpretation of the data the visualizations depict. A "Compare" feature was added to allow users to view two visualizations side-by-side. This feature allows a student to look at students' data and reference set data for the same region and variable or to examine the visualizations for two different but possibly related variables (such as temperature and precipitation). A "tour" of the GLOBE Web site was developed to increase the likelihood that teachers would be aware of the resources available to them there.

Additional materials were added to the GLOBE Web site, increasing its attraction for students and for teachers. In addition to the early posting of the names of schools that had attained various levels of data reporting (number of pieces of data reported), the GLOBE Stars section began featuring stories (with digitized photos and artwork) on schools that had held significant GLOBE-related events (e.g., hosted a visit by a local dignitary). In one month in 1997, for example, the Stars section carried stories on 34 GLOBE schools including 12 international schools. Descriptions of recent training workshops, including photos of and quotes from participants, were included. A GLOBE Visualization Gallery, featuring program-developed visualizations, descriptions and movies of special events (such as hurricanes), advanced visualizations, and sample graphs of students' data plus templates for teachers to use in classroom graphing activities, was another addition to the Web site.

Using Technology To Improve The Program.   We have previously discussed steps taken to try to better support technology use in the program's second year. Another area of activity was the use of technology to ameliorate other aspects of the program. One concern, for example, was the need to provide students and teachers with more interactions with the GLOBE scientists. Although a Scientists' Corner within the GLOBE Web site had provided messages from scientists to students in the program's first year, teachers felt the need for more individualized interactions and for a sense of immediacy in students' communications with the scientists. Scientists' e-mail addresses were added to their messages on the Web site. In addition, live "Web chats" with GLOBE scientists were held during the second school year. The principal investigator (PI) for the atmosphere and climate investigation held a Web chat in November of 1996; the PIs for the soils and hydrology investigations held a chat in December of 1996. The newly appointed Secretary of State Madeline Albright also participated in a GLOBE web chat during her spring, 1997 visit to Moscow. In September of 1997, the atmosphere PI and several of her University of Oklahoma colleagues held another Web chat with GLOBE students.

As the GLOBE Web site has expanded, we have continued to monitor classroom use of its various components. Table 10.3 presents spring, 1997 survey responses from teachers in the most active GLOBE classes. The survey data indicate that the most frequently used components of the GLOBE Web site are the Student Data Archive, GLOBEMail, and the visualizations of students' data. More than 75% of active teachers reported having used these facilities at least occasionally. The lowest utilization rate was found for the Web chats (59% had not used them at

TABLE 10.3

Frequency of Use of GLOBE Web Site Features for 1996–1997 (%)

Features	Reported Frequency of Use			
	Once a Week or More	Occasionally	Once	Not at all
Visualizations of student data	18	64	12	7
Visualizations of reference data	13	58	17	12
Visualization Gallery	11	51	15	23
GLOBEMail	25	53	10	12
GLOBE Stars	5	46	23	27
GLOBE Student Data Archive	22	58	13	7
Scientist Corner	3	51	26	20
Web chat	1	19	21	59

Note. Sample sizes: 323 < n > 343.

all) and the Frequently Asked Questions (29% said they had not used them at all). In viewing these data, it should be remembered that Web chats are time dependent and therefore allow much less opportunity for use (for "live" participation) than ongoing features such as the Data Archive, GLOBEMail, and the visualizations. Teachers who did have their classes participate in the Web chats were very positive about them, as indicated in their responses to open-ended survey questions.

On the positive side, most active GLOBE teachers used the main Web site features at least occasionally. However, if one supposes that a truly intensive implementation of GLOBE would involve students in using the Student Data Archive and data visualizations once a week or more, this intensity is relatively infrequent. For the Student Data Archive, just 22% of teachers in the survey sample reported weekly use. The percentages for the students' data visualizations and the reference data visualizations are 18% and 13%, respectively. The aspect of the GLOBE Web site most likely to be used at least once a week was GLOBEMail, which 25% of the teachers surveyed said was used at least once a week.

Another concern that surfaced during the Year 1 evaluation was teachers' need for follow-up to their GLOBE training (Means, Middleton, Lewis, Quellmalz, & Valdes, 1996). Teachers wanted to sustain the sense of community developed during their week of GLOBE training and to have access to informal advice and support as they were grappling with the challenges posed by setting up the equipment, technology, and learning and data collection activities of GLOBE. A teacher Internet listserv was initiated for exclusive use by the GLOBE teachers.

Finally, technology was brought to bear in trying to improve students' ability to implement the data collection protocols correctly. One of the protocols GLOBE students found difficult in the program's first year was the classification of the types of clouds at their local site. Distinguishing among the 10 different cloud categories used by meteorologists is, in fact, a cognitively complex task. In the spring, 1996 pilot assessment of GLOBE students, only 36% of fourth graders and 44% of seventh and tenth graders, on average, answered cloud type questions correctly (compared to 64% and 75% for air temperature readings and 97% for all ages for precipitation readings).

A GLOBE systems developer, a meteorologist, and a GLOBE teacher teamed up to develop a Web-based "exploration" of cloud types. The Cloud Exploration offers an introduction to cloud categories with a verbal description and set of pictorial examples for each of the 10 categories. The exploration uses 150 different pictures, giving students multiple exemplars of each category, to prevent learning the "right answer" on the basis of irrelevant features in a limited set of photographs (e.g., "the photo with the billboard is cumulonimbus"), as they might with a traditional textbook. A "Cloud Quiz" allowed students to self-test their ability to classify clouds, using a rotating set of cloud photos as the quiz items. A similar exploration and quiz was developed subsequently for the classification of Landsat images into land cover types (e.g., agricultural, desert, coastline).

Increased Teacher Leadership In Technology Use. Another significant trend that emerged during the program's second and third years was increasing involvement and leadership in the technology area on the part of GLOBE teachers and students. Although the GLOBEMail facility provided point-to-point communication, the program's treatment of data in the first year could be considered a broadcast model. The data visualizations, for example, were developed by NASA programmers and posted on the Web for students' viewing with little mechanism for the kind of interaction that would support forming and testing hypotheses about the data. Similarly, the student database was available for viewing and downloading, but control of the content on the Web appeared to be the province of the program staff.

More recently, GLOBE systems developers have been adding interactive features to the archives, enabling students to develop graphs from subsets of the students' data or to develop and display two graphs for comparison purposes.

In addition, over time, some of the more active GLOBE teachers have begun using the GLOBE technology resources in interesting ways, and the GLOBE program established a mechanism for posting both teachers' (and students') work and teacher-recommended Internet resources on the GLOBE Web site within what they call the "Resource Room." (Ted Habermann, the GLOBE assistant director for systems during 1996, played a major role in encouraging and supporting teachers' efforts to contribute to the GLOBE Web site.) Nancy Burton, an elementary school teacher who has been very active in GLOBE teacher training, heads a group of GLOBE teachers that reviews both submissions from GLOBE classes and non-GLOBE Internet sites that offer resources that complement GLOBE. The April, 1997 contents of the GLOBE Resource Room provide an illustration of the emerging teacher use of technology within GLOBE. That month the Room contained hot links to Internet sites plus five activity descriptions ("Classroom Suggestions") developed by GLOBE teachers and students. One activity, developed by teacher Bob Jost, documents the thinking and resources used by his sixth-grade class as they sought to check the likelihood of a very high temperature reading they obtained from their site in Fresno, California. A GLOBE school in Finland contributed three data explorations. In one, they compared winter temperatures in Akutan, Alaska, to those in Devil's Lake, North Dakota, attempting to understand the factors besides latitude that affect temperature. In another activity, they compared readings from GLOBE schools in Finland, the Czech Republic, and Australia. In a final activity, they recorded snow temperature at ground level and 2 m above the ground and related these temperatures to albedo. Nancy Burton's personal contribution to this section was an exploration of her GLOBE data compared to that for other sites, along with research topics suggested by the differences.

The Resource Room is an important part of the GLOBE Web site, not just because it contains model educational activities using the GLOBE data but also because it is a departure from the one-source broadcast model, moving the GLOBE Web site toward becoming a forum where multiple voices and perspectives are heard. In a similar vein, the GLOBE training has evolved to give those teacher trainees with some technology skills an active role in devising technology-based demonstrations and investigations and sharing them with fellow trainees. In the words of a GLOBE technology trainer:

> I wanted the advanced group to discover how to use the GLOBE systems in their classroom, on their own ...Since I had five people in the group [of more advanced trainees] each one chose a different area to focus on, one was preschool and she tied it into the cloud quiz and making a 3-D cloud chart out of cotton that the kids could use in the field. Another presentation we had was based on "Water, Water Everywhere" and he showed the maps of pH during the different seasons using the GLOBE data. We also had an elementary teacher talk about integrating the systems through a storybook she uses about moving to Australia and what they needed if they were going to move there. This led her into the season activities and graphing an Australia school versus an American school, and using GLOBEMail to contact another GLOBE school. She also learned how to use [options] within the graphing, selecting schools that had a lot of data points. We then had a weather comparison of the deep freeze in North Dakota versus the high heat in South America, she also chose to use the Resource Room to compare lake temperatures, [as] done by a Finnish school. Our last presentation dealt with comparing trends of

reference data with the Multispec image to choose the sites they were going to study within that image (i.e. how snowfall affects bare ground vs. tree covered land, and growth patterns, and what they wanted to study).

In addition to providing the more technology savvy trainees with a head start on using GLOBE technology tools, this activity turned out to be an important motivator for all the teachers, as demonstrated by the following quote:

> I think the most important aspects of doing the presentations in this manner is that it gives all the teachers a higher confidence that they can use the GLOBE systems when they get back, and that there are many different ways to integrate them into the classroom. It was great to see how the other teachers responded to each of the presentations, listening intently and seeing that they can do it from other teachers!

INFLUENCE ON STUDENTS' THINKING AND LEARNING IN SCIENCE

Thus far, we have described the ways in which the GLOBE program is capitalizing on the World Wide Web and on other technologies and how the use of technology is being refined in the face of the program's evolution and feedback from teachers and students. An additional question for the evaluation is the impact of using technology within the GLOBE program on students' thinking in science. Through analysis of interviews, students' survey and assessment responses, and e-mail correspondence, we have begun to identify some examples of GLOBE's influence on students' science learning. In the following sections we describe some of the important themes that characterize GLOBE students' thinking. Although it is difficult—and arguably, inappropriate—to disentangle the influence of technology from that of the program as a whole, we do assert that the use of technology is pivotal in making the program feel authentic and significant to students (in addition to its obvious necessity for making feasible a program of this scope). Moreover, the Web-accessible database, which includes each class's data, provides a rich context for uncovering data patterns and confronting issues of data quality.

Using the Technology That Scientists Use

The use of state-of-the-art technology appears to be a value in and of itself for many GLOBE students. They had reported that they are motivated to work on GLOBE because they get to "use really neat technology" (10th-grade student), or because they have the opportunity to "go outdoors and use new kinds of technology" (9th-grade student). In the same vein, a 10th-grade female student, after describing how she used the satellite image provided by GLOBE to differentiate between certain types of vegetation, land types, roads, and various other land-marks in her area, concluded "using technology makes me feel very modern and up-to-date."

Other students appear to view technology more as a tool. They see the use of technology as a way to advance their knowledge or to empower themselves. An 11th grader, for example, expressed preference for the kind of learning by doing that typically goes along with the incorpora-tion of new technology into classrooms, as well as the belief that the technology skills he is acquiring will be relevant for his future.

> You don't have to sit there and listen to a teacher tell you about it, you can get to use it yourself. The biggest thing that affects me in a lot of things that I do is the GPS unit—It really shows me that technology can help out with some of the things that we had and used before. I can now use the GPS to hunt ...this is all important to me because I will probably be going to the Marine Corps and I will need to know all of this stuff.

For these students, using the GLOBE technology appears to have importance not simply because it is novel or fun, but because it is relevant, useful, and empowering.

Authenticity of Research

During their interviews, students offered a number of reasons and justifications for their sustained participation in GLOBE. For some, using GLOBE technology meant that they were able to collaborate with real scientists on real problems. They reported feelings of accomplish-ment because they were engaged in a scientific enterprise with working scientists who would use the data that they had collected. For example, an 11th grader said that his main reason for continuing work on the GLOBE program was "because the scientists will use our data to solve real problems. I like being a part of that." An additional example highlighting the importance of authentic practice in science learning was provided by a 6th grader who responded to questions we posed via e-mail. In one electronic message he wrote:

> I think GLOBE gives students a chance to learn about their environment. I think
> it also gives them a chance to do work that scientists do and makes it so kids help
> study the earth. I think it gives kids a positive way to learn about science.

For these students, and for many others, the authenticity of their participation in GLOBE research served as a motivational mechanism to sustain further learning and exploration in the program. This finding is consistent with research on problem-based learning that has shown that the interest and value that students place on working on particular tasks appear to be enhanced when the tasks have closure and require the production of authentic artifacts (Blumenfeld et al., 1991; Malone & Lepper, 1987). Submitting data to the GLOBE Student Data Archive provides this level of authenticity, helping to sustain students' interest over time.

Reflection on Data Anomalies

A central aspect of understanding data is uncovering meaningful patterns and identifying and explaining anomalies. GLOBE provides students with a reason to care about the accuracy of data (because it is part of a genuine science investigation) and with an electronic database that gives them convenient access not only to their own data but also to that from other classrooms all over the world. The program's first-year evaluation report suggested that the motivation and context for grappling with issues of data quality may prove to be one of the largest and most distinctive educational successes of GLOBE (see Means et al., 1996).

In conventional science instruction, students either read about causal relationships in the absence of data or perform set laboratory experiments, where the "correct" data are known beforehand. Students repeat the "experiment" until they can report the "right" data. They seldom enter into the kinds of data scrutiny and evaluations that characterize teams of scientists engaged in real investigations (Dama & Dunbar, 1996). In contrast, GLOBE provides students with the context and the motivation for reflection and debate over a complex, extensive set of data. The following excerpts, taken from e-mail correspondence with a class of sixth graders, provide examples of how GLOBE students have searched for and interpreted apparent anomalies in the GLOBE data.

One student reviewed daily rainfall and temperature data in the GLOBE Student Data Archive, and found what he believed to be several errors. He wrote the following:

It (data) can let us explore our worlds. Look at yesterday's data! Does it look anomalous? 695? That looks anomalous. 695 inches of rainfall is huge. Where is Fairlawn? Maybe that will explain my question of why there has been so much rainfall there? Another anomalous: -13 degrees in Celsius that is bigger than -20 Fahrenheit. I think that they entered the data in Fahrenheit. This was in Virginia.

Three other students in this class expressed the same kind of critical stance toward students' data:

We collect data so the scientists at GLOBE can analyze it. Then we can compare our data to data sent in from other places around the world. By collecting this data we can learn a lot about what our climate is like compared to other climates, why this is, how many seasons we have, and how many other places have (not to mention how to read a thermometer, rain gauge and use the Internet). We can also learn to graph this data. I think that -13.30 sent in by Winchester, Frederick Douglas, Virginia, sounds anomalous.

I think that a mistake was made on April 1, 1997; in Winchester, Virginia, they had -13.00 C. My hypothesis is the world was pretty dry on April 1, 1997.

Data is probably the most important thing in GLOBE besides the desire to learn. Data can be a series of numbers, or it can be a look at the weather of the world, depending on the effort put into it. I think data is the archive of information and knowledge on any topic. Data can be weather facts, or weather temperature. Data can even be a gateway to the world of knowledge. Yesterday, it looks like most of the places with lower elevations had colder temperatures, which I think is sort of rare.

To take an example from a different GLOBE school, during one of our site visits a sixth grader examined the GLOBE database of tree heights on the day after his own class had submitted data: "A tree over 200' high in Massachusetts? I don't think so!" The student went on to discuss the entry with several of his peers. They reasoned that only a redwood could be that high and redwoods don't grow in Massachusetts. The students pointed out the anomaly to their teacher who suggested they send e-mail to the school that had made the measurement.

There is a sense of involvement with data here that is often lacking in graduate-level statistics classes. The sixth grade students are examining the database and asking, "Does this make sense? Is this possible?" Students find things in the data that violate their expectations. All of the students have pre-existing ideas or theories about why certain environmental events should or should not occur and they explain why the data are anomalous in terms of their prior beliefs. In some cases, students seek to account for what appears to be anomalous data by inferring that they are due to other students' calculation or conversion errors (e.g., reporting Fahrenheit instead of Celsius temperatures). In other cases, students seek to explain anomalous data as instances of unusual or rare events.

The need to distinguish between unusual, valid data that may provide important new knowledge on the one hand and data errors on the other is an important part of genuine science investigation that is being played out in these GLOBE classrooms. Interestingly, in all of the cases mentioned, students cited anomalies found in data submitted by other schools, but not by their own class. It may well be that one of the values of Internet-based science inquiry projects is that they make students feel more comfortable questioning data submitted by peers because those peers are remotely located.

Attempts to Construct Explanations

Trying to make sense of data anomalies is just one aspect of GLOBE students' use of the database to try to formulate explanations or hypotheses. The following examples illustrate how students work back and forth between their causal explanations and the data from the Student Data Archive. For example, one sixth grader wrote the following:

> From looking at this data I have made a hypothesis. My hypothesis is that the farther south you go, until you get to the South Pole (about 60° negative latitude) it is warm, and the farther north you go the colder it gets. From this data I have learned that two cities in the same state can have entirely different temperatures.

Another sixth grader expresses a more complex emerging view of the dimensions of weather systems as well as insight into the importance of looking at data patterns over extended time periods:

> I have a hypothesis from looking at the max temperature of April 1 is that a school in Maine had the same max temperature as a place that was in Finland. They are totally different latitudes and at different longitudes. I think that this is strange because the place that is in Maine is at sea level and the place that is in Finland is at the altitude of 86 m. Usually places that have higher elevations have colder weather but they are also closer to the sun. Finland is

also closer to the polar ice cap than Maine is. Maine is also closer to the equator than Finland is. These are the many reasons that I think that Maine should have warmer weather than Finland. To try and solve this I have looked at some data from the same schools and I have come up with an idea. This is not a regular thing. Most of the time the school that is in Finland has colder weather than the school that is in Maine.

These students are using the GLOBE technology to access and manipulate data sets on which they can reflect, draw inferences, and formulate hypotheses or explanations as they attempt to advance their knowledge of weather patterns and global conditions. Even though many of their statements are actually conjectures rather than hypotheses, and they contain some naive or erroneous ideas, the students are attempting to say something about the relations between the variables presented in the data and to explain what they mean. These efforts, as students express them not only verbally but also in their science journals and their e-mail, provide teachers with a valuable window into how students are reasoning about earth systems.

An aspect of GLOBE that appears to support students' learning is the provision of multiple contexts for examining the same phenomena. These contexts span the physical, abstract–visual, and numerical levels. For example, GLOBE students read or hear about soil, touch soil, conduct analyses and experiments on soil, see satellite images of soil, and interpret soil data. To take another example, students collect information on the height and diameter of trees in their study site, view their data in tabular form and in reports including comparable data from other sites, and generate tables or graphs showing several related variables or data from several schools over extended time periods. In other words, students can access the same information using multiple representations. In other subject areas, such multiple representations have been shown to increase science learning (Kozma, 1997).

Science Learning

By the spring of 1997, some teachers had been actively implementing the GLOBE program for 2 years. At this point, it was reasonable to start to look for ways in which GLOBE had influenced their teaching and what their students had learned. To represent the elementary, middle, and secondary levels, we elected to investigate classroom teaching practices and students' learning at the 4th, 7th, and 10th grades.

Teachers from 44 GLOBE classes and 27 non-GLOBE classes at these grade levels were recruited to administer SRI-developed assessments to their students. All non-GLOBE students were in classes whose teachers had signed up to take the GLOBE training (and hence were likely to be the same kinds of teachers as those leading GLOBE classes). The assessment items were designed to tap students' knowledge of how to conduct the environmental measurements used in GLOBE, ability to recognize sound measurement and sampling practices more generally, and ability to interpret data and apply earth science concepts in new contexts. Teachers in both GLOBE and in non-GLOBE classrooms were asked about the environmental content areas they had covered with their class so we were able to calculate students' scores based only on items dealing with content their class had covered.

When opportunity to learn was taken into account in this fashion, GLOBE students outperformed their non-GLOBE counterparts, as shown in Table 10.4. At the 4th-grade level, GLOBE students demonstrated strikingly better knowledge of GLOBE measurement procedures, scoring 52% correct on average compared to 29% for students from non-GLOBE classes. GLOBE 4th graders also excelled in their ability to recognize sound sampling and measurement practices, 59% correct versus 50%, and in their ability to interpret data and apply earth science concepts, 49% versus 43% (the latter difference attained only marginal statistical significance, however, at $p < .10$). Differences among groups of 7th graders followed similar patterns: 52% versus 40% for GLOBE measurement procedures, 51% versus 46% for sampling and measurement principles; and 42% versus 36% for data interpretation and inference. Among 10th graders, GLOBE students did significantly better than non-GLOBE students only on items concerning knowledge of measurement procedures, with a mean of 55% correct versus 35% correct. The advantage of GLOBE 10th-graders on their ability to interpret data and apply concepts was in the expected direction, 54% correct versus 48%, but fell short of statistical significance with the smaller sample available at the 10th grade. There was no difference between GLOBE and non-GLOBE students at the 10th-grade level on the items tapping ability to apply sampling and measurement principles (both scoring 59% correct). Taken as a whole, the assessment data are very encouraging. After GLOBE's second year of operation, there is evidence of a positive impact on science and mathematics learning in classrooms where GLOBE is being implemented.

TABLE 10.4

Comparison of GLOBE and Non-GLOBE Students' Assessment Performance,
by Grade Level (mean % correct)

GLOBE Status and Grade	Item Type		
	Taking Measurements	Sampling and Measurement Principles	Data Interpretation
All Grades			
GLOBE students	53***	56**	48***
Non-GLOBE students	36	51	42
Fourth Grade			
GLOBE students	52***	59**	49 *
Non-GLOBE students	29	50	43
Seventh Grade			
GLOBE students	52***	51	42**
Non-GLOBE students	40	46	36
Tenth Grade			
GLOBE students	55***	59	54
Non-GLOBE Students	35	59	48

*** $p < .01$ for t-test between GLOBE and non-GLOBE students.

** $p < .05$ for t-test between GLOBE and non-GLOBE students.

*Marginally significant $p < .10$ for t-test between GLOBE and non-GLOBE students.

The Concept of Science

Learning theorists argue that an important aspect of science learning is the process of becoming socialized into a professional community (Hawkins & Pea, 1987). This socialization process entails knowing the community's standards of explanation and modes of discourse as well as understanding the essential activities within the community. Most classroom science instruction divorces science learning from actual scientific practice and tends to focus rather mechanistically on an idealized presentation of the "scientific method." This method is often presented to the students as a set of steps to be performed (e.g., observing, stating a hypothesis, making predictions, conducting experiments). As a result, many students infer that science consists only of those actions performed in a set order and the social nature of science—the communication and back-and-forth wrestling with ideas, evidence, and alternative explanations—is not represented.

GLOBE students and those in the non-GLOBE comparison classes were asked what they thought scientists spend their time doing. As Table 10.5 illustrates, GLOBE students as well as their non-GLOBE peers identified the "traditional" actions that scientists perform (e.g., planning experiments and writing reports) as things scientists would spend "a lot" of time doing. GLOBE students differed from non-GLOBE students,

TABLE 10.5

Students' Conception of Scientists' Activities: What They Believe Scientists Spend "a lot" of Time Doing, by GLOBE Participation Status (%)

Activity	Fourth Grade		Seventh Grade		Tenth Grade	
	GLOBE	Non-GLOBE	GLOBE	Non-GLOBE	GLOBE	Non-GLOBE
Using evidence to support their theory	49	46	67**	56	69	76
Explaining the results of an experiment	62**	49	57	52	67**	58
Discussing their results with other scientists	53**	43	41	40	62***	41
Finding evidence showing how things happen in the world	62	59	50*	44	56	50
Collecting data	75***	53	75***	61	75***	66
Planning experiments and writing reports	54	58	39	47	52	49
Studying a problem without a clear solution	40***	24	35**	27	53**	39
Using scientific evidence to prove that a theory is true or false	59*	49	56	59	69**	54
Defending their points of view or ideas	47***	33	55	47	71***	53

** $p < .05$ for chi-square on choices between "A lot, Some, A little, and None."

*** $p < .01$ for chi-square on choices between "A lot, Some, A little, and None."

* Marginally significant $p < .10$ for chi-square on choices between "A lot, Some, A little, and None."

Note. Questionnaire items were adapted from the instrument used in Songer and Linn (1991).

however, in their likelihood of asserting that scientists spend extensive time on scientific activities that are more social in nature. Higher proportions of GLOBE students believed that scientists spend a great deal of time explaining the results of their experiments, discussing results with other scientists, and defending their points of view. These kind of activities have been shown to be important aspects of the interactions in scientific laboratories and are associated with scientific insight and discovery (Dunbar, 1996).

In addition, GLOBE students across all three grade levels were more likely than non-GLOBE students to acknowledge that scientists spend a lot of time studying problems without a clear solution, using evidence to support their theory, and using scientific evidence to prove that a theory is true or false. GLOBE students appear to be acquiring a more realistic appreciation of the multifaceted nature of scientific practice. This kind of knowledge does not emerge through textbook learning; rather, it is acquired through the experience of scientific practice and communication with others about that practice.

Becoming More Aware of Their Surroundings

Although it appears that at a gross level the environment is an important concern for many young people, their knowledge base is not always well developed or applied to their daily activities. For many students, using GLOBE technology to conduct research on their own local environment has made them more aware and knowledgeable about their surroundings. For example, an 11th grader who had recently participated in a GLOBE research study on ultraviolet radiation in his area said the following during his interview:

> The UV study. I mean I never thought of that before, now, when I walk down the street and it is very hot outside I wonder about what the UV reading is–maybe it is a "3" today like last Saturday. I never knew that there was a liquid that I could test the UV with.

His classmate described that by using GLOBE technology, he was now able to understand what temperature data visualizations referred to when the weather channel person was describing them on television. Similarly, a 10th grade student reported that he was able to discuss with his father the likelihood of rainfall during the following day because he had studied the cloud types and cloud coverage during that particular day. A 6th grade female student explained in an e-mail message how using the GLOBE data had helped her learn more about the weather conditions in her area:

> From this data I have learned that two cities in the same state can have entirely different temperatures. The state that I am talking about is Colorado where I live. I have noticed that the temperatures in Boulder, Denver, and Colorado Springs and other places are almost always significantly different.

For these students, the involvement in GLOBE investigations supported by technology appears to have increased their awareness and knowledge of their local weather conditions in a way that increases the likelihood that they will apply their knowledge in their day-to-day lives.

SUMMARY

The GLOBE program illustrates how the World Wide Web and other technologies can be used to support the involvement of students in authentic science investigations. The uses of technology within the program were described as well as the enhancements and accommodations made in response to the experiences of the program's first year of operation. The GLOBE experience suggests that the combination of authentic science activity, the scaffolding provided by human teachers and scientists, and the affordances of technology, have great promise for helping students to become enthusiastic partners in the generation and interpretation of scientific data.

ACKNOWLEDGMENT

The research on the GLOBE program described in this chapter was supported in part by a grant from the National Science Foundation (ESI-9509718). The views expressed are those of the authors and do not necessarily reflect policies either of the foundation or of the GLOBE program.

REFERENCES

Blumenfeld, P., Soloway, E., Marx, R., Krajcik, J., Guzdial, M., & Palincsar, A. (1991). Motivating project-based learning: Sustaining the doing, supporting the learning. *Educational Psychologist, 26*(3-4), 369–398.

CTGV. (1997). *The Jasper project: Lessons in curriculum, instruction, assessment, and professional development.* Mahwah, NJ: Lawrence Erlbaum Associates.

Dama, M., & Dunbar, K. (1996). Distributed reasoning: Where social and cognitive worlds fuse. In *Proceedings of the 18th Meeting of the Cognitive Science Conference* (pp. 166–170). Mahwah, NJ: Lawrence Erlbaum Associates.

de La Beaujardiere, J-F., Cavallo, J., Hasler, A. F., Mitchell, H., O'Handley, C., Shiri, R., & White, R. (1997). The GLOBE visualization project: Using the WWW in the classroom. *Journal of Science Education and Technology, 6*(1), 15–22.

Dunbar, K. (1996). How scientists really reason: Scientific reasoning in real-world laboratories. In R. J. Sternberg & J. E. Davidson (Eds.), *The nature of insight* (pp. 365–395). Cambridge, MA: MIT Press.

Goldman, S., Petrosino, A., Sherwood, R., Garrison, S., Hickey, D., Bransford, J., & Pellegrino, J. (1996). Anchoring science instruction in multimedia learning environments. In S. Vosniadou, E. De Corte, R. Glaser, & H. Mandl (Eds.), *International perspectives on the design of technology supported learning environments* (pp. 257–284). Mahwah, NJ: Lawrence Erlbaum Associates.

Gore, A. (1992). *Earth in the balance: Ecology and the human spirit.* New York: Houghton Mifflin.

Hawkins, J., & Pea, R. (1987). Tools for bridging the cultures of everyday and scientific thinking. *Journal of Research in Science Teaching, 24*(4), 291–307.

Kozma, R. (1997). Multimedia and understanding: Expert and novice responses to different representations of chemical phenomena. *Journal of Research in Science Teaching, 43*(9), 949–968.

Malone, T., & Lepper, M. (1987). Making learning fun: A taxonomy of intrinsic motivation for learning. In R. Snow & M. Farr (Eds.), *Aptitude, learning, and instruction: Conative and affective process analyses* (Vol. 3, pp. 223–253). Hillsdale, NJ: Lawrence Erlbaum Associates.

Means, B., Middleton, T., Lewis, A., Quellmalz, E., & Valdes, K. (1996). *GLOBE year 1 evaluation: Findings.* Menlo Park, CA: SRI International.

Songer, N. B., & Linn, M. C. (1991). How do students' views of science influence knowledge integration? In M. C. Linn, N. B. Songer, & E. L. Lewis (Eds.), Students' models and epistemologies of science (Special Issue). *Journal of Research in Science Teaching, 28*(9), 761–784.

11

Technological Tools and Instructional Approaches for Making Scientific Inquiry Accessible to All

Barbara Y. White
University of California at Berkeley

John R. Frederiksen
Educational Testing Service

Our focus in this chapter is on science education and on investigating what advances in computer technology and socio cognitive theory can do to make science more interesting and accessible to a wide range of students and teachers. Our work started with an emphasis on facilitating students' conceptual understanding of physics (White, 1981, 1983, 1984; White & Horwitz, 1988), which is an interesting challenge because physics is generally regarded as the most abstract and difficult of all the scientific disciplines. As our research progressed, the emphasis shifted increasingly toward enabling students to learn about the nature of scientific models and the processes of scientific inquiry (White, 1993b; White & Frederiksen, 1998; White & Schwartz, in press; White, Shimoda, & Frederiksen, 1999).

Since the late 1970s, we have been working in a variety of urban and suburban classrooms to develop new educational tools and instructional approaches and have been investigating whether they do indeed make physics and scientific inquiry accessible to all students. This has included research on the use of various metacognitive tools and activities designed to enable students to create explicit models of both subject matter and inquiry expertise, as well as to learn how to monitor and reflect on their inquiry processes. In addition, we have been working on the important issue of preparing teachers to implement such new approaches and to use these technological tools effectively within their classrooms.

Whether we are concerned with students' development of conceptual models, with their ability to engage in and reflect on scientific inquiry, or with teachers' pedagogical expertise for fostering these skills, technology can play a central role. Computer and video technologies enable new types of cognitive and social environments. They make it possible to create conceptual tools that provide new discourse contexts and that facilitate new types of social activities in which inquiry related conversations can take place. In designing our software, we thus need to consider these larger contexts and to envision how students and teachers could use the software in the classroom to create a community of learners engaged in scientific inquiry. In this chapter, we present a set of computer-based tools that we developed and describe how they can be used instructionally to facilitate scientific inquiry, conceptual change, and reflective learning.

MODELING AND SIMULATION TOOLS

Our starting premise was that advances in the fields of computer modeling and simulation can change our view of what it means to understand and engage in science. For example, we now have formal models of reasoning processes, such as causal discrete-state reasoning, that can employ various visual representations and reasoning forms that have always played an important role in scientific theorizing. However, until they were incorporated within formal models, they had not been given the prominence and respectability that they deserve, particularly regarding their potential use in science education. Furthermore, simulation tools that incorporate these new types of formal models can enable students to learn in new ways—ways that engage them in the processes of inquiry and modeling as they create explicit theories of not only the subject matter but also of their own inquiry processes.

We begin by presenting an example of the type of conceptual model that we have been using to help students understand physics. These models can be embodied in computer simulations and can also serve as conceptual models that students create and use to solve problems. They can be characterized as reasoning structures in which one steps through time and analyzes the events that are occurring using basic laws of physics to predict and explain what will happen next. An example of such model-based reasoning in the domain of force and motion is illustrated in Fig. 11.1. This particular model is useful for predicting how forces affect the motion of an object in a one-dimensional world with no friction. In the example shown in Fig. 11.1, the model was used to predict the effects of a sequence of impulses on an object's motion. It uses laws and representations to calculate and encode what is happening. For example, the following are versions of Newton's first two laws of motion that are used by this model.

> *Basic Principle*: When no impulses are applied to an object, its speed stays the same, because there is nothing to make it change. But, whenever an impulse is applied, it causes the object to change speed.

> *Prediction Law*: If the impulse is in the same direction that the object is moving, it adds one to its speed (+1); in the opposite direction, it subtracts one from its speed (-1).

The basic principle determines what events to pay attention to (i.e., the application of impulses) and why (i.e., they cause changes in an object's velocity). The prediction law determines how to calculate the effects of those events. In conjunction with these laws, the model uses the various representations shown in Fig. 11.1 to calculate and to depict the resulting changes in velocity. This type of model can be used to run a computer simulation, which can illustrate its behavior visually and can also explain its reasoning verbally (using a speech output device). It can also serve as the type of conceptual model that we want students to invent as they develop their theory of force and motion.

An example of a pedagogical tool that incorporates such conceptual models is the THINKERTOOLS software that we developed for the Macintosh computer. This software enables students to create and experiment with Newtonian models of force and motion (see Fig. 11.2). Using simple drawing tools, students can construct and run computer simulations. Objects (such as the large circle shown in Fig. 11.2) and barriers can be placed on the screen. (The objects are introduced to students as generic objects, simply called "dots," which are the pictorial equivalent of variables that students can map onto different objects such as space ships or billiard balls.) Students can define and change the properties of any object, such as its mass, elasticity (e.g., bouncy or fragile), and velocity.

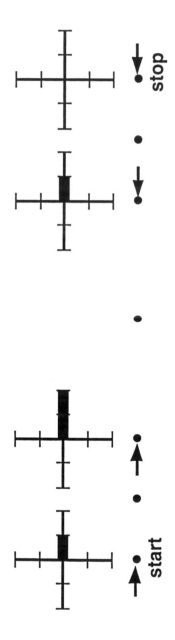

FIG. 11.1 A model-based prediction of the effects of a sequence of four impulses on an object's motion. The "dotprints" show the position of the object as time passes. The arrows indicate the direction and timing of each impulse. The "datacross" is used to calculate and show the effect that each impulse has on the object's velocity.

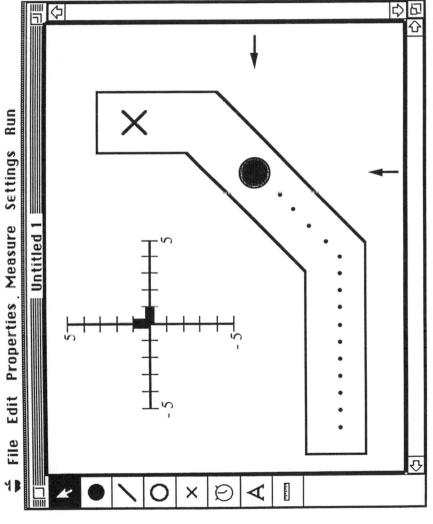

FIG. 11.2 An example of a ThinkerTools activity. This software provides an inquiry tool for creating and experimenting with models of force and motion.

They can then apply impulses to the object to change its velocity using the keyboard or a joystick as in a video game. (*Impulses* are forces that act for a specified—usually short—amount of time like a kick or a hit.) Students can thus create and experiment with a "dot-impulse model," and they can discover, for example, that when one applies an impulse in the same direction that the dot is moving, it increases the dot's velocity by one unit of speed. In this way, they can use simulations to discover the laws of physics and their implications.

Such software enables students to create experimental situations that are difficult or impossible to create in the real world. For example, they can turn friction and gravity on or off and can select different friction laws (i.e., sliding friction, gas-fluid friction). They can also vary the amount of friction or gravity to see what happens. Such experimental manipulations in which students dramatically alter the parameters of the simulation allow students to use inquiry strategies, such as "look at extreme cases," which are hard to utilize in real-world inquiry. This type of inquiry enables students to see more readily the behavioral implications of the laws of physics and to discover the underlying principles.

Another advantage of having students experiment with such simulations is that the software includes measurement tools that allow students to easily make accurate observations of distances, times, and velocities. These observations would often be very difficult to make in the corresponding real-world experiments. The software also includes graphical representations of variables. There is also a "datacross," which shows its x and y velocity components, and students can have the software keep a table or graph to record, for example, the velocity of the dot. In addition, there are analytic tools such as "stepping through time," which allows students to pause the simulation and to proceed time step by time step so they can better see and analyze what is happening to the motion of the dot. In this mode, the simulation runs for a small amount of time, leaves one dotprint on the screen, and then pauses again. The students have control over whether the simulation remains paused, proceeds to the next time step, or returns to continuous mode. These analytic tools and graphical representations help students determine the underlying laws of motion. They can also be incorporated within the students' conceptual model to represent and reason about what might happen in successive time steps. In this way, such dynamic interactive simulations can provide a transition from students' intuitive ways of reasoning about the world to the more abstract, formal methods that scientists use for representing and reasoning about the behavior of a system (White, 1993a).

This type of software is a powerful tool for inquiry. As shown in Fig. 11.3, it allows students to create and experiment with models that are less abstract than algebraic laws, but are more abstract than real-world phenomena. Because the essence of developing physics expertise is learning to deal with such simplified, idealized, abstract models, these "intermediate causal models" are a good starting point for science education (White, 1993a). As students work with the THINKERTOOLS software, which embodies such models, they typically begin by focusing solely on the behavior of the dot. The teacher then gives them tasks to illustrate the utility of the more abstract representations, such as the datacross. For example, in one such activity the dot is off the screen and the only way that students can determine its velocity is to look at its datacross and see the effect that impulses they apply have on its velocity. By focusing on the datacross and applying impulses, they can bring the dot back onto the screen and stop it on the target "X." Through activities such as this, students learn the power and utility of such abstract representations.

INSTRUCTIONAL APPROACHES
FOR INQUIRY AND MODELING

Having illustrated the type of conceptual model and modeling tools that embody new ways of understanding and engaging in science, we now turn to describing the types of instructional approaches that are made possible by such technological tools (see also, Mellar, Bliss, Ogburn, & Tompsett, 1994; White, 1993a; White & Frederiksen, 1990). To exemplify our instructional theories, we developed the THINKERTOOLS Inquiry Curriculum that centers on the THINKERTOOLS force and motion software. This curriculum employs a constructivist approach in which the focus is on inquiry and modeling. It is aimed at developing students' *metacognitive knowledge*—their knowledge about the nature of scientific laws and models, their knowledge about the processes of modeling and inquiry, and their ability to monitor and reflect on these processes so they can improve them. It contains scaffolded inquiry activities that make use of our computer-based, conceptual tools for modeling. The

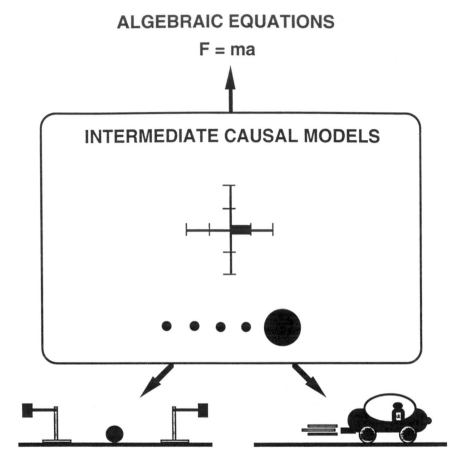

FIG. 11.3 Causal models that portray sequences of events at an intermediate level of abstraction can provide a bridge between real-world phenomena and more abstract mathematical formalisms.

pedagogical strategies include having students make their conceptual models and inquiry processes explicit, supplying materials to support their inquiry process, and introducing them to methods for monitoring and reflecting on their progress.

Our general thesis is that if one combines what cognitive scientists have discovered about the nature and importance of metacognition with new conceptual tools made possible by technology, then it should be feasible for all students to learn science (see also, Brown & Campione, 1996; Collins, Brown, & Newman, 1989; Driver, Asika, Leach, Mortimer, & Scott, 1994; Scardamalia, Bereiter, & Lamon, 1994; Schauble, Raghavan, & Glaser, 1993; Shute, Glaser, & Raghavan, 1989; White & Gunstone, 1989). Our curriculum centers around a generic inquiry cycle, shown in Fig.11.4, which provides a top level model of the inquiry process. This cycle is made explicit to students and is presented as a sequence of goals to be pursued:

- Question: The students start by formulating a research question.
- Hypothesize: They then generate predictions and come up with alternative, competing hypotheses related to their question.
- Investigate: Next, they design and carry out experimental investigations in which they try to determine which of their hypotheses, if any, is accurate. (In our force and motion curriculum, they conduct their experiments in the context of both the THINKERTOOLS computer simulations and the real world. The computer simulations make it easy for them to conduct and see the results of their experiments. Experimentation in the real world is more difficult and is a good vehicle for enabling students to learn about problems that occur in the design and implementation of real-world experiments.)
- Analyze: After the students have completed their investigations, they analyze their data to see if there are any patterns.
- Model: Next they try to summarize and explain their findings by formulating a law and a causal model to characterize their conclusions. (Students' models typically take the form: "If A then B because ..." For example, "if there are no forces like friction acting on an object, then it will go forever at the same speed, because there is nothing to slow it down.")
- Evaluate: Once the students have developed their laws and causal models, they then try to apply them to different real-world situations to investigate their utility and their limitations. Determining the limitations of their conceptual models raises new research questions, and the students begin the inquiry cycle again.

The inquiry cycle thus starts with formulating a research question, which is perhaps the single most difficult step in scientific research. Even doctoral students have great difficulty with this step in their dissertation research. In the THINKERTOOLS Inquiry Curriculum, the process of

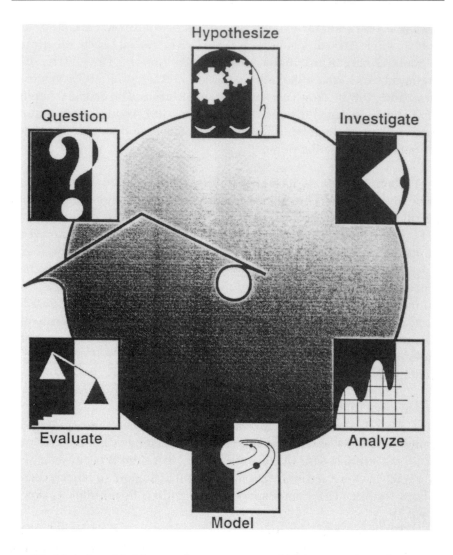

FIG. 11.4 A model of the scientific inquiry process, which is presented to students as a sequence of high-level goals to be pursued.

formulating a research question is heavily scaffolded for students. For example, the teacher begins the curriculum by tossing a beanbag around the room and asking the students to describe all of the factors affecting its motion. In this way, they see that this apparently simple motion is actually very complicated. The teacher then asks the students to think about how they could simplify this situation. The research strategy is to start with simplified, idealized, force-and-motion situations, such as one-dimensional motion in a world with no friction or gravity, and then gradually add complexity. The sequence of complexities considered includes the following: thinking about friction, varying the mass of the object, dealing with two-dimensional motion, understanding gravity, and, finally, reasoning about trajectories, which is where the curriculum started with students tossing a bean bag around their classroom. This strategy of starting with simplified situations and gradually adding complexity is made clear to the students.

The inquiry cycle is repeated with each module of the curriculum. As it is repeated, the conceptual models the students are creating increase in complexity. In addition, the inquiry that they are doing becomes less and less scaffolded. By the end of the curriculum, the students are engaging in independent inquiry projects on research topics of their own choosing. To guide them, they are provided with the project outline and checklist shown in Fig. 11.5.

Reflective Assessment

In addition to the inquiry cycle and the project outline, which provide the students with a goal structure for guiding their scientific inquiry, we also introduce students to a set of criteria for reflecting on their research. These are shown in Fig. 11.6 and include high-level goals, such as "understanding the processes of inquiry," and cognitively oriented criteria, such as "being inventive" and "reasoning carefully," as well as socially oriented criteria, such as "communicating well" and "team-work." The definitions for these criteria were designed to help students understand the nature and purpose of research. The students use these criteria in a process we call *reflective assessment* in which they evaluate their own and each others' research (cf., Frederiksen & Collins, 1989; Miller, 1991; Towler & Broadfoot, 1992). For example, Fig. 11.7 provides a sample reflective assessment page from the students' research books in which they use these criteria. In this case, "being systematic" and "communicating well" are defined for the students who then rate the research they have just completed using a 5-point scale for each criterion. Then, they have to justify their scores by describing how their work deserves those scores.

Our hypothesis is that this reflective assessment process will help students to better understand the purpose and steps of the inquiry cycle.

An Outline and Checklist for Your Project Report

☐ **Question:**

     🍎 Which general topic did you choose?
         • Explain why you choose that topic.
     🍎 What specific question(s) did you choose to investigate?
         • Why did you choose that question(s)?

☐ **Hypothesize:**

     🍎 Write down some hypotheses, or predictions, that relate to your question.
         • You should have at least two different hypotheses.
     🍎 For each hypothesis, explain why someone might believe it.

☐ **Investigate:**

     🍎 Describe how you did your investigation.
         • Give enough detail so that someone else could repeat what you did.
             – Include a list of the laboratory equipment, computer databases, questionnaires, or other information sources that you used.
             – If you did an experiment, draw a sketch of how you set it up.
     🍎 Justify why you did your investigation this way.
         • Explain how it allowed you to test your hypotheses.
     🍎 Show your data in a table, graph, or some other representation.

☐ **Analyze:**

     🍎 Describe how you analyzed your data and show your work.
         • Be specific and refer to your table or other representations of your data.
     🍎 Describe any patterns that you found in your data.
     🍎 Discuss the parts of your data, if any, that do not make sense.
         • Could there have been any serious errors in your investigation?

☐ **Model:**

     🍎 Summarize your conclusions.
         • State any laws or findings that you discovered.
         • Present your theory about why this happens?
     🍎 Illustrate how your data support your conclusions.
     🍎 How do your conclusions relate to your research question?
         • Which of your hypotheses, if any, do your data support?

☐ **Evaluate:**

     🍎 Show how what you learned could be useful.
         • Give examples to illustrate.
         • Can your model (laws & theory) be applied to new situations to predict and explain what will happen?
     🍎 What are the limitations of your model?
         • Are there situations where your laws would make wrong predictions or your theory could not explain what happens?
     🍎 What are the limitations of your research?
         • What remains to be learned about your chosen topic?
         • What further investigations would you do if you had more time?

FIG. 11.5 An outline and checklist that is provided to students to guide them as they undertake their research projects and write their reports. It unpacks the subgoals that need to be pursued as students follow the inquiry cycle.

Criteria for Judging Your Work

HIGH-LEVEL CRITERIA

	Understanding the Science. Students show that they understand the relevant science and can apply it in solving problems, in predicting and explaining phenomena, and in carrying out inquiry projects.
	Understanding the Processes of Inquiry. Students are thoughtful and effective in all phases of the inquiry process, including: raising questions for study, developing hypotheses, designing an investigation, collecting and analyzing data, drawing conclusions in the form of laws and models, and reflecting on the limitations of their investigation and their conclusions.
	Making Connections. Students see the big picture and have a clear overview of their work, its purposes, and how it relates to other ideas or situations. They relate new information, ideas, and findings to what they already know.

COGNITIVELY-ORIENTED CRITERIA

	Being Inventive. Students are creative and examine many possibilities in their work. They show originality and inventiveness in thinking of problems to investigate, in coming up with hypotheses, in designing experiments, in creating new laws or models, and in applying their models to new situations.
	Being Systematic. Students are careful, organized, and logical in planning, carrying out, and evaluating work. When problems come up, they are thoughtful in examining their progress and deciding whether to alter their approach or strategy.
	Using the Tools of Science. Students understand the representations and tools of science and use them appropriately in their investigations. These may include diagrams, graphs, tables, formulas, calculators, computers, and lab equipment.
	Reasoning Carefully. Students reason appropriately and carefully using scientific concepts and models. They can argue whether or not a prediction or law fits a model. They can show how their observations support or refute a model. And they can evaluate the strengths and limitations of a model.

SOCIALLY-ORIENTED CRITERIA

	Writing and Communicating Well. Students clearly express their ideas to each other or to an audience through writing, diagrams, and speaking so that others will understand their research and how they carried it out.
	Teamwork. Students work together as a team to make progress. They respect each others' contributions and support each others' learning. They divide their work fairly so that everyone has an important part.

FIG. 11.6 The criteria for judging research that students use in the reflective assessment process.

It should also motivate them in that their work will be constantly evaluated by themselves, their peers, and their teachers. This process also encourages the students to continually monitor and reflect on their work, which should improve their inquiry skills. Furthermore, we hy-

Now you will evaluate the work you just did.

Being Systematic

 Being Systematic. Students are careful, organized, and logical in planning, carrying out, and evaluating work. When problems come up, they are thoughtful in examining their progress and deciding whether to alter their approach or strategy.

Circle the score that you think your work deserves

1	2	3	4	5
not adequate		adequate		exceptional

Explain how your experimental work justifies the score you have given yourself. _____

_____

_____

Communicating Well

 Communicating Well. Students clearly express their ideas to others or to an audience through writing, diagrams, and speaking so that others will understand their research as well as how they carried it out.

Circle the score that you think your work deserves

1	2	3	4	5
not adequate		adequate		exceptional

Explain how your experimental write-ups justify the score you have given yourself. _____

_____

_____

FIG. 11.7 An example of a reflective assessment page found in the students' research books. This sample page is located at the end of the investigate phase of the inquiry cycle.

pothesize that this metacognitive reflective assessment process should be particularly important for disadvantaged, low-achieving students, because one reason these students are low achieving is that they lack metacognitive skills, such as monitoring and reflecting on their work

(Campione, 1987; Nickerson, Perkins, & Smith, 1985). If this process is introduced and scaffolded as we illustrated, it should enable low-achieving students to learn these valuable metacognitive skills and their performance should therefore be closer to that of high-achieving students.

INSTRUCTIONAL TRIALS

The THINKERTOOLS Inquiry Curriculum—which centers on the modeling software, the inquiry cycle, and the reflective assessment process—was implemented by three teachers in their urban classrooms. We saw these instructional trials of the curriculum as an opportunity to conduct a controlled study on the value of the reflective assessment process, in particular, and the development of metacognitive skills in general. For each of the participating teachers, half of his or her classes engaged in the reflective assessment process and the other half did not. Thus, all of the classes completed the same THINKERTOOLS Inquiry Curriculum, but half of the classes included reflective–assessment activities, such as that shown in Fig. 11.7, whereas the control classes included alternative activities in which students commented on what they did and did not like about the THINKERTOOLS Inquiry Curriculum.

These 3 teachers were teaching 12 classes in Grades 7 through 9. Two of the teachers had no prior formal physics education. They were all teaching in urban situations in which their class sizes averaged almost 30 students, two thirds of whom were minority students, and many were from very disadvantaged backgrounds. Regarding their students' achievement levels on a standardized achievement test (the Comprehensive Test of Basic Skills [CTBS]), the distribution of percentile scores was almost flat, indicating that there were many low- , middle- , and high-achieving students, which is an ideal population for research purposes.

We now turn to the results of these instructional trials of the THINKERTOOLS Inquiry Curriculum, including our experimental test of the reflective assessment process. In presenting the results, we first focus on the students' learning of inquiry and the impact that the reflective assessment process had on that learning. Then, we turn to the students' learning of physics. As these findings are presented in depth in White and Frederiksen (1998), we summarize only the major findings here.

The Development of Inquiry Expertise

One of our assessments of students' scientific inquiry expertise was an inquiry test that was given both before and after the THINKERTOOLS curriculum. In this written test, the students were asked to investigate a specific research question: "What is the relationship between the weight of an object and the effect that sliding friction has on its motion?" In this test, the students were asked to come up with alternative, competing hypotheses that relate to this question. Next, they had to design on paper an experiment that would determine what actually happens, and then they had to pretend to carry out their experiment. In other words, they had to conduct it as a thought experiment and make up the data that they thought they would get if they actually carried out their experiment. Finally, they had to analyze their made-up data to reach a conclusion and relate this conclusion back to their original, competing hypotheses.

In scoring this test, the focus was entirely on the students' inquiry skills. Whether or not the students' theories embodied the correct physics was regarded as totally irrelevant. Fig. 11.8 presents the gain scores on this test for both low- and high-achieving students, and for students in the reflective assessment and the control classes. Notice, first, that students in the reflective assessment classes gained more on this inquiry test. Second, notice that this was particularly true for the low-achieving students. This is the first piece of evidence that the reflective assessment process is beneficial, particularly for the academically disadvantaged students.

If we examine this effect of reflective assessment in more detail by looking at the difference in the gain scores for each component of the test, as shown in Fig. 11.9, one can see that the difference in the gain scores is significantly greater for the more difficult aspects of the test: making up results, analyzing those made-up results, and relating them back to the original hypotheses. In fact, the difference in the gain scores on this test is greatest for a measure we call *coherence*, which measures the extent to which the experiments the students designed related to their hypotheses, the results they made up related to their proposed experiment, the conclusions they reached related to the data they made up, and whether they related these conclusions back to their original hypotheses. This kind of overall coherence in research is, we think, a very important indication of sophistication in scientific inquiry. It is on this coherence measure that we see the greatest difference in favor of students who engaged in the reflective assessment process.

Inquiry Gain Scores

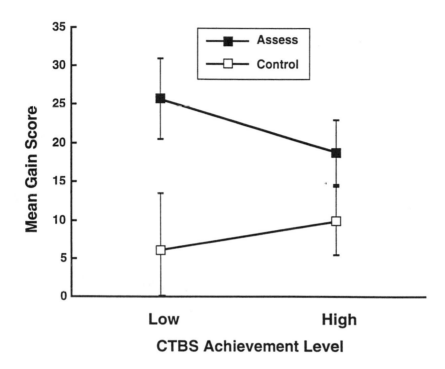

FIG. 11.8 The mean gain scores on the inquiry test for students in the reflective assessment and the control classes, plotted as a function of their achievement level.

Students carried out two research projects in this course, one about halfway through the curriculum and one at the end. For the sake of brevity, we added the scores for these two projects together as shown in Fig. 11.10. These results indicate that students in the reflective assessment classes perform significantly better on their research projects than students in the control classes. In addition, the reflective assessment process is particularly beneficial for the low-achieving students: low-achieving students in the reflective assessment classes performed almost as well as the high-achieving students. These findings were the same across all three teachers and all three grade levels.

To investigate further this reflective assessment effect, we looked at the composition of the students' research groups. The students worked together in pairs and in some cases a low-achieving student was paired

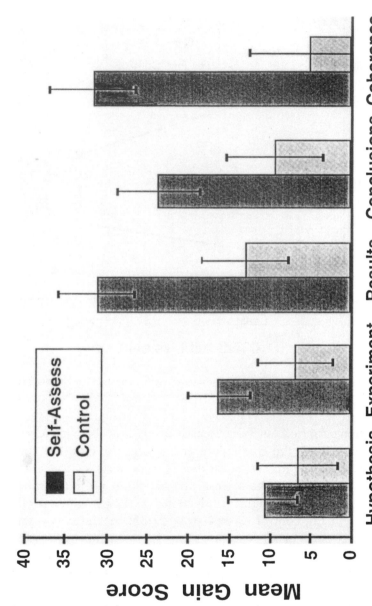

FIG. 11.9 Average gains on the inquiry test subscores for students in the reflective assessment and the control classes.

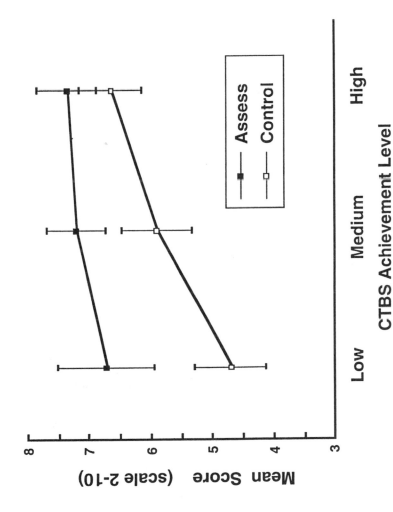

FIG. 11.10 The mean combined scores on their research project for students in the reflective assessment and the control classes, plotted as a function of their achievement level.

with a high-achieving student and in other cases it was a low–low or a high–high pairing. This analysis revealed that the reflective assessment effect is enhanced if low-achieving students collaborate with high-achieving students. For example, in the reflective assessment classes, a low-achieving student paired with a high-achieving student performed significantly better on average than two low-achieving students working together. In contrast, this was not the case in the control classes where it did not make any difference for low-achieving students whether they were paired with a high-achieving student or with another low-achieving student. We think that the high–low pairing matters in the reflective–assessment classes because high-achieving students already have metacognitive reflection skills. Thus, when high-achieving students are asked to do a reflective assessment, they can model this metacognitive process for low-achieving students as they collaborate in carrying out their research.

The Development of Physics Expertise

We now summarize the results from the point of view of the students' understanding of physics. We gave the students a test, both before and after the THINKERTOOLS Inquiry Curriculum, that included items, such as the one shown in Fig. 11.11, in which students are asked to predict and explain how forces will affect an object's motion. On this test we found significant pretest to posttest gains. We also found that our middle school THINKERTOOLS students perform better on such items than do high school physics students who are taught using traditional approaches. When we analyzed the effects of the curriculum on items that represent near or far transfer in relation to contexts they had studied in the course, we found that there were significant learning effects for both the near and the far transfer items. Together, these results show that you can teach sophisticated physics in urban, middle school classrooms when you make use of simulation tools combined with teaching and scaffolding the inquiry process.

IMPLICATIONS OF THE INSTRUCTIONAL TRIALS

There are several implications of these findings to which we want to draw attention. The first is that scientific inquiry and reflective assessment should be introduced to students early in their school careers.

Imagine that you kick a ball horizontally (→) off a cliff. Drawn below are three paths that someone might think the ball would take as it falls to the ground.

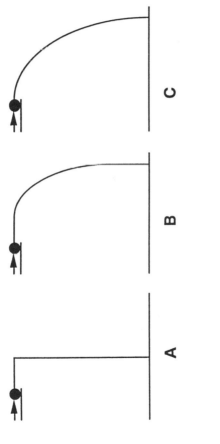

A   B   C

Circle the path you think is correct: A   B   C

Explain the reasons for your choice: _____

_____

_____

FIG. 11.11 A sample problem from the physics test.

Developing skills in inquiry, modeling, and metacognition should enable low-achieving students to perform closer to the high-achieving students. Another implication is that students should benefit from learning how to generalize these inquiry and reflective assessment processes to their other school subjects. In this way, they could "learn how to learn" and develop general inquiry and metacognitive skills.

Our present research is thus focused on finding methods for enabling students to generalize their inquiry expertise. Our hypothesis is that for students to be able to transfer this expertise to other topics, it needs to be introduced in multiple areas of their curriculum. For this reason, we created a genetics curriculum around the GENSCOPE software (Horwitz & Christie, chap. 6, this volume) which follows the same inquiry cycle and utilizes the same reflective assessment process that we described earlier. We also created an "inquiry about inquiry" THINKERTOOLS curriculum, which not only enables students to generalize the inquiry cycle and reflective assessment processes to research in the cognitive sciences but also enables them to engage in research on metacognitive skills and inquiry processes. The goal in this curriculum is to make it possible for young students to become cognitive researchers who create articulate computer models of sociocognitive processes related to inquiry, reflection, and self-improvement. Students then design and carry out educational experiments to investigate the utility of their sociocognitive models with the aim of improving them (White, Shimoda, & Frederiksen, 1999).

THE NEED FOR ADDITIONAL PEDAGOGICAL TOOLS

Our instructional trials of the THINKERTOOLS Inquiry Curriculum indicated that students and teachers would benefit if we developed additional pedagogical tools and incorporated their use within our curricula. Specific areas of need include the following: facilitating students' understanding of the nature of scientific models, further scaffolding of the inquiry process, and facilitating students' and teachers' use of reflective assessment processes. In what follows, we elaborate on each of these in turn.

Tools for Understanding Modeling

We found that many students had problems understanding the modeling phase of the inquiry cycle. In general, they were confused about what conceptual models are and about the relationship between their own conceptual model, the computer simulation, and the real world.

Computer simulation software, such as THINKERTOOLS, can potentially help students to understand the nature of both scientific and conceptual models. To elaborate, the computer is not the real world; it can only simulate real-world behavior by stepping through time and using rules to determine how forces that are acting (like friction and gravity) will change the dot's velocity on that time step. Thus, the computer is actually using a conceptual model to predict behavior, just as the students will use the conceptual model they construct to predict behavior. In working with the computer, the students' task is to design experiments that will help them induce the laws that are used by the simulation. This is more straightforward than the corresponding real-world inquiry task. After all, objects in the real world are not driven by laws; rather, the laws simply characterize their behavior.

One example of a modeling activity, which is carried out early in the curriculum, has students explain how their computer and real-world experiments could lead to different conclusions. They might say, for instance, "The computer simulation does not have friction, which affects our real-world experiments." Alternatively, they might say, "The real world does not behave perfectly and does not follow rules." Working with a computer simulation can thus potentially help students to develop metaconceptual knowledge about what scientific models are and about how laws can be used to predict and control behavior. It can also enable them to appreciate the utility of creating computer simulations that embody scientific laws and idealized abstractions of real-world behavior and then of using such simulations to conduct experiments to see the implications of a particular theory.

To facilitate the development of such expertise, we modified the software to allow more authentic scientific modeling. In the version of the software described earlier, students work with the software to discover its conceptual model. In the new improved version, students use the software to express their own conceptual model based on the findings from their real-world experiments. Thus, the new software allows students to create models that obey non-Newtonian laws of physics. For example, Fig. 11.12 illustrates how students can choose from among alternative laws for determining what will happen to the motion of an object when no forces are acting on it. By choosing laws that predict how objects will behave when various forces are (or are not) acting,

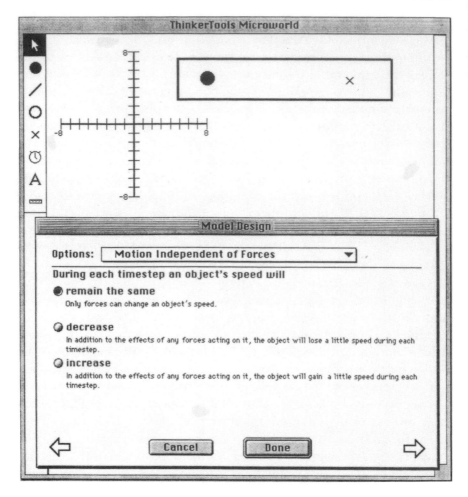

FIG. 11.12 An example of the model design feature of the ThinkerTools force and motion software.

students can create a computer model that embodies their theory of force and motion. They can then experiment with the computer model to see the implications of their theory.

In instructional trials with a curriculum that utilizes this revised version of the THINKERTOOLS force and motion software, Schwarz found that students gain a more sophisticated view of the nature of conceptual models, as well as a more sophisticated view of the scientific inquiry process for creating models (Schwarz, 1998). However, she also found that they do not necessarily develop Newtonian theories. This result is not too surprising, because the students are no longer constrained to working with Newtonian computer simulations. In our present research, we are trying to synthesize this "model creation" use of the software with our earlier "model discovery" approach to enable students to develop a sophisticated understanding of inquiry and modeling as well as a Newtonian conception of force and motion.

Tools for Scientific Inquiry

The success of the THINKERTOOLS Inquiry Curriculum, particularly the reflective assessment component, supports our view that making students aware of cognitive and social processes related to inquiry will enable them to acquire metacognitive expertise, which will then play an important role in enabling them to learn via inquiry. However, our findings also suggest that students and teachers could benefit from additional computer-based tools designed to assist them as they design, carry out, and reflect on their research. Furthermore, the students' research books, which include the scaffolding and reflection activities described previously, are in printed form and suffer from the limitations of the print medium.

These considerations motivated us to create software that can do an even better job of making inquiry goals and processes explicit and of getting students to reflect on their inquiry processes with the aim of improving them. We are thus creating computer software, called SCI-WISE THINKERTOOLS, which supports students as they carry out research projects (White et al., 1999). This system provides user-modifiable models of cognitive and social processes related to inquiry in the form of articulate agents, such as a Hypothesizer, an Inventor, and a Collaborator, who pop up in appropriate contexts. These agents, known as Advisors, aid students as they engage in research and encourage students to reflect on and revise their inquiry processes. For instance, the Collaborator can pop up and say, "Hi, I'm the Collaborator. My goal is to help you work effectively with your research partners. Here are some strategies that might help you do that." Once the students have tried some of the suggested collaboration strategies, the Collaborator then encourages the students to reflect on their utility and to modify the strategies if needed.

The SCI-WISE system supports a variety of Task Contexts and makes available suitable Task Advisors for each context. Our prototype system includes four Task Contexts: research projects, preparing presentations, evaluating research reports, and modifying the inquiry support system. These are authentic tasks in which scientists engage as they conduct research. They also correspond to important steps in the process of learning how to learn via inquiry, mainly engaging in inquiry, explaining your work to others, reflecting on your work, and modifying your inquiry processes to make them better.

Associated with each Task Context is a Head Advisor. So, we are creating an Inquirer, a Presenter, an Assessor, and a Modifier. Each Head Advisor provides possible goal structures for that task. The Inquirer, for example, makes use of the inquiry cycle to provide a structure for the inquiry process (i.e., Question, Hypothesize, Investigate). Each step in the cycle has a Task Specialist associated with it, such as the Hypothesizer, who can advise students concerning how to achieve its particular goals (as shown in the top half of Fig. 11.13).

In addition to Task Advisors, there are General Purpose Advisors who can assist students no matter what task they are engaged in. General Purpose Advisors include both Cognitive Advisors, such as the Reasoner and the Inventor, as well as Social Advisors, such as the Communicator and the Collaborator. These correspond to the assessment criteria, such as Reasoning Carefully and Communicating Well, that we developed for the THINKERTOOLS Inquiry Curriculum to get students to reflect on their inquiry processes. The SCI-WISE General Purpose Advisors, however, have a broader range of expertise and serve a larger number of functions than our prior reflective assessment criteria and process. For example, they incorporate heuristics for achieving goals as well as knowledge of when these heuristics might be useful along with examples to illustrate their use. The Inventor, for instance, includes heuristics such as "relax and turn your mind loose" (see the bottom of Fig.11.13). Advisors can "pop up" when their advice might be most useful (e.g., the Inventor's heuristics might be useful at the beginning of each step in the inquiry cycle).

The students collaborate with the General Purpose and the Task Advisors in a virtual inquiry support environment (see Fig. 11.14), which includes artifacts such as a research journal, a project report, and a project evaluation. It also contains a meeting room, where students can go to find the various advisors if they have not already popped up in a particular context, and a dialogue box for communication (Shimoda, White, & Frederiksen, 1999). In addition to Task Advisors and General Purpose Advisors, there are also System Development Advisors, such as

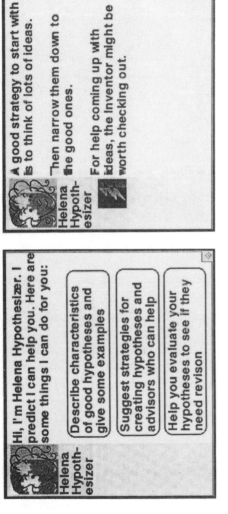
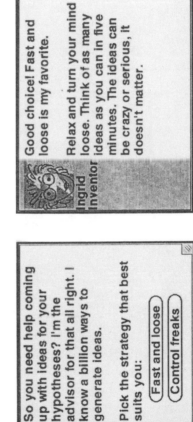

FIG. 11.13 An illustration of students interacting with a task advisor, Helena hypothesizer, and a general purpose advisor, Ingrid inventor, who are guiding the students as they undertake the task of generating hypotheses.

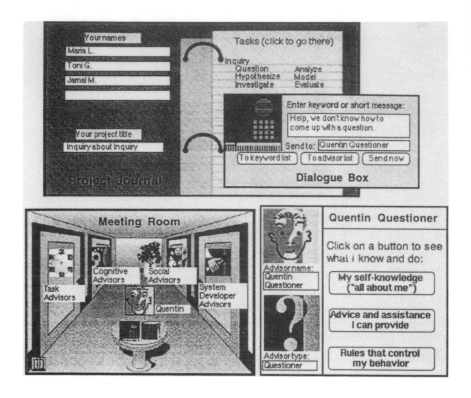

FIG. 11.14 An example of students using the SCI-WISE system, which supports them as they design and carry out research projects. It provides modifiable software advisors who suggest strategies and help students to reflect on and improve their inquiry processes.

a Modifier and a Pedagogue, who assist students as they work to improve the inquiry support system itself. For example, students can modify the various advisors, such as the Hypothesizer, so that they can embody the students' own theories about the goals that should be pursued (such as help the user come up with competing hypotheses), the type of advice that should prove helpful (such as offer a strategy or recommend consulting the Inventor), and the circumstances in which the advice should be offered (such as when the user is in the Hypothesize step of the inquiry cycle and asks for help). Students can thus modify an advisor's goals, its advice, and how it gets activated, as well as other features of the system. In this way, different students can develop alternative, competing hypotheses concerning how best to support inquiry and reflection.

Students can use the modifiability of the system to conduct research on the inquiry process itself. For example, a class could generate a variety of strategies for facilitating collaboration, such as "take turns" and "listen to others," and could create alternative versions of the system with different Collaborators who recommend and support different strategies. The class can then conduct empirical research to determine which Collaborator's advice proves most helpful. Such "inquiry about inquiry" is carried out as students use their alternative versions of the inquiry support system to design and conduct research projects in domains such as physics, genetics, nutrition, and cognitive science (White et al., 1999).

The SCI-WISE THINKERTOOLS system thus has several features that may foster learning how to learn via inquiry: It guides students as they do their various research projects, it encourages them to become aware of and reflect on sociocognitive processes related to inquiry, and it enables students to engage in inquiry about these processes with the aim of improving them. Our hope is that by modifying the system to test their own theories of how inquiry could best be modeled and supported, and by working with it to conduct research on a wide variety of topics, students will internalize aspects of the advisors' expertise related to inquiry learning, reflection and self-improvement, and will learn how to generalize the use of such expertise to a wide variety of contexts.

Tools for Reflective Assessment

Another need emanating from instructional trials of the THINKERTOOLS Inquiry Curriculum is concerned with enabling teachers' use of the reflective assessment process. This process is more authentic and effective if the criteria for judging research (shown in Fig. 11.6) are used not only by the students to score their own and each other's work but are also used by the teachers when they evaluate the students' research projects. Unfortunately, because the teachers taught as many as 150 students each (5 classes of approximately 30 students), they did not have time to judge and characterize their students' work on each of the criteria. Instead, they gave students much more limited feedback, usually just a letter grade often with no written comments. To help remedy this problem, we developed a computer-based scoring system called the

Inquiry Scorer. Teachers can use this system to generate a written evaluation as the students give oral presentations of their research project to the class.

In this tool, shown in Fig. 11.15, each of the criteria for characterizing good scientific research is presented on the screen. The teachers can click on the name of any criterion and see its definition. If they click on the icon for a given criterion, a 5-point scoring rubric appears that characterizes each of the levels on the 5-point scale. The teachers can then type in the score that they feel characterizes the students' research for each of the criteria. The software then generates a written report that provides students with a score and corresponding level descriptor for each of the criteria. The teachers can edit these descriptors if the ones provided do not characterize the students' research appropriately. In this way, the teachers can quickly generate a customized, written evaluation of each research group's project.

We found that the process of working with teachers to decide what each level descriptor should say was very worthwhile and helped teachers to think about the characteristics of good research. If this reflective assessment tool had been available for use in the instructional study summarized in this paper, the positive effects of the reflective assessment process might have been even greater. In addition, the students could be provided with this scoring tool so they too could participate in conversations about what each level descriptor should say. This would be a potentially interesting and useful pedagogical activity.

Recently, we expanded the Inquiry Scorer so it allows students and teachers to score research projects using two complementary methods: an Overall Assessment and a Project Analysis. The Overall Assessment is the method described previously and illustrated in Fig. 11.15. It is based on the reflective assessment criteria, such as Reasoning Carefully and Communicating Well, that apply to all aspects of a research project. In the Project Analysis, the scorer evaluates specific features of each section of the research project (the Research Question, Hypotheses, Investigation, Analysis, Modeling, and Evaluation). For each section, a series of questions are presented asking for judgments about specific aspects of the work in that section (as shown in Fig. 11.16 for the Question and Hypotheses sections). These questions are based on the analytic scoring rubric that we developed for the inquiry test, as well as on the sequence of inquiry goals and subgoals presented to students in the "Outline and Checklist for Your Project Report" (see Fig. 11.5). Our

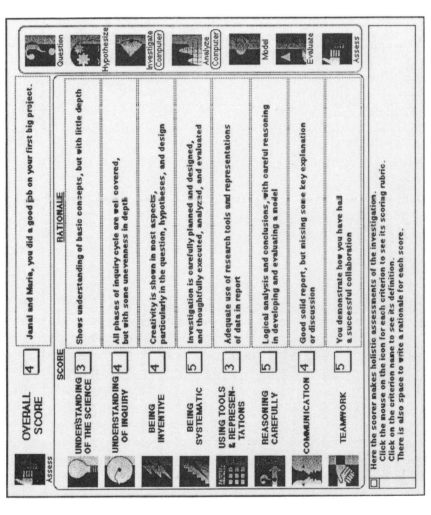

FIG. 11.14 An illustration of the inquiry scorer system that we developed to enable teachers to more easily use the "criteria for judging your work" when assessing students' research projects.

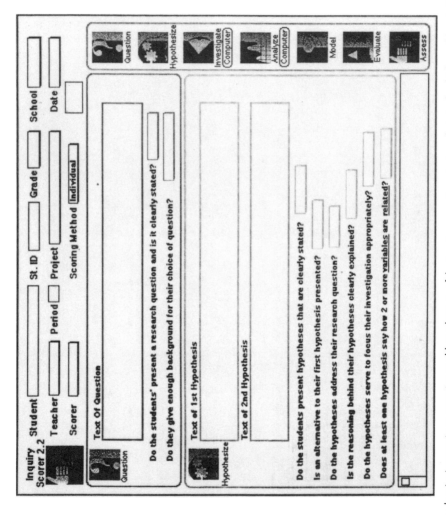

FIG. 11.16 The beginning sections, question and hypothesize, of the inquiry scorer's project analysis tool, which enables students and teachers to analyze and evaluate research projects.

intention in introducing the Project Analysis was to make the scorer's reading of the project more systematic and, in so doing, to influence the evidential basis for the Overall Assessment. Our collaborating teachers have reported that reading a student's research report and performing a Project Analysis followed by an Overall Assessment provides a thorough analysis of a research project in a form that enables both students and teachers to better understand the goals and processes of scientific inquiry.

Tools for Teacher Preparation

Another need emerged when we began to disseminate the THINKER-TOOLS Inquiry Curriculum. We sent the curriculum "mail order" to eight teachers who requested it (all at a great distance from us). We had no direct contact with any of these teachers and simply had them fill out questionnaires that asked them to outline their goals for science teaching and to describe what they did and did not like about THINKERTOOLS. They also gave their students our inquiry test and our physics test before and after they completed the curriculum. These data revealed some interesting findings. Four of the teachers said that their primary goal was to teach scientific inquiry, and they described the THINKERTOOLS materials as a good way to teach inquiry. For the students of these teachers, we found the same significant gains in physics and inquiry expertise as in the study summarized in this chapter. The other four teachers said, in contrast, that their focus was on teaching physics, and they described THINKERTOOLS as a good way to teach physics. For the students of these teachers, we found significant gains on our physics test but not on our inquiry test. When we later asked the teachers whether they taught the entire curriculum, we found that the "physics-focused" teachers dropped many of the inquiry components.

Furthermore, when we analyzed videotapes of six local teachers teaching THINKERTOOLS, we found that the ways in which they implemented the curriculum often did not match what we envisioned regarding good inquiry teaching. For example, in the prediction phase of the inquiry cycle, when the teachers were trying to get students to articulate a set of competing hypotheses, they often did not ask students to justify their predictions with some form of causal explanation. Also, when students were having difficulty in designing and conducting their experiments, the teachers sometimes gave a procedural solution without getting the students to analyze the design problem for themselves. Furthermore, in the model phase of the inquiry cycle, the goal was to try to reach a consensus about the law(s) that best characterize what the students had discovered from their experiments. Here, some teachers used aspects of the activities suggested in the teachers' guides, such as asking students to vote on the best law, but they did not ask their students to cite theory and evidence to support their choice or to engage in debates using evidence from their experiments. In short, there were numerous missed opportunities for students to engage in inquiry and reflection.

Based on these findings, we determined that it is not enough to simply provide teachers with teacher's guides that attempt to outline goals, describe activities, and suggest, in a semiprocedural fashion, how the lessons might proceed. We now believe that, in addition, teachers need to develop a conceptual framework for characterizing good inquiry teaching and for reflecting on their teaching practices (Schön, 1983, 1987) in the same way that students need to develop criteria for characterizing good scientific research and for reflecting on their inquiry processes.

To achieve the goal of enabling teachers to characterize and reflect on inquiry teaching, we are now using a framework that we developed for the National Board for Professional Teaching Standards (Frederiksen, Sipusic, Sherin, & Wolfe, 1998). This framework, which attempts to characterize expert teaching, includes five major criteria: worthwhile engagement, adept classroom management, effective pedagogy, good classroom climate, and explicit thinking about the subject matter, to which we added engaging in inquiry. In this characterization of expert teaching, each of these criteria for good teaching is unpacked into a set of "aspects." For example, Fig. 11.17 illustrates the criterion of "classroom climate," which is defined as "the social environment of the class empowers learning." Under this general criterion, there are five different aspects: engagement, encouragement, rapport, respect, and sensitivity to diversity. Each of these aspects is defined in terms of specific characteristics of classroom practice, such as "humor is used effectively" or "there is a strong connection between students and teacher." Furthermore, each of these specific characteristics of classroom practice is indexed to video clips, called "video snippets," that illustrate it. This framework characterizes good inquiry teaching and provides teachers with video exemplars of teaching practice. It could easily be embodied in a CD-ROM system.

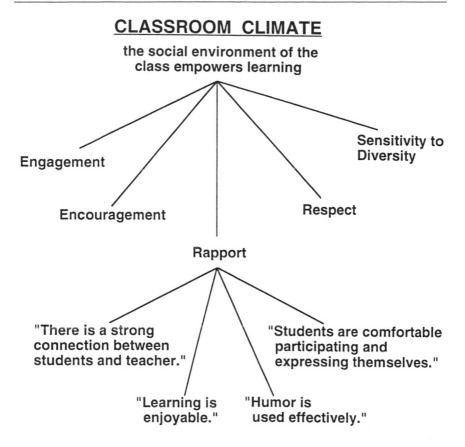

FIG. 11.17 An example of the hierarchical definitions created for each criterion, such as classroom climate, that are used to characterize expert teaching and that help teachers reflect on their teaching practices.

Such materials can be used to enable teachers to learn about inquiry teaching and its value, as well as to reflect on their own and on each other's teaching practices. For example, recently we tried the following approach with a group of 10 student-teachers. The student-teachers first learned to use the framework outlined previously by scoring some of our THINKERTOOLS videotapes. Then, they used the framework to facilitate discussions of videotapes of their own teaching. In this way, they participated in what we call "video clubs," which enable them to reflect on their own teaching practices and to hopefully develop better approaches for inquiry teaching. (Video clubs incorporate social activities designed to help teachers reflectively assess and talk about their teaching practices [Frederiksen et al., 1998]). The results so far have been very encouraging, and our findings indicate that engaging in this reflective activity enabled the student-teachers to develop a shared language for viewing and talking about teaching that, in turn, led to highly productive conversations in which they explored and reflected on their own teaching practices (Frederiksen & White, 1997).

We thus argue that the same emphases on scaffolding inquiry, meta-cognition, and reflection that we have illustrated are important and effective for students are important for teachers as well. This can partly be achieved by providing teachers with teacher's guides that scaffold each step in the inquiry cycle; that is, outlining the pedagogical goals and describing the instructional activities and how they can be intro-duced. The teacher's guides, however, are not enough. In addition, teachers need to be introduced to a reflective assessment process in which they learn about the characteristics of good inquiry teaching and then learn to reflect on their teaching practices. We are presently conducting research with in-service as well as preservice teachers to further investigate these hypotheses about how to enable teachers to adopt inquiry oriented approaches to their teaching.

SUMMARY AND CONCLUSION

In this chapter, we have described various technological tools and their instructional use in facilitating inquiry oriented approaches to science education. Our work is based on the premise, derived from cognitive and educational research, that students need to be made explicitly aware of their theories and inquiry processes as well as to develop an ability to monitor and reflect on their theory-building processes. We described software modeling tools that enable students to create explicit theories. These theories are in the form of conceptual models that incorporate stepping through time, analyzing events as cause–effect sequences, and employing visual representations and verbal laws to calculate and depict what happens. We went on to demonstrate how software modeling tools that incorporate this type of conceptual model make physics under-standable and interesting to a wide range of students. Furthermore, we illustrated how focusing on creating conceptual models enables students to learn about the subject matter, in this case physics, as well as about the properties of scientific models and the inquiry processes needed for creating them.

In our research, we found that the learning of inquiry was greatly facilitated not only by making the inquiry process explicit but also by introducing a reflective assessment process. This metacognitive process helped students learn about the characteristics of good inquiry and encouraged them to monitor and reflect on their inquiry processes. We found that this metacognitive, reflective process was particularly beneficial for low-achieving students and enabled them to gain more on the inquiry test and to perform closer to high-achieving students on their research projects. We went on to illustrate a variety of software tools for introducing metacognitive reflection into the collaborative work of students as they carry out scientific inquiry projects. For example, one of the software tools enables students to work with and modify an inquiry support system (SCI-WISE). Another tool helps teachers and students to evaluate their research using criteria that focus on the cognitive and social processes involved in scientific inquiry (Inquiry Scorer).

We argued that the same emphasis on making cognition explicit and creating theories about what one is doing applies to teachers as well as to students. This explicitness was achieved for teachers by scaffolding each step in the inquiry cycle via teachers' guides that outline the pedagogical goals and describe the instructional activities and how they could be implemented. This explicitness can be further enhanced by enabling teachers to build a theory about the characteristics of good inquiry teaching. Our strategy has been to introduce teachers to a reflective assessment process in which they learn about the characteristics of good inquiry teaching. They then participate in video clubs, which include social activities designed to help them reflectively assess and talk about their teaching practices. In this way, teachers learn to implement such new approaches to science education and to use the associated technological tools effectively.

Our conclusion is that a synthesis of sociocognitive theory with the development of technological tools and the design of new instructional approaches can transform the nature of science education for both students and teachers. It may even play a role in transforming how scientists themselves engage in and think about the scientific enterprise.

ACKNOWLEDGMENTS

This work was supported by the James S. McDonnell Foundation, the National Science Foundation, the United States Department of Education's Office of Educational Research and Improvement, and the Educational Testing Service. We are grateful for the support of these sponsors and would also like to express our gratitude to all members of the ThinkerTools team for their contributions to the project. This chapter incorporates material from White and Frederiksen (1998).

REFERENCES

Brown, A., & Campione, J. (1996). Psychological theory and the design of innovative learning environments: On procedures, principles, and systems. In L. Schauble & R. Glaser (Eds.), *Innovations in learning: New environments for education* (pp. 289–325). Mahwah, NJ: Lawrence Erlbaum Associates.

Campione, J. (1987). Metacognitive components of instructional research with problem learners. In F. E. Weinert & R. H. Kluwe (Eds.), *Metacognition, motivation, and understanding* (pp. 117–140). Hillsdale, NJ: Lawrence Erlbaum Associates.

Collins, A., Brown J., & Newman, S. (1989). Cognitive apprenticeship: Teaching the craft of reading, writing, and mathematics. In L. Resnick (Ed.), *Knowing, learning, and instruction: Essays in honor of Robert Glaser* (pp. 453–494). Hillsdale, NJ: Lawrence Erlbaum Associates.

Driver, R., Asika, H., Leach, J., Mortimer, E., & Scott, P. (1994). Constructing scientific knowledge in the classroom. *Educational Researcher, 23*(7), 5–12.

Frederiksen, J., & Collins, A. (1989). A systems approach to educational testing. *Educational Researcher, 18*(9), 27–32.

Frederiksen, J., Sipusic, M., Sherin, M., & Wolfe, E. (1998). Video portfolio assessment: Creating a framework for viewing the functions of teaching. *Educational Assessment, 5*(4), 225–297.

Frederiksen, J., & White, B. (1997). Cognitive facilitation: A method for promoting reflective collaboration. In the *Proceedings of the Second International Conference on Computer Support for Collaborative Learning.* Toronto, Canada: University of Toronto.

Mellar, H., Bliss, J., Boohan, R., Ogborn, J., & Tompsett, C. (1994). *Learning with artificial worlds: Computer based modeling in the curriculum.* London: The Falmer Press.

Miller, M. (1991). Self-assessment as a specific strategy for teaching the gifted learning disabled. *Journal for the Education of the Gifted, 14*(2), 178–188.

Nickerson, R., Perkins, D., & Smith, E. (1985). *The teaching of thinking.* Hillsdale, NJ: Lawrence Erlbaum Associates.

Scardamalia, M., Bereiter, C., & Lamon, M. (1994). The CSILE Project: Trying to bring the classroom into World 3. In K. McGilly (Ed.), *Classroom lessons: Integrating cognitive theory and classroom practice* (pp. 201–228). Cambridge, MA: MIT Press/Bradford Books.

Schauble, L., Raghavan, K., & Glaser, R. (1993). The discovery and reflection notation: A graphical trace for supporting self-regulation in computer-based laboratories. In S. P. Lajoie & S. J. Derry (Eds.), *Computers as cognitive tools* (pp. 319–337). Hillsdale, NJ: Lawrence Erlbaum Associates.

Schön, D. (1983). *The reflective practitioner.* New York: Basic Books.

Schön, D. (1987). *Educating the reflective practitioner.* San Francisco, CA: Jossey-Bass.

Schwarz, C. (1998). *Developing students' understanding of scientific modeling.* Unpublished doctoral dissertation. University of California at Berkeley.

Shimoda, T., White, B., & Frederiksen, J. (in press). Acquiring and transferring intellectual skills with modifiable software advisors in a virtual inquiry support environment. In *Proceeding of the Thirty-Second Annual Hawaii's International Conference on System Sciences*, Los Alamitos, CA: IEEE Computer Society.

Shute, V., Glaser, R., & Raghavan, K. (1989). Inference and discovery in an exploration laboratory. In P. Ackerman, R. Sternberg, & R. Glaser (Eds.), *Learning and individual differences: Advances in theory and research* (pp. 279–326). New York: W. H. Freeman.

Towler, L., & Broadfoot, P. (1992). Self-assessment in primary school. *Educational Review, 44*(2), 137–151.

White, B. (1981). *Designing computer games to facilitate learning [physics]*, (Technical Report AI-TR-619). Cambridge, MA: Artificial Intelligence Laboratory, MIT.

White, B. (1983). Sources of difficulty in understanding Newtonian dynamics. *Cognitive Science, 7*(1), 41–65.

White, B. (1984). Designing computer activities to help physics students understand Newton's laws of motion. *Cognition and Instruction, 1*, 69–108.

White, B. (1993a). Intermediate causal models: A missing link for successful science education? In R. Glaser (Ed.), *Advances in instructional psychology, Vol. 4* (pp. 177–252). Hillsdale, NJ: Lawrence Erlbaum Associates.

White, B. (1993b). ThinkerTools: Causal models, conceptual change, and science education. *Cognition and Instruction, 10*(1), 1–100.

White, B., & Frederiksen, J. (1990). Causal model progressions as a foundation for intelligent learning environments. *Artificial Intelligence, 24*, 99–157.

White, B., & Frederiksen, J. (1998). Inquiry, modeling, and metacognition: Making science accessible to all students. *Cognition and Instruction, 16*(1), 3–118.

White, R., & Gunstone, R. (1989). Metalearning and conceptual change. *International Journal of Science Education, 11*(5), 577–586.

White, B., & Horwitz, P. (1988). Computer microworlds and conceptual change: A new approach to science education. In P. Ramsden (Ed.), *Improving learning: New perspectives* (pp. 69–80). London: Kogan Page.

White, B., Shimoda, T., & Frederiksen, J. (1999). Enabling students to construct theories of collaborative inquiry and reflective learning: Computer support for metacognitive development. *International Journal of Artificial Intelligence in Education, 10*(2).

White, B. & Schwartz, C. (in press). Alternative approaches to using modeling and simulation tools for teaching science. In N. Roberts, W. Feurzeig, & B. Hunter (Eds.), *Computer modeling and simulation in science education.* New York: Springer-Verlag.

12

The Design of Immersive Virtual Learning Environments: Fostering Deep Understandings of Complex Scientific Knowledge

Chris Dede and Marilyn Salzman
George Mason University

R. Bowen Loftin
University of Houston

Katy Ash
George Mason University

The simple fact is that the world of sensory experience is not Newtonian. More than a little research shows that children and adults learn many things about the physical world through their experience, but do not learn about Newton's Laws. In a deep sense, physics is not about the world as we naturally perceive it, but about abstractions that have been put together with effort over hundreds of years, which happen to be very powerful when we learn to interpret the world in their terms ... The trick is not to turn experience into abstractions with a computer, but to turn abstractions like laws of physics into experiences. Science is reorganized intuition. (diSessa, 1986, p. 208)

Imagine launching and catching balls in an environment with neither gravity nor friction. Imagine creating and altering electrostatic fields and releasing charged particles to be propelled through those fields. Imagine manipulating atoms and observing the forces created when molecules bond. Then, as a giant step further, imagine being able to directly experience these phenomena by becoming a part of them "inside" a virtual world: being a ball as it bounces, riding on a test charge as it moves through an electrostatic field, or becoming an atom as it

361

bonds. These are the kinds of learning activities enabled in the virtual worlds of ScienceSpace. Our research suggests that such immersive, multisensory experiences enhance students' abilities to conceptualize and integrate complex, abstract scientific ideas.

Many groups are developing sophisticated instructional designs with well-understood, conventional technologies, such as today's personal computing and telecommunications devices. In contrast, our work explores the strengths and limits for learning of a very powerful emerging technology, virtual reality (VR). However, Project ScienceSpace does not focus solely on developing educational worlds using an interface that enables multisensory immersion. Our studies are exploring new ideas about the nature of learning based on the unique capabilities for research that virtual reality provides. ScienceSpace worlds enable unique, extraordinary educational experiences that help learners challenge their intuitions and construct new understandings of science. Our evaluations are designed to examine various aspects of these learning experiences, processes, and outcomes. Sophisticated experimentation along these dimensions is critical to determining the educational potential of three-dimensional, sensorily immersive virtual environments, a medium that the entertainment industry will place "under the Christmas tree" by the year 2000.

One of the challenges in working with instructional media is that developers and educators are confronted with rapidly increasing capabilities for information technology. The business and entertainment sectors are driving a fast-paced evolution of the devices people have in their workplaces and homes. Researchers and educators are scrambling to assess the potential, develop pedagogical strategies, create instructional materials, and implement a school-based infrastructure for today's technologies—only to find that computers and communications are "morphing" into new media of even greater power. Not since the dawn of the Industrial Revolution has a generation of students faced a future environment so dramatically different than what their parents experience at present. Charting the strengths and limits of emerging media for learning is imperative, so this group of learners has educational tools capable of preparing them for future workplace and citizenship responsibilities.

In particular, people's understanding of what computers can do has shifted dramatically as the size and cost of these devices has decreased while their power has grown. First, computers were seen as "number-crunching" machines, then came data processing devices, and now we live in the age of tools to manipulate symbols and information. Our VR research is based on the growing certainty that the next evolutionary stage is a fusion of computers and telecommunications into virtual environments. "Cyberspace" is not simply a channel through which content can flow, but a virtual place to live that (for better or for worse) competes directly with reality for the attention of many, especially this generation of students. For this reason, charting the strengths and limits of VR, long before it is ubiquitous in the form of video games, is vital for educational technology as a field.

To help in understanding the advanced learning tools we are developing, this chapter begins with a brief introduction to our worlds and to the virtual reality technology on which they are built. We then describe our learner-centered strategy for design and evaluation and identify issues that have shaped the development and assessment of our immersive, multisensory environments. Next, we discuss the evolution and evaluation of each ScienceSpace world. Finally, we describe insights gained both about learning and about emerging educational technologies such as VR and then delineate our plans for future research.

SCIENCESPACE WORLDS

ScienceSpace consists of three worlds in various stages of development: NewtonWorld, MaxwellWorld, and PaulingWorld. In NewtonWorld, users experience laws of motion from multiple points of view. In this world with neither gravity nor friction, balls hover above the ground. Users can become a ball; they can see, hear, and feel its collisions; and they can experience the ensuing motion (see Fig. 12.1). In Maxwell-World, users build electrostatic fields and manipulate multiple representations of force and energy. They can directly experience the field by becoming a test charge that is propelled by the forces of the electric field (see Fig. 12.2). In PaulingWorld, users learn about molecular structure and chemical bonding. They can explore the atoms and bonds of a simple molecule, such as water, and can manipulate the amino acids of complex proteins, such as hemoglobin (see Fig. 12.3).

The interface of our immersive, multisensory environments is typical of current high-end VR. ScienceSpace's hardware architecture includes a four-processor Silicon Graphics Onyx Reality Engine2 graphics workstation, Polhemus magnetic tracking systems utilizing a stylus or 3Ball (a three-dimensional mouse), and a Virtual Research VR4 head-mounted display (HMD). Sound is produced by a Silicon Graphics Indy worksta-

FIG. 12.1   Balls in NewtonWorld.

tion and is experienced via HMD headphones and external speakers. Vibrations are delivered to a subject's torso using a "vest" with embedded subwoofers. This interface enables us to immerse students in three-dimensional virtual worlds using the visual, auditory, and haptic (touch and pressure) senses.

The software interface relies on three-dimensional models and qualitative representations controlled through NASA-developed physical simulation applications. Visual models are built using a polygonal geometry; colored, shaded polygons and textures are used to produce detailed objects. These objects are linked together and given behaviors through the use of NASA-developed software (VR-Tool) that displays the virtual worlds while connecting them to underlying physical simulations. User interactivity is achieved through the linkage of external devices (e.g., a head-mounted display) using this same software. Finally, graphics rendering, collision detection, and lighting models are provided by other NASA-developed software.

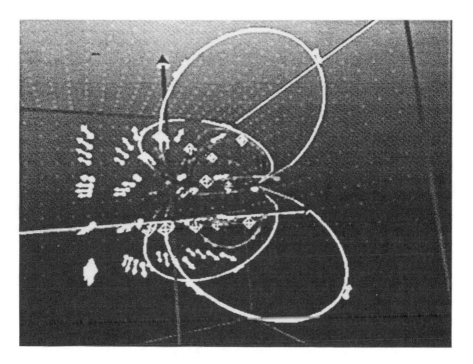

FIG. 12.2 A dipole in MaxwellWorld.

Students use a virtual hand (controlled by the 3Ball), menus, and direct manipulation to perform tasks in these immersive virtual environments. One Polhemus tracker is in the 3Ball held by the participant in one hand, a second is mounted on a fixture and held in the other hand, and a third is mounted on the HMD. The user's hand holding the 3Ball or the stylus is represented in the virtual world as a hand with the index finger extended, aligned with the user's hand. The menu system is attached to the tracker held by the other hand. Displaying the menu in this manner allows students to remove the menu from their field of view, while keeping it immediately accessible.

Students select menu items by holding up the menu with one hand, pointing to the menu option with the virtual hand, and depressing the 3Ball button. Therefore, menu selection in our ScienceSpace worlds is similar to menu selection on two-dimensional interfaces in which users manipulate the menu with a cursor controlled by a mouse. Figure 12.4 shows a student immersed in one of ScienceSpace's worlds. She is using the 3Ball and tracker to control a virtual hand and menu system.

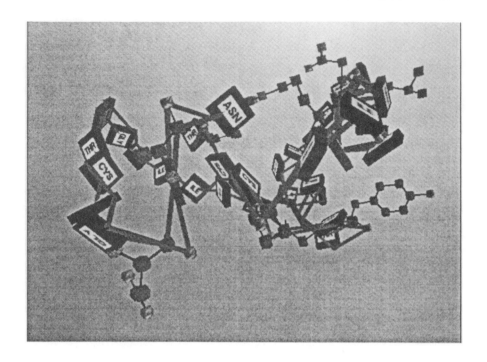

FIG. 12.3   A molecule in PaulingWorld.

Our worlds also utilize direct manipulation, empowering students to interact with objects in the space. For example, MaxwellWorld enables learners to place source charges in a three-dimensional space, to move them around, and to delete them. In NewtonWorld, students can "beam" (teleport) among cameras located in various frames of reference and can launch and catch balls. Learners in PaulingWorld can grasp and rotate molecular structures. Also, users can change their location ("fly") by selecting the navigation mode on the menu, pointing the virtual hand in the desired direction, and depressing the 3Ball button.

OUR APPROACH

Throughout the development of our ScienceSpace worlds, we have employed a learner-centered design strategy that focuses simultaneously on interface issues, users' subjective experiences in virtual reality, and learning outcomes (Salzman, Dede, & Loftin, 1995; Soloway, Guzdial, &

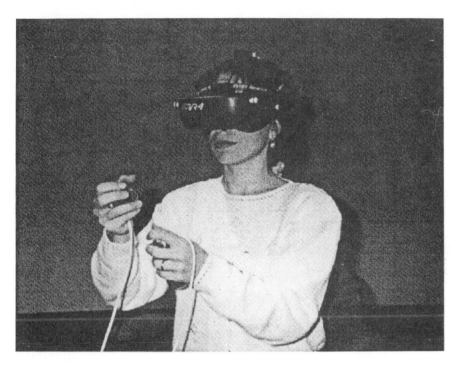

FIG. 12.4   A student immersed in ScienceSpace.

Hay, 1994). The issues and strategies underlying this learner-centered design and evaluation approach may be generalized to a wide range of synthetic environments beyond virtual reality.

In our continuing work on each of our worlds, we establish learning objectives and design goals through a careful initial analysis of what students need to enable their learning (including the types of experiences that might aid in mastering the complexities of the particular scientific domain) and the capabilities and limits of virtual reality technology (the role multisensory immersion in three-dimensional virtual environments could play in meeting these learner needs). We then proceed through iterative cycles of design and evaluation. Four issues are critical to our evaluations:

• *The learning experience.* The VR experience can be characterized along several dimensions. We focus on participants' subjective judgments of usability, simulator sickness, immersion, meaningfulness of our models and representations, and motivation. In designing our evaluations, we not only assess usability but also attempt to minimize usability problems through calibration of our equipment to each individual participant's idiosyncratic strategy for interacting with three-dimensional space. For example, portions of our protocols center on customizing the virtual world's interface to that particular learner's visual perception. We also measure simulator sickness (caused by changes in vestibular and ocularmotor functions due to the optics in the head-mounted display) to ensure users' comfort. The remaining measures—immersion, meaningfulness of our models and representations, and motivation—are designed to yield further insights into which factors provide greatest leverage for learning.

• *Learning.* We are interested in both the learning process and learning outcomes. Throughout the learning process, we monitor how students are progressing through activities within the virtual environment. Asking students to make verbal predictions about a certain activity, to describe what they observe when performing the activity, and to compare their predictions to their observations had been a useful way to monitor the learning process (White, 1993). As discussed in detail later, to assess learning outcomes we examine mastery of concepts at both the "descriptive" and the "causal" levels using multiple measures (e.g., conceptual, two-dimensional, and three-dimensional understanding).

• *The learning experience versus learning.* Our focus in this contrast is to understand the relation between the VR experience and learning and to identify when the VR experiences help or hinder learning. For example, increased student motivation may aid learning, whereas simulator sickness may reduce educational gains.

• *Educational utility.* This contrast centers on whether, for particularly complex and abstract domains, the virtual reality medium is a better (or a worse) teaching tool than other pedagogical approaches. We compare the quality and efficiency of learning among different alternatives of varying cost, instructional design, and teaching strategy. In particular, we compare our learning outcomes to less-complex technology based scientific modeling approaches such as two-dimensional "microworlds."

We collect information along these four dimensions using a variety of techniques. Throughout sessions with students, we carefully monitor the learning process and log users' comments and reactions. The learning sessions are also videotaped so that we can study these records for additional insights. We use sketches, demonstrations, and various assessment instruments that are based on short answer, open-ended response, true–false, and matching items to capture dimensions of learning. Also, questionnaires and interviews are used to gather users' perceptions about the learning experience.

With each cycle of evaluation, we add to a pool of knowledge that is helping us make design decisions and more fully understand how multisensory immersion can enhance learning. By focusing on the students' experience as well as on their learning, we gain insights that guide the refinement of the user interface and aid us in understanding the strengths and limits of VR's capabilities for conveying complex scientific concepts.

AN ANALYSIS OF HOW MULTISENSORY IMMERSION MIGHT AID LEARNING

To understand how to help students master complex scientific concepts, examining the general nature of learning is vital. First, a prerequisite for learning is attention: students must focus on or be engaged in an experience for learning to occur. Second, meaningful representations are necessary to communicate information (Hewitt, 1991). Third, multiple mappings of information can enhance learning (Kozma, Chin, Russell, & Marx, 1997). Additionally, learning by doing and reflective inquiry are both effective in inducing learning as, through experience, students can extend and modify their knowledge constructs (mental models) based on discontinuities between expected and actual behaviors of phenomena. In addition, researchers are finding that the social construction of knowledge among students—even when their interactions are mediated by virtual environments—enables innovative, powerful types of collaborative learning (Bruckman & Resnick, 1995; Turkle, 1995).

In particular, mastery of abstract science concepts requires learners to build generic and runnable mental models (Larkin, 1983). These often must incorporate invisible factors that represent intangible forces and other abstractions (diSessa, 1983). Frequently, the ability to translate among reference frames is crucial. Unfortunately, learners have trouble identifying important factors or imagining new perspectives (Redish, 1993). They also lack real-life analogies on which to build their mental models. For example, in scientific domains such as quantum mechanics, relativity, and molecular bonding, learners cannot draw on personal experiences to provide metaphors for these phenomena.

Additionally, real-life experiences (which are confounded with invisible factors) often distort or contradict the principles students need to master. For example, the universal presence of friction makes objects in motion seem to slow and stop "on their own," undercutting the face validity of Newton's First Law. As a result, most learners—including many science majors—have difficulty understanding science concepts and models at the qualitative level, let alone the problems that occur with quantitative formulation (Reif & Larkin, 1991). These misconceptions, based on a lifetime of experience, are very difficult to remediate with instructionist pedagogical strategies.

Traditional lectures and laboratory sessions are not adequate for teaching difficult science concepts. For example, researchers in physics education have demonstrated that students typically enter and leave high school and college-level physics courses with faulty mental models (Halloun & Hestenes, 1985a). Some of these misconceptions may have little effect on learners' understanding of science or on their ability to cope with everyday phenomena, but the cumulative effect of large numbers of misconceptions may undermine students' comprehension.

To master complex scientific concepts, learning tools and pedagogical strategies should provide learners with experiential metaphors and analogies to aid in understanding abstractions remote or contradictory to their everyday experience and enable students to participate in shared virtual contexts within which the meaning of this experience is socially constructed. To date, uses of information technology to apply these pedagogical principles have centered on creating computational tools and two-dimensional virtual representations that students can manipulate to complement their memory and intelligence in constructing more accurate mental models. Perkins (1991) classified types of "constructivist" paraphernalia instantiated through information technology: information banks, symbol pads, construction kits, phenomenaria, and task managers. Transitional objects (such as Logo's "turtle") are used to facilitate translating personal experience into abstract symbols (Fosnot, 1992; Papert, 1988). Thus, technology enhanced constructivist learning currently focuses on how representations and tools can be used to mediate interactions among learners and natural or social phenomena.

VRs for guided inquiry have the potential to complement existing approaches to science instruction (Dede, 1995). VR has several characteristics that make it promising as a constructivist tool for learning science via students' manipulation of models:

- *Immersion.* Learners develop the subjective impression that they are participating in a "world" comprehensive and realistic enough to induce the willing suspension of disbelief (Heeter, 1992; Witmer & Singer, 1994). By engaging students in learning activities, immersion may make important concepts and relationships more salient and memorable, helping learners to build more accurate mental models. Also, inside a head-mounted display, the learner's attention is focused on the virtual environment without the distractions presented in many other types of educational environments.
- *Multiple three-dimensional representations and frames of reference.* Spatial metaphors can enhance the meaningfulness of data and can provide qualitative insights (Erickson, 1993). Enabling students to interact with spatial representations from various frames of reference may deepen learning by providing different and complementary insights.
- *Multisensory cues.* Using high-end VR interfaces, students can interpret visual, auditory, and haptic displays to gather information while employing their proprioceptive system to navigate and control objects in the synthetic environment. This potentially deepens learning and recall (Psotka, 1996).
- *Motivation.* Learners are intrigued by interactions with well-designed immersive worlds, inducing them to spend more time and concentration on a task (Bricken & Byrne, 1993).
- *Telepresence.* Geographically remote learners can experience a simultaneous sense of presence in a shared virtual environment (Loftin, 1997).

Full immersion and telepresence depends on actional, symbolic, and sensory factors. Inducing actional immersion involves empowering the participant in a virtual environment to initiate actions that have novel, intriguing consequences. For example, when a baby is learning to walk, the degree of concentration this activity creates in the child is extraordinary. Discovering new capabilities to shape one's environment is highly motivating and sharply focuses attention. In contrast, inducing a participant's symbolic immersion involves triggering powerful semantic associations via the content of a virtual environment. As an illustration, reading a horror novel at midnight in a strange house builds a mounting sense of terror, even though one's physical context is unchanging and rationally safe. Invoking intellectual, emotional, and normative archetypes deepens one's experience in a virtual environment by imposing a complex overlay of associative mental models.

Beyond actional and symbolic immersion, advances in interface technology also enable sensory immersion in virtual realities designed to enhance learning. Inducing a sense of physical immersion within a synthetic context involves manipulating human sensory systems (especially the visual system) to enable the suspension of disbelief that one is surrounded by a virtual environment. The impression is that of being inside an virtual world rather than looking through a computer monitor "window" into a synthetic environment—the equivalent of diving rather than riding in a glass-bottomed boat. A weak analog to sensory immersive interfaces that readers may have experienced is the IMAX motion picture theater, in which a movie projected on a 2-story by 3-story screen can generate in observers strong sensations of motion. Adding stereoscopic images, highly directional and realistic sound, tactile force feedback, a visual field even wider than IMAX and the ability to interact with the virtual world through natural physical actions produces a profound sensation of "being there," as opposed to watching.

The multisensory immersion learners experience through VR technology has the potential to complement other, less complex educational tools and strategies. VR makes possible new kinds of learning experiences that are highly perceptual in nature. By means of this technology, students can be immersed within a phenomenon visually, auditorily, and haptically, and they can experience that phenomenon from multiple, novel frames of reference. These kinds of activities increase the saliency of important factors and relations and help learners gain experiential intuitions about how the natural world operates. For complex, abstract material that is difficult to teach in any other manner, VR seems a promising educational medium.

However, despite its strengths, current virtual reality technology has many limitations and problems that can potentially interfere with students' mastery of scientific concepts. These include the following:

- Virtual reality's physical interface is cumbersome (Krueger, 1991). HMDs, cables, three-dimensional mice, and computerized clothing all can interfere with interaction, motivation, and learning.

- Display resolution is inversely proportional to field of view. A corresponding trade-off exists between display complexity and image delay (Piantanida, Boman, & Gille, 1993). The low resolution of current VR displays limits the fidelity of the synthetic environment and prevents virtual controls from being clearly labeled.
- VR systems have limited tracking ability with delayed responses (Kalawsky, 1993).
- Providing highly localized three-dimensional auditory cues is challenging, due to the unique configuration of each person's ears. Also, some users have difficulty localizing three-dimensional sounds (Wenzel, 1992).
- Haptic feedback is extremely limited and expensive. Typically, only a single type of haptic feedback can be provided by computerized clothing; for example, one glove may provide heat as a sensory signal but cannot simultaneously provide pressure. In addition, using computerized clothing for output can interfere with accurate input on users' motions.
- Virtual environments require users to switch their attention among the different senses for various tasks (Erickson, 1993). To walk, users must pay attention to their haptic orientation; to fly, users must ignore their haptic sense and focus on visual cues. Also, as Stuart & Thomas (1991) described, multisensory inputs can result in unintended sensations (e.g., nausea due to simulator sickness) and unanticipated perceptions (e.g., awareness of virtual motion, but feeling stationary in the real world).
- Users often feel lost in VR environments (Bricken & Byrne, 1993). Accurately perceiving one's location in the virtual context is essential to both usability and learning.
- The magical (unique to the virtual world) and literal (mirroring reality) features of VR can interact, reducing the usability of the interface (Smith, 1987). Also, some researchers have demonstrated that realism can detract from rather than enhance learning (Wickens, 1992).

As virtual reality technology evolves, some of the challenges to educational design will recede. At present, however, achieving the potential of immersive, synthetic worlds to enhance learning requires transcending these interface barriers through careful attention to usability issues.

Another class of potential problems with the use of immersive virtual worlds for education is the danger of introducing new or unanticipated misconceptions due to the limited nature of the "magic" possible via this medium. For example, learners will not feel their sense of personal physical weight alter, even when the gravity field in the virtual reality they have created is set to zero. The cognitive dissonance this mismatch creates, due to conflicting sensory signals, may create both physiological problems (e.g., simulator sickness) and possibly false intellectual generalizations. One part of our research is to examine the extent to which manipulating learners' visual, auditory, and tactile cues may induce subtle types of misconceptions about physical phenomena. The medium (VR) should not detract from the message (learning scientific principles).

DESIGNING AND EVALUATING SCIENCESPACE

ScienceSpace worlds rely on the three-dimensional representations, multiple perspectives and frames of reference, multimodal interaction, and simultaneous visual, auditory, and haptic feedback afforded by VR technology. Our design of each of the worlds and the kinds of activities they support is based on a detailed assessment of what learning experiences are required to master complex scientific material. In the following sections, we discuss the design, evaluation, and iterative evolution of our immersive virtual worlds.

MAXWELLWORLD

MaxwellWorld is designed to help students understand the difficult concepts underlying electrostatic fields (distribution of force and energy). Our early work with students and with our domain expert, Dr. Edward Redish of the University of Maryland, uncovered the following about pupils' learning of electric fields. (Many of these insights also apply to mastering concepts about any type of vector field.) Electric fields and their associated representational formalisms are three-dimensional, abstract, and have few analogies to learners' everyday experience. As a result, students have trouble understanding the relation of abstractions about electric fields to phenomenological dynamics. Learners also often confuse the concepts of force and energy, indicating that they do not understand the meaning of the representations that are traditionally used (e.g., two-dimensional field lines, two-dimensional equipotential lines) to convey information about these abstractions.

In addition, learners have trouble understanding how the electric field would propel a test charge through the field if it were free to move. This is because they lack the ability to visualize the distribution of forces throughout a vector field, to relate how that distribution of force translates into the motion of the test charge, or even to understand the concept of superimposed forces at a distance. This is another example of an instance in which students lack real-life referents that provide metaphors for these behaviors, as well as an experimental environment in which to test and validate their mental models.

Overall, students lack a qualitative understanding of these electric field concepts. Such qualitative mental models are believed to lay the foundation for more scientific, abstract understanding (Reimann & Spada, 1996; White, 1993). Therefore, we began our design by exploring ways to help students develop generic, qualitative three-dimensional mental models of these phenomena, models that incorporate intangible, abstract factors such as force and energy.

In the design of MaxwellWorld, we enable learners to virtually experience scientifically accurate models of electric fields, make factors salient that are not perceptible in the real world through multisensory cues (e.g., how the forces at each point in space continually accelerate a test charge), motivate learners by immersing them within the phenomena, and capture and direct learners' attention to relations between force and energy through enhancing traditional scientific formalisms that are used by experts, but are "cognitively opaque" to novices.

MaxwellWorld allows learners to explore electrostatic forces and fields, learn about the concept of electric potential, explore how test charges would move through the space, and "discover" the nature of electric flux. The field space in this virtual world occupies a cube approximately 1 m on a side, with Cartesian axes displayed for convenient reference. The small size of the world produces large parallax when viewed from nearby, making its three-dimensional nature quite apparent.

Students use a virtual hand, a menu, direct manipulation, and navigation to interact with this world (see Fig. 12.5). Learners can place both positive and negative charges of various relative magnitudes into the world. Once a charge configuration is established, users can instantiate, observe, and interactively control three-dimensional representations of the force on a positive test charge, on electric field lines, potentials, on surfaces of equipotential, and on lines of electric flux through surfaces. For example, a small, positive test charge can be attached to the tip of

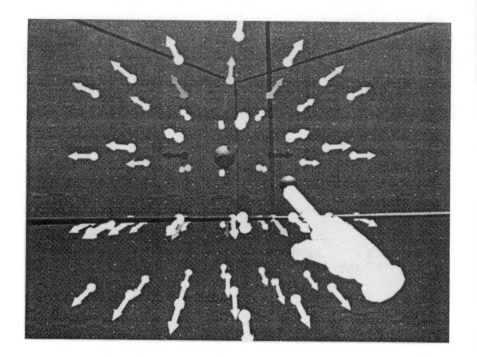

FIG. 12.5 User exploring a field with a test charge.

the virtual hand. A force meter associated with the charge then depicts both the magnitude and the direction of the force of the test charge (and, hence, the electric field) at any point in the workspace (see Fig. 12.6). A series of test charges can be "dropped" and used to visualize the nature of the electric field throughout a region. In our most recent version of MaxwellWorld, learners can first release a test charge and watch its dynamics as it moves through the field space (see Fig. 12.7), then "become" the test charge and travel with it as it moves through the electric field.

An electric field line can also be attached to the virtual hand. Learners can then move their hands to any point in the workspace and see the line of force extending through that point. MaxwellWorld can also display many electric field lines to give students a view of the field produced by a charge configuration. In another mode of operation, the tip of the virtual hand becomes an electric "potential" meter that, through a simple color map and an " = " or a " - " sign on the finger tip,

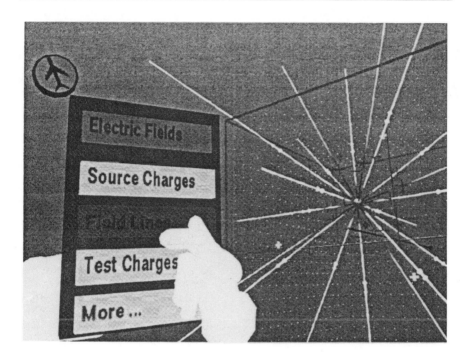

FIG. 12.6 Activating the menu via the virtual hand.

allows students to explore the distribution of potential in the field space. Through the production and manipulation of equipotential surfaces, learners can watch how the shapes of these surfaces alter in various portions of the field space (see Fig. 12.8). The surfaces are colored to indicate the magnitude of the potential across the surface; however, the student can also choose to view the electric forces as they vary across the surface. This activity helps students to contrast the concepts of electric force and potential.

Using the production of a Gaussian surface, the flux of the electric field through that surface can be visually measured. Gaussian surfaces can be placed anywhere in the workspace by using the virtual hand to anchor the sphere; the radius (small, medium, and large) is selected from the menu. This representation enables students to explore flux through a variety of surfaces when placed at various points in the field. All of these capabilities combine to enable representing many aspects of the complex scientific models underlying vector field phenomena.

FIG. 12.7 Bipole with moving test charge.

Formative Evaluations of MaxwellWorld

During the summer of 1995, we conducted formative evaluations of MaxwellWorld. We examined MaxwellWorld's effectiveness as a tool for learning and remediating misconceptions about electric fields, electric potential, and Gauss's law. A total of 14 high school and 4 college students completed from 1 to 3 lessons in MaxwellWorld. Of the 14 high school students, 13 had recently completed their senior year; 1 student had recently completed his junior year. All students had completed one course in high school physics. Each session lasted for approximately 2 hours. Students were scheduled on consecutive days for the first two sessions, whereas the third session was conducted approximately 2 weeks later.

Below is a brief overview of some of the findings:

- Overall, students felt MaxwellWorld was a more effective way to learn about electric fields than either textbooks or lectures. College-level

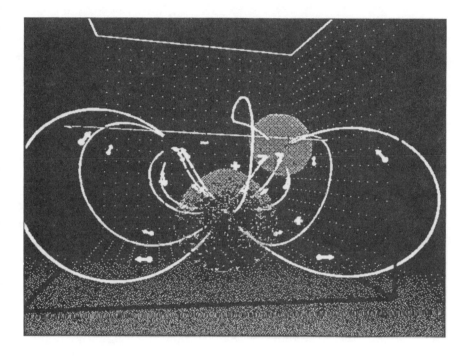

FIG. 12.8 Tripole with equipotential surface.

students found that they were better able to visualize and understand electrostatic phenomena. They cited the three-dimensional representations, interactivity, the ability to navigate to multiple perspectives, and the use of color as characteristics of MaxwellWorld important to their learning experience.

- Pre- and postlesson evaluations showed that, while using Maxwell-World, students developed an in-depth understanding of the distribution of forces in an electric field, as well as of representations such as test charge traces and field lines.

- Manipulating the electric field in three-dimensional space appeared to play an important role in students' ability to visualize the distribution of energy and force. For example, several students who were unable to describe the distribution of forces in any electric field prior to using MaxwellWorld gave clear descriptions during the posttest interviews and demonstrations.

- We observed substantial individual variability in the students' abilities to work in the three-dimensional environment and with three-dimensional controls (usability), and their susceptibility to symptoms of simulator sickness (eyestrain, headaches, dizziness, and nausea). Typical usability problems occurred when navigating, using menus, and deleting source charges.

These evaluations showed that lessons in MaxwellWorld helped students learn advanced concepts using MaxwellWorld, and remediate misconceptions. However, they did not allow us to establish whether learning was due to the unique capabilities of MaxwellWorld's multisensory immersion, to the lessons students received, or to instructional capabilities than could be replicated in a less complex two-dimensional microworld.

Comparative Evaluations of MaxwellWorld

In January, 1996, we initiated an extended study designed to compare learning and usability outcomes from MaxwellWorld to those from a highly regarded and widely used two-dimensional microworld, EM Field™, which covers similar material (Dede, Salzman, Loftin, & Sprague, in press). Stage 1 of this study compared MaxwellWorld and EM Field on the extent to which representational aspects of these simulations influenced learning outcomes. EM Field runs on standard desktop computers and presents learners with two-dimensional representations of electric fields and electric potential, using quantitative values to indicate strength (Trowbridge & Sherwood, 1994). To make the two learning environments comparable, we designed lessons to utilize only those features of MaxwellWorld for which EM Field had a counterpart; this limited version of MaxwellWorld we designated MW_L. Thus, the primary differences between the simulations were representational dimensionality (EM Field's two-dimensions vs. MW_L's three) and type (EM Field's quantitative vs. MW_L's qualitative; see Fig. 12.9).

In the second stage of the study, we utilized MaxwellWorld's full range of capabilities (including multisensory input) to ascertain the value these features added to the learning experience. Through the pretest for Phase 2, we also examined the extent to which students, after a period of 5 months, retained mental models learned in either environment. Through this two-stage approach, we hoped to separate the relative

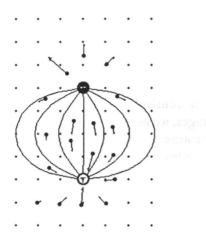

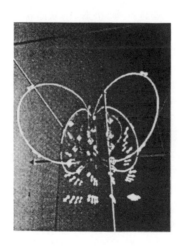

FIG. 12.9 A dipole with field lines and test charge traces in MaxwellWorld and EM Field.

contributions of three-dimensional representation versus multisensory stimulation as instrumental to the learning potential of virtual reality.

During Stage 1, we examined whether representational aspects of the microworlds influenced learning outcomes. All 14 high school students completed lessons in MW_L or in EM Field. Lessons leveraged the visual representations used in EM Field and in MW_L. During Stage 2, we examined the "value added" by unique VR features (e.g., multisensory cues) supported by MaxwellWorld. Seven EM Field and MW_L students returned for Stage 2 approximately 5 months after participating in Stage 1. All students received an additional lesson in the full version of MaxwellWorld that utilized multisensory cues as well as visual representations. During both stages, we examined pre- and postlesson understanding for each of the groups. We also assessed Stage 1 retention for those students that returned for Stage 2. Finally, we examined whether factors such as motivation, simulator sickness, and usability differed across groups and whether these predicted learning outcomes. Following is a summary of Stage 1 outcomes:

- Both groups demonstrated significantly better conceptual 2-D and 3-D understanding postlesson than for prelesson. (All t-tests were significant at p .05.) Therefore, lessons in both EM Field and in MW_L were meaningful.
- MW_L students were better able to define concepts than EM Field students. Although not statistically significant, differences also occurred in the students' ability to describe electric fields in three-dimensional on the test given to measure retention after 5 months (see Table 12.1).
- MW_L students did not perform any worse than the EM Field students at sketching concepts in two-dimensional space. Although MW_L students performed better on the force sketches, they performed worse on the sketches relating to potential, resulting in total sketch scores that were similar for the two groups. An explanation for this outcome may be that representations of force (lines and arrows) are more easily translated from three-dimensional space to two-dimensional space than representations of potential surfaces (see Table 12.1).
- MW_L students were better able to demonstrate concepts in three-dimensional space than EM Field students. For example, despite the inherent three-dimensionality of the lessons and demonstration exercises, all but one of the EM Field students restricted answers to a single

TABLE 12.1

Adjusted Postlesson Means, Retention Means, and Ancova Outcomes
for Stage 1 (Covariate = Prelesson Scores)

Learning	Postlesson		Retention	
	EMF	MW	EMF	MW
Concepts	.58	.70	.69	.66
	$F(1,11) = 3.17^*$		$F(1,5) = .27$	
2-D	.80	.82	.42	.43
sketches	$F(1,11) = .24$		$F(1,5) = 0.00$	
3-D	.67	.87	.31	.57
demos	$F(1,11) = 9.99^*$		$F(1,5) = 2.40$	

$^* p .05$

plane, drew lines when describing equipotential surfaces, and used
terms such as "oval" and "line." In contrast, MW_L students described
phenomena using three-dimensional gestures and phrases such as
"sphere" and "surface." Although not statistically significant, differences also occurred in the students' ability to describe electric fields
in three-dimensional space on the retention test (see Table 12.1).
• Students' ratings indicated that they felt more motivated by MW_L than
EM Field, experienced greater simulator sickness symptoms in MW_L
than EM Field, and had more trouble using MW_L than EM Field.
However, none of these factors significantly predicted learning outcomes, indicating that the unique capabilities of the virtual reality
interface accounted for the differences in educational outcomes.

Data for Stage 2 yielded insights into the value of multisensory representations:

• Students demonstrated significantly better understanding of concepts, two-dimensional sketches, and three-dimensional demos for
postlesson than for prelesson. (All t-tests were significant at $p .05$.)
Students learned from visual and multisensory representations used
in the lesson. Ratings concerning multisensory representations (haptic and sound), postlesson understanding, and students' comments all
suggest that students who experienced difficulty with the concepts
found that multisensory representations helped them understand
visual representations.

- Mean motivation, simulator sickness, and usability ratings were similar to the ratings for MW_L in Stage 1.

Both stages lend support to the thesis that immersive, three-dimensional multisensory representations can help students develop more accurate causal mental models than two-dimensional representations. Learning outcomes for Stage 1 show that MW_L learners—more than EM Field learners—were able to understand the space as a whole, recognize symmetries in the field, and relate individual visual representations (test charge traces, field lines, and equipotential surfaces) to the electric field and the electric potential. MW_L students appeared to visualize the phenomena in 3-D, whereas EM Field students did not.

Subjective ratings for Stage 1 yielded converging evidence that the representational capabilities VR enables were responsible for differences in learning. First, motivation, though higher in MW_L than in EM Field, was not a predictor of learning. Second, despite MW_L's usability and simulator sickness problems, students learned more using this virtual environment than they did using EM Field. In Stage 2, the enhancement of visual representations with multisensory cues appeared to facilitate learning, especially for students who had trouble grasping the concepts. Dede, Salzman, Loftin, & Sprague (in press) provide additional detail concerning this study, as well as other early research results for MaxwellWorld.

PAULINGWORLD

PaulingWorld is still under development and has not yet undergone formative evaluation. Currently, learners can view, navigate through, superimpose, and manipulate five different molecular representations: wireframe, backbone, ball-and-stick, amino acid, and space-filling models. See Figs. 12.10 and 12.11 for some examples of these models.

We are working on extending PaulingWorld to address concepts underlying quantum–mechanical bonding—these kinds of concepts have no real-life referents, are difficult to represent, and are hard for students to comprehend. They include probability density and wave functions; molecular bonding and antibonding orbitals; multiple, interacting determinants of bond angles and bond length; the role of electronegativity in ionic versus covalent bonding; and three-dimensional molecular geometries—culminating in Pauling's seminal insights on Valence Shell

FIG. 12.10 Ball-and-stick with some amino acids.

Electron Pair Repulsion (VSEPR). To design the immersive multisensory representations and underlying scientific models we plan to use for quantum–mechanical bonding phenomena, we are coordinating our design activities with a NSF-funded project, "Quantum Science Across the Disciplines," led by Peter Garik at Boston University (http://qsad.bu.edu/).

NEWTONWORLD

NewtonWorld addresses many well-documented misconceptions learners have about Newtonian mechanics. Clement (1982) referred to such misconceptions as "conceptual primitives"; these reflect erroneous generalizations from personal experience about the nature of mass, acceleration, momentum, Newton's laws, and the laws of conservation. Conceptual primitives form mental constructs, the understanding of which is a basic prerequisite for many higher order concepts. Among

FIG. 12.11 Space-filling model.

common misconceptions about motion documented by Halloun &
Hestenes (1985b) are the "motion implies force" notion, the "impetus"
theory (an object's past motion influences the forces presently acting on
it), and "position–speed confusion" (i.e., ahead = faster).

Not only are these misconceptions strongly held by students entering
physics courses, but they are also very difficult to change with conventional
approaches to instruction. Reinforced by their own real-world experiences,
learners persist in believing that motion requires force (rather than that a
change in motion requires force), that constant force produces constant
velocity (rather than producing constant acceleration), and that objects
have intrinsic impetus (rather than moving based on instantaneous forces).
Thus, making these factors and their relations salient is crucial to the
teaching of Newton's laws and the laws of conservation.

Building on model-based pedagogical strategies for teaching complex
scientific concepts, the challenges of learning Newtonian physics, and
VR's strengths and limitations, we constructed learning objectives and

general design guidelines for NewtonWorld. Learning goals are framed by the realization that students have deeply rooted misconceptions concerning Newton's laws, momentum, energy, and reference frames. Consequently, we determined that NewtonWorld should help learners to challenge and to reconstruct these mental models. For example, after being guided through a series of inquiry activities focusing on conservation of momentum and of energy, students should be able to identify important factors, accurately predict how each factor influences momentum and energy, describe the momentum and energy of objects under various dynamic and static conditions, explain how the laws are reflected in the behavior of objects, and use these insights to explain real-world phenomena.

NewtonWorld's Original Design

In NewtonWorld, we rely on sensorial immersion to enhance the saliency of important factors and relations, as well as to provide experiential referents against which learners can compare their intuitions. In our original version of NewtonWorld, learners can be "inside" a moving object and feel themselves moving; this three-dimensional, personalized frame of reference centers attention on velocity as a variable. Multisensory cues are used to further heighten the saliency of factors such as force, energy, and velocity. Students begin their guided inquiry inside an immersive virtual environment in which gravity and frictional forces are set to zero, allowing observation of Newton's three laws operating without other superimposed phenomena clouding their perceived effects. These three laws are summarized as follows:

- Newton's First Law states that if the net force on an object is zero, an object originally at rest remains at rest, and an object in motion remains moving in a straight line with constant velocity.
- Newton's Second Law states that the acceleration of an object is directly proportional to the net force acting on it and inversely proportional to its mass. The direction of the acceleration is in the direction of the applied net force.
- Newton's Third Law states that, whenever one body exerts a force on a second body, the second body always exerts an equal and opposite force on the first body.

Studying the collision of objects also enables the introduction of other scientific principles, such as conservation of momentum and of energy and reversible conversions between kinetic and potential energy.

The original version of NewtonWorld provides an environment for investigating the kinematics and dynamics of one-dimensional motion. Once immersed in NewtonWorld, students spend time in and around an activity area, which is an open "corridor" created by colonnades on each side and a wall at each end (see Fig. 12.12). Students interact with NewtonWorld using a "virtual hand" and a menu system. Learners can launch and catch balls of various masses and can "beam" (teleport) from the ball to cameras strategically placed around the corridor. The balls move in one dimension along the corridor, rebounding when they collide with each other or with the walls. Equal spacing of the columns and lines on the floor of the corridor aids learners in judging distance and speed. Signs on the walls indicate the presence or absence of gravity and of friction.

Multisensory cues help students experience phenomena and direct their attention to important factors such as mass, velocity, and energy. For example, potential energy is made salient through tactile and visual cues, and velocity is represented by auditory and visual cues. The presence of potential energy before launch is represented by a tightly

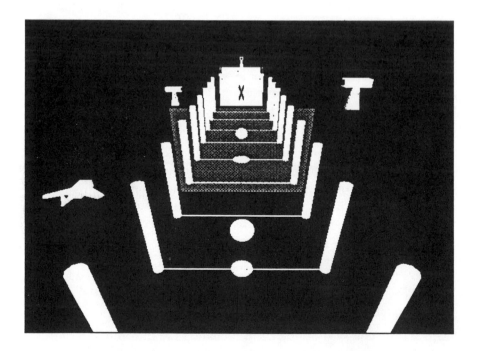

FIG. 12.12 Above the corridor, showing cameras, balls with shadows, and the far wall.

coiled spring, as well as via vibrations in the vest users wear. As the ball is launched (see Fig. 12.13) and potential energy becomes kinetic energy, the spring uncoils and the energy vibrations cease. The balls then begin to cast shadows whose areas are directly proportional to the amount of kinetic energy associated with each ball. On (perfectly elastic) impact, when kinetic energy is instantly changed to potential energy and then back to kinetic energy again, the shadows disappear and the vest briefly vibrates. To aid students in judging the velocities of the balls relative to one another, the columns light and chime as the balls pass.

Additionally, we provide multiple representations of phenomena by allowing students to assume the sensory perspectives of various objects in the world. For example, students can "become" one of the balls in the corridor, a camera attached to the center-of-mass of the bouncing balls (see Fig. 12.14), a movable camera hovering above the corridor, and so forth. Figure 12.15 shows a collision seen from just outside one colonnade. These features aid learners in understanding the scientific models underlying Newton's three laws, potential and kinetic energy, and conservation of momentum and of energy.

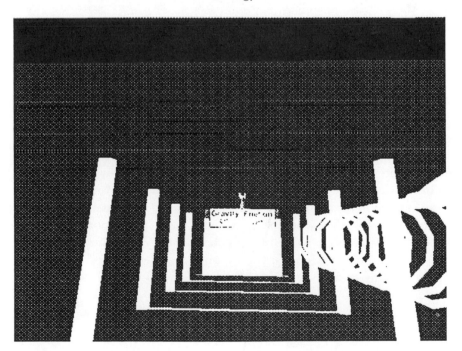

FIG. 12.13 After launch, illustrating the spring-based launching mechanism.

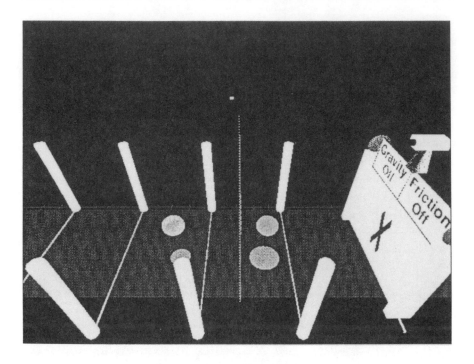

FIG. 12.14 A collision seen from the center-of-mass reference frame.

In scaffolding the learning in NewtonWorld, our approach draws on recent research that places an emphasis on aiding learners to construct causal models as they experience dynamic, intriguing natural phenomena (Frederiksen & White, 1992; White, 1993; White & Frederiksen, chap. 11, this volume). Phenomena are selected that exemplify misconceptions in learners' current models of reality, thereby heightening student interest by exhibiting counterintuitive behaviors. Through gamelike inquiry activities in simulations that are sequenced to present increasingly complex situations, students make predictions, conduct experiments, and derive qualitative rules against which they can assess and modify their predictions. For example, learners might be asked to predict the motion of an object as a force is applied to it; one rule a student might generalize (incorrectly) is "If a force is applied to an object, its velocity increases." By instructing students to make predictions about upcoming events, directly experience them, and then explain what they experienced, we encourage learners to question their intuitions and refine their mental models.

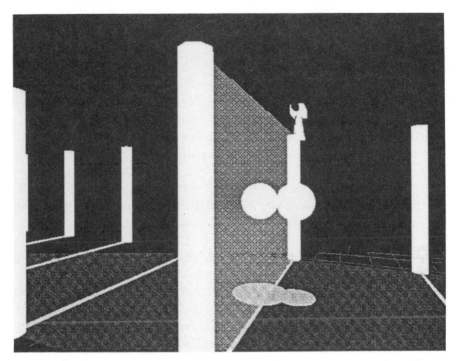

FIG. 12.15 A collision seen from just outside a colonnade.

To illustrate an activity a student might undertake in the original version of NewtonWorld, imagine that the learner is "inside" a ball that has an initial velocity relative to the corridor. Neither gravitational nor frictional forces are activated, and objects have a perfect coefficient of restitution (i.e., the balls will rebound with perfect elasticity and will not transfer kinetic energy to heat). The walls at the end of the corridor have infinite mass; the student (as a ball) has a unitary mass of 1. Through a sequence of experiences, the student is asked to answer the following questions: "If you launch a ball equal in mass to the ball that you are within, what will be the subsequent behavior of both balls?" "What will occur if you 'catch' the other ball when the two masses are moving in opposite directions—or in the same direction?" "If instead you launch a ball whose mass is not equal to the mass of the ball you are within, will the balls' behaviors be different; if so, how?" "What rules can you derive that predict the balls' dynamics in other similar situations?"

By launching and catching balls of various masses, and by viewing the collisions from various viewpoints (e.g., a ball, a camera at the center of mass, a camera outside the corridor), the student immersively experiences a variety of counterintuitive phenomena such as the following:

- The relative motion of the ball the student is within is affected by launching the other ball.
- The momenta of two unequal masses are equal but opposite after launch, but their kinetic energies are not.
- If the student catches a ball when it is moving with exactly opposite momentum to the ball he or she is within, both balls will come to a complete stop.
- Whether traveling in the same direction or in opposite directions at the time of collision, two balls of equal mass interchange relative velocities when colliding.

After observing one or more of the previously mentioned phenomena, students are asked to describe what they observed, determine whether observations supported their predictions, and refine their predictions. After completing a series of related activities, students are encouraged to synthesize what they observed by describing and explaining relations among important factors. Ultimately, our goal is for students to be able to transfer and generalize their insights concerning the phenomena they experienced in NewtonWorld to a wide variety of analogous real-world situations.

NewtonWorld Evaluations

We have conducted several formative evaluations for our first version of NewtonWorld. As our design and evaluation is iterative, the original version of NewtonWorld evolved slightly from evaluation to evaluation. Therefore, we briefly describe how each evaluation impacted NewtonWorld's design.

Evaluating The Learning Experience With Students.   In the summer of 1994, we examined the earliest version of NewtonWorld, which contained no sound or tactile cues and no visual cues representing energy or velocity. This version provided only two points of reference: the ball and a movable camera. Additionally, a Gamebar for accessing menu items was displayed at all times in the upper right field of view in the HMD.

We compared interaction alternatives, determined whether users could perform typical tasks with relative ease, assessed the overall metaphor used in NewtonWorld, and examined the general structure of learning activities. We modeled these evaluations after a usability test, asking a small, diverse set of students to perform a series of "typical" activities and provide feedback about their experiences.

Nine high school students (five females and four males) participated in this study; two of these students participated as pilot volunteers. Participants had a range of science, computer, and video experience to ensure that our sample was representative. Using each of four variations of the user interface (menu-based, gesture-based, voice-based, and multimodal), participants performed a series of typical and "critical" activities, thinking aloud as they performed them. Students performed activities such as becoming a ball, using the menus, selecting masses of the balls they were to launch (throw), launching balls, catching balls, and changing camera views. Task strategies, task completion, error frequency, and students' comments were recorded as they attempted each of the tasks. Following the sessions, students rated the ease of use of various aspects of the interaction, ranked interaction alternatives, and listed what they liked and disliked about the system. The following is a summary of the lessons we learned from this evaluation:

- Participants were comfortable with the bouncing ball metaphor, liked the virtual hand, and intuitively understood that this interface enabled them to interact with objects in the world. Seven of nine students ranked the multimodal interface above the others, and eight students used one or more of the options (voice, gestures, and menus) available to them while using the multimodal interface. Of the interaction alternatives, voice was the preferred and most error-free method of interaction. Menus also were well liked, yet students experienced difficulty selecting menu items. Gestures were unreliable and were the least preferred interaction method. Additionally, all students experienced slight to moderate levels of discomfort and eyestrain after wearing the HMD for approximately 11/4 hours (even with one or two breaks during that period).
- Students' comments suggested that the ability to observe phenomena from multiple viewpoints was motivating and crucial to understanding. However, additional visual, auditory, or tactile cues seemed necessary to smooth the interaction and to help the students focus on important information.

- Students interpreted the size of the ball as a cue for mass. From a usability perspective, this might suggest utilizing size as an indicator of mass. However, from an educational perspective, this is problematic, as such a representation reinforces the misconception that larger objects are more massive. Using color to distinguish the balls, and labels or color intensity as a cue for mass, meets both usability and learning criteria.

Based on these outcomes, we made a number of modifications to the early design of NewtonWorld. We maintained the ball metaphor and the general nature of the activities, but expanded the possible viewpoints from two to five and implemented the more flexible "beaming" (teleporting) method for moving among frames of reference. We also implemented sound cues to supplement visual cues.

Evaluating Design Concepts With Physics Educators.   T o obtain feedback and guidance from experienced educators, at the 1994 Summer Meeting of the American Association of Physics Teachers, 107 physics instructors and researchers used NewtonWorld and gave us their insights. Participants observed a 10-minute demonstration of Newton-World via a computer monitor, then received a personal experience while immersed in the virtual learning environment. After the demonstration, they completed a survey that focused on their interactive experiences, recommendations for improving the system, and perceptions of how effective this three-dimensional learning environment would be for demonstrating Newtonian physics and conservation laws. The following is a summary of evaluation outcomes:

- A majority of those surveyed found the basic activities easy to perform. However, as with the students in the usability tests, many participants experienced difficulty using the menus and focusing the optics of the HMD.
- A large majority of physics education experts felt that NewtonWorld would be an effective tool for demonstrating Newtonian physics and dynamics. Participants were enthusiastic about the three-dimensional nature of this learning environment and appreciated the ability to observe phenomena from a variety of viewpoints. However, several participants expressed concerns regarding the limitations of the prototype and encouraged expanding the activities, environmental controls, and sensory cues provided.

- Several participants felt a broader field of view would have improved their experiences; however, some reported slight eyestrain and dizziness. Thus, identifying an appropriate solution to this problem was difficult because increased field of view could have resulted in usability problems due to eyestrain and nausea.

Physics educators' feedback indicated that, although we had improved on the version of NewtonWorld tested in the usability sessions, we needed to more fully utilize the multisensory nature of VR. We expanded the interface to include a haptic vest and more extensive visual and sound cues. We also refined the menus to make selecting menu items easier. Finally, because the menus were not used during the observation portion of activities, we changed the menu bar to a small 3-Ball icon, resulting in an increased visual field of view and improving users' abilities to experience motion and see important visual cues.

Evaluating Learning. From December of 1994 through May of 1995, we conducted formative learnability evaluations on Newton-World, focusing both on the importance of the multisensory experience and on reference frame usage in learning.

A total of 30 high school students with at least 1 year of high school physics participated. Each individual trial required 21/2 to 3 hours; learning tasks in the VR required 1 to 11/4 hours. During the sessions, students thought aloud as they performed learning tasks that focused on relations among force, mass, velocity, momentum, acceleration, and energy during and between collisions. For each task, students began by predicting what the relationships or behaviors would be, then experienced them, and finally assessed their predictions based on what they observed. To evaluate the utility of the multisensory experience, we formed three groups of subjects differentiated by controlling the visual, tactile, and auditory cues that students received while performing learning tasks: visual cues only, visual and auditory cues, or visual, auditory, and haptic cues.

Our observations during the sessions, students' predictions and comments, usability questionnaires, interview feedback, and pre- and posttest knowledge assessments helped to determine whether this "first generation" version of NewtonWorld aided students in better understanding relations among force, motion, velocity, and energy. Below is a summary of the outcomes of these evaluations:

- Most students found the activities interesting and enjoyed their learning experience. Additionally, many users stated that they felt NewtonWorld provided a good way to explore physics concepts. When asked to list the features they liked most, almost all students cited the ability to beam to various cameras and to navigate in the movable camera. As positive aspects of NewtonWorld, students also cited multisensory informational cues used to represent velocity, energy and collisions, as well as feedback cues.

- Single-session usage of NewtonWorld was not enough to dramatically transform users' mental models. Students did not demonstrate significant learning from pre- to posttest knowledge assessments, and no significant differences were found among groups.

- Students appeared to be more engaged in activities when multisensory cues were provided. In fact, students receiving sound or sound plus haptic cues rated NewtonWorld as easier to use and rated the egocentric reference frame as more meaningful than those receiving visual cues only. Useful ideas about the design of these multisensory cues emerged. For example, students who received haptic cues in addition to sound and visual cues performed slightly better than students in other groups on questions relating to velocity and acceleration. Additionally, lesson administrators observed that students receiving haptic and sound cues were more attentive to these factors than students without these cues. However, those same students performed slightly worse on predicting the behavior of the system. One possible explanation is that haptic cues may have caused students to attend more to factors at play just before, during, and after collisions—and less to the motions of the balls.

- Most learners found the environment easy to use. Nevertheless, students suggested that we could improve the learning experience by expanding the features and representations used in NewtonWorld and by adding more variety to the nature of the learning activities. Also, as in earlier tests, several students experienced difficulty with eyestrain, navigating, and selecting menu items. At times, these problems appeared to distract users from the learning activities and contributed to fatigue.

Outcomes encouraged us to further refine the interface and learning activities. We moved the menu from its fixed location in the HMD's field of view to the user's second virtual hand, allowing users to freely adjust menu position and to judge menu location based on the physical position of their own hands. We also investigated ways to enhance multisensory cues. Perhaps the most significant design change, however, was our reconceptualization of NewtonWorld to shift the emphasis of educational activities. Our analysis of the learnability data suggested that younger users might gain more from virtual experiences in sensorily immersive Newtonian environments than would high school students. By means of virtual reality experiences, early interventions may undercut Aristotelian mental models just at the time when young learners are developing these misconceptions. This in turn might promote a less difficult, accelerated transition to a Newtonian paradigm.

The Redesign of NewtonWorld

We are currently in the process of making substantial changes to the original version of NewtonWorld. As mentioned in the previous section, we have reconceptualized the learning objectives and the target audience for NewtonWorld. We will use the revised NewtonWorld to target younger users and to focus specifically on Newton's laws as they relate to the conservation of momentum.

Because NewtonWorld was the first virtual environment we built, its original interface did not incorporate sophisticated features we developed in designing MaxwellWorld and PaulingWorld. Accordingly, we are redesigning NewtonWorld to take advantage of these new capabilities. Following are two sketches illustrating our redesign, at present under construction. New features include a "scoreboard" (Fig. 12.16) to aid learners in relating qualitative and quantitative representations, an improved interface based on a "endless roadway" metaphor (Fig. 12.17), shifts in the representations used to connote mass and momentum, and the inclusion of both perfectly elastic and perfectly inelastic collisions.

This "second generation" version of NewtonWorld is intended to target concepts relating to Newton's laws and to the conservation of momentum, presented at a level appropriate for learners around Grades 5 through 7. Our revision of NewtonWorld has three levels of activities. In Level 1, the student can explore the relation between force, mass, velocity, and momentum with a single object. By allowing the learner to observe the behavior of one object as a function of mass, force, and velocity, the student can better understand the contribution of mass and velocity to momentum before observing the motions of two colliding objects. In Level 2, two objects—each of varying masses, velocities, and elasticities—are involved in collisions. These collisions allow students to

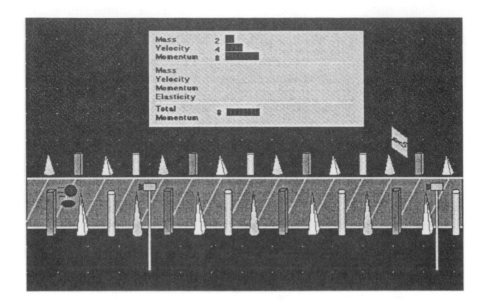

FIG. 12.16 Redesigned NewtonWorld showing "scoreboard" and "roadway."

observe the relations between mass, velocity, momentum, conservation of momentum, and elasticity. Level 3 will incorporate aspects of Levels 1 and 2 and will test students' mastery of concepts within a gamelike environment.

A major enhancement to the revised version of NewtonWorld is a scoreboard that displays information about the mass, velocity, momentum, and elasticity of each object, as well as the total system momentum. This information is represented both numerically and as a graphical segmented line. The latter allows for rapid approximation by learners (e.g., large velocity and large mass yields large momentum), whereas the numerical value will be helpful when students need more exact values of variables.

In a shift from the original version of NewtonWorld, mass is represented visually by different levels of transparency. The more massive an object, the greater its opacity; an object of low mass will be relatively transparent (but still readily visible). Elasticity is also represented visually, via textures. Elastic objects appear shiny and hard, whereas inelastic

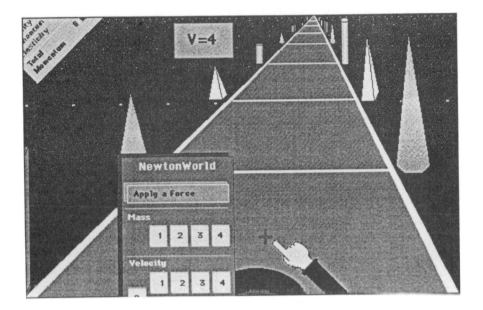

FIG. 12.17 Within the "roadway" view.

objects seem soft and "squishy" like a piece of gum. Momentum is represented by haptic cues (differing intensities of haptic vibration) and visual cues (varying shadow areas under the objects). This is a change from the original version of NewtonWorld, in which shadows represented kinetic energy. As an added feature in the new version, the total momentum between two objects involved in the collision is represented by a cloud hovering above and between the two objects.

Evaluating Redesign Concepts with Teachers and their Students

We involved teachers and students in the formative stages of Newton-World's redesign. Specifically, we wanted to gauge students' level of understanding of the concepts covered in NewtonWorld—Newton's laws and the conservation of momentum, to validate learners' interest in the kinds of activities we planned to use in Levels 1 and 2 of NewtonWorld, and to generate ideas about designing motivating and educational activities for NewtonWorld.

We began this process by interviewing three teachers from the fifth, seventh, and eighth grades concerning the skills of their students and the content and learning activities of NewtonWorld. (As described as follows, we later conducted focus groups with students in their science classes.) The teachers helped us understand which scientific terms might be familiar and how they had been covered in the curriculum. They also aided our thinking about how to work with different age levels in a focus group setting.

We then conducted three focus groups (one per teacher). Fifth-grade students represented a wide range of academic performance. The seventh-grade students were in a gifted-and-talented (GT) science class and embodied the top of their class with respect to academic achievement. Eighth-grade students were from an average class and represented a wider range of abilities than the GT students. In each case, about 30 students participated in the focus group; in all cases, approximately equal proportions of males and females were involved. Through this strategy, we obtained insights from students of a broad range of academic capabilities.

Focus group activities included the following: an interactive discussion of concepts relating to Newton's Laws and conservation of momentum, completion of a series of learning activities using a two-dimensional simulation of NewtonWorld programmed in the Macintosh-based Interactive Physics II™software, and a brainstorming session in which students identified liked and disliked features of their favorite video and educational games and generated ideas for gamelike activities in NewtonWorld. The following is a summary of focus group outcomes:

NewtonWorld Concepts.   Topics discussed included mass (variable and zero), gravity, velocity (for the fifth graders, we referred to velocity as "speed" to the left and to the right), elasticity (in the framework of gooey or bouncy), and momentum. All levels of students were unfamiliar with some of the scientific terminology necessary to describe Newton's laws and the law of conservation of momentum. Therefore, prior to completing learning activities, we defined key factors and found that they quickly grasped these definitions. On relating factors during the learning activities, we found that the fifth graders received the physics content well above expectation. Compared to older students, fifth graders progressed through the activities a little more slowly and had more difficulty predicting how factors interrelated, but they demonstrated increased understanding as the sessions progressed, as well as a high degree of enthusiasm and intellectual curiosity. These young learners seemed quite capable of comprehending this material. Although most seventh-grade and eighth-grade students were able to define gravity and speed, some hesitation and disagreement arose in each group about mass and momentum. They also experienced difficulties predicting the outcomes of some collisions. Similar to the fifth-grade students, older students demonstrated increased understanding as the sessions progressed.

NewtonWorld Simulations Based On The Interactive Physics II Software. As a group, students engaged in a series of activities similar to those planned for our immersive, multisensory NewtonWorld, but contextualized in a two-dimensional microworld with no multisensory capabilities. The format used to present activities to the group was the predict observe-compare cycle central to our research. Students responded positively to this pedagogical approach, and the progression of activities (discussing single objects in Level 1 and discussing collisions in Level 2) also worked well for all groups of students. Students, the youngest group in particular, seemed to be motivated by the activities.

Gamelike Activities. Brainstorming revealed that all groups of students were attracted to adventure games with good graphics (e.g., Dark Forces, Outlaws, Doom). Several racing games and fighting games were mentioned, but for the most part the focus was on adventure games. Students felt that the flexibility of the environment (e.g., having various types of activities and levels of difficulty) is an important part of making it gamelike. The following features were seen as assets in educational games: side activities, puzzles, reward factors (for example, a "Hall of Fame"), and multiple representations of information (e.g., mathematics presented not only as numbers but also as pictorial symbols). In general, an impression left by all three focus groups was that students seemed appreciative of games in which players have ultimate control over their fate.

On balance, the focus groups' results have reinforced our strategy of targeting younger learners just when they are developing Aristotelian, rather than idiosyncratic, concepts of motion. Additionally, these discussions reinforced our content and approach. Finally, the focus groups helped us generate design ideas for Level 3, in which we want to engage students in gamelike activities where success depends on the application of concepts learned in Levels 1 and 2. However, making Level 3 gamelike for students creates some task goals that are somewhat removed from our primary objective of mastering scientific concepts. Therefore, careful design of Level 3 will be required to ensure that motivational features reinforce learning rather than interfering with it.

In early 1998 (prior to the publication of this text), we plan to begin formative evaluations of the revised version of NewtonWorld. Once these are complete, we plan to conduct a comparative study to a comparable two-dimensional virtual environment (similar to the MaxwellWorld–EM Field contrast described earlier).

LESSONS LEARNED

For all three of our virtual worlds, the research we have conducted to date provides insights into strategies for investigating advanced learning technologies, as well as assessments of virtual reality's potential for teaching complex scientific knowledge. Lessons learned concerning formative research on advanced educational technologies are as follows:

- A learner-centered development approach that focuses simultaneously on the learning experience, the learning process, and learning outcomes has been invaluable in yielding insights into the strengths and weaknesses of VR technology. Additionally, continuous evaluation of progress through lessons coupled with assessments of factors such as usability, simulator sickness, and motivation has helped us to explain learning outcomes. We would expect such an approach to work for the evaluation of any educational technology.
- We have found talk-aloud protocols employing a cycle of prediction–observation–comparison are highly effective for monitoring the learning process, as well as for identifying usability problems.
- A careful initial analysis of learners' needs and the capabilities and limits of the technology were critical to understanding how to leverage that educational medium to support the learner. However, fully anticipating learners' needs is not possible. The iterative process of design and evaluation has helped us to make our worlds more enjoyable and educational.

- Spreading lessons over multiple VR sessions may be more effective than covering many topics in a single session. We have found that although students began to challenge their misconceptions during the first session, many had trouble synthesizing ideas during posttesting. Fatigue and cognitive overhead in mastering the interface may have influenced these outcomes. When we spread lessons over multiple, shorter sessions, students were better able to retain and integrate information in posttesting.

Additionally, we have discovered several challenges that must be considered when designing immersive educational VR worlds.

- To help learners utilize educational virtual worlds, calibrating the display and virtual controls for each individual is vital. Additionally, monitoring and systematically measuring "simulator sickness" is important, as its onset signals interface problems and can explain why a learner is having trouble with certain activities.
- Students exhibit noticeable individual differences in their interaction styles, abilities to interact with the three-dimensional environment, and susceptibility to simulator sickness. In terms of the latter, our extensive work with MaxwellWorld indicates that most learners' ocularmotor and vestibular problems are mild, typically occur only after at least 1/2 hour of immersion, and for almost all students do not interfere with learning if sessions are held to 45 minutes or less. About 3% of our subjects experience more substantial problems with simulator sickness (upon which we immediately end the VR experience) and are therefore not good candidates for learning environments that utilize HMDs.
- Immersion presents some challenges for lesson administration. For example, students in the HMD cannot access written instructions or complete written questions. Verbal interaction works well.
- Standard approaches to building two-dimensional microworlds (graphical user interfaces [GUIs] and activities based on a planar context) do not scale well to three-dimensional worlds. Multimodal interaction and multisensory communication are important parts of an immersive experience. The development of VR interface tools that facilitate these interactions is a much-needed advance.
- Our work with students and teachers in ScienceSpace suggests that collaborative learning can be achieved by having several learners take turns administering lessons, recording observations, and exploring the virtual worlds.

Finally, we have found the following aspects of immersive VR technology promising for learning complex science.

- Multimodal interaction (voice, virtual, and physical controls) facilitates usability and appears to enhance learning. Multimodal commands offer flexibility, allowing individuals to adapt the interaction to their own style and to distribute attention when performing learning activities. For example, some learners prefer voice commands so they need not shift attention from phenomena of interest to manipulating the menu system.
- Multisensory cues can engage learners, direct their attention to important behaviors and relations, help them understand new sensory perspectives, prevent errors through feedback cues, and enhance ease of use.
- Enabling students to experience phenomena from multiple perspectives appears to facilitate the learning process. As discussed later, we plan additional research to more fully investigate the potential leverage that frames of reference can provide.
- Three-dimensional representations seem to aid learners in understanding phenomena that pervade physical space. Being immersed in a three-dimensional environment is also motivating for learners.
- Qualitative representations (e.g., shadows showing kinetic energy in NewtonWorld) can make salient crucial features of phenomena and representations, thereby aiding learning.
- The creation of new representations that leverage VR's features (e.g., enabling students to become objects or to feel force and energy) may help students challenge misconceptions formed through traditional instruction, as well as aid learners in developing correct mental models.

NEXT STEPS IN OUR VIRTUAL REALITY RESEARCH

From 1999 to 2001, we plan to extend our current research on the ScienceSpace worlds along several dimensions. Described as follows is a study that we will have conducted on MaxwellWorld to examine the contribution of immersive frames of reference to understanding complex science concepts. Using the revised version of NewtonWorld, we also intend to examine how, by facilitating innovative types of students' collaborations, VR may enhance the nature of social constructivist learning. These two planned studies are described in more detail as follows. In addition, as PaulingWorld matures, we will study whether multisensory immersion enables students to master counterintuitive chemistry concepts such as complex as quantum-level phenomena. Finally, to examine challenges in curriculum integration and in classroom implementation, we will move our VR worlds out of laboratory environments into pre-college classroom settings.

Understanding the Potential Utility of Frames of Reference for Learning Complex Science

We believe that by making the learning experiences more perceptual, we can augment their power for visualizing complex information and for learning. We have documented that adding multisensory perceptual information aided students struggling to understand the complex scientific models underlying NewtonWorld and MaxwellWorld. Providing experiences that leverage human pattern recognition capabilities in three-dimensional space, such as shifting among various frames of reference (points of view), may also make the learning experience more perceptual. These enhanced "perceptualization" techniques create experiences that may increase the saliency and memorability of abstract scientific concepts and may potentially benefit learning.

Psychological research on spatial learning, navigation, and visualization suggests that frames of reference make salient different aspects of an environment and influence what people learn (Barfield, Rosenberg, & Furness, 1995; Darkin & Sibert, 1995; Ellis, Tharp, Grunwald, & Smith, 1991; Presson & Hazelrigg,1984; Thorndike & Hayes-Roth, 1982). Although there are numerous FORs, most classification systems converge to two types: exocentric or egocentric (McCormick, 1995; Wickens & Baker, 1995). See Fig. 12.18 for an example of FORs in MaxwellWorld.

By using frames of reference in VR, we can provide learners with experiences that they would otherwise have difficulty in imagining. For example, we can enable students to become part of a phenomenon and experience it directly. Alternately, we can let learners step back from the phenomenon to allow a global view of what is happening. One frame of reference may make salient information that learners might not notice in another frame-of-reference. Furthermore, multiple frames of refer-

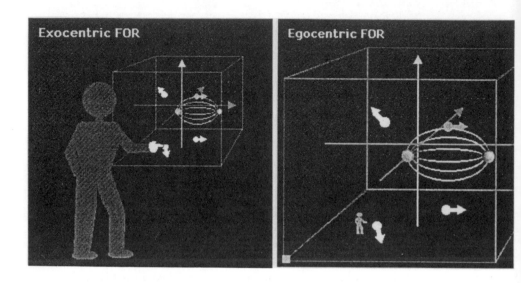

FIG. 12.18   Exocentric versus Egocentric Frames of Reference in MaxwellWorld.

ence might help students to fill in gaps in their knowledge and to become
more flexible in their thinking.

In the MaxwellWorld study on frames of reference and perceptualization that Salzman will have conducted as her doctoral dissertation,
the two concepts learners will be asked to master are the distribution of
force in electric fields and the motion of test charges through electric
fields. These two learning tasks were selected because they differ in the
extent to which global and local knowledge is important—the kinds of
knowledge believed to be afforded by different frames of reference.
Comprehending distribution depends more heavily on global judgments than on local judgments, whereas understanding motion requires
more local judgments than global judgments.

Salzman also will have assessed students' mastery of scientific concepts at two levels: descriptive and causal. Descriptive mastery measures
a student's understanding of symbolic, or what, information and causal
mastery measures student's understanding of conceptual, or why, information (Shute, 1995). Thus, descriptive mastery indicates that an indi-

vidual remembers the representations and behaviors and causal mastery shows that he or she understands what the representations and their pattern of relations mean about the nature of the reality. The latter reflects a deeper understanding of the information and is what we seek to accomplish in teaching learners about scientific phenomena.

To try to identify the unique potential of different frames of reference, Salzman will have examined mastery concerning the concepts of force and motion at both descriptive and causal levels. Additionally, she will have examined the relations between frames of reference and mastery within the context of several other factors (e.g., individual characteristics and dimensions of the learning experience) that are likely to play a role in influencing the learning process and mastery outcomes. Outcomes of these analyses will provide insights into the strengths and weaknesses of frames of reference and into perceptualization in mastering various kinds of complex information and will help us to describe the relation between frames of reference and mastery in a broader context.

This study may bring us one step closer to understanding how we can leverage the human perceptual system in the visualization process. Given that the ability to comprehend complex scientific concepts is becoming increasingly important for success both for workers and for citizens, investigating how to enhance people's perceptual abilities with augmented visualization tools is an important issue. In addition, we intend to extend our explorations on how multisensory immersion influences learning. For example, various sensory modalities can provide similar, mutually confirming input or can increase the amount of information conveyed to the learner through each sensory channel conveying different data. Little is known about what level of redundancy in sensory input is optimal for learning and about how much information learners can process without sensory overload. Moreover, each sense uniquely shapes the data it presents (e.g., perceived volume and directionality of sound is nonlinear, varies with the pitch of the input, and is idiosyncratic to each person). This poses complex considerations in deciding which sensory channel to use in presenting information to learners.

The nature of the electric field domain should be sufficiently representative of other kinds of visualization problems that we can gain insights not only into how to leverage frames of reference for learning, but also to utilize perceptualization to facilitate scientific discovery and the communication of complex ideas in research and industry. However, additional studies will be necessary to help understand how frames of references, multisensory cues, and other features can be integrated in visualization tools. VR provides a good research environment for exploring these design issues, as well as for exploring how multisensory immersion shapes collaborative learning.

Immersive Collaborative Learning as a Means of Enhancing the Shared Construction of Knowledge

As a near-term research initiative in our ScienceSpace worlds, we will investigate the effectiveness of collaborative learning situations in which three students in the same location rotate roles in the following ways: interacting with the world via the HMD, serving as external guide, and participating as a reflective observer. We also plan to experiment with collaborative learning among distributed learners inhabiting a shared virtual context. The student would act and collaborate not as himself or herself, but behind the mask of an "avatar": a surrogate persona in the virtual world. Loftin (1997) has already demonstrated the capability of two users simultaneously manipulating a shared immersive environment using communications bandwidth as low as a standard ISDN telephone line. By adapting military developed distributed simulation technology, we could scale up to many users in a shared, interactive virtual world.

Collaboration among learners' avatars in shared synthetic environments may support a wide range of pedagogical strategies (e.g., peer teaching, Vygotskian tutoring, apprenticeship). In addition, adding a social dimension aids in making technology based educational applications more intriguing to those students most motivated to learn when intellectual content is contextualized in a social setting. However, in virtual environments, interpersonal dynamics provide leverage for learning activities in a manner rather different than typical face-to-face collaborative encounters. Various researchers (Bruckman & Resnick, 1995; Sproull & Kiesler, 1991; Turkle, 1995), as well as virtual community participants like Rheingold (1993), are documenting the psychological phenomena that result when people interact as avatars or depersonalized entities rather than face-to-face. These include disinhibition, fluidity of identity, mimesis, and a wider range of group participation via increased interaction from people who are shy or who want time to think before responding.

Virtual environments that illustrate the challenges and opportunities of these psychological phenomena for education include learning-oriented multi-user virtual environments (MUSEs). These are text-based "worlds" in which users can assume fluid, anonymous identities and vicariously experience intriguing situations cast in a dramatic format. In contrast to standard adventure games, where one wanders through someone else's fantasy, the ability to personalize an environment and to receive recognition from others for a contribution to the shared context is attractive to users (as is also true in face-to-face constructivist learning). The continual evolution of shared virtual environments based on participants' collaborative interactions keeps these educational settings from becoming boring and stale.

We believe that our ScienceSpace worlds offer an intriguing context for extending such work on "social constructivism" in virtual environments. Physical immersion and multisensory stimulation may intensify many of the psychological phenomena noted previously, and "psychosocial saliency" may be an interesting counterpart to perceptual saliency in enhancing learning. Important questions to be answered include the relative value of providing learners with graphically generated bodies and the degree to which the "fidelity" of this graphical representation affects learning and interaction (here fidelity is not simply visual fidelity, but also the matching of real body motions to the animation of the graphical body). Our research plans include studies to explore these possibilities.

CONCLUSION

At the beginning of this chapter, we argue that our research is important in part because information technology is developing powerful capabilities for creating virtual environments. By the year 2010, the video game industry will develop devices capable of multisensory immersion ubiquitously available in homes of varying socioeconomic status, in urban and in rural areas. To compete with the captivating but mindless types of entertainment that will draw on this power, educators will need beautiful, fantastic, intriguing environments that also foster deep and effective learning. Project ScienceSpace is beginning to chart these frontiers, as well as revealing which parts of VR's promise are genuine and which parts are "hype".

Exploring the potential of home-based devices for learning is particularly important because of the high costs of keeping school-based instructional media current with technologies routine in business set-tings. The goal espoused by many people today of multimedia-capable, Internet-connected classroom computers for every 2 to 3 pupils carries a staggering price tag— especially if those devices are obsolete 5 to 7 years after installation. Although providing adequate, sophisticated school-based instructional technologies is extremely important, it is vital to leverage this investment via simultaneous utilization of entertainment and information-services devices in family and in community settings. In other words, using technology to aid educational reform through systemic innovation must occur on two levels simultaneously: drawing one boundary of the system around the school, with stu-dent–teacher–technology partnerships, and another system boundary around the society, with classroom–family–workplace–commu-nity–technology partnerships. Such an innovation strategy necessitates developing learning materials—including "edutainment"—for emerging technologies such as Web-TV and VR (Dede, 1996).

In the long run, research on multisensory immersion will also pro-duce another important outcome: a deeper understanding of the nature of human learning. As biological organisms, our brains have evolved very sophisticated mechanisms for comprehending three-dimensional spatial environments that provide input on various sensory modalities. To date, however, these "perceptualized" learning capabilities have provided little aid in mastering phenomena whose causes are abstract, complex, or counterintuitive. Being a worker and citizen in the 21st century will require comprehension of sophisticated scientific content, material most people do not learn through the best of the instructional approaches available today. Through the types of representations and learning activities Project ScienceSpace is exploring, insights are emerg-ing into how we can leverage the full capabilities of the brain—and advanced information technologies—to attain this type of learning.

ACKNOWLEDGMENTS

This work is supported by NSF's Applications of Advanced Technology Program, Grants RED-93-53320 and 95-55682, and by NASA through a grant (NAG 9-713) and through access to equipment and computer software. The authors gratefully acknowledge the aid of Kim Adams, Katy Ash, Brenda Bannan, Craig Calhoun, Jim Chen, Leslye Fuller, Erik

Geisler, Pam Heishman, Wayne Herbert, Jeff Hoblit, Belinda Hyde, Pat Hyde, Deirdre McGlynn, Edward (Joe) Redish, Saba Rofchaei, Chen Shui, Debra Sprague, Dane Toler, Susan Trickett, and Mike Walsh.

Note: Further information about our project, including QuickTime™ and QuickTime VR™ files for "viewing" the worlds we have developed, can be obtained from our Web site: http://www.virtual.gmu.edu.

REFERENCES

Barfield, W., Rosenberg, C., & Furness, T. A. (1995). Situation awareness as a function of frame of reference, virtual eyepoint elevation, and geometric field of view. *International Journal of Aviation Psychology, 5*(3), 233–256.

Bricken, M., & Byrne, C. M. (1993). Summer students in virtual reality. In A. Wexelblat (Ed.), *Virtual reality: Applications and exploration* (pp. 199–218). New York: Academic Press.

Bruckman, A., & Resnick, M. (1995). The Mediamoo project: Constructivism and professional community. *Convergence, 1*(1), 94–109.

Clement, J. (1982). Students' preconceptions in introductory mechanics. *American Journal of Physics, 50*, 66–71.

Darkin, R. P., & Sibert, J. L. (1995). Navigating large virtual spaces. *International Journal of Human–Computer Interaction, 8*(1), 49–71.

Dede, C. (1995). The evolution of constructivist learning environments: Immersion in distributed, virtual worlds. *Educational Technology, 35*(5), 46–52.

Dede, C. (1996). Emerging technologies and distributed learning. *American Journal of Distance Education, 10*(2), 4–36.

diSessa, A. (1986). Artificial worlds and real experience. *Instructional Science, 14*, 207–227.

Dede, C., Salzman, M., Loftin, B., & Sprague, D. (in press). Multisensory immersion as a modeling environment for learning complex scientific concepts. In N. Roberts, W. Feurzeig, and B. Hunter (Eds.), *Computer modeling and simulation in science education*. New York: Springer-Verlag.

diSessa, A. (1983). Phenomenology and the evolution of intuition. In D. Gentner & A. Stevens (Eds.), *Mental models* (pp. 15–33). Hillsdale, NJ: Lawrence Erlbaum Associates.

Ellis, S. R., Tharp, G. K., Grunwald, A. J., & Smith, S. (1991). Exocentric judgments in real environments and stereoscopic displays. In *Proceedings of the 35th annual meeting of the Human Factors Society* (pp. 1442–1446). Santa Monica, CA: Human Factors Society.

Erickson, T. (1993). Artificial realities as data visualization environments. In A. Wexelblat (Ed.), *Virtual reality: Applications and explorations* (pp. 1–22). New York: Academic Press.

Fosnot, C. (1992). Constructing constructivism. In T. M. Duffy & D. H. Jonestown (Eds.), *Constructivism and the technology of instruction: A conversation* (pp. 167–176). Hillsdale, NJ: Lawrence Erlbaum Associates.

Frederiksen, J., & White, B. (1992). Mental models and understanding: A problem for science education. In E. Scanlon & T. O'Shea (Eds.), *New directions in educational technology* (pp. 211–226). New York: Springer-Verlag.

Halloun, I. A., & Hestenes, D. (1985a). Common sense concepts about motion. *American Journal of Physics, 53*, 1056–1065.

Halloun, I. A., & Hestenes, D. (1985b). The initial knowledge state of college students. *American Journal of Physics, 53*, 1043–1055.

Heeter, C. (1992). Being there: The subjective experience of presence. *Presence: Teleoperators and Virtual Environments, 1*(1), 262–271.

Hewitt, P. G. (1991). Millikan lecture: The missing essential—A conceptual understanding of physics. *American Journal of Physics, 51*, 305–311.

Kalawsky, R. S. (1993). *The science of virtual reality and virtual environments*. New York: Addison-Wesley.

Kennedy, R. S., Lane, N. E., Berbaum, K. S., & Lilienthal, M. G. (1993). Simulator sickness questionnaire: An enhanced method for quantifying simulator sickness. *The International Journal of Aviation Psychology*, *3*(3), 203–220.

Kozma, R., Chin, E., Russell, J., & Marx, N. (1997). *The use of linked multiple representations to understand and solve problems in chemistry*. Menlo Park, CA: SRI.

Krueger, M. (1991). *Artificial reality II*. New York: Addison-Wesley.

Larkin, J. (1983). The role of problem representation in physics. In D. Gentner & A. Stevens, (Eds.), *Mental models* (pp. 75–98). Hillsdale, NJ: Lawrence Erlbaum Associates.

Loftin, R. B. (1997). Hands across the Atlantic. *IEEE Computer Graphics & Applications*, *17*(2), 78–79.

McCormick, E. P. (1995). *Virtual reality features of frames of reference and display dimensionality with stereopsis: Their effects on scientific visualization*. Unpublished master's thesis, University of Illinois at Urbana–Champaign, Urbana, IL.

McDermott, L. C. (1991). Millikan lecture 1990: What we teach and what is learned—Closing the gap. *American Journal of Physics*, *59*, 301–315.

Papert, S. (1988). The conservation of Piaget: The computer as grist for the constructivist mill. In G. Foreman & P. B. Pufall (Eds.), *Constructivism in the computer age* (pp. 3–13). Hillsdale, NJ: Lawrence Erlbaum Associates.

Perkins, D. (1991, May). Technology meets constructivism: Do they make a marriage? *Educational Technology*, *31*(5), 18–23.

Piantanida, T., Boman, D. K., & Gille, J. (1993). Human perceptual issues and virtual reality. *Virtual Reality Systems*, *1*(1), 43–52.

Presson, C. C., & Hazelrigg, M.D. (1984). Building spatial representations through primary and secondary learning. *Journal of Experimental Psychology: Learning, Memory, and Cognition*, *10*, 716–722.

Psotka, J. (1996). Immersive training systems: Virtual reality and education and training. *Instructional Science*, *23*(5–6), 405–423.

Redish, E. (1993). The implications of cognitive studies for teaching physics. *American Journal of Physics*, *62*(9), 796–803.

Reif, F., & Larkin, J. (1991). Cognition in scientific and everyday domains: Comparison and learning implications. *Journal of Research in Science Teaching*, *28*, 743–760.

Reimann, P., & Spada, H. (1996). *Learning in humans and machines: Toward an interdisciplinary learning science*. New York: Pergamon.

Rheingold, H. (1993). *The virtual community: Homesteading on the electronic frontier*. New York: Addison-Wesley.

Salzman, M. C., Dede, C., & Loftin, R. B. (1995). Learner-centered design of sensorily immersive microworlds using a virtual reality interface. In J. Greer (Ed.), *Proceedings of the 7th International Conference on Artificial Intelligence and Education* (pp. 554–564). Charlottesville, VA: Association for the Advancement of Computers in Education.

Shute, V. (1995). SMART: Student modeling approach for responsive tutoring. *User Modeling and User-adapted Interaction*, *5*, 1–44.

Smith, R. B. (1987). Experiences with the alternate reality kit: An example of the tension between literalism and magic (pp. 324–333). In *Proceedings of CHI+GI 1987*. New York: Association for Computing Machinery.

Soloway, E., Guzdial, M., & Hay, K. E. (1994, April). Learner-centered design. The challenge for HCI in the 21st century. *Interactions*, *1*(1), 36–48.

Sproull, S., & Kiesler, S. (1991). *Connections: New ways of working in the networked world*. Cambridge, MA: MIT Press.

Stuart, R., & Thomas, J. C. (1991). The implications of education in cyberspace. *Multimedia Review*, *2*, 17–27.

Thorndike, P. W., & Hayes-Roth, B. (1982). Differences in spatial knowledge acquired from maps and navigation. *Cognitive Psychology*, *14*, 560–589.

Trowbridge, D., & Sherwood, B. (1994). *EMField* [computer software]. Raleigh, NC: Physics Academic Software.

Turkle, S. (1995). *Life on the screen: Identity in the age of the internet*. New York: Simon & Shuster.

Wenzel, E. M. (1992). Localization in virtual acoustic displays. *Presence*, *1*(1), 80–107.

White, B. (1993). Thinkertools: Causal models, conceptual change, and science education. *Cognition and Instruction, 10,* 1–100.

Wickens, C. (1992). Virtual reality and education. *IEEE Spectrum,* 842–847.

Wickens C. D., & Baker, P. (1995). Cognitive issues in virtual reality. In W. Barfield & T. Furness (Eds.), *Virtual environments and advanced interface design* (pp. 56–72). New York: Oxford University Press.

Witmer, B. B., & Singer, M. J. (1994). *Measuring Presence in Virtual Environments* (ARI Tech Report No. 1014). Alexandria, VA: U.S. Army Research Institute for the Behavioral and Social Sciences.

Author Index

Subject Index

Graphs, 12, 15–16, 23, 26, 37, 48, 51–52, 54–55, 62–65, 67, 70–71, 74, 78, 88, 93, 98, 114, 303, 306, 313
Grounding, 50, 86, 93, 114

H

High school, 3–4, 17, 48, 72, 77–78, 80–81, 92, 112–113, 124, 139, 141, 144, 150, 158, 164, 185, 224, 259, 262–263, 265, 271, 279, 281, 283, 286, 340, 370, 378, 380, 393, 395, 397
History, 45–46, 53, 123, 136, 143, 166, 212, 232, 277, 279, 288
Hyperlinks, 3, 130, 137
Hypermedia, 3, 7–8, 74, 117–120, 122–124, 126, 131–132, 134, 136,137, 139, 142–144, 148, 150–154, 156–157, 159–161, 256
Hypertext, 118, 160–162

I

Ill-defined, 123
Ill-structured, 123, 161
Imagery, 53
Immersion, 120, 227, 365, 367–368, 371–372, 387, 394, 403–404, 409, 411
Indexing, 126, 155
Innovation, 1, 10, 49–50, 55, 57, 72, 158, 264, 284, 285, 410
Inquiry, 5, 8, 34–35, 43–44, 49–50, 53, 74, 155, 217, 288, 312, 321–322, 326–329, 331, 333, 335–336, 340, 342–343, 345–346, 348, 349–350, 353–358, 369–370, 386–387, 390
 activities, 35, 327, 386, 390
 skills, 329, 331, 333, 335–336, 342, 346, 348, 353–354, 356–357
Instruction, 74–75, 158, 160–161, 225–226, 286, 359, 413
Instructional approaches, 5, 153, 321, 327, 357, 410
Intelligent tutoring systems, 45, 132
Interactive learning environments, *see* Environments, interactive learning
International, 48, 282, 287, 289–290, 301, 303

Internet, 412
Interviews, 123–124, 141, 156, 182, 186, 263, 308–309, 369, 379
Investigation, 5, 37, 159, 189, 193, 261, 265, 279, 281–282, 289, 291, 303–304, 310, 312

K

Knowledge, 1–4, 6, 8–10, 12, 16, 31, 35, 48–50, 57–58, 73–74, 78–79, 81, 83, 86, 117–120, 122–123, 126, 130–131, 134, 136–137, 142–143, 145, 148, 152–156, 158–161, 164–165, 170, 180, 182–184, 186–189, 194–197, 199, 206, 209, 211, 217, 222–226, 228, 236–237, 255–256, 260, 268, 296, 309, 311–314, 317–319, 327, 343, 346, 358, 369, 395–396, 402, 406, 411–412
 abstract conceptual, 118
 component, 145, 148, 152
 contextualized, 118
 deep structure, *see* Deep structure, knowledge
 difficult, 2, 4, 153, 156, 370
 in-context, 3, 123
 inert, 136–137
 interconnection, 153
 metaconceptual, 130, 156, 343, *see also* Scaffolding, metaconceptual
Knowledge Integration Environment (KIE), 4, 8, 193–195, 200–201, 204, 206, 209, 211–215, 217, 221–224
Knowledge Mediator
 Evolution Knowledge Mediator, 3, 118, 122–124, 126, 130, 132, 134, 136–137, 154, 157
Knowledge Mediator Framework (KMF), 3, 117–120, 123, 130–131, 136–137, 139, 153–156

L

Learning, 2–10, 13, 26, 35, 45–46, 48, 50, 53, 55–57, 63–64, 70–75, 77, 79–83, 88, 92–93, 96, 103–104, 111, 113–114, 117–118, 120,